FINAL INJUNCTIONS IN TORT LAW

This book is the first considered study of final injunctions in tort law. It devises a novel taxonomy of such injunctions and explores the implications of the law on injunctions for the way in which scholars think about tort law more generally.

The book begins by analysing how the injunction in aid of legal rights came to be developed as a remedy in the Court of Chancery. It then provides definitive guidance as to the range of final injunctions that may be available to restrain or remedy torts. A clear, structured framework to guide legal reasoning in injunction cases is constructed. The book concludes by making several claims about tort law in the light of the availability of injunctive relief.

In addition to the taxonomy that is developed, the overarching message of the book is that injunctive relief is a central component of the law of tort. The way in which tort law is expounded in textbooks and monographs, and taught in universities, needs revising. Specifically, we must not overemphasise the award of damages and neglect to highlight the importance of the injunction. The true position is that injunctive relief is as crucial as damages are to enforcing the rights that are generated by tort law.

Volume 57 in the series Hart Studies in Private Law

Hart Studies in Private Law

This monograph series brings together in one place two types of book: works which examine in-depth the fundamental doctrines and principles of private law, and works which engage with the theoretical underpinnings of private law. The series thus aims to contribute to ever-evolving debates about the nature of private law such as problems of classification and taxonomy, remedies, the relationship with public law and the boundaries of private law generally.

The series includes, but is not confined to, works on contract, tort, unjust enrichment, equity, property and the conflict of laws, welcoming work which intersects with other fields of study to enable a deeper understanding of private law theory and practice.

Final Injunctions in Tort Law

Aiden Lerch

• HART •
OXFORD • LONDON • NEW YORK • NEW DELHI • SYDNEY

HART PUBLISHING

Bloomsbury Publishing Plc

Kemp House, Chawley Park, Cumnor Hill, Oxford, OX2 9PH, UK

1385 Broadway, New York, NY 10018, USA

Bloomsbury Publishing Ireland Limited, 29 Earlsfort Terrace, Dublin 2, D02 AY28, Ireland

HART PUBLISHING, the Hart/Stag logo, BLOOMSBURY and the Diana logo are trademarks of Bloomsbury Publishing Plc

First published in Great Britain 2025

A catalogue record for this book is available from the British Library.

A catalogue record for this book is available from the Library of Congress.

Library of Congress Control Number: 2025942501

ISBN: HB: 978-1-50998-971-3
ePDF: 978-1-50998-973-7
ePub: 978-1-50998-972-0

Typeset by Compuscript Ltd, Shannon

For product safety related questions contact productsafety@bloomsbury.com

To find out more about our authors and books visit www.hartpublishing.co.uk. Here you will find extracts, author information, details of forthcoming events and the option to sign up for our newsletters.

For my mother and father

FOREWORD

The final injunction is a powerful and flexible remedy. Just over a century ago, Justice Isaacs of the High Court of Australia considered it 'self-evident' that a competent court has 'power to prevent by prohibitory injunction unauthorized persons from committing an illegal act calculated to imperil in advance the liberty of an accused person'.[1]

Final injunctions to vindicate common law rights for the protection of autonomy and personal interests have been ordered in a variety of contemporary contexts. In 2016, the Federal Court of Australia granted an injunction to a woman in immigration detention to restrain a government Minister from breaching their duty of care in negligence to procure a safe and lawful termination of a pregnancy, where the failure to do so would cause physical and psychological harm.[2] In Western Australia, an injunction was granted to restrain the State from unlawfully holding youth detainees in solitary confinement.[3] In Queensland, an injunction required spermatozoa retrieved from the body of a widow's recently deceased husband to be dealt with in accordance with her directions.[4]

Final injunctions also respond to the contemporary media environment to protect reputational interests, for example by restraining the republication of defamatory material following a 'sustained campaign of tweets repeating the defamation';[5] or by restraining a publisher, through a national television broadcaster, from continuing to make available online for download or otherwise, so much of a television programme that conveyed specified defamatory imputations.[6]

Dr Lerch's accomplishment in the publication of this work, the first comprehensive examination of final injunctions in tort law, is remarkable. The book is the product of passion, which I have witnessed first hand, for the general law and the protection it offers for individual rights and interests. Dr Lerch's comprehensive doctrinal research is located in a masterful examination of private law more generally. Its logically structured and informative contents, aided by Dr Lerch's elegant

[1] *R v MacFarlane, ex parte O'Flanagan* (1923) 32 CLR 518, 540.
[2] *Plaintiff S99/2016 v Minister for Immigration and Border Protection* (2016) 243 FCR 17.
[3] *CRU v Chief Executive Officer of the Department of Justice* [2023] WASC 257.
[4] *Re Denman* [2004] 2 Qd R 595.
[5] *Tribe v Simmons (No 2)* [2021] FCA 1164.
[6] *Chau v Australian Broadcasting Corporation (No 3)* (2021) 386 ALR 36.

prose, will be welcomed particularly by practitioners, judges and the academy, who seek to navigate an area of law that is complex, important and perennially relevant.

Justice Jacqueline Gleeson
High Court of Australia
Canberra
April 2025

ACKNOWLEDGEMENTS

When I first studied tort law as an undergraduate student, what struck me about the subject was that our most fundamental individual rights are given to us not by Parliament but by the courts. I was interested to learn that, provided legislation does not state otherwise, our common law rights can be enforced against the Crown. To me, this meant (and still means) that our legal system is more than just a tool for the political elite. It is a system that, in certain circumstances, will protect ordinary individuals against the dominant will of the majority. When I spoke to my friends and family about the law, however, none of them had any idea that our most basic rights are given to us by the courts. So, ever since I learnt about tort law myself, I have had a passion to inform those around me about the subject and to deepen my own knowledge of it.

Being given the opportunity to write and publish this book has therefore been a dream come true. The book is a revised version of a doctoral thesis that I completed at the University of Oxford. I will always be grateful for the generous funding provided by the Clarendon Fund and St Edmund Hall, as the reality is that without it this book would not have been written. But the book would also not have been possible without a great number of people, to all of whom I wish to express my thanks.

First and foremost, I must thank my supervisor, Professor Donal Nolan. I could not have hoped for a better person to guide me in my work. Donal has been supportive, energetic and, most importantly, a constant source of testing comments. I will only ever be able to aspire to achieve Donal's level of knowledge about tort law, and I will forever be grateful for being able to learn so much from someone who is so brilliant at what he does.

My doctoral thesis was examined by a number of scholars whom I deeply respect and admire. My final examiners, Professor James Goudkamp and Nick McBride, provided penetrating and insightful comments that improved the quality of this book greatly. As well as James Goudkamp, Professor Ciara Kennefick and Professor Ben McFarlane served as examiners at other stages. I owe them a huge debt of gratitude for saving me from making errors of law and for gently persuading me to abandon some of my misconceived arguments. I owe a special thanks to Ciara for supervising my BCL dissertation, which formed the building blocks of chapter 6 of the book. Ciara's guidance at the very early stages of my studies led to fundamental changes in my writing and in my approach to legal analysis. I remain immensely grateful for this. Finally, chapter 2 was improved by thought-provoking comments given by Justice Mark Leeming and Professor Mark Lunney.

Next, I must express my thanks to Professor Adrian Briggs and Professor Joanna Bell, my college advisors at St Edmund Hall. They have been a constant source of support over the years and imparted many words of wisdom. I must also thank Yvonne Apolo at the University of Wollongong, and James Goudkamp, for encouraging me to pursue a BCL and then a DPhil. Yvonne and James both taught me tort law as an undergraduate student, and it is their passion for the subject that inspired mine.

During the course of writing the thesis and the book, I worked at a number of institutions. In the early stages of writing the thesis, I worked as an Associate at Floyd Zadkovich LLP in London. Luke Zadkovich, Damon Thompson and Calum Cheyne taught me the nuances of shipping law (some of which feature in this book – see chapter 6) and I owe them a huge thanks for supporting me at the very start of my career.

My time as a lecturer at Worcester College and Christ Church was exceptionally rewarding. I learnt a great deal by teaching students who were so bright and motivated. Dr Chen Chen, Professor James Edwards, Hilary Hogan, Professor Ciara Kennefick and Dr Leah Trueblood were truly wonderful colleagues.

The final portion of the work on this book was completed while I was working as an Associate to the Honourable Justice Jacqueline Gleeson at the High Court of Australia. It was an immeasurable privilege to work for the Court and for someone whose intellectual prowess is matched by their warmth and humility. I will forever be grateful for the many lessons that I learnt at the Court.

I presented a previous version of chapter 7 of the book at the *Intersections of Private Law Colloquium* at the University of Sydney. I would like to thank those in attendance who made many penetrating comments, particularly Professor Jodi Gardner, Justice Mark Leeming and Professor James Penner.

The production team at Hart Publishing have been excellent to work with. Sinéad Moloney and Sasha Jawed have overseen a very smooth publication process. The copy-editing completed by Catherine Minahan was outstanding.

I have also been extremely lucky to be surrounded by a group of truly wonderful friends while writing the book. A number of them kindly read over previous versions of certain chapters. For that I must thank Lucy Cameron, Mitchell Cleaver, Emerson Hynard, Eleanor Makeig, Sophie Ryan, Georgia Speechly, Ben Teng and Sophie Whittaker. Special mention must also be given to Kristen Allison, Nicholas Bradman, Dr Nancy Burrell, Emma Ffrench-Mullen, Alyssa Glass, Jacqueline Krynda, Zoe Linnane, Alice Maxwell, Caroline Miller, Melinda Morris, Monica Perri, Emma Roff, Dr Rhys Thomas, Flyn Wells and Anna Wotherspoon.

Finally, my greatest thanks go to my family, in particular: my mum and dad, Mignon and Michael; my brother and sister-in-law, Callum and Olivia; and my wonderful partner, Ethan. I cannot express in words how grateful I am for their love and support.

Aiden Lerch
Arnold Bloch Leibler
Sydney
April 2025

CONTENTS

AUTHOR'S NOTE

The expressions 'tort law', 'tort' and 'law of tort' are used interchangeably.

When referring to a hypothetical claimant, this book uses the pronoun 'she'. When referring to a hypothetical defendant, this book uses the pronoun 'he'. When describing the facts of a particular case, the relevant pronoun that appears in the report is adopted. When referring to a hypothetical plaintiff or defendant in chapter 2, this book uses the pronoun 'he' in order to be consistent with the historical sources.

TABLE OF CASES

Australia

England and Wales

United States

TABLE OF STATUTES

1

Introduction

There is a large body of contemporary and historical case law in England and Wales, and in other common law jurisdictions, in which injunctions have been granted to restrain or remedy many different torts. Yet if you were to ask an undergraduate law student, or even a private law scholar more generally, when an injunction is available in respect of a right generated by tort law, most would struggle to give an answer that goes beyond identifying that an injunction can be granted to restrain a continuing private nuisance or trespass to land. At first sight, this seems perplexing. To those who are familiar with tort law scholarship, however, there is in fact nothing perplexing about this at all.

In the latter half of the twentieth century, and at least some way into the twenty-first century, most tort scholars believed that the sole function of the law of tort was to determine when a claimant could claim compensation for a loss caused by the defendant. The inevitable consequence of conceptualising tort law in this way was that scholars neglected the availability of injunctive relief in tort. In the past decade or so, thanks to the work of a new generation of tort scholars,[1] more academics have come to conceptualise and teach tort law as it was originally understood when it developed as a category of law in the nineteenth century: as a law of civil wrongs. Nevertheless, the large body of cases in which injunctions have been granted to restrain or remedy torts remains underexplored. Our limited understanding of the availability of injunctive relief in respect of tort law rights, and the function that the injunction performs in tort law, is therefore a remnant of the once pervasive idea that, as Nicholas McBride has put it, 'Tort Law = Compensation for Loss'.[2]

This book is the first considered study of final injunctions in tort. It provides practitioners and academics with definitive guidance as to the range of final injunctions that may be available to be awarded against an actual or putative tortfeasor, and what will have to be shown for such injunctions to be awarded. It also considers what the availability of injunctive relief indicates about tort law itself. In short, the book devises a novel taxonomy of final injunctions in tort and explores the implications of the law on injunctions for the way in which scholars think about tort law more generally.

[1] See, eg, R Stevens, *Torts and Rights* (Oxford University Press 2007); D Nolan and A Robertson (eds), *Rights and Private Law* (Hart Publishing 2012).

[2] N McBride, 'Rights and the Basis of Tort Law' in Nolan and Robertson (eds) (n 1) 331, 333.

In addition to the taxonomy that is developed, the overarching message of this book is that injunctive relief is a central component of the modern law of tort. By focusing solely on damages and reparation, we have been unable to see the full picture of what the law of tort really is. The true position is that injunctive relief is as crucial as damages are to enforcing the rights that are generated by tort law.

Many more arguments are advanced in this book, each of which challenges long-established orthodoxies about tort law and equity. For example, and to provide a glimpse of the conclusions that follow, the book makes the novel claim that two types of mandatory injunctions are granted in tort law, questions the view that damages must be inadequate before an injunction can be granted to restrain tortious conduct, challenges the idea that damages are tort law's 'primary' remedy, disputes the assumption that injunctions are more readily available with respect to property rights and argues that a final injunction can be granted with respect to the tort of negligence.

I. The Neglect of Injunctive Relief in Tort Law

There is a dearth of analysis of injunctions in tort in England and Wales and in other common law jurisdictions. There are four under-explored issues in the case law and the extant literature.

The first, and most important, of these issues concerns the principles governing when injunctive relief can be awarded to restrain or remedy a tort. There is a large body of case law concerning injunctive relief in tort law.[3] Nevertheless, while it is not in doubt that courts have the power to grant prohibitory,[4] mandatory[5] and quia timet[6] injunctions in tort, the precise legal tests governing when such injunctions will be awarded are unclear and under-explored. Each of the tests has been established predominantly in the context of awarding an injunction in respect of a private nuisance.[7] It is uncertain whether the principles established in those cases are broadly applicable across tort law or differ according to the tort pleaded. Precisely what conditions are required to be made out for the award of each type of injunction are also largely undefined.

Little assistance is gained by turning to extant literature. Only John Murphy has critically analysed the role of the injunction in tort law in England and Wales.[8] The leading treatises generally devote limited space to injunctions in tort.[9] When the

[3] As shown in chs 4, 5, and 6.

[4] *Shelfer v City of London Electric Lighting Co* [1895] 1 Ch 287 (CA); *Coventry v Lawrence* [2014] UKSC 13, [2014] AC 822.

[5] *Redland Bricks v Morris* [1970] AC 652 (HL).

[6] *Fletcher v Bealey* (1885) 28 Ch D 688 (Ch); *Bromley LBC v Persons Unknown* [2020] EWCA Civ 12.

[7] Indeed, the leading cases cited above all concern the tort of private nuisance.

[8] J Murphy, 'Rethinking Injunctions in Tort Law' (2007) 27 *OJLS* 509.

[9] A Burrows, *Remedies for Torts, Breach of Contract, and Equitable Wrongs* (4th edn, Oxford University Press 2019) 443–49 (prohibitory); 462–65 (mandatory), 467–68 (quia timet); J Goudkamp

topic is considered more specifically, the discussion is predicated on the remedy's availability to restrain the tort of nuisance.[10] There is also little consideration in the literature of the topic of injunctions more generally. Of the texts that are devoted exclusively to injunctions, generally only one chapter is focused on the injunction in aid of legal rights.[11] The analysis of injunctions is otherwise limited to one chapter in various treatises on equity or remedies more generally.[12] This literature tends to provide a brief account of the necessary conditions for the award of an injunction and the discretionary considerations that militate against, or in favour of, injunctive relief. However, the analytical process that courts employ to determine whether an injunction should be awarded to restrain or remedy torts, and the nature and limits of the discretion that is exercised by the courts, is seldom considered.

The second issue concerns the historical development of the injunction in aid of legal rights. It is well known that the injunction has long served as a remedy to restrain the commission of legal wrongs.[13] However, as Donal Nolan has observed, '[t]he deep history of the injunction as a tort remedy is obscure'.[14] Some consideration has been given to the general history of the injunction,[15] as well as the injunction in aid of public rights.[16] But it seems that only William Gummow, former Justice of the High Court of Australia, has considered briefly the history of the injunction in aid of private legal rights in England and Wales.[17] The way in

and D Nolan, *Winfield & Jolowicz on Tort* (20th edn, Sweet & Maxwell 2020) [23.124]–[23.132]; A Tettenborn, 'Injunctions' in M Jones and A Dugdale (eds), *Clerk & Lindsell on Torts* (23rd edn, Sweet & Maxwell 2020) [28-01]–[28-22]. The exceptions are: K Oliphant (ed), *The Law of Tort* (3rd edn, LexisNexis 2015) [8.1]–[8.50]; N McBride and R Bagshaw, *Tort Law* (6th edn, Pearson Education 2018) ch 27. But in these last two texts, the authors do not attempt to impose an intelligible order on (or cite all of) the relevant cases.

[10] See, eg, S Tromans, 'Nuisance – Prevention or Payment?' (1982) 41 *CLJ* 78; B Pontin, *Nuisance Law and Environmental Protection: A Study of Nuisance Injunctions in Practice* (Lawtext Publishing 2013); P Davies, 'Injunctions in Tort and Contract' in G Virgo and S Worthington (eds), *Commercial Remedies: Resolving Controversies* (Cambridge University Press 2017) 127; D Nolan, 'Injunctions' in W Day and S Worthington (eds), *Challenging Private Law: Lord Sumption on the Supreme Court* (Hart Publishing 2020) 155.

[11] S Gee, *Commercial Injunctions* (7th edn, Sweet & Maxwell 2020) (no consideration of final injunctions in respect of torts); D Bean et al, *Injunctions* (14th edn, Sweet & Maxwell 2022) ch 2; D Capper, *Injunctions in Private Law* (Edward Elgar Publishing 2024) chs 4, 5. See also R Sharpe, *Injunctions and Specific Performance* (4th edn, Thomson Reuters 2012) chs 1, 4, 5 (although Sharpe's text contains numerous chapters on final injunctions, his primary focus is on the law of Canada).

[12] I Spry, *Equitable Remedies* (9th edn, Thomson Reuters 2014) ch 4; JD Heydon, MJ Leeming and PG Turner, *Meagher, Gummow & Lehane's Equity: Doctrines & Remedies* (5th edn, LexisNexis 2015) ch 21; P Davies, 'Injunctions' in J McGhee and S Elliott (eds), *Snell's Equity* (34th edn, Sweet & Maxwell 2021) ch 18; J Glister and J Lee, *Hanbury on Modern Equity* (22nd edn, Sweet & Maxwell 2021) ch 28; Burrows (n 9) ch 23; R Zakrzewski, *Remedies Reclassified* (Oxford University Press 2009) ch 8.

[13] F Maitland, *Equity: A Course of Lectures* (Cambridge University Press 1909) Lecture XX, 261.

[14] Nolan (n 10) 156.

[15] D Raack, 'A History of Injunctions in England Before 1700' (1986) 61 *Indiana Law Journal* 539. See also J Baker, *An Introduction to English Legal History* (5th edn, Oxford University Press 2019) ch 6.

[16] E Sykes, 'The Injunction in Aid of Public Law' (1953) 2 *University of Queensland Law Journal* 114.

[17] Justice William Gummow, 'The Injunction in Aid of Legal Rights – An Australian Perspective' (1993) 56 *Law & Contemporary Problems* 83. See also the treatises written by 19th-century authors cited in ch 2.

which the Court of Chancery ('the Chancery') developed its jurisdiction to grant injunctions in aid of legal rights has therefore never been the subject of detailed analysis.

The third issue concerns the formal distinctions between prohibitory, mandatory and quia timet injunctions. There is debate in the existing literature surrounding the classification of injunctions in particular tort cases.[18] However, although a number of modern treatises on equitable remedies provide short definitions of the different types of injunction,[19] sustained analysis directed at identifying the precise distinctions between prohibitory, mandatory and quia timet injunctions is rare.[20] It follows that the formal distinctions between such injunctions are under-explored, even though the classification of an injunction directly determines what law governs whether a particular type of injunction should be granted to restrain or remedy a tort.

The final issue is what the availability of the injunction as a tort remedy indicates about tort law itself. Some doctrinal claims about tort law are predicated on suggestions about the availability (or otherwise) of injunctive relief in tort law. For example, the (un)availability of injunctive relief has been used to make arguments that damages are tort law's primary remedy,[21] that property law can be distinguished from tort law[22] and that tort law operates as 'first-order' law while equity operates as 'second-order' law.[23] The validity of these claims is difficult to evaluate, however, as the law governing when injunctions can be granted to restrain or remedy torts has never been explored in detail. Several widely accepted assumptions about tort law therefore remain largely untested. Moreover, in the extant literature there is little consideration of what function the injunction performs in tort and whether this may shed new light on the contested nature of tort law. Indeed, in the leading theoretical accounts of tort law, the role of the injunction is almost entirely overlooked.[24]

[18] See J Jolowicz, 'Damages in Equity – A Study of Lord Cairns' Act' (1975) 34 *CLJ* 224, 244–45; Burrows (n 9) 442–43; S Smith, *Rights, Wrongs and Injustices: The Structure of Remedial Law* (Oxford University Press 2019) 149.

[19] See, eg, Spry (n 12) 332; Heydon, Leeming and Turner (n 12) [21-010], [21-440]; Davies (n 12) [18-003]; Burrows (n 9) 442; Glister and Lee (n 12) [28-004]–[28-007].

[20] For an exception, see Sharpe (n 11) [1.10]–[1.50], [1.500]–[1.650].

[21] J Gardner, 'Torts and Other Wrongs' (2011) 39 *Florida State University Law Review* 43.

[22] G Calabresi and AD Melamed, 'Property Rules, Liability Rules, and Inalienability: One View of the Cathedral' (1972) 85 *Harvard Law Review* 1089.

[23] J Goldberg and H Smith, 'Wrongful Fusion: Equity and Tort' in J Goldberg, P Turner and H Smith (eds), *Equity and Law: Fusion and Fission* (Cambridge University Press 2019) 309.

[24] See, eg, R Posner and W Landes, *The Economic Structure of Tort Law* (Harvard University Press 1987) 43–48 (discussion limited to property torts); E Weinrib, *The Idea of Private Law* (Oxford University Press 1995) 195; Stevens (n 1) 57–58; A Ripstein, *Private Wrongs* (Harvard University Press 2016) 12 (one-sentence introductory mention), 139–40 (two-sentence mention in respect of nuisance), 240 (one-sentence mention in respect of remedies), 276 (one-sentence mention); J Goldberg and B Zipursky, *Recognizing Wrongs* (Harvard University Press 2020) 164.

II. Why is Injunctive Relief in Tort Worth Investigating?

The four under-explored issues in the extant literature demonstrate that there is a lack of sustained and thoroughgoing study of injunctions in tort law. But it still needs to be asked: why is this area of law worth investigating?

There are at least three clear reasons why injunctive relief in tort law deserves significant attention. The first is that an injunction, like an award of damages, is a means by which the rights generated by tort law can be protected. Yet, unlike an award of damages, when an injunction is granted it does not compensate the claimant for her damage or loss.[25] The availability of injunctive relief therefore offers claimants a distinct means by which they can enforce their tort law rights. Hence, a detailed study of the topic is essential to fully understand the ways in which (and limits on when) tort law rights can be protected. From a practical perspective, this is extremely important for practitioners and judges who are required to determine when claimants can enforce their tort law rights by injunction.

The second reason is that the availability of injunctive relief bears directly upon the contested nature of the law of tort (and its relationship with equity). When an injunction is granted in respect of a right generated by tort law, it means that courts are providing a remedy to the claimant because of that right. The circumstances in which injunctive relief is available in respect of a tort law right therefore reveals how tort law operates. It follows that unless adequate attention is given to injunctive relief in tort, the law of tort will not be fully understood by scholars.

The third reason why the topic deserves significant attention is related to the fact that injunctions can be granted not only in respect of tort law rights, but also in respect of contractual, equitable and public rights. It is obvious that the ways in which injunctions operate in these areas of law have a great deal in common (such as, for example, the formal distinctions between different types of injunctions, and the operation of the discretionary considerations). A clear picture of how the injunction operates in tort law can therefore shed light on the way in which injunctions operate in these other areas of law.

III. Methodology

The primary aim of this book is not to propose reform of the law. Rather, it is to advance our understanding of injunctive relief in the law of tort. To achieve this aim, the book has four objectives, which have been designed to address the dearth of analysis of injunctions in tort. The objectives are stated in an order

[25] This book adopts Nolan's distinction between damage and loss, see D Nolan, 'Rights, Damage and Loss' (2017) 37 *OJLS* 255.

that ensures the first and second objectives will assist in achieving the third and fourth objectives:

1. The first objective is to analyse how the injunction in aid of legal rights came to be advanced as a remedy by the Chancery before the passing of the Judicature Act reforms of 1873–75.
2. The second objective is to identify the formal distinctions between prohibitory, mandatory and quia timet injunctions in tort law. This objective enables the book to offer a fresh way of analysing the law of injunctions as, by meeting the objective, the law governing prohibitory, mandatory and quia timet injunctions can then be analysed in stand-alone chapters.
3. The third objective is to provide definitive guidance on when final prohibitory, mandatory and quia timet injunctions can be awarded to restrain or remedy torts.
4. The final objective is to explore what the award of injunctive relief indicates about tort law itself. This objective enables the book to engage further with scholarly debates in this area of law and to make novel claims about the law of tort.

To achieve these objectives, this book employs a primarily doctrinal method. The book does not merely describe the results and the reasoning in the relevant cases. It engages in analytical jurisprudence by defining legal concepts, applying logic to determine how legal principles fit together, and identifying the formal distinctions that are employed in this area of law.[26] The book also engages in a form of Dworkinian interpretivism, as it imposes an intelligible order on a body of law. In the chapters that follow, it is argued on numerous occasions that certain cases have been wrongly decided or that a judge's reasoning is incorrect, as the decision or the reasoning does not fit the law as a whole or cannot be justified.[27] In this sense, this book is concerned with what justice requires.

Nevertheless, consistently with Dworkin's method, this book is committed to placing faith in the reasons that courts have given for making their decisions. It does not ignore or fail to engage meaningfully with cases that do not fit the suggested model of the law. Rather, the method adopted in writing this book has been to devise a taxonomy that shows fidelity to the decisions in the case law and to the reasons given by the courts, and that otherwise departs from decisions or reasons only where they are shown to be contrary to prior authority, inconsistent with principles of logic or plainly wrong. This enables the book to advance a faithful account of the principles that govern the award of final injunctions in tort, such that practitioners and judges can meaningfully be assisted in arguing and deciding cases, and scholars can understand and rationalise this area of law more coherently.

[26] See J Stone, *The Province and Function of Law* (Associated General Publications 1946) 52.

[27] R Dworkin, *Law's Empire* (Fontana 1980) 225. See also S Smith, *Contract Theory* (Oxford University Press 2004) 5; R Stevens, 'Professor Sir Frederick Pollock (1845–1937): Jurist as Mayfly' in J Goudkamp and D Nolan (eds), *Scholars of Tort Law* (Hart Publishing 2019) 75, 91–94.

Why is a doctrinal method of this nature worthwhile? At least two reasons can be given. First, bearing in mind the objectives stated above, what this book sets out to do is investigate a large body of case law in order to advance arguments as to how an area of law is best understood. Engaging in a doctrinal study, rather than a theoretical, philosophical or empirical one, is the only method that can be employed to achieve this stated goal. To assist courts and practitioners in identifying what the positive law is, it is necessary to employ a doctrinal method.

Furthermore, although the importance of theoretical and philosophical accounts of tort law should not be underestimated, such accounts cannot be given without a clear picture of what the law is. This observation has been made repeatedly, both in the courts and in the academy. For example, Lord Rodger has written extra-judicially that 'one has to wonder whether it is altogether satisfactory for academic writers to go direct to the more theoretical aspects of a subject without ever really engaging with the nitty-gritty of how it actually operates in practice'.[28] Similarly, Stephen Smith has explained in his monograph on remedial law that 'it is difficult to say much about the law's normative foundations without having a clear picture of its structure'.[29] Because injunctive relief in tort is under-analysed, it means that the existing theoretical and philosophical accounts of tort law do not grapple with a significant body of cases that make up the law of tort. A doctrinal study of injunctive relief in tort law will therefore enable other scholars to take the doctrinal findings and use them in theoretical or philosophical studies.

IV. Scope

This book is primarily about when final injunctions are granted in respect of a right generated by tort law in England and Wales. Where appropriate, references are made to other common law jurisdictions such as Australia and the United States. There are numerous references to the cases in Australia in particular, as the law governing the award of injunctions in Australia is very similar to that in England and Wales. To contextualise the analysis that follows, it is necessary to make some general remarks about tort law and injunctions that demarcate the scope of this book.

A. Tort Law

This book is about when injunctions are granted in respect of a right generated by tort law. It is not concerned with when injunctions are granted in respect of other

[28] Lord Rodger, 'Judges and Academics in the United Kingdom' (2010) 29 *University of Queensland Law Journal* 29, 36.

[29] Smith (n 18) 12. See also S Smith, 'Taking Law Seriously' (2000) 50 *University of Toronto Law Journal* 241.

rights generated in private law, such as, for example, contract, equity and unjust enrichment. It is therefore necessary to articulate what causes of action are encompassed by the label 'tort law'.

Tort law is not a body of law with bright-line boundaries. No scholar has put forward a satisfactory definition of a 'tort' as distinct from other causes of action.[30] Nevertheless, one cannot deny that there is a conventional understanding of what 'tort law' is. As James Goudkamp has explained, '[i]f no [conventional] understanding existed it would be impossible to have meaningful discussions about tort law, and this is self-evidently not the case'.[31]

This book is about 'tort law' as it is conventionally understood. Provided the limits of that understanding are identified, it is therefore not necessary to engage in the debate over what a 'tort' is. One way of articulating the conventional understanding would be to adopt a definition of tortious liability provided by one or more tort theorists. However, there are two reasons why this approach would be problematic. The consensus in the literature is that no definition of a tort has commanded 'anything approaching universal support'.[32] It follows that cherry picking the 'best' definition would be unlikely to reflect the generally accepted understanding of which causes of action fall within the subject. Furthermore, even if it could be said that one definition is better than most and is therefore generally accepted in the literature, there is a risk that adopting such a definition would erroneously include or exclude causes of action for the sake of conforming with a particular theoretical perspective. For example, consider Winfield's influential definition:

> Tortious liability arises from the breach of a duty primarily fixed by the law; this duty is towards persons generally and its breach is redressable by an action for unliquidated damages.[33]

Although this definition has merit, adopting it would mean that copyright and patent infringements, and discrimination actions for compensation under the Equality Act 2010, would be included in the analysis in order to conform with Winfield's theoretical position. As any tort lawyer would recognise, including these causes of action within the area of tort law would be problematic, as such actions are plainly not included within the conventional understanding of tort.

i. An Atheoretical Definition

The better way to articulate the conventional understanding of what tort law comprises is to adopt, and expand upon, an atheoretical definition. This book

[30] 'Numerous attempts have been made to define a "tort" with varying degrees of lack of success': Goudkamp and Nolan (n 9) [1-001].

[31] J Goudkamp, *Tort Law Defences* (Hart Publishing 2013) 21.

[32] ibid.

[33] Goudkamp and Nolan (n 9) [1-003].

adopts Tony Weir's definition of tort law: 'Tort is what is in the tort books.'[34] What this definition comprises is the common law and statutory causes of action that are examined in the tort textbooks in England and Wales.[35] It would be superfluous to set out a list of what causes of action fall within this definition. There is one difficulty with adopting Weir's definition, however. It is that the tort textbooks give different answers as to whether certain causes of action, which sit at the intersection of tort and another area of law, fall within or outside tort law. This problem can be remedied by identifying whether those causes of action fit within the conventional understanding of tort law. Four points are worth highlighting.

First, although copyright and patent infringements have recently been included in one tort textbook,[36] they are excluded from the analysis as they are not examined in the remaining tort textbooks and therefore straightforwardly do not fall within the conventional understanding of tort law. Nevertheless, the tort of passing off is included in the analysis. That is because the tort is a common law cause of action and has therefore traditionally fallen within the conventional understanding of tort law (hence why it is analysed in all of the leading tort texts).

The second point is that equitable wrongs (such as, for example, breach of confidence, breach of fiduciary duty, breach of trust, and knowing receipt of trust assets) are excluded from the analysis. Although it has been argued that equitable wrongs are torts,[37] they are not analysed in tort textbooks as the conventional understanding of tort law does not include the equitable causes of action. There is, however, one exception. A brief discussion of breach of confidence is found in one textbook.[38] This would suggest that perhaps this cause of action should be considered in the analysis. However, there are two reasons why the action must be excluded. First, the other tort textbooks do not analyse breach of confidence and it therefore cannot be said that the action falls within the conventional understanding of tort law. Further, breach of confidence was developed by the Chancery and it is well established that the Chancery had a separate jurisdiction to restrain equitable wrongs by injunction.[39] The modern law reflects this position, as a claimant is not required to meet a jurisdictional threshold (such as, for example, by proving that damages would be an inadequate remedy) before a court will consider whether it should award an injunction in respect of equitable wrongs.[40] The principles upon which injunctions are granted to restrain a breach of confidence are therefore distinct from the equivalent principles in respect of legal wrongs. Hence,

[34] T Weir, *An Introduction to Tort Law* (2nd edn, Oxford University Press 2006) ix.

[35] The tort textbooks that are referred to have been chosen because they set out to provide the most comprehensive account of tort law. Those texts are: Oliphant (ed) (n 9); McBride and Bagshaw (n 9); Goudkamp and Nolan (n 9); Jones and Dugdale (eds) (n 9).

[36] Jones and Dugdale (eds) (n 9) ch 24.

[37] J Edelman, 'Equitable Torts' (2002) 10 *Torts Law Journal* 64.

[38] See Jones and Dugdale (eds) (n 9) [26-05].

[39] See, eg, Spry (n 12) 333, 343; Heydon, Leeming and Turner (n 12) [21-015].

[40] *Attorney General v Mayor of Liverpool* (1835) 1 My&C 171, 210; *Fouche v Superannuation Fund Board* (1952) 88 CLR 609, 639.

in the context of a book that aims to investigate the principles governing when an injunction can be granted in aid of a *legal* right generated by tort law, it would be misconceived to classify breach of confidence as a tort.

The third point is that the action of misuse of private information, as distinct from the equitable action of breach of confidence, is included in the analysis. That is because the current prevailing view in the case law and the literature is that misuse of private information is a tort.[41] Finally, for the avoidance of doubt, breaches of contract and unjust enrichments are excluded from the analysis as they are straightforwardly not classified as torts.

ii. The Exceptions

There are two exceptions to the general position that the scope of this book is limited to causes of action that fall within the conventional understanding of 'tort law'. First, before the Judicature Act reforms of 1873–75 were passed, copyright and patent infringements were conceptualised by the Chancery as legal wrongs that were akin to actions that we would now conceptualise as torts (such as waste, trespass to land, and public and private nuisance). Accordingly, when analysing the development of the injunction in aid of legal rights in chapter 2, it is necessary to examine cases involving intellectual property infringements to give greater depth to the analysis.

Second, throughout this book several equitable discretionary considerations are analysed. These considerations are general in nature as they can be considered by a court when deciding to grant an injunction in respect of *any* legal or equitable right. It follows that some of the leading cases concerning particular discretionary considerations involve the protection of non-tort law rights, such as contractual, intellectual property and equitable rights. It is therefore necessary to examine these cases for the purpose of analysing the law in respect of the discretionary considerations.

B. The Injunction

The injunction is a complex remedy and it is worth analysing its intricacy by reference to five main points: (i) the meaning of an injunction; (ii) how an injunction in aid of a tort law right is a remedy in equity and in tort law; (iii) how such an injunction operates in practice; (iv) this book's focus on final injunctions; and (v) how the power to award damages in lieu of an injunction is separate from the power to grant an injunction and is therefore not analysed comprehensively in this book.

[41] See, eg, *McKennitt v Ash* [2006] EWCA Civ 1714 [8]; *Imerman v Tchenguiz* [2010] EWCA Civ 908 [65]; Oliphant (ed) (n 9) ch 24; McBride and Bagshaw (n 9) 23, ch 17; Goudkamp and Nolan (n 9) ch 13; Jones and Dugdale (eds) (n 9) [26-37].

i. *What is an Injunction?*

An injunction is often described as a court order forbidding the person to whom it is addressed from doing something or commanding that person to do something.[42] However, as Heydon, Leeming and Turner have explained, there is a problem with accepting this description as a *definition* of an injunction.[43] It would mean that any court order that required a person to do something (eg, to pay a litigant's costs after judgment in her favour) would be classified as an injunction. This is obviously not what is meant by the term 'injunction'. It is therefore necessary to set out what the best way is to define, or at least describe, an injunction.

An injunction could be defined as a court order that, if breached, is punishable for civil contempt of court. As explained by the authors of *Arlidge, Eady & Smith on Contempt*, '[b]reaches of injunctions are always traditionally addressed as falling within the category of civil contempt',[44] and therefore a defendant who acts in breach of an injunction can be fined or imprisoned for a maximum of two years, or his assets can be sequestrated.[45] The problem with this definition, however, is that it captures court orders that are not injunctions. As the authors of *Arlidge, Eady & Smith on Contempt* explain, civil contempt 'may arise in a variety of circumstances … during the course of civil litigation' as civil contempt 'consists principally in disobedience to an order of the court'.[46] To give just one example, a defendant will act in contempt of court for breaching a search order requiring him to preserve documents relevant to a claimant's claim.[47] Obviously, such an order is not an injunction.

Another way an injunction could be defined is as a court order that expressly uses the word 'injunction' to describe the remedy that is granted. There are two problems with this definition, however. First, court orders, as distinct from court judgments, are not always publicly available. It would therefore be impossible to employ this definition in practice. Second, requiring a court to expressly use the word 'injunction' in its order or judgment would be unduly formal, as it would exclude cases in which what appear to be injunctions have been granted even though the word 'injunction' was not used.

Finally, an injunction could be defined by reference to the courts' power to award injunctions. An injunction is classified as an equitable remedy because it was developed as a remedy by the Chancery. Immediately before the passing of the Judicature Act reforms of 1873–75, the Chancery had an inherent power to

[42] See, eg, Spry (n 12) 332; Heydon, Leeming and Turner (n 12) [21-005]; Davies (n 12) [18-003]; Glister and Lee (n 12) [28-001].

[43] Heydon, Leeming and Turner (n 12) [21-005].

[44] P Londono (ed), *Arlidge, Eady & Smith on Contempt* (5th edn, Sweet & Maxwell 2019) [3-18]. See also *Scott v Scott* [1913] AC 417 (HL) 456.

[45] See Contempt of Court Act 1981, s 14; Civil Procedure Rules 1998, pt 81; *Jennison v Baker* [1972] 2 QB 52 (CA).

[46] Londono (ed) (n 44) [12-1].

[47] *Ocado Group v McKeeve* [2021] EWCA Civ 145.

grant an injunction (and the common law courts had a statutory power to grant an injunction pursuant to section 79 of the Common Law Procedure Act 1854).[48] Those powers were then transferred to the Supreme Court of Judicature (now known as the 'Senior Courts of England and Wales'[49]) pursuant to section 16 of the Supreme Court of Judicature Act 1873 (the '1873 Act'). In the present day, the powers have been preserved by section 19(2)(b) of the Senior Courts Act 1981 (the '1981 Act') and are embodied in section 37(1) of the same Act,[50] which provides:

> The High Court may by order (whether interlocutory or final) grant an injunction or appoint a receiver in all cases in which it appears to the court to be just and convenient to do so.

It has been held at the highest judicial level that section 37(1) 'merely confirms and restates the powers of the Chancery (and common law) courts to grant injunctions which existed before [the Judicature Act reforms]'.[51] What this means is that section 37(1) does not confer a fresh power on courts to grant injunctions, the nature of which is *res integra*. Rather, every time an order is made by a court which is in substance an injunction, the court's power to make that order is confirmed by section 37(1) of the 1981 Act but derives from the pre-1873 Act powers of the courts to grant injunctions.[52] It is in this way that injunctions could be said to be distinguished robustly from all other court orders.

However, even this definition has problems. Other remedies may be awarded pursuant to the power confirmed by section 37(1) of the 1981 Act, such as an order appointing a receiver. Moreover, there are other legal sources that give courts the power to award injunctions, such as section 3A of the Protections from Harassment Act 1997. It follows that a definition limited by the power to award an injunction confirmed by section 37(1) is, at the same time, overly broad and overly narrow.

Consistently with the observation made by Dawson, Toohey, Gaudron, McHugh, Gummow and Kirby JJ in the High Court of Australia's observations that 'the term "injunction" in the parlance of equity has no fixed minimum definition' and that 'it is legal usage which decides which court orders are to be identified as injunctions',[53] the approach taken in this book is that it would be futile to advance and defend a bright-line definition of an injunction. The better view is that an

[48] These powers are examined in detail in ch 2.

[49] Constitutional Reform Act 2005, s 59.

[50] *Fourie v Le Roux* [2007] 1 WLR 320 (HL) [25]; *Convoy Collateral Ltd v Broad Idea International Ltd* [2021] UKPC 24, [2023] AC 389 [40]; *Wolverhampton City Council v London Gypsies and Travellers* [2023] UKSC 47, [2024] AC 983 [17]. Note that the courts' power to grant interim injunctions is also embodied in CPR, pt 25.

[51] *Convoy v Broad* (n 50) [40]; *Wolverhampton* (n 50) [17]. See also *Mercedes Benz AG v Leiduck* [1996] AC 284 (PC) 295, 308 (in indirect terms); *Fourie* (n 50) [25].

[52] *Convoy v Broad* (n 50) [40]; *Wolverhampton* (n 50) [17]. See also *Mercedes Benz* (n 51) 308; *Fourie* (n 50) [25].

[53] *CSR Ltd v Cigna Insurance Australia Ltd* (1997) 189 CLR 345, 390, citing Millett J in *ISC Technologies Ltd v Radcliffe* (Chancery Division, 7 December 1990) 10–12.

injunction is a remedy that can only be described by general remarks. Those remarks should be conceptualised to be sign-posts that point someone in the right direction in answering the question whether a court order is an injunction (rather than as concrete boundaries that are capable of strict application).

Accordingly, when this book refers to a case concerning an injunction, it means any judgment in which a party asks a court to make an order where: (i) breach of that order is punishable for civil contempt of court; and (ii) in most cases, the court's power to make the order is confirmed by section 37(1) of the 1981 Act and derives from the courts' pre-1873 Act powers (irrespective of whether this is stated explicitly in the judgment).

ii. A Remedy in Equity and in Tort Law

An injunction is classified as an equitable remedy because the courts' power to grant injunctions derives from the Chancery's inherent power to do so. Importantly, however, it should not be thought that when an injunction is granted in respect of a tort law right this indicates nothing about tort law and can only illustrate how equity operates as a distinct body of law. It is necessary to consider the effects of the Judicature Act reforms of 1873–75 and a fundamental principle of injunction law to fully understand this point.

Although there have been some debates about the effects of the Judicature Act reforms, this book adopts the orthodox view that these reforms did not change the substance of the law but were purely procedural in effect.[54] Given that an injunction is an equitable remedy, at first sight this would suggest that injunctions granted in respect of a tort law right are remedies solely in equity.

However, a fundamental principle of injunction law (that existed both before and after the passing of the Judicature Act reforms) is that a claimant must establish a legal or equitable right before she can obtain an injunction.[55] The effect of this principle is that when an injunction is granted to restrain or remedy a tort, equity can operate to award an injunction only because of the right generated by tort law in the first place. As Zipursky has observed, when a court grants an injunction in respect of tortious conduct, 'it is doing so because of the parties' [duties and corresponding] rights under tort law'.[56] The grant of an injunction in aid of a tort law right therefore does not create equitable rights (like, for example, the doctrine of proprietary estoppel). Rather, when such an injunction is granted, it enforces a *legal* duty that is generated by tort law. In this sense, equity and tort operate

[54] *Salt v Cooper* (1880) 16 Ch D 544, 549; *Ind Coope & Co v Emmerson* (1887) 12 App Cas 300, 309. See, generally, S Degeling and J Edelman (eds), *Equity in Commercial Law* (Lawbook Co 2005).

[55] *Day v Brownrigg* (1878) 10 Ch D 294; *Cowley v Cowley* [1901] AC 450 (HL); *Waterside Workers' Federation of Australia v JW Alexander Ltd* (1918) 25 CLR 434. Although, exceptions have been made for some particular types of injunctions: see *Convoy v Broad* (n 50); A Tettenborn, 'Injunctions Without Damages' (1987) 38 *Northern Ireland Legal Quarterly* 118.

[56] BC Zipursky, 'Civil Recourse, Not Corrective Justice' (2003) 91 *Georgetown Law Journal* 695, 713.

together as one body of law: the common law of England and Wales. It necessarily follows that injunctions granted in respect of tort law rights are remedies in equity *and* in tort law.

The award of injunctive relief therefore reveals as much about tort law as it does about equity. Indeed, it is important to remember that 'equity' and 'tort law' are organising labels that have been employed by courts and scholars to help make sense of complex bodies of principles. At times, however, these labels can obscure the interactions between legal phenomena.[57] While the injunction has traditionally been classified as an 'equitable' remedy, we should not let this classification prevent us from recognising that an injunction in aid of a tort law right is also a remedy in tort law.

iii. The Operation of the Injunction in Practice

It is well established that an injunction can be granted in aid of a legal right generated by tort law.[58] Moreover, such an injunction can take interim or final, and prohibitory, mandatory or quia timet, form.[59] Because an injunction is a discretionary remedy, an injunction is not available as of right, even if a claimant's legal right has been infringed by a defendant.[60] Not only must additional facts be proved by the claimant in order to satisfy the court that an injunction can be awarded, but there are also a number of equitable discretionary considerations that, if engaged by the defendant, may persuade a court not to exercise its discretion in favour of the claimant (or, conversely, if engaged by the claimant, may persuade a court that there are additional reasons why an injunction should be granted). If a court ultimately decides to grant an injunction, serious consequences follow. As explained in section IV.B.i, a defendant who acts in breach of an injunction will be liable in civil contempt, and he can be fined or imprisoned for a maximum of two years, or his assets can be sequestrated.

Finally, it is important to bear in mind that while injunctions can be granted against an officer of the Crown when sued in his or her personal capacity,[61] injunctions cannot be granted against the Crown itself. That is because section 21(1)(a) of the Crown Proceedings Act 1947 provides that:

> where in any proceedings against the Crown any such relief is sought as might in proceedings between subjects be granted by way of injunction or specific performance, the court shall not grant an injunction or make an order for specific performance, but may in lieu thereof make an order declaratory of the rights of the parties …

[57] See, generally, T Khaitan and S Steel, 'Areas of Law: Three Questions in Special Jurisprudence' (2023) 43 *OJLS* 76.

[58] See ch 2.

[59] See ch 3.

[60] *Law Debenture Trust Corporation v Ural Caspian Oil Corporation Ltd* [1995] Ch 152 (CA).

[61] See *M v Home Office* [1994] 1 AC 377 (HL).

iv. Final Injunctions

The scope of this book is limited to cases in which *final* injunctions are sought. That is because the book is concerned with what the award of injunctions indicates about tort law. It is the remedy *after* the rights of the parties have been determined that is most indicative of the law's response to the defendant's infringement, or threatened infringement, of the claimant's tort law right. Interim injunctions are awarded pursuant to principles that are distinct from those that govern the award of final injunctions.[62] Furthermore, those principles are sensitive to what the law's response should be *before* the rights of the parties have been determined. It necessarily follows that the principles governing when an interim injunction can be granted are not considered. Nevertheless, many cases concerning interim injunctions are analysed in this book. That is because they are helpful in illuminating the law on final injunctions (as where the defendant admits to committing the tort alleged by the claimant) and the law on the discretionary considerations that govern when an injunction can be granted.

The focus on final injunctions also means that all other remedies that are not classified as an injunction (pursuant to how the remedy is described above) are excluded. Any court orders that are analogous to an injunction are *not* analysed in this book. For example, orders for specific delivery under the Torts (Interference with Goods) Act 1977 are excluded. The exclusion of remedies that are akin to injunctive relief is justified for two reasons. First, it would be problematic to analyse such remedies as if they were identical to injunctions because the power to make such orders, and the principles governing their award, is straightforwardly distinct from that governing the award of injunctive relief. Moreover, the remedies that are akin to injunctive relief are not general tort remedies in the same way that injunctive relief is. Such orders therefore do not indicate how tort law operates on a wider scale.

Although, generally speaking, only final injunctions are considered, there are two exceptions. First, it is explained in section V that chapter 2 examines how the injunction in aid of legal rights came to be developed by the Chancery. In that chapter, cases concerning both interim and final injunctions are examined because, as we will see, an appreciation of the Chancery's jurisdictional basis for awarding interim injunctions is crucial to understanding the basis for the award of final injunctions.

The second exception is related to declarations. Declarations straightforwardly do not fall within the definition of an injunction adopted in this book. However, it was said in section IV.B.iii that, pursuant to section 21(1)(a) of the Crown Proceedings Act 1947, only declarations (and not injunctions) can be granted against the Crown. Declarations are therefore functionally equivalent to injunctions when they are awarded against the Crown.[63] It follows that it is necessary to

[62] See *American Cyanamid Co v Ethicon Ltd* [1975] AC 396 (HL).
[63] See, eg, *Dennis v Ministry of Defence* [2003] EWHC 793 (QB) [80].

analyse the (rare) cases in which a declaration is sought against the Crown in aid of a tort law right.

v. Damages in Lieu

The final limitation on the scope of this book is that it does not include a chapter on the remedy of damages awarded in lieu of an injunction. That is because the question of when damages are awarded in lieu of an injunction is separate from, and considered after, the question of whether an injunction should be awarded to restrain or remedy a tort. As Jolowicz has observed, the power to grant damages in lieu is 'a discretion upon a discretion'.[64] Therefore, exclusion of the topic does not detract from the doctrinal findings in respect of injunctions in tort. It is also worth recognising that the topic gives rise to quite different subsidiary questions that would require extensive consideration (for example, how damages in lieu are calculated, and what the implications are of their award).

Importantly, however, this limitation certainly does not mean that all cases in which damages have been awarded in lieu of an injunction are excluded from this book. On the contrary, many such cases are analysed. This is for two reasons. First, damages in lieu of an injunction can be awarded only where the court has jurisdiction to grant an injunction, in other words once the claimant has established a case for an injunction by proving the necessary conditions for relief.[65] Accordingly, as in cases in which injunctions are granted, the cases in which damages have been awarded in lieu of an injunction demonstrate when the necessary conditions for injunctive relief in tort law are engaged. Second, such cases readily demonstrate the limits of the equitable discretionary considerations. In some cases, damages have been awarded in lieu of an injunction because the defendant has engaged a countervailing discretionary consideration that has persuaded the court that an injunction should not be granted, but the court decides in its discretion that damages should be awarded in lieu of an injunction. In some other cases, a claimant specifically seeks damages in lieu of an injunction because the claimant has accepted that damages would be an adequate remedy. These cases are highly relevant to the analysis of the discretionary considerations and are therefore included.

V. Overview of the Book

This book consists of eight chapters in total; an introduction (chapter 1), six substantive chapters (chapters 2 to 7), and a conclusion (chapter 8). The substantive chapters mirror the objectives of the book as previously set out.

[64] Jolowicz (n 18) 240. See also RA Buckley, *The Law of Nuisance* (Butterworths 1981) 131–32; M Bryan, 'Injunctions and Damages: Taking *Shelfer* off the Shelf' (2016) 28 *Singapore Academy of Law Journal* 921, 924–25.

[65] *Leeds Industrial Co-operative Society Ltd v Slack* [1924] AC 851 (HL), 859; *Jaggard v Sawyer* [1995] 1 WLR 269 (CA), 287; *One Step (Support) Ltd v Morris-Garner* [2018] UKSC 20, [2019] AC 649 [44].

Chapter 2 analyses historical case law and literature to consider how the Chancery came to develop its jurisdiction to award injunctions in aid of legal rights from the seventeenth century until the passing of the Judicature Act reforms of 1873–75. It offers the first chapter-length account of how final injunctions in aid of tort law rights came to be developed by the Chancery. The chapter draws out three key lessons that are integral to the analysis of the modern law.

Chapter 3 examines the formal distinctions between prohibitory, mandatory and quia timet injunctions. Although modern treatises on equitable remedies provide short definitions of the different types of injunction, sustained analysis directed at identifying the precise distinctions between prohibitory, mandatory and quia timet injunctions is rare and is not the subject of a stand-alone chapter in texts on injunctions. This chapter offers a new perspective by making three key arguments about the formal distinctions between prohibitory, mandatory and quia timet injunctions, which enables the book to analyse the law with respect to each type of injunction in later chapters. The chapter argues that two types of mandatory injunction are awarded to restrain or remedy torts. One is a desisting mandatory injunction, which orders a defendant to do a positive act to stop his tort from continuing. The other is a restorative mandatory injunction, which orders a defendant to do a positive act to remedy a tort that has been completed.

Chapters 4, 5 and 6 represent the doctrinal core of the book. Each of the chapters concludes by summarising the analytical process that is employed by the courts to determine whether to grant a particular type of injunction to restrain or remedy a tort.

Chapter 4 advances a coherent account of the positive law governing when prohibitory injunctions can be awarded to restrain future torts. The law in respect of prohibitory injunctions is analysed first because a prohibitory injunction was the first type of injunction that was developed by the Court of Chancery, and such injunctions have been granted in respect of the greatest number of different torts. Chapter 4 is the largest in the book. It is argued that damages are not required to be an inadequate remedy for a final injunction to be granted in tort, and that any tort (except causes of action generating primary liabilities) can be restrained by a prohibitory injunction. The chapter also examines the equitable discretionary considerations that militate against, and in favour of, the award of injunctive relief. The arguments centre on what is required to engage the discretionary considerations.

Chapter 5 advances a coherent account of the positive law governing when desisting and restorative mandatory injunctions can be granted to restrain or remedy a tort. The core argument of chapter 5 is that a desisting mandatory injunction can be granted where a defendant is continuing to commit any tort and it is necessary for the defendant to do a positive act to stop his tort from continuing. By contrast, a restorative mandatory injunction can be granted where damages would be an inadequate remedy for a particular consequence caused by a defendant's completed tort and it is necessary for the defendant to do a positive act to rectify that consequence.

Chapter 6 advances a coherent account of the positive law governing when quia timet injunctions can be awarded to restrain future torts. The primary contention in chapter 6 is that quia timet relief in tort law can be granted upon the establishment of two distinct sets of necessary conditions by the claimant: first, that there is a real and imminent risk that a tort will be committed; and, second, that the claimant is unable to protect herself from a real risk that the defendant will commit a tort against her that will cause irreparable harm.

Chapter 7 considers the implications of the doctrinal findings for tort law more generally. This enables the book to engage further with debates about the nature of tort law. It is argued that the findings give rise to at least three main implications. The first is that it cannot be said that damages are tort law's 'primary' remedy as the availability of the injunction as a general remedy is essential to understanding tort law. The second is that tort law and property law cannot be distinguished on the basis that property rights are generally protected by injunctive relief, while other rights generated by tort law are generally protected by liability rules. The third implication is that although the tort of negligence can be restrained by an injunction, one should not conclude from this that the duty of care in negligence is a primary duty.

Chapter 8 concludes by reflecting on the importance of the main findings of the book. Although several reasons are given for why the findings are important, the most significant point is that the way in which tort law is expounded in textbooks and monographs, and taught in universities, needs revising. Specifically, we must not overemphasise the award of damages and neglect to highlight the importance of the injunction. The true position is that injunctive relief is as crucial as damages are to enforcing the rights that are generated by tort law.

2

Equity's Development of the Injunction in Aid of Legal Rights Before the Judicature Acts

I. Introduction

The injunction has long served as a remedy to restrain the commission of legal wrongs. From as early as the seventeenth century, the Court of Chancery ('the Chancery') was willing to award an injunction to prohibit a defendant from committing legal waste in order to protect a plaintiff's legal right.[1] By the time the Judicature Act reforms of 1873–75 were passed, courts routinely granted injunctions to restrain various causes of action that we would now classify as 'torts', as well as negative breaches of contract and intellectual property infringements. As Maitland observed in his lectures at the end of the nineteenth century, 'a very large part of the whole province of Tort is a proper field for the injunction'.[2]

The courts' practice of granting injunctions in aid of legal rights is therefore age-old and, as explained in chapter 1, is still predicated on the Chancery's jurisdiction to award such injunctions in the nineteenth century. However, little consideration has been given to the history of the injunction in aid of legal rights. Gummow has considered the topic briefly.[3] He posits that the Chancery had jurisdiction to award such an injunction when a legal wrong would risk causing the plaintiff irreparable harm.[4] Nineteenth-century treatises on the law of injunctions also provide a general analysis of the relevant case law at this time.[5] However, they do not provide a historical account of how the injunction in aid of legal rights emerged.

It goes without saying that historical legal research is indispensable to a proper understanding of the modern law. As Sir Percy Winfield observed, it is 'often

[1] See, eg, *Cole v Peyson* (1637) Rep Ch 106 and n 17.

[2] F Maitland, *Equity: A Course of Lectures* (Cambridge University Press 1909) Lecture XX, 261.

[3] Justice William Gummow, 'The Injunction in Aid of Legal Rights – An Australian Perspective' (1993) 56 *Law & Contemporary Problems* 83.

[4] ibid 91–92.

[5] See generally R Eden, *A Treatise on the Law of Injunctions* (Butterworth 1821); C Drewry, *A Treatise on the Law and Practice of Injunctions* (S Sweet 1841); W Joyce, *The Doctrines and Principles of the Law of Injunctions* (Stevens & Haynes 1877); W Kerr, *A Treatise on the Law and Practice of Injunctions in Equity* (3rd edn, Maxwell & Sons 1888).

difficult to state what the law is without knowing something of its history and always dangerous to attempt reform of the law without it'.[6] This chapter engages in historical legal research in order to contextualise and enhance the analysis of the modern law in the later chapters of this book. The chapter examines seventeenth-, eighteenth- and nineteenth-century cases and literature, and provides an account of the development of the injunction in aid of legal rights in the Chancery from the remedy's inception in the seventeenth century until the passing of the Judicature Act reforms of 1873–75. Throughout the chapter, litigants are referred to as 'plaintiffs' and 'defendants', and injunctions are referred to as 'perpetual' and 'interlocutory'.[7] The cases examined are those reported in the *English Reports*, *The Jurist*, and the *Weekly Reporter*.[8] Four caveats must, however, be noted in respect of the scope of this chapter.

First, for the reasons given in chapter 1, this chapter examines perpetual and *interlocutory* injunctions, and it considers cases concerning copyright and patent infringements.

Second, the title of this chapter refers to injunctions in aid of 'legal rights' instead of injunctions in aid of 'tort law rights'. That is because 'tort law' was not recognised as a distinct legal category before the passing of the Judicature Acts and the Chancery did not conceptualise an injunction to be awarded in aid of a 'tort law' right. It is important to recognise, however, that this chapter does not analyse the cases concerning injunctions in aid of negative contractual rights. As was explained in chapter 1, breaches of contract are beyond the scope of this book.

Third, the principal focus of this chapter is *prohibitory* and *mandatory* injunctions. The chapter does not consider cases concerning quia timet injunctions as, for reasons explained in chapter 6, it is more appropriate to analyse the history of such injunctions in that chapter.

Fourth, it is important to appreciate that the Chancery was not the only court granting injunctions in aid of legal rights before the passing of the Judicature Act reforms. The Court of Exchequer Chamber also granted injunctions in its equitable jurisdiction until such jurisdiction was abolished in 1841.[9] Furthermore, after the enactment of the Common Law Procedure Act 1854, the Courts of Common Law had the power to grant injunctions.[10] This chapter therefore includes the cases

[6] PH Winfield, 'Law and Other Things' (1938) 6 *CLJ* 461, 462.

[7] Although this terminology is not in accordance with the Civil Procedure Rules, it is used in order to complement the 17th- to 19th-century sources.

[8] This chapter is unable to take into account the likely legions of unopposed injunctions, and unreported decisions on opposed injunctions, all of which bear upon the practice and beliefs of judicial officers and practitioners.

[9] DB Fowler, *The Practice of the Court of Exchequer: Upon Proceedings in Equity* (2nd edn, Butterworth 1817) vol 1, 1; Administration of Justice Act 1841, s 1.

[10] There are very few cases involving such injunctions, however, as the common law judges took a restrictive view of their equitable powers under the Act: WF Finlason, *An Exposition of Our Judicial System and Civil Procedure as Reconstructed Under the Judicature Acts* (Longmans, Green and Co 1877) 42–46; M Lobban, 'Preparing for Fusion: Reforming the Nineteenth-Century Court of Chancery, Part II' (2004) 22 *Law and History Review* 565, 590.

in which these courts granted injunctions. However, for simplicity, the remainder of this chapter will refer to 'the Chancery's' jurisdiction to award an injunction.

The chapter is divided into five main sections. Section II briefly considers the origins of the Chancery injunction, explores the meaning of 'irreparable harm' and examines the reasons put forward by Gummow for his contention that a risk of irreparable harm was the sole criterion for the Chancery's jurisdiction to award an injunction in aid of a legal right. Section III examines the historical case law and literature to determine why the Chancery found that it had jurisdiction to intervene to restrain legal wrongs (which we would now conceptualise to be torts) by injunction. Section IV considers to what extent the discretionary considerations influenced whether injunctions in aid of legal rights were ultimately awarded. Section V examines how the mandatory injunction in aid of legal rights came to be developed. Section VI concludes by summarising the three main lessons of broader importance that are advanced in this chapter.

II. The Origins of the Injunction and the Irreparable Harm Requirement

An injunction was a writ issuing from a Court of Equity directing a person to do or not do a specified act.[11] In the fifteenth century, the Chancery developed the 'common' injunction.[12] This injunction restrained litigants from commencing or maintaining proceedings at common law or executing common law judgments. Over the course of the sixteenth century, the Chancery also developed the 'special' injunction.[13] This injunction was awarded in cases where the Chancellor, motivated by his conscience, believed that equitable relief was necessary in the particular circumstances of the case. Although there is some evidence to suggest that special injunctions were granted to restrain the tort of legal waste during this period,[14] the special injunction was awarded in a variety of cases and there seem to have been no guiding principles underlying the award of such injunctions.[15]

After the famous and well-documented dispute between Coke and Ellesmere, which crystallised in the 1615 decision of the *Earl of Oxford's Case*,[16] the Chancery's power to award injunctions was confirmed. In the years that followed,

[11] Eden (n 5) 1–2. Note, however, that the usage of the term 'injunction' was not uniform, as chancery 'orders' were also sometimes described as injunctions: see ibid 290; DG Lubé, *An Analysis of the Principles of Equity Pleading* (Sweet 1823) 67–68.

[12] J Baker, *An Introduction to English Legal History* (5th edn, Oxford University Press 2019) 114; W Holdsworth, *A History of English Law* (Sweet & Maxwell 1909) vol V, 335; D Raack, 'A History of Injunctions in England Before 1700' (1986) 61 *Indiana Law Journal* 539, 568–70.

[13] See, eg, I Spry, *Equitable Remedies* (9th edn, Thomson Reuters 2014) 333; P Davies, 'Injunctions' in J McGhee and S Elliott (eds), *Snell's Equity* (34th edn, Sweet & Maxwell 2021) [18-004].

[14] See *Anonymous* (1603) Cary 26.

[15] See, eg, Holdsworth (n 12) 323, 336; Raack (n 12) 564.

[16] *Earl of Oxford's Case* (1615) Chan Rep 1.

the Chancery developed a practice of awarding perpetual injunctions to restrain waste, which continued into the eighteenth century.[17] From about the early eighteenth century, injunctions were awarded to restrain nuisance,[18] breach of a negative contractual stipulation,[19] and copyright and patent infringement.[20] By the beginning of the nineteenth century, interlocutory injunctions were granted to restrain trespass to land.[21] This raises the question: on what doctrinal bases did the Chancery believe that it had jurisdiction to intervene and grant injunctions to protect legal rights?

Gummow has written that to 'support its decisions against allegations of arbitrary and unprincipled interference in common law proceedings', in the eighteenth century the Chancery founded the doctrine of 'irreparable harm' to govern when the Chancery could award an injunction to protect legal rights.[22] Other scholars also take this view, although without providing an explicit historical basis.[23] For example, Heydon, Leeming and Turner state that 'the reason why during the eighteenth century the only five cases in which equity would grant injunctions in the auxiliary jurisdiction were to restrain waste, nuisance, infringement of patents, infringement of copyright, and breach of negative stipulations in contract' was because a risk of irreparable harm needed to be proved in order for such an injunction to be granted.[24]

Gummow traced the irreparable harm doctrine back to the 1773 decision of the House of Lords in *Welby v Duke of Rutland*.[25] In that case, the appellant disputed the respondent's title to the manor of Denton. He sought an injunction restraining the respondent from appointing any steward or game keeper for the manor in the future on the basis that these actions would perpetuate the respondent's allegedly false title.[26] The respondent reportedly submitted that because the appellant's claim was a legal one, the Chancery would not have jurisdiction to intervene,

[17] See, eg, *Cole v Peyson* (n 1); *Jane Roberts an Infant* (1657) Hardres 97; *Lady Katharine Jacob Widow v John Thasker Gent* (1675) Rep t Finch 197; *John Cornish Gent v Thomas New Esq* (1675) Rep t Finish 219; *Goring v Goring* (1677) 3 Swans 662; *Tracy v Tracy* (1681) 1 Vern 23; *Robinson v Litton* (1744) 3 Atk 209 (interlocutory, quia timet), 1 Dick 210 (perpetual, quia timet); *Anonymous* (1747) 3 Atk 485; *Cuddon v Morley* (1848) 7 Hare 202 (perpetual). See also the remarks in *Garth v Cotton* (1753) 3 Atk 752.

[18] See, eg, *Dean and Chapter of Durham v The Member and Burgesses of Newcastle upon Tyne* (1698) Colles 18; *Cherrington v Abney Mill* (1709) 2 Vern 646; *Ryder v Bentham* (1750) 1 Ves Sen 543 (quia timet); *Duke of Grafton v Hilliard* (1751) 4 De G & Sm 326 (although the injunction was later discharged); *Fishmongers' Company v East India Company* (1752) Dick 163; *Baines v Baker* (1752) 3 Atk 750.

[19] See *Martin v Nutkin* (1724) 2 P Wms 266; *East-India Company v Vincent* (1740) 2 Atk 83.

[20] See, eg, *Pope v Curl* (1741) 2 Atk 342 (copyright); *Hicks v Raincock* (1783) Dick 647 (patent).

[21] See, eg, *Mitchell v Dors* (1801) 6 Ves Jr 984.

[22] Gummow (n 3) 91–92. See also E Williams and F Guthrie-Smith (eds), *Daniell's Chancery Practice* (8th edn, Stevens & Sons 1914) 16.

[23] See, eg, Spry (n 13) 396; JD Heydon, MJ Leeming and PG Turner, *Meagher, Gummow & Lehane's Equity: Doctrines & Remedies* (5th edn, LexisNexis 2015) [21-040].

[24] Heydon, Leeming and Turner (n 23) [21-040].

[25] *Welby v Duke of Rutland* (1773) 2 Bro PC 39.

[26] ibid 41.

> unless there are particular circumstances stated in the bill, shewing the necessity of the Court's interposition, either for preventing multiplicity of suits, or other vexation, or for preventing an injustice irremediable by a Court of Law.[27]

The respondent accordingly submitted that the injunction should not be granted, as not only was there no 'pretence for vexation, or multiplicity of suits' but the appellant's alleged damage was also common to every legal claim to real property before it was tried.[28] The House of Lords was reported to have dismissed the appeal, apparently accepting the arguments of the respondent.[29]

Although it was argued in *Welby* that the Chancery could only intervene where, inter alia, there was 'irremediable injustice', Gummow posits that the decision established that injunctions would be granted to protect legal rights only where the plaintiff would suffer 'irreparable harm'.[30] Two cases in the highest appellate courts in England and Australia also interpret the decision in *Welby* in this way. In the 1904 House of Lords decision of *Colls v Home and Colonial Stores Ltd*,[31] Lord Macnaghten, in the context of reflecting upon the Chancery's power to award injunctions to restrain nuisances, observed:

> Courts of Equity had no original jurisdiction in the matter. Their province was simply to grant an injunction in aid of the legal right where there was danger of irreparable mischief, or where an injunction was required to prevent multiplicity of actions ...[32]

Furthermore, and as Gummow notes, this also was the view of two judges of the High Court of Australia in *Heavener v Loomes*.[33] In that case, Isaacs and Rich JJ stated that the doctrine of 'irreparable damage' was founded in *Welby v Duke of Rutland* and that the decision stood for the proposition that 'where the title sued upon is purely legal, some equity must be shown to justify the intervention of the Court, such as "an injustice irremediable by a Court of law"'.[34]

The assumption made by Gummow, Lord Macnaughten, and by Isaacs and Rich JJ, that the expression 'irremediable injustice' was in fact intended to mean 'irreparable mischief/harm/damage', should be accepted. Indeed, following *Welby v Duke of Rutland*, in the late eighteenth century there were numerous decisions of the Chancery in which it was remarked, either in argument or by the Chancellor himself, that an interlocutory injunction to protect a legal right would be granted only where the defendant's actions threatened to cause the plaintiff irreparable harm.[35]

[27] ibid 41–42.
[28] ibid 42.
[29] ibid 43.
[30] Gummow (n 3) 92.
[31] *Colls v Home and Colonial Stores Ltd* [1904] AC 179 (HL).
[32] ibid 188.
[33] *Heavener v Loomes* (1924) 34 CLR 306.
[34] ibid 325.
[35] See, eg, *Mogg v Mogg* (1786) Dick 670, 671; *Earl Bathurst v Burden* (1786) 2 Bro CC 64, 65 (in argument); *Mortimer v Cottrell* (1789) 2 Cox Eq Cas 205, 205 (in argument).

The meaning of 'irreparable harm', however, was apparently not subject to clear judicial elucidation until the 1847 decision of the Court of Exchequer in *Attorney-General v Hallett*.[36] In that case, the Attorney-General alleged that the defendant had trespassed onto Crown land, enclosed part of it for his own use, and cut down trees and undergrowth. The defendant admitted to doing these acts but contended that he was entitled to do them pursuant to an easement by prescription. Before the trial at law, the Attorney-General sought an interlocutory injunction restraining the defendant from cutting down any further trees.[37] The Court of Exchequer refused to grant the injunction on the basis that the defendant's actions were not causing irreparable harm. Alderson B stated:

> I take the meaning of irreparable injury to be that which, if not prevented by injunction, cannot be afterwards compensated by any decree which the Court can pronounce … If extraordinary damage was to be apprehended, the Court would prevent it by its interposition.[38]

Rolfe B also reasoned that the Court would not intervene unless 'there is a bona fide subject of litigation, and the reasonable apprehension of great damage, amounting to irreparable injury, being done to the property in question in the meantime, if the Court does not so interfere'.[39]

The remarks of Alderson B and Rolfe B suggest that what the nineteenth-century courts meant by irreparable harm was that the claimant was threatened with damage or loss that: (i) was substantial (that is, 'extraordinary' or 'great'); and (ii) which a pecuniary payment would not rectify.[40] So, in the instant case, the Court reasoned that the trespass would not risk causing irreparable harm because damages were an adequate remedy: they would fully compensate the Crown for the small number of trees that were being cut down by the defendant.[41]

This definition of 'irreparable harm' also seems to accord with how contemporary writers understood the term. Although the leading scholars and practitioners all referred frequently to the doctrine of irreparable harm in their treatises, it was only Kerr who specifically analysed the meaning of the doctrine. Kerr stated:

> By the term 'irreparable injury' it is not meant that there must be no physical possibility of repairing the injury; all that is meant is, that the injury would be a grievous one, or at least a material one, and not adequately reparable by damages … and by the term 'inadequacy of the remedy by damages' is meant that the remedy by damages is not such a compensation as will in effect, though not in specie, place the parties in the position in which they formerly stood.[42]

[36] *Attorney-General v Hallett* (1847) 16 M & W 569.
[37] It is unclear why the Court of Exchequer had jurisdiction to hear this case given that its equitable jurisdiction was abolished in 1841: see n 9.
[38] *Attorney-General v Hallett* (n 36) 581–82.
[39] ibid 582.
[40] See also *Attorney-General v Johnson* (1819) 2 Wils Ch 87, 101–02.
[41] *Attorney-General v Hallett* (n 36) 581 (Parke B), 581–82 (Alderson B), 582–83 (Rolfe B), 583 (Platt B).
[42] Kerr (n 5) 14.

Thus, in line with Gummow's view, this definition of irreparable harm explains why the Chancery had jurisdiction to intervene and award an injunction: the common law courts did not have the power to adequately remedy an infringement of the plaintiff's legal rights that would cause substantial damage or loss.

What should not be overlooked, however, is that in the cases quoted above, it was not stated that the doctrine of irreparable harm was the *sole* basis for an injunction to restrain a legal wrong. As we shall see, there was another jurisdictional basis upon which the Chancery would countenance the award of a perpetual injunction.

III. Two Bases for Jurisdiction

By examining the cases in which injunctions were awarded to restrain or rectify waste, nuisance, trespass to land, and patent and copyright infringement, this section challenges the assumption that the Chancery had jurisdiction to grant injunctions to restrain legal wrongs only if the plaintiff would otherwise suffer irreparable harm. It is divided into two subsections.

Section III.A shows that the Chancery first began to award *perpetual* injunctions to restrain a defendant from continuing to commit waste in order to prevent a multiplicity of suits. No risk of irreparable harm was required for the Court to countenance whether it would award an injunction. Inevitably, by the mid-nineteenth century, it came to be established that the Chancery could award a perpetual injunction to restrain any legal wrong simply on the basis that it was proved to be continuing.

Section III.B explains that when the Chancery came to grant *interlocutory* injunctions to restrain nuisance, trespass to land, and copyright and patent infringement, the Court established the irreparable harm doctrine to justify its jurisdiction to award injunctive relief to restrain these wrongs before a trial was had at law.

A. Preventing a Multiplicity of Suits

When a plaintiff filed a bill for an injunction in the Chancery in the seventeenth to nineteenth centuries, he was required to plead 'one or more of the grounds upon which the jurisdiction of the [C]ourt is founded'.[43] A well-established ground upon which the Chancery would intervene to protect a plaintiff was that, without relief, there would be a 'multiplicity of suits'.[44] Indeed, 'Equity prevents multiplicity

[43] J Mitford and JW Smith, *A Treatise on the Pleadings in Suits in the Court of Chancery* (5th edn, V&R Stevens and GS Norton 1847) 8.

[44] ibid 5, 133, 169.

of suits' was an eighteenth-century maxim.[45] Pomeroy traced its history and examined its meaning.[46] He explained that although it often had numerous meanings and was applied in a range of different contexts, the 'first class' in which the maxim came to be developed was:

> [w]here, from the nature of the wrong, and from the settled rules of the legal procedure, the same injured party, in order to obtain all the relief to which he is justly entitled, is obliged to bring a number of actions against the same wrongdoer, all growing out of the one wrongful act and involving similar questions of fact and law. To this class would belong cases of nuisance, waste, continued trespass and the like.[47]

Pomeroy stated that it was in order to avoid a multiplicity of suits that in this first class of case 'a court of equity interferes … and awards some specific equitable remedy, which gives, perhaps, in one proceeding more substantial relief than could be obtained in numerous actions at law'.[48] Such relief, he stated, 'might include a perpetual injunction'.[49]

A close analysis of the cases reveals that it was the multiplicity of suits doctrine, and not the irreparable harm doctrine, that was employed by the Chancery to develop a jurisdiction to award a *perpetual* injunction to stop a defendant from continuing to commit a legal wrong against the plaintiff. However, it should not be thought that this proposition went without saying throughout the seventeenth to nineteenth centuries. As we shall see, it took until 1859 for this proposition to be accepted at the highest judicial level, and even then there were still competing views in the case law and literature.

i. Perpetual Injunctions to Restrain Waste

As explained in section II, there is evidence to suggest that 'special' injunctions were granted to restrain waste in the sixteenth century. Throughout the seventeenth century (and into the eighteenth century), the Chancery frequently awarded perpetual injunctions to restrain both legal and equitable waste.[50] However, it is important to recognise that the common law was also providing specific relief to plaintiffs to restrain the commission of waste during this period. Since the thirteenth century, the common law courts could award a writ of prohibition in which an order, known as a 'prohibition', was made against a defendant at the conclusion of an action to prevent waste and nuisance.[51] Furthermore, the

[45] R Francis, *Maxims of Equity* (3rd edn, Savoy 1746) 35. See also J Story, *Commentaries on Equity Jurisprudence: As Administered in England and America* (Maxwell & Sons 1836) vol 1, 30–31.
[46] J Pomeroy, *A Treatise on Equity Jurisprudence* (AL Bancroft 1881–83) vol 1, ch 2, sec IV.
[47] ibid 256. See also 264–65.
[48] ibid 255.
[49] ibid 261.
[50] See n 17.
[51] HD Hazeltine, 'The Early History of English Equity' in P Vinogradoff (ed), *Essays in Legal History* (Oxford University Press 1913) 270–76; Holdsworth (n 12) 248–49; Raack (n 12) 545–48.

common law courts issued writs of estrepement, which prohibited the commission of waste during the course of proceedings concerned with real actions.[52] There is good evidence that the writ of prohibition continued to be awarded in respect of waste until at least the seventeenth century,[53] while the writ of estrepement was issued well into the eighteenth century.[54]

Given that these writs provided plaintiffs with a remedy to prevent acts that amounted to waste, on either a final or an interlocutory basis, it is difficult to maintain that the available common law remedies were inadequate at remedying the damage or loss caused by legal waste where such writs were available to a plaintiff. Indeed, Eldon LC expressly recognised this in the 1802 decision of *Smith v Collyer*, when he stated '[i]t was always surprising to me, that the jurisdiction by injunction was taken so freely in waste, and not in trespass; for there is a writ at common law after action to restrain waste'.[55]

The Chancery reasoned that injunctions to restrain legal waste were granted not to prevent irreparable harm but to prevent a multiplicity of suits. There are numerous cases in the sixteenth and seventeenth centuries in which, upon waste's being proved to have been committed, an injunction restraining future waste is granted almost as of right.[56] Indeed, Purlevent wrote in his treatise on the law of waste published in 1786 that the Chancery 'very widely interpreted' its powers to restrain waste by injunction on the basis that 'preventing justice is infinitely preferable to punishing [justice]'.[57] In these early cases, however, the reported reasons do not explain why the injunctions were granted. It seems the reason for Chancery's intervention in these cases was not explicitly recognised until the 1745 case of *Jesus College v Bloom*.[58] There, Jesus College bought a bill for an account of profits after the defendant had committed waste on land owned by the College. Lord Hardwicke LC stated in obiter dicta:

> Waste is a tort, and the remedy lies at law. … The ground of coming into this court is, to stay the waste, and not by way of satisfaction for the damages, but by way of prevention of the wrong, which courts of law cannot do in those instances, where a prohibition of waste will not strictly lie. But in all these cases, this court has gone further, *merely upon the maxim of preventing multiplicity of suits, which is the reason that determines this court in many cases.* … So, in bills for injunctions, the court will make a complete decree, and give the party a satisfaction, and not oblige him to bring an action at law, as well as a bill here.[59]

[52] Hazeltine (n 51) 275–76; Raack (n 12) 549.

[53] Coke wrote in the first half of the 17th century that the writ of prohibition 'may be used to this day': Sir Edward Coke, *The Second Part of the Institutes of the Lawes of England* (M Flesher 1644) 299.

[54] See, eg, *William Plunket v Lord Viscount Kingsland* (1746) 1 Bro PC 322.

[55] *Smith v Collyer* (1803) 8 Ves Jr 90, 90. Similar remarks were made in *Courthope v Mapplesden* (1804) 10 Ves Jr 290, 291.

[56] See n 17.

[57] J Purlevent, *Two Law Tracts: The One Being Reflections Upon Estates for Life, the Doctrine of Waste, and the Principles of Injunctions* (His Majesty's Law Printers 1786) 11.

[58] *Jesus College v Bloom* (1745) 3 Atk 262.

[59] ibid 263 (emphasis added).

Lord Hardwicke LC is making the point that although in some cases a prohibition of waste will not strictly lie, the underlying reason why the Chancery granted perpetual injunctions to restrain waste was to prevent a multiplicity of suits. Although Hardwicke LC does not explicitly use the word 'continuing', his reasoning is to the effect that once it is proved that a defendant has committed waste against a plaintiff and will continue to do so in the future, the Chancery will intervene to prevent future waste by making 'a complete decree', so that a plaintiff is not required to bring fresh proceedings each time waste is committed against him. Indeed, as Hardwicke LC stated in the later 1746 case of *Smith v Cooke* after citing *Jesus College v Bloom*, 'where the [defendant] continues in possession, and consequently in a condition of committing more waste, there a [plaintiff] is proper to come into equity for an injunction to stay waste'.[60] In the light of Hardwicke LC's reasoning, it seems that early in the eighteenth century it was accepted that the Chancery had jurisdiction to award perpetual injunctions to restrain defendants from continuing to commit waste on the basis of preventing a multiplicity of suits.

Interestingly, however, there are conflicting views from the nineteenth century that suggest that perpetual injunctions were readily granted in these cases only because there was privity of estate between the parties. The common law tort of waste is unique because it is predicated on the privity of estate; that is, where two or more persons hold an interest in the same real property.[61] The tort is committed when a defendant, rightfully in possession of land, fails to exercise his or her duty to care for the land, which subsequently causes a diminution in the value of the inheritance of the plaintiff reversioner or remainderman.[62]

The view that privity of estate was a necessary condition for the grant of a perpetual injunction first came to be developed in two cases in the late 1780s. In those cases, Thurlow LC refused to grant an injunction restraining a trespass to land because, in his view, the Chancery could not interfere if the party was a 'mere trespasser'[63] or a 'mere stranger'.[64] As Eldon LC later suggested in *Crockford v Alexander*,[65] this reasoning indicated that Thurlow LC believed it was the privity of estate between the parties that justified the grant of an injunction. Because this feature was lacking in the context of a trespass, Thurlow LC refused to grant an injunction. Thus, by the mid-nineteenth century, Chancery judges frequently made obiter statements that injunctions were originally awarded to restrain waste only because there was privity of estate between the parties. For example, in the context of analysing the law on injunctions when considering whether to restrain

[60] *Smith v Cooke* (1746) 3 Atk 378, 381.
[61] J Law (ed), *A Dictionary of Law* (9th edn, Oxford University Press 2018) 168.
[62] Michael Jones and Anthony Dugdale (eds), *Clerk & Lindsell on Torts* (23rd edn, Sweet & Maxwell 2020) [18-97]–[18-98]. See also RH Helmholz, 'The Law of Waste and the Law of Dilapidations: A Comparative History' (2021) 9 *Comparative Legal History* 154, 154.
[63] *Mogg v Mogg* (n 35) 671.
[64] *Mortimer v Cottrell* (n 35) 205.
[65] *Crockford v Alexander* (1808) 15 Ves Jr 138, 138–39.

a trespass, Wigram VC remarked in 1849 that '[t]he jurisdiction of the Court in cases of injunction, originally, no doubt, arose in cases of waste, where there was privity between the parties'.[66]

The authors of the leading treatises on injunctions and equity in the nineteenth century differed on the correctness of the above statements. On the one hand, albeit in the context of a discussion that focused predominantly on the grant of interlocutory injunctions, Eden[67] and Story[68] wrote that privity of estate (and the threat of irreparable harm) was necessary for the award of an injunction to restrain waste. Eden also explicitly interpreted the decision in *Jesus College v Bloom* to be concerned with when equity would permit a decree for an account and satisfaction of past waste.[69] He otherwise did not consider this case in his analysis on injunctions.

On the other hand, Pomeroy, Joyce and Kerr seemed to think that privity of estate was not a necessary condition for the award of a perpetual injunction. Pomeroy, consistent with his examination of the multiplicity of suits doctrine, simply stated that 'an injunction will be granted in all cases where a legal action would lie to recover possession of the land wasted or to recover damages'.[70] Joyce was more explicit, stating that a bill for an injunction could be 'filed to prevent future waste, to avoid a multiplicity of suits'.[71] Kerr stated, in his discussion of interlocutory injunctions in respect of waste, that there must be privity of estate and irreparable damage for an injunction to issue.[72] However, in his discussion of perpetual injunctions in aid of legal rights, he simply stated that 'a man is in general entitled as of course to a perpetual injunction to prevent the recurrence of the wrong'.[73]

The claim that privity of estate was a precondition for the award of a perpetual injunction to restrain waste should be rejected and the view of the latter authors should be accepted. This is for three reasons. First, the claim developed in the nineteenth century. It therefore seems to be a retrospective explanation of how cases decided decades earlier had been reasoned. Second, and relatedly, no authority is given for the proposition that privity of estate was a precondition for the award of an injunction. Nor do the nineteenth-century cases make any reference to the statements made by Hardwicke LC in *Jesus College v Bloom*.[74] Finally, the claim is made in the case law and literature in the context of a consideration of the principles relevant to the grant of interlocutory injunctions. It is therefore unclear whether the claim was also intended to apply to the award of *perpetual* injunctions.

[66] *Davenport v Davenport* (1849) 7 Hare 217, 222. See also *Attorney-General v Hallett* (n 36) 578, 582.
[67] Eden (n 5) 195.
[68] Story (n 45) vol 2, 200.
[69] Eden (n 5) 206–07.
[70] Pomeroy (n 46) 379.
[71] Joyce (n 5) 121.
[72] Kerr (n 5) 52, 109.
[73] ibid 42.
[74] *Jesus College v Bloom* (n 58).

For these reasons, it is difficult to accept the claim that privity of estate was a precondition for the award of a perpetual injunction. The better view is that provided by Hardwicke LC in the mid-eighteenth century: the Chancery awarded perpetual injunctions to restrain defendants who were continuing to commit waste to prevent a multiplicity of suits.

It might be expected that once the multiplicity of suits doctrine was used to justify the grant of perpetual injunctions to restrain waste, the doctrine would have been employed to enable the Chancery to award perpetual injunctions to restrain a continuing nuisance, trespass, or copyright or patent infringement. Although this did ultimately eventuate in the 1859 decision of the House of Lords in *Imperial Gas and Coke Company v Broadbent*,[75] some confusion ensued before this decision.

ii. Initial Confusion

Throughout the eighteenth and nineteenth centuries, the Chancery held that it had jurisdiction to award interlocutory injunctions to restrain alleged nuisances, trespasses to land and intellectual property infringements where they were causing the plaintiff irreparable harm. Importantly, however, it seems that perpetual injunctions were not initially granted in respect of these causes of action.[76] This is reflected by the dearth of cases cited in the treatises of Eden, Story and Drewry, all of whom wrote before 1859. Eden cited only two cases in which a perpetual injunction was granted to restrain infringements of legal rights.[77] Interestingly, Drewry stated that perpetual injunctions in aid of legal rights were 'rare' but did not cite a case in which such an injunction had been granted.[78] Story purported to cite cases in which perpetual injunctions were granted to restrain nuisances,[79] but the English cases that he cited all concerned interlocutory injunctions.

Before the Court of Chancery Procedure Act 1852 (and later the Chancery Regulation Act 1862) was passed to provide the Chancery with the power to decide points of law, unless an infringement of a plaintiff's legal right had been determined at law the Chancery would refuse to award perpetual injunctive relief.[80] This seems to be the reason why perpetual injunctive relief was rare.[81] However,

[75] *Imperial Gas and Coke Company v Broadbent* (1859) 7 HLC 600, 11 ER 239.

[76] Only one case in this period could be located in which it was reported (in one paragraph) that acts by a defendant, which seem to amount to a nuisance, were restrained by a perpetual injunction: see *Thomas v Jones* (1844) 7 Jur 170.

[77] See *Robinson v Litton* (n 17) (waste, quia timet); *Millar v Taylor* (1769) 4 Burr 2303 (copyright infringement) (not including cases in which perpetual injunctions were granted in respect of vexatious litigation).

[78] Drewry (n 5) 343.

[79] Story, *Commentaries on Equity Jurisprudence: As Administered in England and America* (7th edn, Little, Brown 1857) 235.

[80] C Rotherham, 'Remedies for Breaches of Rights to Light: Averting a Tragedy of the Anticommons' in B McFarlane and S Agnew (eds), *Modern Studies in Property Law* (Hart Publishing 2019) 154.

[81] See, in particular, *Holyoake v Shrewsbury and Birmingham Railway Company* (1848) 5 Rail Cas 421, 427.

as Rotherham has explained, following the passing of the above statutes, perpetual injunctions in aid of private legal rights came to be awarded more frequently.[82] Indeed, Kerr devoted a particular section in his treatise to perpetual injunctions in aid of legal rights, and highlighted the relevant cases decided in the 1850s.[83] Interestingly, in these cases it was a continuing nuisance that was sought to be restrained, and two conflicting approaches were taken by the Chancery.

On the one hand, it was thought that perpetual injunctions to restrain a continuing nuisance could be granted only where the plaintiff could prove that the damage he was suffering amounted to irreparable harm. So, in the 1851 decision of *Wood v Sutcliffe*,[84] Kindersley VC refused to grant an injunction restraining the defendants from polluting a stream because, in his view, it was not causing the plaintiffs irreparable harm. He reasoned that he could not accept the proposition that 'on the mere dry fact of the Plaintiffs having the abstract right, a Court of Equity will, as a matter of course, on that right being established at law, grant an injunction if the right be infringed ever so minutely'.[85]

On the other hand, it was thought that irrespective of whether or not the defendant was causing the plaintiff irreparable harm, the fact that a nuisance was continuing meant that the Chancery had jurisdiction to award an injunction to prevent a multiplicity of suits.[86] For example, in *Attorney-General v Birmingham*,[87] Page Wood VC granted an interlocutory injunction restraining the defendant local authority from continuing to discharge sewage into the River Tame. He stated in obiter dicta that once it had been proved at trial that the defendant was committing a nuisance and was continuing to do so, the Chancery would exercise its discretion by 'granting an injunction, to relieve [the plaintiff] from the necessity of bringing a series of actions, in order to obtain the damages to which such continual and daily annoyance entitles him'.[88]

iii. Clarification by the House of Lords

In *Imperial Gas and Coke Company v Broadbent*,[89] the House of Lords confirmed that the Chancery had jurisdiction to award a perpetual injunction solely upon proof that a defendant was continuing to infringe a plaintiff's legal rights. The facts were that the defendants owned a gas company and had been found to have

[82] Rotherham (n 80) 154.

[83] Kerr (n 5) 42–43, 165, 190.

[84] *Wood v Sutcliffe* (1851) 2 Sim NS 163 (legal right had been established at law). See also *Soltau v De Held* (1851) 2 Sim NS 133, 159-60; *Attorney-General v Sheffield Gas Consumers Co* (1853) 3 De Gm & G 304, 315.

[85] *Wood v Sutcliffe* (n 84) 166.

[86] See, eg, *Potts v Levy* (1854) 2 Drewry 272; *Bostock v North Staffordshire Railway Company* (1856) 3 Sm & G 283; *Jessel v Chaplin* (1856) 2 Jurist (NS) 931 (injunction granted at common law).

[87] *Attorney-General v Birmingham* (1858) 4 K & J 528.

[88] ibid 540.

[89] *Imperial Gas and Coke Company v Broadbent* (n 75).

committed a nuisance by allowing noxious fumes to escape from one of their gas retort houses, which killed flowers, fruit and vegetables grown by the plaintiff market gardener. As the defendant refused to abate the nuisance, the plaintiff sought a perpetual injunction. Wood VC granted the injunction, and it was later confirmed by Cranworth LC. On appeal to the House of Lords, the defendants argued that the injunction should not have been granted because, inter alia, '[t]he granting of a perpetual injunction is not a matter of course, even after a verdict at law; all the circumstances must be looked to'.[90] The House of Lords explicitly rejected this argument and dismissed the appeal. Giving the leading speech, Lord Campbell LC (with whom Lord Cranworth agreed) remarked:

> If there has once been a trial at law and the Plaintiff's right has been established at law, I think it is for the Equity Judge to determine, when the application is made for the injunction, whether the nuisance continues, or whether it has been abated, and if he is of opinion that it has not been abated but that it still continues, then it is his duty to grant an injunction. … [U]nless there is something peculiar in this case, it would be a matter of course to grant an injunction.[91]

In his speech, Lord Kingsdown (with whom Lord Cranworth also agreed) stated:

> The rule I take to be clearly this: if a Plaintiff applies for an injunction to restrain a violation of a common law right, if either the existence of the right or the fact of its violation be disputed, he must establish that right at law; but when he has established his right at law, I apprehend that unless there be something special in the case, he is entitled as of course to an injunction to prevent the recurrence of that violation.[92]

It should be recognised that when making the above statements, their Lordships conceptualised a continuing wrong to be a distinct ground for the Chancery's intervention. Indeed, Lord Kingsdown makes no mention of the irreparable harm principle. And although Lord Campbell LC observed later in his speech that damages would not have adequately remedied the plaintiff,[93] he emphasised this fact *after* explaining that because Wood VC had found that the nuisance was continuing, the injunction should be granted as of course. It seems, therefore, that Lord Campbell LC believed that the fact that damages were inadequate was a discretionary factor that weighed in favour of the grant of the injunction, rather than the underlying reason why the Chancery had jurisdiction to intervene.

It follows that the House of Lords considered that the Chancery had jurisdiction to award injunctions to prevent continuing legal wrongs not because there was irreparable harm, but for a different reason. Two things indicate that the House of Lords believed it was to prevent a multiplicity of suits.

First, one of the arguments made by the defendants was that the plaintiff would not suffer any injustice if an injunction were refused because he could bring an

[90] ibid 604.
[91] ibid 609.
[92] ibid 612.
[93] ibid 610.

action in nuisance each time he suffered damage. Lord Campbell LC rejected this contention by stating:

> Then we are told that an action is to be brought, I know not how often, I suppose an annual action, *that actions are to be multiplied indefinitely*. I cannot but think that this would be a denial of justice to a person who has proved the injury he has sustained, especially when the party of whom he complains still obstinately persists in doing what produces effects so injurious to him.[94]

Although Lord Campbell LC does not cite *Jesus College v Bloom*, his remark that requiring the plaintiff to bring further actions each time his right is infringed would be 'a denial of justice' bears a strong resemblance to the reasoning of Hardwicke LC. The point being made is that it is necessary for the Chancery to interpose by injunction to prevent a multiplicity of suits, as otherwise the plaintiff would be left to bring action after action to protect his legal right.

Second, in some of the cases that immediately followed *Imperial*, it was expressly identified that the Chancery had jurisdiction to grant perpetual injunctions to restrain continuing wrongs in order to prevent a multiplicity of suits. For example, it was acknowledged by James LJ in the 1872 case of *Clowes v Staffordshire Potteries Waterworks Co* that the Chancery could award perpetual injunctions to restrain continuing nuisances because of 'the absolute necessity of preventing a continued series of actions'.[95] The nineteenth-century authors took the same view. Kerr, after citing the decision in *Imperial v Broadbent*, explained:

> After the establishment of his legal right and of the fact of its violation, a man is in general entitled as of course to a perpetual injunction to prevent the recurrence of the wrong, unless there be something special in the circumstances of the case. The jurisdiction is founded on the equity of relieving a man from the necessity of bringing action after action at law for every violation of a common law right, and of finally quieting the right …[96]

Similarly, Story and Redfield, Joyce and Pomeroy, all stated that one of the bases for the Chancery's jurisdiction to grant injunctions in respect of nuisance and trespass to land was to prevent a multiplicity of suits.[97] Thus, by 1859, it was well

[94] ibid 610 (emphasis added).

[95] *Clowes v Staffordshire Potteries Waterworks Co* (1872–73) LR 8 Ch App 125, 143. See also ibid 142–43 (Mellish LJ); *Goodson v Richardson* (1873–74) LR 9 Ch App 221, 227; *Pennington v Brinsop Hall Coal Co* (1877) 5 Ch D 769 (Ch), 773–74; *Fullwood v Fullwood* (1878) 9 Ch D 176 (Ch), 179. cf *Swaine v Great Northern Rly Co* (1864) 4 De GJ & Sm 211 (where the Court fails to refer to the House of Lords decision in *Imperial v Broadbent*). For later cases explicitly stating that a multiplicity of suits is a basis for injunctive relief or specific performance, see: *Cruickshank v Bidwell* 176 US 70 (1900), 81 (Supreme Court of the United States); *Colls* (n 31) 188; *Angelides v James Stedman Hendersons Sweets Ltd* (1927) 40 CLR 43, 63, 66 (High Court of Australia); *Beswick v Beswick* [1968] AC 58 (HL) 81, 97.

[96] Kerr (n 5) 42. See also ibid 8, 165, 190.

[97] J Story and I Redfield, *Commentaries on Equity Jurisprudence: As Administered in England and America* (9th edn, Little, Brown 1866) vol 2, 102 (nuisance), 110 (trespass to land); Joyce (n 5) 99–100, 102 (nuisance), 219 (trespass to land); Pomeroy (n 46) vol 3, 381 (nuisance), 388 (trespass to land). See also E Snell, *Snell's Principles of Equity* (Stevens and Haynes 1868) 466.

established that the Chancery had jurisdiction to grant injunctions to restrain continuing legal rights invasions to prevent a multiplicity of suits. However, there is a point of contention that must be recognised here.

In his statement of principle quoted above, Lord Campbell LC limited his analysis to a continuing nuisance. He did not go as far as Lord Kingsdown, who stated that a continuing invasion of *any* legal right can be restrained as of course by injunction. Lord Campbell LC's statement seems to reflect a line of reasoning in the Chancery that suggests that injunctions could be awarded only in respect of property rights. For example, in *Gee v Pritchard*, when asked to grant an interlocutory injunction to restrain the publication of a libel, Eldon LC stated that:

> [t]he publication of a libel is a crime, and I have no jurisdiction to prevent the commission of crimes. ... The injunction then must rest on one of two grounds: 1. That the Plaintiff possesses, in the letters, a property either general or literary; 2. That the publication of them is a breach of trust.[98]

Similarly, in *Emperor of Austria v Day*, Campbell LC and Turner LJ were in agreement that the Chancery had 'no jurisdiction to prevent the commission of acts which are merely criminal or merely illegal, and do not affect any rights of property'.[99]

There are, however, difficulties with this restrictive view of the Chancery's powers to grant injunctive relief. First, although the Chancery refused to restrain libel on the basis that it was a crime, it readily awarded injunctions to restrain the crime of public nuisance.[100] Second, it was well established that the Chancery would restrain the infringement of negative contractual stipulations.[101] The injunctions that were granted in these cases were clearly not in respect of property rights. Third, section 79 of the Common Law Procedure Act 1854 was passed to give the common law courts the same powers to grant injunctions as were possessed by the Chancery. The provisions in the 1854 Act were enacted upon the *Second Report of Her Majesty's Commissioners for Inquiring Into the Process, Practice, and System of Pleading in the Superior Courts of Common Law*.[102] In that report, the Commissioners noted that the Chancery had gradually enlarged its jurisdiction to grant injunctions in aid of legal rights, originally by granting injunctions in respect of waste. The Commissioners then stated that the common

[98] *Gee v Pritchard* (1818) 2 Swans 402, 414. See also *Prudential v Knott* (1874–75) LR 10 Ch App 142.

[99] *Emperor of Austria v Day* (1861) 3 De GF & J 217, 253. See also *Maxwell v Hogg* (1866–7) LR 2 Ch App 307. This view was accepted in the Court of Appeal in 1891 in *Bonnard v Perryman* [1891] 2 Ch 269 (CA) 283. However, Lord Coleridge CJ's statements could be taken to be *per incuriam* as they were made without consideration of the House of Lords decision in *Imperial v Broadbent*.

[100] See, eg, *Attorney-General v Johnson* (n 40).

[101] See, eg, *Martin v Nutkin* (n 19); *Lord Grey De Wilton v Saxon* (1801) 6 Ves Jr 106; *Morris v Colman* (1812) 18 Ves 437; *Rankin v Huskisson* (1830) 4 Sim 13; *Earl of Mexborough v Bower* (1843) 7 Beav 127; *Dickenson v Grand Junction Canal Company* (1852) 15 Beav 260; *Lumley v Wagner* (1852) 1 De M & G 604; *Tipping v Eckersley* (1855) 2 Kay & J 264; *Lord Manners v Johnson* (1875) 1 Ch D 673.

[102] *Second Report of Her Majesty's Commissioners for Inquiring Into the Process, Practice, and System of Pleading in the Superior Courts of Common Law* (Eyre and Spottiswoode 1853).

law courts should be empowered to 'exercise the same jurisdiction, and restrain violation of legal rights in the case in which an injunction now issues for that purpose from the courts of equity'.[103] Importantly, section 79 of the 1854 Act specifically stated that a litigant might bring a writ of injunction against the repetition or continuance of a breach of contract or '*other Injury*', irrespective of whether or not that injury was concerned with property. It seems, therefore, that the Commissioners (and the legislature) believed that the Chancery's power to restrain continuing wrongs was not restricted to restraining causes of action that protected property rights.[104]

For these reasons, one should be cautious before accepting the nineteenth-century cases stating that injunctions could be awarded only in respect of property rights.[105] As Jessel MR remarked in 1878, because injunctions were granted by different Chancellors, 'in course of time various vexatious and inconvenient restrictions were adopted'.[106] Ultimately, even though there were conflicting views in the nineteenth century, Lord Kingsdown's statement of principle in *Imperial v Broadbent* should be accepted as reflecting the correct position. The Chancery had jurisdiction to award a perpetual injunction upon proof of the continuing infringement of *any* legal right. There was no need to prove that the right being infringed was a proprietary one, or that there was a risk of irreparable harm.

B. Preventing Irreparable Harm

In the reported eighteenth-century cases, some references were made to the doctrine of irreparable harm in the context of refusing to award an interlocutory injunction to restrain waste.[107] However, as we shall see, it was not until the Chancery began to award interlocutory injunctions to restrain nuisance, trespass and intellectual property infringements that the doctrine of irreparable harm came to be fully developed.

i. Nuisance

Given that the assize of nuisance is said to have fallen into disuse during the seventeenth century,[108] it might be expected that the Chancery would have begun granting injunctions to restrain nuisance during this period. However, as McLaren has observed, '[f]or reasons which are obscure the Chancery did not begin

[103] ibid 43.
[104] See also *Beddow v Beddow* (1878) 9 Ch D 89 (Ch) 92.
[105] Spry has also come to this conclusion: (n 13) 348–50. cf P Turner, 'Equity and Administration' in P Turner (ed), *Equity and Administration* (Cambridge University Press 2016) 1, 29–30.
[106] *Beddow* (n 104) 91–92.
[107] See, eg, *Filewood v Palmer* (1729) Mos 169; *Anonymous* (1750) 1 Ves Sen 476.
[108] Baker (n 12) 454.

regularly to grant injunctions in nuisance cases until the end of the eighteenth century'.[109] Furthermore, even when the Chancery did begin to grant injunctions in this context, the Court would only grant *interlocutory* injunctions restraining a defendant from engaging in certain acts before a trial was had at law to determine if those acts were a nuisance. As already explained, not a single case can be located where a perpetual injunction was awarded to restrain a nuisance until the 1850s.

Nineteenth-century writers were unanimously of the view that irreparable harm was the central justification for equity's intervention to restrain nuisances at the interlocutory stage.[110] The first example of the use of the irreparable harm doctrine by the Chancery to justify its intervention in a case concerning nuisance was the 1785 decision in *Robinson v Lord Byron*.[111] In that case, the River Lyme flowed through the defendant's lands and into the plaintiffs' property, and the river water was used by the plaintiffs to operate their cotton mills. It was alleged by the plaintiffs that, in an attempt to extort money from them, the defendant prevented the water from flowing into the plaintiffs' property, and at other times let out the water in great quantities, so as to prevent the mills from operating. In a short judgment, Thurlow LC reasoned that because the defendant's actions were causing 'mischief, the Court may interpose'.[112] He therefore awarded an injunction to restrain the defendant from acting 'to prevent the water flowing to the mill in such regular quantities as it had done ordinarily' before the trial.[113]

What is significant about this case is that it was the first time that the Chancery had awarded an injunction before an infringement of a legal right had been proved because the defendant's nuisance was causing serious, and possibly irreparable, harm to the plaintiffs. This was recognised explicitly by Eldon LC in 1802 in *Hanson v Gardner*.[114] In the context of explaining how the 'principle' of irreparable harm was developed to allow the Chancery to intervene in certain categories of case, he remarked:

> This led to *Robinson v Lord Byron* and the other cases; in which also this principle operated; that unless there was some jurisdiction to prevent it, there would be a great failure of justice in the country. The ground of that case was irreparable mischief; and irreparable mischief, that would have been done, before there could have been any trial at law as to the right claimed to let off the water.[115]

[109] JPS McLaren, 'Nuisance Law and the Industrial Revolution: Some Lessons from Social History' (1983) 3 *OJLS* 155, 186.

[110] Eden (n 5) 259; Drewry (n 5) 237; Joyce (n 5) 99-100; Story (n 68) 230; Kerr (n 5) 166, 172–74.

[111] *Robinson v Lord Byron* (1785) 1 Bro CC 589. See also *Robinson v Lord Byron* (1788) 2 Cox Eq Cas 4; (1788) Dick 703. Although it was noted by Eldon LC that the injunction in *Robinson v Lord Byron* was ultimately made perpetual (see *Crowder v Tinkler* (1816) 19 Ves Jr 617), from a reading of the reports it is difficult to see that this was in fact the case given that the injunction was always granted 'upon further order'.

[112] *Robinson v Lord Byron* (1785) (n 111) 589.

[113] ibid.

[114] *Hanson v Gardner* (1802) 7 Ves Jr 305.

[115] ibid 308. See also *Crockford v Alexander* (n 65) 138–39.

Thus, from the nineteenth century onwards, the doctrine of irreparable harm was the explicit basis upon which the Chancery intervened to award *interlocutory* injunctions to restrain a nuisance.[116] There are numerous examples of this. First, consider the 1816 decision of *Crowder v Tinkler*.[117] In that case, Eldon LC awarded an interlocutory (quia timet) injunction restraining the defendants from storing a large amount of gun powder in their warehouse, to protect relator plaintiffs who owned paper mills next door to the defendants and had brought an action in public nuisance. When explaining why the Chancery had jurisdiction to intervene, Eldon LC remarked:

> The complaint is … to be considered as of, not a public nuisance simply, but what, being so in its nature, is attended with extreme probability of irreparable injury to the property of the Plaintiffs, including also danger to their existence; and on such a case, clearly established, I do not hesitate to say, an Injunction would be granted.[118]

Lord Eldon emphasised that it was the risk of 'irreparable injury' being suffered by the plaintiffs (that is, the fact that the nuisance threatened the plaintiffs' neighbouring paper mills, and indeed their lives) that gave the court jurisdiction to interfere and grant an injunction. Similar sentiments were expressed by Plummer MR in *Wynstanley v Lee*, where he stated, in the context of considering whether to restrain the defendant from constructing a building that would interfere with the plaintiff's light, that the Chancery would grant an injunction 'upon seeing that that injury might be irreparable … without waiting [for] the slow process of establishing the legal right, when delay would be itself a wrong'.[119]

In the light of these cases, there can be no doubt that it was in the context of awarding injunctions to restrain a nuisance that the irreparable harm doctrine first came to be employed by the Chancery to justify an extension of its jurisdiction to award *interlocutory* injunctions in aid of legal rights.

ii. Trespass to Land

The irreparable harm doctrine was also employed by the Chancery to justify the grant of interlocutory injunctions to restrain trespass to land. For most of the eighteenth century, the Chancery refused to award injunctions to restrain trespass to land.[120] However, nineteenth-century authors noted that Thurlow LC, with reluctance, later awarded an injunction to restrain a trespass to land in *Flamang's case*.[121] Despite this, no citation is given for the decision by these authors, and

[116] In addition to the cases discussed immediately below, see also: *Attorney-General v Johnson* (n 40); *Blakemore v Glamorganshire Canal Company* (1832) 1 My & K 181; *Earl of Ripon v Hobart* (1834) 3 My & K 169; *Dawson v Paver* (1847) 5 Hare 415.

[117] *Crowder v Tinkler* (n 111).

[118] ibid 622.

[119] *Wynstanley v Lee* (1818) 2 Swans 333, 335–36.

[120] See *Coulson v White* (1743) 3 Atk 21; *Mogg v Mogg* (n 35) 671; *Mortimer v Cottrell* (n 35) 205.

[121] Eden (n 5) 232; Drewry (n 5) 183–84; Kerr (n 5) 109.

although the case is frequently referred to by Eldon LC in later decisions,[122] he similarly provides no citation.

The earliest decisions that can be located in which injunctions were granted to restrain trespass to land were decided by Eldon LC in the early 1800s. Initially, the Chancery would award an injunction to restrain a trespass to land only where the plaintiff could prove that the defendant's trespass would risk causing irreparable harm *and* the defendant did not dispute that he had committed trespass.[123] However, as was identified by the nineteenth-century authors,[124] an analysis of the later cases indicates that the Chancery came to hold that even where the plaintiff's legal right was disputed bona fide by the defendant, a risk of irreparable harm would still justify interlocutory injunctive relief. In *Crockford v Alexander*,[125] for example, the plaintiff contracted to sell an estate to the defendant. After the defendant obtained possession, but before he had paid the purchase price and gained title, he began to cut large amounts of timber. Eldon LC granted an interlocutory injunction restraining the defendant from cutting timber until the purchase price had been paid.[126] Relying on *Robinson v Lord Byron*,[127] Eldon LC reasoned that the Chancery would restrain a 'destruction', which the effects of the alleged trespass amounted to in the instant case.

iii. Copyright and Patent Infringement

Finally, the doctrine of irreparable harm was also the basis upon which the Chancery intervened to restrain copyright and patent infringement. Like the cases involving nuisance and trespass, a review of the reported cases indicates that the injunctions awarded in the first half of the nineteenth century were interlocutory rather than perpetual. However, as we shall see, the doctrine of irreparable harm operated slightly differently where intellectual property rights were alleged to have been infringed.

Although there are cases that report that injunctions were granted to restrain patent and copyright infringement in the eighteenth century,[128] the Chancery did not begin to intervene regularly in this area until Eldon LC explained the reason for equity's interposition in the 1802 decision of *Universities of Oxford and Cambridge v Richardson*.[129] In that case, the universities had been granted an injunction that

[122] See *Mitchell v Dors* (n 21); *Twort v Twort* (1809) 16 Ves Jr 128.

[123] *Smith v Collyer* (n 55) (interlocutory injunction refused as the defendant disputed the plaintiff's title); *Kinder v Jones* (1810) 17 Ves Jr 110 (injunction granted until further order because the defendant did not appear).

[124] Eden (n 5) 233; Kerr (n 5) 115–17.

[125] *Crockford v Alexander* (n 65). See also *Grey v The Duke of Northumberland* (1809) 17 Ves Jr 281; *Earl Cowper v Baker* (1810) 17 Ves Jr 128; *Chalk v Wyatt* (1810) 3 Mer 688.

[126] *Crockford v Alexander* (n 65) 138.

[127] *Robinson v Lord Byron* (n 111).

[128] For a comprehensive overview of the relevant cases in the eighteenth century, see *Donaldson v Beckett* (1774) 2 Bro PC 129, 137–38.

[129] *Universities of Oxford and Cambridge v Richardson* (1802) 6 Ves Jr 689.

restrained the defendants from printing and selling certain books until a trial was had at law to determine who owned the intellectual property in the books. The defendants brought an application to dissolve the injunction, but Eldon LC refused the application. He indicated that the reason the Chancery could intervene in the case was that if the defendants continued to infringe the universities' intellectual property rights, they would have great difficulty in determining the profits made by the defendants:

> One question … is, whether, if the Court cannot find an accurate mode of estimating the profits, an injunction can be granted. … [C]an it be contended, that on account of that difficulty [the universities] should not have that equity, which this Court administers as preventive justice … I am of opinion, that, … the right to the injunction, to prevent in future that, which is unjustly done or threatened, would be sufficient to support the bill.[130]

Although Eldon LC does not explain why it would be difficult for the profits to be calculated, his reasoning suggests that he employed the doctrine of irreparable harm. What Eldon LC is suggesting is that without the injunction to restrain the continuing infringement, the universities would face difficulties in calculating the profits made by the defendants, and ultimately the universities' own losses. The result would therefore be that the compensation provided at law would be inadequate and accordingly equity had a basis to intervene.

This analysis was more clearly expressed by Eldon LC in the later 1803 decision of *Hogg v Kirby*.[131] In that case, Eldon LC granted an injunction before the trial restraining the defendants from publishing a magazine series which intentionally used the title of a successful magazine series owned by the plaintiff. After referring to the previous decisions in which the Court had restrained copyright and patent infringement, Eldon LC explained:

> The principle of granting the injunction in those cases is, that damages do not give adequate relief; and that the sale of copies by the Defendant is in each instance not only taking away the profit upon the individual book, which the Plaintiff probably would have sold, but may injure him to an incalculable extent, which no inquiry for the purpose of damages can ascertain.[132]

As the nineteenth-century authors identified,[133] it follows that the Chancery awarded injunctions to restrain infringements of copyright and patents so that the plaintiff could be adequately remedied at law. Although the threat of future harm caused by the infringements was purely economic, the longer it continued the greater the risk that the plaintiff's economic loss would be incalculable and would not be adequately remedied by a damages award. As Kerr observed more generally,

[130] ibid 705–06.

[131] *Hogg v Kirby* (1803) 8 Ves Jr 215.

[132] ibid 225. For similar statements, see *Harmer v Plane* (1807) 14 Ves Jr 130; *Wilkins v Aikin* (1810) 17 Ves Jr 424; *Rundell v Murray* (1821) Jac 311.

[133] Eden (n 5) 264; Drewry (n 5) 191, 220; Story (n 45) vol 2, 237–38.

'[t]he fact that the amount of damage [or loss] cannot be accurately compensated may constitute irreparable damage'.[134]

It is important to recognise, however, that the above reasoning differs radically from the cases involving nuisance and trespass. The risk of irreparable harm identified in the *Universities of Oxford and Cambridge v Richardson* and *Hogg v Kirby* was not specific to the facts of the cases. Rather, the risk of the plaintiff's economic loss being incalculable arose from the general nature of the wrongs of copyright and patent infringement. This meant that once it was alleged that the wrongs had been committed and were continuing, the Chancery presumed that the plaintiff would suffer irreparable harm. Accordingly, the Court was concerned only with the strength of the legal right (that is, the plaintiff's case that an infringement had occurred and would continue) and any applicable discretionary factors before it would award interlocutory relief.[135]

C. Overview

In the light of the above analysis, it cannot be said that the doctrine of irreparable harm was the exclusive basis upon which equity intervened to award injunctions in aid of legal rights. The irreparable harm doctrine was limited to justifying *interlocutory* injunctions. By contrast, the Chancery awarded *perpetual* injunctions in aid of legal rights where a legal wrong was continuing to be committed against the plaintiff because the Chancery was motivated to prevent a multiplicity of suits.

In addition to clarifying the reasons why the Chancery believed that it had jurisdiction to award injunctions in aid of legal right, it is worth pausing to highlight three equally significant points that can be derived from the foregoing analysis. First, it is important to appreciate that the multiplicity of suits doctrine still operated to show that the remedies at law were inadequate. As Pomeroy explained:

> The multiplicity of suits to be avoided, which are generally actions at law, shows that the legal remedies are inadequate, and can not meet the ends of justice; and therefore a court of equity interferes, and although the primary rights and interests of the parties are legal in their nature, it takes cognizance of them, and awards some specific equitable remedy, which gives, perhaps, in one proceeding more substantial relief than could be obtained in numerous actions at law.[136]

Importantly, however, the multiplicity of suits doctrine was conceptually distinct from the narrower irreparable harm doctrine. The former doctrine focused on whether the remedies at law were inadequate because they could not stop the

[134] Kerr (n 5) 14.
[135] See, eg, *Hill v Thompson* (1817) 3 Mer 622; *Mawmen v Teg* (1826) 2 Russ 385; *Kay v Marshall* (1836) 1 My & C 373; *Bacon v Jones* (1839) 4 My & C 433; *Collard v Allison* (1840) 4 My & C 487.
[136] Pomeroy (n 46) 255.

defendant from continuing to commit a wrong against the plaintiff. The latter concept focused solely on whether a monetary award would sufficiently remedy the plaintiff for his future damage or loss.

The second point to note is that the jurisdictional basis for the Chancery's intervention (for example, because there was a multiplicity of suits) was the core justification for the award of the injunction. It did not mean that the Chancery could merely hear the dispute, as is connoted by the ordinary meaning of the word 'jurisdiction'.

The final point is that if the Chancery found that it had jurisdiction to intervene, this was not a discretionary finding. For example, whether there was a risk of irreparable harm, or whether the defendant was committing a continuing wrong against the plaintiff, was a question of fact.[137] Chancery judges were not given any discretion in determining these issues.

IV. The Discretionary Considerations

It is well established that over the seventeenth to nineteenth centuries, the Chancery developed numerous discretionary considerations that governed whether equitable remedies were awarded. As can be gleaned from nineteenth-century equity treatises, these considerations, such as hardship, laches, the doctrine of unclean hands and acquiescence, were not neatly developed in a specific area of equity. Rather, they were applied broadly by the Chancery when it believed that a particular consideration was applicable to the specific facts of a case.

It is beyond the scope of this chapter to provide an account of how the discretionary considerations developed in equity more generally. What is more pertinent to the analysis is the extent to which injunctions in aid of legal rights were ultimately awarded on a discretionary basis. As we shall see, the width of the discretion differed greatly, depending upon whether the injunction sought was perpetual or interlocutory.

A. Perpetual Injunctions

When it came to the award of perpetual injunctions, the discretionary considerations were more relevant in theory than they were in practice. It was explained in section III.A that before the mid-nineteenth century, it seems that the Chancery would grant perpetual injunctions only to restrain waste. In respect of these cases, the author could locate only one case in which a perpetual injunction to restrain waste that was being repeated was refused due to an applicable discretionary

[137] In the context of a discussion of the topic of adequacy of damages, this is explicitly recognised in *Snell's Equity*, see Davies (n 13) [18-034].

factor: *Woodward v Gyles*.[138] In that case, the defendant had leased land from the plaintiff pursuant to a covenant not to plough the land; but if he did engage in ploughing, he would pay the plaintiff 20 shillings for every acre ploughed. After the defendant ploughed the land, the plaintiff sought an injunction restraining the defendant from continuing to do so on the basis that the defendant's actions amounted to waste. The Court accepted that waste had been committed; however, it refused to exercise its discretion and grant an injunction as '[t]he parties themselves have here agreed the damage'.[139] It seems, therefore, that the Court was willing to refuse to award an injunction to restrain the defendant from continuing to commit waste only because the plaintiff had consented to its commission.

Other than the cases concerning waste, it was not until after the mid-nineteenth century that Chancery began to grant perpetual injunctions in aid of legal rights. In the cases that were discussed in section III involving perpetual injunctions, once the plaintiff had demonstrated that his legal right had been infringed, an injunction was granted almost as of right. From the mid-nineteenth century until the Judicature Act reforms of 1873–75, it seems that there were only two categories of case in which such a perpetual injunction was refused due to an applicable discretionary consideration: where there was acquiescence or laches. As both Joyce and Kerr observed,[140] the Chancery would refuse to restrain a continuing wrong by injunction where the plaintiff had acquiesced in the commission of the wrong or had otherwise delayed bringing proceedings to restrain the defendant from committing the wrong. There are numerous examples of the Chancery's making statements to this effect.[141] However, only a handful of cases could be located in this period in which a perpetual injunction was in fact refused for acquiescence or laches.[142] That reflects the fact that the Chancery was hesitant to permit a defendant to continue infringing a plaintiff's legal right. As was stated by Turner LJ in *Johnson v Wyatt*, 'to justify the Court in refusing to interfere at the hearing of a cause there must be a much stronger case of acquiescence than is required upon an interlocutory application'.[143]

It follows that it was only in quite narrow circumstances that the Chancery would refuse to restrain a continuing tort. Indeed, the nineteenth-century authors did not identify in their treatises any other grounds on which a *perpetual* injunction would be restrained once the legal right was proved to have been infringed. This fact, as well as the dearth of cases in which perpetual injunctions were in fact refused due to an applicable discretionary factor, aligns with the statements in *Imperial v Broadbent* that once the plaintiff has proved that a defendant is continuing to infringe his legal right, an injunction will be granted as of course unless

[138] *Woodward v Gyles* (1690) 2 Vern 119.
[139] ibid 119.
[140] Joyce (n 5) 35, 38; Kerr (n 5) 16–20, 46.
[141] See, eg, *Attorney-General v Leeds Corporation* (1869–70) LR 5 Ch App 583.
[142] *Wood v Sutcliffe* (n 84); *Senior v Pawson* (1866–67) LR 3 Eq 330; *Gaunt v Fynney* (1872) 8 Ch App 8.
[143] *Johnson v Wyatt* (1863) 2 De GJ&S 18, 25.

there is something peculiar or special in the case. It is important to recognise that in *Imperial*, the defendants had argued that even if the plaintiff could show that his legal right was being continuously infringed, 'he must also show that the balance of convenience is in his favour'.[144] Therefore, by holding that an injunction should be granted 'as of course', both Lord Campbell and Lord Kingsdown explicitly rejected the defendants' contention that a continuous rights invasion would be stopped only where the balance of convenience was in the plaintiff's favour.

Taking stock of the above cases, what they indicate is that the discretionary considerations were rarely decisive in the analysis of whether a perpetual injunction should be awarded to restrain a legal wrong. Once it was proved that the defendant had infringed the plaintiff's legal right, and was continuing to infringe that right, it was only in exceptional circumstances that the Chancery refused to act.

B. Interlocutory Injunctions

By contrast, a highly discretionary approach was adopted when it came to deciding whether to grant an interlocutory injunction where the infringement of the plaintiff's legal right was disputed by the defendant.[145] The reason for this was that, beginning in cases concerning nuisance, a balance-of-convenience test came to be developed.

As explained in section III, injunctions to restrain nuisances were first awarded on an interlocutory basis. The interlocutory injunction was a critical remedy for plaintiffs, as otherwise the plaintiff would continue to suffer damage until his rights had been established at law.[146] In early cases in the late eighteenth century, the Chancery was only concerned with ensuring that the plaintiff had an actionable case at law before interlocutory relief was awarded.[147] For example, in *Fishmongers' Company v East India Company*,[148] Hardwicke LC refused to grant an interlocutory injunction to prevent a defendant from continuing to build a brick wall before the trial, because he was 'of the opinion that it [was] not a nuisance contrary to law'.[149]

By the nineteenth century, however, defendants were concerned with ensuring that their activities, particularly when they involved a trade that employed several people, were not restrained prematurely. Hence, the Chancery, under Eldon LC, became increasingly reluctant to award interlocutory injunctions to restrain

[144] *Imperial v Broadbent* (n 75) 604.

[145] Where the defendant admitted to infringing the plaintiff's legal right, less discretion was involved, see *Saunders v Smith* (1838) 3 My&C 711, 728–29.

[146] Spry (n 13) 467.

[147] This is neatly summarised in the first footnote in *Baines v Baker* (n 18) (involving an interlocutory quia timet injunction).

[148] *Fishmongers' Company v East India Company* (n 18).

[149] ibid 165.

nuisance.[150] In addition to considering whether the plaintiff had good prospects at law and would suffer irreparable harm, the Chancery assessed the effects that the proposed injunctive relief would have on the defendant. As McLaren points out,[151] Eldon LC first considered this factor in *Attorney-General v Cleaver.*[152] In that case, the plaintiff sought an interlocutory injunction restraining the defendants from manufacturing soap on the basis that it was a nuisance. Lord Eldon refused to grant the injunction and remarked that 'some caution is necessary, before the Court should interpose to suspend, which may destroy concerns of this nature, that cannot be established without immense expenditure'.[153] In *Crowder v Tinker*,[154] Eldon LC expressed similar concerns despite the fact that an interlocutory injunction limiting the amount of gun powder that could be stored in the defendants' warehouse was ultimately granted. He wrote that 'great caution is required in granting an [i]njunction of this nature, where the effect will be to stop a large concern in lucrative trade'.[155]

The result of this reasoning was that whenever an interlocutory injunction was sought to restrain actions of defendants that were alleged to amount to a nuisance, the Court would exercise a wide discretion that took into account the probabilities of success of the parties and the effects that the proposed injunction would have on each party. Indeed, it was in the 1819 decision of *Attorney-General v Johnson* that the well-established phrase 'balance of convenience' was used to describe the process undertaken to determine whether injunctive relief should be awarded before a trial for nuisance was had at law.[156]

Once established by Eldon LC in the context of restraining a nuisance, the balance-of-convenience test also came to be employed in the context of interlocutory injunctions sought to restrain intellectual property right infringements, and later waste and trespass. So, for example, in *Hill v Thompson*,[157] Eldon LC refused to grant an interlocutory injunction restraining the defendants from making smelted iron on the basis that their entire business operation was alleged to infringe a patent. He reasoned that halting the defendants works for a significant time period would be a 'much greater inconvenience than any that can result from my refusal [to grant the injunction]'.[158] Furthermore, in *Clowes v Beck*, when deciding whether to continue an interlocutory injunction restraining a trespass to land, Langdale MR said 'What I really have to consider is this: which party is most likely to suffer by the continuing or dissolving the injunction?'[159]

[150] Drewry (n 5) 238; Kerr (n 5) 169; McLaren (n 109) 186.
[151] See McLaren (n 109) 186–89 for a detailed analysis of this consideration.
[152] *Attorney-General v Cleaver* (1811) 18 Ves Jr 211.
[153] ibid 217.
[154] *Crowder v Tinker* (n 111).
[155] ibid 622.
[156] *Attorney-General v Johnson* (n 40) 96.
[157] *Hill v Thompson* (n 135).
[158] ibid 631.
[159] *Clowes v Beck* (1851) 13 Beav 347, 354.

Thus, as the nineteenth-century authors also explained,[160] a highly discretionary analysis was employed when deciding whether to award interlocutory injunctions in aid of legal rights. The 'balance-of-convenience' test that came to be developed was ultimately a reflection of the fact that the Chancery was justifiably slow to intervene when a defendant disputed that it had interfered with a plaintiff's legal right.

C. Overview

In the light of the foregoing analysis, including the findings of section III, it can be determined that the Chancery came to develop a meaningful two-stage approach to the discretionary analysis of cases for the award of an injunction to restrain legal wrongs.

First, the Chancery was required to be satisfied that the Court *could* award an injunction. This jurisdictional question did not involve the exercise of a discretion. If satisfied, it was the core, underlying reason in favour of granting an injunction.

Second, if the Chancery found it had jurisdiction to interpose, the Court would then go on to conduct a discretionary analysis that weighed its reason for interposing against any countervailing discretionary factors to ultimately determine whether an injunction *should* be awarded on the facts of the case. If the plaintiff sought a perpetual injunction, little discretion was involved, as the defendant was already proved to be a wrongdoer and it was only in 'special' or 'peculiar' circumstances that such an injunction would be refused. By contrast, if the plaintiff sought an interlocutory injunction, the analysis was highly discretionary, as the Chancery sought to balance the conveniences between the parties.

V. The History of the Mandatory Injunction

The analysis so far has focused on prohibitory injunctions. This raises the question: how did the mandatory injunction come to be developed?

A. Initial Reluctance

Throughout the eighteenth century and the first half of the nineteenth century, the Chancery did not believe that it had jurisdiction to grant mandatory injunctions. Indeed, it is notable that in the treatises written by Eden, Drewry and Story before 1850, not one of these authors referred to a 'mandatory' injunction. Although there are numerous judicial statements indicating that the Chancery

[160] See Joyce (n 5) 43; Kerr (n 5) 25–26; Pomeroy (n 46) vol 3, 368.

doubted its jurisdiction to grant mandatory injunctions,[161] this opinion was most clearly expressed by Brougham LC in the 1832 case of *Blakemore v Glamorganshire Canal Navigation*.[162] There, the defendant had widened its canal on the River Taff, which caused the supply of water to the plaintiff's ironworks to be significantly reduced. As a result, the plaintiff sought an interlocutory injunction compelling the defendant to fill in the canal on the basis that it was causing a private nuisance. In his judgment, Brougham LC accepted that the defendant had likely committed a nuisance. Yet he refused to grant the mandatory injunction because 'the injunction has been to restrain; to prohibit, not to abate; to prevent irreparable mischief, not to undo what has been done'.[163]

Lord Brougham LC's statement was influential in the case law throughout the remainder of the nineteenth century,[164] and is still quoted in the modern literature.[165] It is therefore necessary to pause for a moment and consider how Brougham LC conceptualised the operation of a mandatory injunction. Lord Brougham LC explained that the mandatory injunction was inappropriate because it would 'undo what has been done'. In the context of granting an *interlocutory* injunction on the facts of *Blakemore* this makes sense, as if the mandatory injunction had been granted, it would have operated to reverse the defendant's actions before the rights of the parties were determined at law, rather than simply maintaining the status quo until the trial. It seems, therefore, that Brougham LC's understanding of the operation of a mandatory injunction was predicated on the fact that on the case before him it was an interlocutory injunction.

Beyond this more conceptual point, it has been observed by numerous authors that because of the Court's jurisdictional concerns Chancery judges would instead award *prohibitory* injunctions that had the effect of compelling defendants to do positive acts.[166] Such injunctions were often granted to restrain defendants from continuing acts that were alleged to amount to a nuisance. There are numerous examples of this.[167] Consider the decision in *Manchester, Sheffield, &c, Railway Company v Worksop Board of Health*.[168] In that case, the plaintiff owners of a canal sought injunctive relief after the defendant health authority constructed a sewerage system that discharged raw sewage into the canal. Sir John Romilly MR granted an 'injunction to restrain the Defendants from … permitting privies or cesspools

[161] See, eg, *Ryder* (n 18) 543; *Corporation of London v Bolt* (1799) 5 Ves Jr 129, 130.

[162] *Blakemore v Glamorganshire Canal Navigation* (n 116). See also *Gale v Abbott* (1862) 8 J NS 987.

[163] *Blakemore v Glamorganshire Canal Navigation* (n 116) 182.

[164] See, eg, Joyce (n 5) 57.

[165] See, eg, Davies (n 13) [18-003]; Heydon, Leeming and Turner (n 23) [21-440].

[166] Kerr (n 5) 48; Williams and Guthrie-Smith (n 22) vol 1, 42; J Klein, 'Mandatory Injunctions' (1898) 12 *Harvard Law Review* 95, 97; Spry (n 13) 620-621; Heydon, Leeming and Turner (n 23) [21-440]. See also *Smith v Smith* (1875) LR 20 Eq 500, 504.

[167] See, e.g., *Robinson v Lord Byron* (n 111); *Lane v Newdigate* (1804) 10 Ves 192; *Spencer v London and Birmingham Railway Company* (1836) 8 Sim 193; *Great North of England Clarence and Hartlepool Junction Railway Company v The Clarence Railway Co* (1844) 1 Coll 507.

[168] *Manchester, Sheffield, &c, Railway Company v Worksop Board of Health* (1857) 23 Beav 198.

from such houses to drain into or communicate with the [plaintiff's canal]'.[169] Although framed in negative form, the injunction was mandatory in effect as its terms required the defendant to take the positive step of stopping the sewerage system from operating until the trial for nuisance was had at law.

What is important about the fact that the Chancery ordered positive action to be taken in negative form is that no distinction was made between mandatory and prohibitory injunctions. Accordingly, both types of injunction were awarded pursuant to the same principles that guided the exercise of the Chancellor's discretion. The law governing the grant of prohibitory injunctions therefore applied equally to the grant of mandatory injunctions.

B. Further Development

It was only after the passing of the Chancery Amendment Act 1858 ('Lord Cairns' Act') that the distinction between mandatory and prohibitory injunctions was brought into sharper focus. That was because, following the decision of the Court of Appeal in Chancery in *Isenberg v East House India Estate Co*,[170] the fact that an injunction was classified as mandatory was relevant to whether damages should be awarded in lieu of the injunction.

In *Isenberg*, the defendant had constructed a building that reduced the natural light in the plaintiff's neighbouring premises. On the basis that the defendants' actions amounted to a nuisance, at first instance the Master of the Rolls granted a *perpetual* mandatory injunction in prohibitory form, which had the effect of requiring the defendant to reduce the height of its building.[171] On appeal, Westbury LC suspended the order of the Master of the Rolls and directed an inquiry to assess the plaintiff's loss so that he could make an award of damages in lieu.

Lord Westbury LC's reasoning is noteworthy for two reasons. First, although the injunction granted at first instance was in prohibitory form, Westbury LC assumed that a mandatory injunction operates differently from a prohibitory injunction. He stated:

> This jurisdiction of this Court, so far as it partakes of the nature of a *preventive remedy*, that is, prohibition of further damage or an intended damage, is a jurisdiction that may be exercised without difficulty, and rests upon the clearest principles. But there has been superadded to that the power of the Court to grant what has been denominated a mandatory injunction, that is, an order compelling a Defendant to *restore things* to the condition in which they were at the time when the Plaintiff's complaint was made.[172]

[169] ibid 209.
[170] *Isenberg v East House India Estate Co* (1863) 3 De GJ & S 263.
[171] The decree made was 'final' according to the definition provided in E Daniell, *A Treatise on the Practice of the High Court of Chancery* (J & WT Clarke 1838) vol 2, 638.
[172] *Isenberg* (n 170) 272 (emphasis added).

This was the first time it had been said that a *perpetual* prohibitory injunction operates to prevent future damage, while a *perpetual* mandatory injunction operates to restore a plaintiff to his previous position by rectifying previously inflicted damage. Although the decision in *Blakemore* was not cited, Westbury LC conceptualised a perpetual mandatory injunction to operate in the same way as the interlocutory mandatory injunction sought in *Blakemore*. Treatise writers at the time similarly conceptualised mandatory injunctions in this way.[173] However, as will be explained more fully in chapter 3, there are serious difficulties with conceptualising the operation of a perpetual mandatory injunction in this way.

Second, the reason why Westbury LC accentuated the distinction between mandatory and prohibitory injunctions was so that he could use it as a justification to award damages in lieu of an injunction. After explaining that on the evidence before him it was 'doubtful' that the plaintiff had sustained any damage, he went on to observe:

> This is a case in which the benefit of the recent statute giving power to this Court to assess and ascertain damages is peculiarly felt; and I hold it, therefore, to be the duty of the Court in such a case as the present not, by granting a mandatory injunction, to deliver over the Defendants to the Plaintiff bound hand and foot, in order to be made subject to any extortionate demand that he may by possibility make, but to substitute for such mandatory injunction an inquiry before itself, in order to ascertain the measure of damage that has been actually sustained.[174]

Lord Westbury LC's remarks indicate that a reason favouring the award of damages in lieu was that the mandatory injunction sought would cause loss to the defendants and potentially allow the plaintiff to make an extortionate demand. The distinction between prohibitory and mandatory injunctions was therefore emphasised, because it meant that Westbury LC could use the fact that the injunction was a mandatory one to better justify his decision to award damages in lieu of the injunction.

Following the decision in *Isenberg*, courts implicitly understood prohibitory injunctions to operate to restrain future acts, and mandatory injunctions to 'undo' past wrongs and 'restore' the state of affairs that existed before the defendant committed his wrong. Additionally, although the courts continued to grant mandatory injunctions in prohibitory form, courts became much more conscious of when injunctions had a mandatory effect. In this sense, the distinction between mandatory and prohibitory injunctions had crystallised.

It should not be thought, however, that following *Isenberg* courts preferred to award damages in lieu of a mandatory injunction. On the contrary, there was an abundance of cases in the late nineteenth century (and indeed beyond the passing of the Judicature Act reforms) in which courts granted mandatory injunctions to restrain the continued commission of nuisance and trespass to land on

[173] Story and Redfield (n 97) 113; Joyce (n 5) 57; Kerr (n 5) 48–51; Pomeroy (n 46) 367, 391.
[174] *Isenberg* (n 170) 273.

the same principles that governed the award of prohibitory injunctions.[175] These injunctions, although framed in prohibitory form, ordered defendants to do a variety of positive acts, including: to remove 2,000 tons of combustible jute from a property;[176] to remove water pipes wrongfully laid on the plaintiff's land;[177] to remove a footpath;[178] to pull down a party wall;[179] to pull down a building that obstructed the plaintiff's right of way;[180] and to pull down a wall or a building that substantially interfered with the plaintiff's right to light,[181] or was built in breach of a negative covenant.[182] Damages were, however, much more likely to be awarded in lieu of a mandatory injunction. In the 1895 decision of *Shelfer v City of London Electric Lighting Co (No 1)*, AL Smith LJ noted that counsel had submitted that 'fourteen cases are to be found in the books since the year 1858 in which damages in lieu of an injunction have been awarded by the Chancery, and that all these are cases in which mandatory injunctions were sought'.[183]

C. Overview

The foregoing analysis demonstrates that mandatory injunctions in aid of legal rights came to develop out of, and were awarded pursuant to, the same principles as governed prohibitory injunctions. Indeed, because of the Chancery's reluctance to confirm its jurisdiction to grant mandatory injunctions, such injunctions were always expressed in prohibitory form. It was not until the 1899 case of *Jackson v Normanby Brick Co*[184] that it was explicitly held that courts must award mandatory injunctions in positive form. In that case, the Court of Appeal stated:

> The registrar has called our attention to the form in which orders of this kind have hitherto been made, namely, restraining the defendant from allowing the buildings to remain on the land; *but in future it will be better for the Court to say in plain terms what it means, and in direct words to order the buildings to be pulled down and removed. The order will therefore go.*[185]

Nevertheless, courts and scholars in the nineteenth century understood mandatory injunctions (irrespective of whether they were interlocutory or perpetual) to operate differently from prohibitory injunctions. Mandatory injunctions were

[175] cf *Durell v Pritchard* (1865–66) LR 1 Ch App 244.
[176] *Hepburn v Lordan* (1865) 2 Hem & M 345.
[177] *Goodson v Richardson* (n 95).
[178] *Milward v Redditch Local Board of Health* (1873) 21 WR 429.
[179] *Smith v Smith* (n 166).
[180] *Krehl v Burrell* (1879) 11 Ch D 146 (CA).
[181] See, eg, *Beadel v Perry* (1866–67) LR 3 Eq 465 (interlocutory); *Staight v Burn* (1869–70) LR 5 Ch App 163 (interlocutory); *Kelk v Pearson* (1870–1) LR 6 Ch App 809.
[182] *Lord Manners* (n 101).
[183] *Shelfer v City of London Electric Lighting Co (No 1)* [1895] 1 Ch 287 (CA) 319.
[184] *Jackson v Normanby Brick Co* [1899] 1 Ch 438 (CA).
[185] ibid 438–39 (emphasis added).

thought to restore the plaintiff to the position he was in before the wrong occurred. By contrast, prohibitory injunctions were thought to simply restrain the defendant from committing future wrongs.

VI. Concluding Lessons

This chapter has offered an account of the development of the injunction in aid of legal rights from the seventeenth century until the Judicature Act reforms of 1873–75. The purpose in doing so has been to understand what the law *was* so that it can afford guidance in analysing what the law *is*. The chapter has highlighted three main lessons of broader importance.

The first lesson is that, although there is some contention in the historical sources, the evidence indicates that there was not one but two jurisdictional bases upon which the Chancery could intervene in aid of legal rights by awarding an injunction. It was the multiplicity of suits doctrine that justified the Chancery's award of a perpetual injunction in aid of legal rights, while the irreparable harm doctrine was what justified the Chancery's award of such an interlocutory injunction.

The second lesson is that the Chancery developed a two-stage analytical process to determine whether an injunction in aid of legal rights should be granted. Specifically, the Chancery would find that it *could* award an injunction (that is, there was a jurisdictional reason to interpose by granting an injunction), after which it would then ask whether it *should* award the injunction by weighing the reason for interposing against any countervailing discretionary factors. There was, however, a notable difference in the amount of discretion involved in the analysis, depending on whether the injunction sought was perpetual or interlocutory.

The third lesson is that although the mandatory injunction in aid of legal rights developed after the prohibitory injunction, mandatory injunctions were awarded on the same principles as prohibitory injunctions. Nevertheless, mandatory and prohibitory injunctions were said to operate differently.

Armed with a greater understanding of the historical development of the injunction in aid of legal rights, the modern law governing when injunctions can be awarded in tort law will now be analysed.

3

The Formal Distinctions between Prohibitory, Mandatory and Quia Timet Injunctions

I. Introduction

It was explained in chapter 1 that one of the objectives of this book is to provide a comprehensive account of the positive law governing when prohibitory, mandatory and quia timet injunctions can be awarded to restrain or remedy torts. As was explained in chapter 2, to achieve this objective it is essential to understand how the Chancery developed its jurisdiction to award injunctions in aid of legal rights. Equally as important, however, is an examination of the formal distinctions between prohibitory, mandatory and quia timet injunctions. Without identifying and analysing these distinctions, it would be impossible to articulate the law governing when each of these injunctions can be granted.

To assist in the analysis of the modern law in later chapters, the purpose of this chapter is to identify the precise distinctions between prohibitory, mandatory and quia timet injunctions. It is also necessary to briefly examine the effects of those distinctions. Although those effects will be explored in detail in chapters 4, 5, and 6, reflecting on them at a higher level of generality in this chapter emphasises the importance of correctly classifying an injunction as prohibitory, mandatory or quia timet.

The chapter is structured as follows. Section II examines the distinction between prohibitory injunctions and mandatory injunctions, and the alleged effects of the distinction. Section III examines the distinction between prohibitory and mandatory injunctions, on the one hand, and quia timet injunctions, on the other, and the alleged effects of that distinction. Section IV concludes by summarising the three main claims advanced in this chapter.

II. The Distinction between Prohibitory and Mandatory Injunctions

A. Prohibitory Injunctions

The view adopted in the existing literature is that a prohibitory injunction is granted to restrain a defendant from doing an act that amounts to a wrong in circumstances where the defendant has already committed the wrong against the claimant and it is likely to be committed again in the future.[1] This definition is reflected in the case law. There are two circumstances in which an injunction that restrains tortious conduct will be classified as a prohibitory injunction by the courts.

First, where a tort is ongoing (or would have been ongoing had an interim injunction not been granted) because the tort is being committed day after day, an injunction that restrains the defendant from doing an act that amounts to that tort is classified as a prohibitory injunction. For example, consider cases where injunctions have been granted to restrain defendants from: using a sewerage system that continuously polluted waterways;[2] allowing trees to interfere with an easement over the defendant's airspace;[3] or leaving trees to grow unchecked, which causes their roots to damage the claimant's property.[4]

Second, where a tort is being committed repeatedly on a regular basis (that is, it is recurring) but it is not occurring every day, an injunction that restrains the defendant from doing an act that amounts to the tort is also classified as a prohibitory injunction. Noise on a particular day that amounts to a private nuisance is a good example of a recurring tort, such as in *Coventry v Lawrence*, where the nuisance arose from car racing that would occur on different occasions, estimated at 16 to 27 times each year.[5] Harassment[6] and repeated defamatory statements[7] are also examples of recurring torts that courts will restrain by injunction.

[1] I Spry, *Equitable Remedies* (9th edn, Thomson Reuters 2014) 389–90; JD Heydon, MJ Leeming and PG Turner, *Meagher, Gummow & Lehane's Equity: Doctrines & Remedies* (5th edn, LexisNexis 2015) [21-035]; A Burrows, *Remedies for Torts, Breach of Contract, and Equitable Wrongs* (4th edn, Oxford University Press 2019) 443; P Davies, 'Injunctions' in J McGhee and S Elliott (eds), *Snell's Equity* (34th edn, Sweet & Maxwell 2021) [18-027]–[18-028]; K Oliphant (ed), *The Law of Tort* (3rd edn, LexisNexis 2015) [8.18]; A Tettenborn, 'Injunctions' in M Jones and A Dugdale (eds), *Clerk & Lindsell on Torts* (23rd edn, Sweet & Maxwell 2020) [28-06]; D Bean, I Parry and A Burns, *Injunctions* (14th edn, Sweet & Maxwell 2022) [2-09]; D Capper, *Injunctions in Private Law* (Edward Elgar Publishing 2024) [1-02].

[2] See, eg, *Stollmeyer v Trinidad Lake Petroleum Co Ltd* [1918] AC 485 (PC); *Haigh v Deudraeth RDC* [1945] 2 All ER 661 (Ch); *Pride of Derby and Derbyshire Angling Association Ltd v British Celanese Ltd* [1953] Ch 149 (CA).

[3] *Bockenfield Aerodrome Ltd v Clarehugh* [2021] EWHC 848 (Ch).

[4] See, eg, *McCombe v Read* [1955] 2 QB 429 (QB); *King v Taylor* [1976] 1 EGLR 132 (QB).

[5] *Coventry v Lawrence* [2014] UKSC 13, [2014] AC 822 [11].

[6] Cases in which final injunctions have been granted to restrain harassment are not wanting. See, eg, *Norwich City Council v Famuyiwa* [2004] EWCA Civ 1770; *Mitton v Benefield* [2011] EWHC 2098 (QB); *SKA v CRH* [2012] EWHC 2236 (QB); *Nursing and Midwifery Council v Nowak* [2014] EWHC 2945 (QB); *Brand v Berki* [2015] EWHC 3373 (QB); *GYH v Persons Unknown* [2018] EWHC 121 (QB); *Oliver v Shaikh* [2019] EWHC 3389 (QB); *Hodson v Person Unknown A* [2022] EWHC 1960 (QB).

[7] '[P]erpetual injunctions to restrain publication of a libel are commonly granted, either after a trial, or after judgment is entered in default of defence': *Law Society v Kordowski* [2011] EWHC 3185 (QB) [3]. See, eg, *John v MGN Ltd* [1997] QB 586 (CA); *Brett Wilson LLP v Persons Unknown* [2015] EWHC 2628 (QB); *Zahawi v Press TV* [2017] EWHC 1010 (QB); *Burgon v News Group Newspapers Ltd* [2019] EWHC 195 (QB); *Glenn v Kline* [2020] EWHC 3182 (QB); *Mirza v Ali* [2021] EWHC 1494 (QB); *Dudley v Phillips* [2022] EWHC 930 (QB). See also *Grobbelaar v News Group Newspapers Ltd* [2002] 1 WLR 3024 (HL); Richard Parkes et al, *Gatley on Libel and Slander* (13th edn, Sweet & Maxwell 2022)

What the above examples demonstrate is that prohibitory injunctions are focused on preventing *continuing* wrongs (that is, ongoing *or* recurring wrongs).[8] As explained by Lord Burrows in *Jalla v Shell International Trading and Shipping Co Ltd*, continuing wrongs are wrongs that occur 'day after day [that is, the wrong is ongoing] or on another regular basis [that is, the wrong is recurring]'.[9] Accordingly, as both Stevens and Smith have recognised,[10] the operative purpose of a prohibitory injunction is to prevent wrongs from occurring in the future.

B. Mandatory Injunctions

The extant literature suggests that a mandatory injunction is an injunction that orders a defendant to do a positive act.[11] The literature explains that there are two types of mandatory injunction. The first type is the *enforcing* mandatory injunction. This type of injunction orders a defendant to carry out a positive obligation that he promised to do for valuable consideration.[12] As this category of injunction is awarded to enforce contractual duties, it is beyond the scope of this book.

The second type of mandatory injunction is the *restorative* injunction. This type of injunction requires the defendant to 'repair the consequences of some wrongful act done by him or her'.[13] According to the literature, each time a mandatory injunction is awarded to remedy a tort, it operates to restore the claimant to the position she would have been in before the tort occurred. The restorative mandatory injunction is therefore said to be entirely distinct from a prohibitory injunction, as the former restores the claimant to her previous position, while the latter prevents a future infringement of legal rights. This understanding is consistent with how the Chancery originally understood the mandatory injunction to operate, as was explained in chapter 2.

Interestingly, however, little attention has been paid to whether it is correct to classify all mandatory injunctions in tort law in this way. In each of the relevant

[10-040]. In Australia, see *Zaia v Eshow* [2017] NSWSC 1540; *Capilano Honey Ltd v Dowling (No 4)* [2021] NSWSC 264.

8 'For this purpose there is no distinction between continuance and repetition': *Mayfair Trading Co Pty Ltd v Dreyer* (1958) 101 CLR 428, 451. Hereinafter, what is meant by a 'continuing' tort is any tort that is ongoing or recurring.

9 *Jalla v Shell International Trading and Shipping Co Ltd* [2024] AC 595 [26]. See also ibid [31].

10 R Stevens, *Torts and Rights* (Oxford University Press 2007) 57; S Smith, *Rights, Wrongs and Injustices: The Structure of Remedial Law* (Oxford University Press 2019) 134, 146–47.

11 Burrows (n 1) 462; Heydon, Leeming and Turner (n 1) [21-440]; RJ Sharpe, *Injunctions and Specific Performance* (4th edn, Thomson Reuters 2012) [1.30]; J Glister and J Lee, Hanbury on Modern Equity (22nd edn, Sweet & Maxwell 2021) [28-108]; Davies (n 1) [18-010]; Spry (n 1) 555; Oliphant (ed) (n 1) [8.20]; Tettenborn (n 1) [28-05]; N McBride and R Bagshaw, *Tort Law* (6th edn, Pearson Education 2018) 799.

12 Burrows (n 1) 462; Heydon, Leeming and Turner (n 1) [21-445]; Sharpe (n 11) [1.10]; Glister and Lee (n 11) [28-018]; Davies (n 1) [28-108]; Spry (n 1) 556–58.

13 Heydon, Leeming and Turner (n 1) [21-445]. For similar statements, see Burrows (n 1) 462; Glister and Lee (n 11) [28-018]; Sharpe (n 11) [1.10]; Davies (n 1) [28-108]; Spry (n 1) 555–59.

texts, only a brief statement is made to the effect that the mandatory injunction remedies torts by restoring the claimant to her former position, before the discussion then moves on to the relevant discretionary considerations. The existing literature therefore adopts uncritically what was said by Lord Westbury LC in *Isenberg v East House India Estate Co*.[14] A closer examination of the cases reveals, however, that there are in fact *two* distinct types of final mandatory injunctions that are awarded in tort law.

The first is the (true) restorative mandatory injunction. This injunction operates solely to undo the consequence(s) of a tort already committed. In this context, the injunction is not focused on stopping a continuing tort (as on the facts there is no risk that the tort will occur again in the future) but aims to restore the claimant to the position she would have been in had the tort not been committed. The injunction therefore draws its justificatory basis from the fact that damages (or any other legal remedy) will not adequately remedy the past damage or loss suffered by the claimant.[15]

A good example is found in the decision of *Esso Petroleum Co Ltd v Kingswood Motors (Addlestone) Ltd*.[16] In that case, it was likely (if not certain) that the second and third defendants had procured the first defendant to breach its solus tie agreement with the claimant by, inter alia, transferring the title to the land that was the subject of the agreement to the third defendant. After the title had been transferred and the damage had been done, the claimant was granted a mandatory (interlocutory[17]) injunction, ordering the third defendant to retransfer the title in the land back to the first defendant. Bridge J reasoned that damages would not be able to remedy the fact that the title to the land remained with the third defendant, which would mean that the solus tie agreement could not be enforced by the claimant against the first defendant.[18] Accordingly, an injunction was granted ordering the third defendant to retransfer title to the land to the first defendant. Just like an award of damages,[19] the injunction placed the claimant in the position it would have been in had the tort not occurred.

The restorative mandatory injunction therefore operates to redress *past* damage or loss, and is entirely distinct from an injunction that operates to stop a tort from continuing and hence to prevent *future* damage. As was explained by Patten J in *Perlman v Rayden*, when determining whether to award a restorative mandatory injunction to knock down a second-floor extension constructed by the defendant allowing builders to trespass over the claimant's land:

[14] *Isenberg v East House India Estate Co* (1863) 3 De GJ & S 263. See ch 2. cf Capper (n 1) [1.02].
[15] This point is elaborated on in ch 5.
[16] *Esso Petroleum Co Ltd v Kingswood Motors (Addlestone) Ltd* [1974] QB 142 (CA).
[17] Although the injunction in that case was an interlocutory one, the same injunction would have been available on a final basis. This was recognised explicitly by Edelman J in the High Court of Australia in *Smethurst v Commissioner of Police* (2020) 272 CLR 177 [256].
[18] *Esso Petroleum* (n 16) 157.
[19] *Livingstone v Rawyards Coal Co* (1880) 5 App Cas 25 (HL) 39.

> Mr Perlman seeks an injunction ordering the removal of the second floor extension and the lights as a remedy for the trespass on the roadway. Neither the dormer window nor the lights project over the roadway so as to constitute a continuing trespass. I am not therefore concerned with the type of issue that arose in cases like *Shelfer v City of London Electric Lighting Co* [1895] 1 Ch 287, as to whether the Court should allow a wrong to continue by refusing an injunction and ordering the payment of damages in lieu. The issue for me is whether an injunction is an appropriate remedy for a past trespass.[20]

The second type of mandatory injunction is what the author will label the *desisting* mandatory injunction. It is distinct from a restorative mandatory injunction as it operates to compel a defendant to do a positive act to stop a tort from continuing. This type of injunction is awarded most frequently in the context of nuisance and trespass to land cases, where an act by a defendant leads to an ongoing wrong. For example, consider the numerous cases in which mandatory injunctions have been granted to order a defendant to pull down buildings and fences that were substantially interfering with the claimant's light and amounted to a private nuisance.[21] The direct effect of such an injunction is to stop the tortious infringement of the claimant's light from continuing and to prevent the occurrence of future identical private nuisances.[22] Accordingly, the justificatory basis for the *desisting* mandatory injunction is to stop the relevant tort from continuing, not to redress any past damage or loss.

The obvious retort to classifying the injunction in this way (which is implicit in the literature) is to say that although the injunction is stopping a tort from continuing, it is also restoring the claimant to her previous position. Indeed, in the example described above, the defendant is being forced to pull down a building, and this seems to restore the claimant back to the position she was in before the nuisance was committed. However, there is a major difficulty with this line of reasoning. The award of a desisting mandatory injunction on its own (that is, without damages) will not compensate the claimant for the damage or loss that she suffered before the tort was stopped. So, in the above example, the effect of the injunction is that the claimant's right will no longer be interfered with in the future. But it will not remedy the loss of the reasonable enjoyment of her land during the period in which the nuisance was committed. It is the award of damages that rectifies this past loss.

[20] *Perlman v Rayden* [2004] EWHC 2192 (Ch) [99].

[21] See, eg, *Staight v Burn* (1869-70) LR 5 Ch App 163; *Smith v Smith* (1875) LR 20 Eq 500; *Daniel v Ferguson* [1891] 2 Ch 27 (CA); *Allen v Greenwood* [1980] Ch 119 (CA); *Pugh v Howells* (1984) 48 P&CR 298 (CA); *Regan v Paul Properties Ltd* [2006] EWCA Civ 1391. As for trespass to land, see *Martyr v Lawrence* (1864) 2 De GJ & S 261; *Goodson v Richardson* (1873-74) LR 9 Ch App 221; *Harrow LBC v Donohoe* [1995] 1 EGLR 257 (CA); *Jones v Stones* [1999] 1 WLR 1739 (CA).

[22] Such a nuisance was expressly referred to as a continuing one by Lord Burrows in *Jalla* (n 9) [44]. This classification is undoubtedly correct, as it explains why damages in lieu of an injunction (and not common law damages for one nuisance) are awarded in such cases.

Preventing a future rights infringement is, of course, exactly what a final prohibitory injunction achieves. Consider the classic case of *Pride of Derby and Derbyshire Angling Association Ltd v British Celanese Ltd*.[23] Here, the defendants were restrained by a prohibitory injunction from continuing to discharge untreated effluent into two rivers. The direct effect of the injunctions was that the effluent would no longer be discharged into the rivers in the future and the claimants would be put in the position that they were in before the nuisances were committed. Yet it is not generally thought that these injunctions 'restored' the claimants to their previous position. What the prohibitory injunctions were doing was stopping the nuisances from continuing. Only an award of damages would remedy the claimants for their past damage caused by the untreated effluent that had already flowed into the rivers. Given that a desisting mandatory injunction also operates to prevent a future rights infringement (and not to remedy past damage or loss), it necessarily follows that it is misconceived to conceptualise such an injunction as a 'restorative' injunction.

In the light of the above analysis, it can be determined that there are in fact *two* types of final mandatory injunction that remedy torts: (i) a restorative mandatory injunction; and (ii) a desisting mandatory injunction. It seems the extant literature has obscured the different ways in which a mandatory injunction operates to remedy a tort, depending on whether that tort has been completed or is continuing. It is with this in mind that we can now assess how these mandatory injunctions are distinct from prohibitory injunctions.

C. The Distinction

Existing literature suggests that it is quite simple to distinguish a prohibitory injunction from a mandatory injunction. Although it is often said that the distinction is one of substance rather than form,[24] the consensus is that

> [a] mandatory injunction is an injunction which directly orders the person to whom it is addressed to do something, as opposed to the much more usual prohibitory injunction which restrains the person to whom it is addressed from doing something.[25]

There is, however, a problem with adopting this method of distinction. From the very inception of the mandatory injunction, it was recognised that the distinction between mandatory and prohibitory injunctions is not as straightforward as examining the form of the words used in the court's order. As was explained in chapter 2, mandatory injunctions were historically awarded in prohibitory form. So, a defendant who was committing an ongoing nuisance was not ordered to do a

[23] *Pride of Derby* (n 2).

[24] See McBride and Bagshaw (n 11) 799; Spry (n 1) 560–61; Sharpe (n 11) [1.510]; Heydon, Leeming and Turner (n 1) [21-440].

[25] Heydon, Leeming and Turner (n 1) [21-440]. See also the other works cited in n 1.

positive act to stop the nuisance. Instead, the courts would grant an injunction, for example, 'to restrain the Defendants from ... permitting privies or cesspools from such houses to drain into or communicate with the [claimant's canal]'.[26] Despite the negative form of the words used, the Chancery conceptualised this injunction as mandatory in substance. Therefore, merely because an injunction was framed in prohibitive form did not necessarily mean that it was prohibitive in substance.

The better way to understand the distinction between mandatory and prohibitory injunctions is to examine the underlying reason *why* the injunction is being awarded. It was explained in section II.A that a final prohibitory injunction requires abstention from acting to prevent a future infringement of legal rights. Looking first to the *restorative* mandatory injunction, this injunction is plainly distinguishable from a prohibitory injunction as it operates to remedy past damage or loss, after a tort is complete. It is therefore not future-focused and is in no way concerned with preventing a further infringement of legal rights.

As explained in section II.B, the *desisting* mandatory injunction operates to stop a tort that is continuing, to prevent a future infringement of legal rights. Other than the form of the words used in the court's order, as a matter of substance a desisting mandatory injunction is therefore identical to a prohibitory injunction and cannot be distinguished from it. A retort that could be made here (which is implicit in the existing literature) is that desisting mandatory injunctions are distinct from prohibitory injunctions because a mandatory injunction requires the taking of positive steps that often cause the defendant to expend money. Accordingly, the argument would run, a mandatory injunction is more coercive and irreversible in effect, and that is why it must be distinguished from a prohibitory injunction.

The difficulty with this view is that it is predicated on a misconception. It presumes that because prohibitory injunctions restrain a defendant from doing something, they do not require the defendant to do a positive act or to expend money and are therefore less coercive. However, as Robert Sharpe has observed, prohibitory injunctions often have the practical effect of requiring a positive course of action or expenditure of money.[27] Sharpe explains that in nuisance cases, for example, 'a negative injunction restraining the continuation of a nuisance in effect usually requires the defendant to take positive steps to correct a situation and these steps may be extremely costly'.[28] The correctness of this statement is evident by way of numerous examples.

Consider the classic case where a defendant's tree roots cause damage to a neighbouring claimant's land. The injunctions that are granted in these cases restrain 'the defendant ... from causing or permitting roots from any tree on the defendant's land to encroach on to the [claimants'] land so as to cause a nuisance'.[29]

[26] *Manchester, Sheffield, &c, Railway Company v Worksop Board of Health* (1857) 23 Beav 198, 209.
[27] Sharpe (n 11) [1.540].
[28] ibid.
[29] *King v Taylor* (n 4) 133. For a prohibitory injunction requiring positive action in another context, see, eg, *Fawcett v Phoenix Inns Ltd* [2003] EWCA Civ 128 [37].

The direct effect of the injunction is to compel the defendant to take positive action to remove the tree roots. This 'prohibitory' injunction is therefore identical to a desisting mandatory injunction: it requires the defendant to take positive action in order to stop committing a nuisance.

A similar kind of injunction is granted in nuisance cases where a defendant causes pollution. For example, in *Pride of Derby*,[30] the second defendant (the Derby Corporation) was restrained by prohibitory injunction from continuing to maintain a sewerage system that discharged sewage into the River Derwent. However, in order to stop its tort, the Derby Corporation could not simply do nothing, as the sewerage system was continuing to discharge sewage into the river. The direct effect of the prohibitory injunction, therefore, was that the Derby Corporation would have to make modifications to its sewerage system to stop the sewage from flowing into the river. Indeed, counsel for the Derby Corporation in argument, and Evershed MR in his judgment, intimated that the injunction was 'mandatory in substance'.[31]

There are also many cases in which prohibitory injunctions granted to prevent trespasses to land require defendants to take positive actions and expend money. For example, in *Jaggard v Sawyer*,[32] the defendants bought a house that was built as part of a residential development of 10 houses served by a private cul-de-sac ('Property A'). Each plot had been conveyed subject to covenants binding on successive owners not to use any part of the unbuilt land other than as a private garden. Believing the cul-de-sac to be a public road, the defendants built a house on a plot of land ('Property B') next to Property A. The only way to access Property B was by building a laneway in the garden of Property A, which was linked to the cul-de-sac. The claimant, who also owned a house on the cul-de-sac, brought an action for a *prohibitory* injunction restraining the defendants from using the cul-de-sac to access Property B, on the basis that it was a trespass to land and in breach of covenant. Both Bingham MR and Millett LJ accepted that the direct effect of the injunction would be the same as a mandatory injunction ordering the defendants to demolish their house.[33] In the words of Millett LJ, 'the house would not have to be pulled down, but it would be rendered landlocked and incapable of beneficial enjoyment'.[34]

The same point can be made in respect of prohibitory injunctions granted to restrain a continuing libel or malicious falsehood. For example, in *Pirtek (UK) Limited v Robert Jackson*,[35] after the defendant carried out a campaign in which he intentionally made disparaging and false comments about the claimant's products on social media, Warby J granted a prohibitory injunction restraining the

[30] *Pride of Derby* (n 2).
[31] ibid 162.
[32] *Jaggard v Sawyer* [1995] 1 WLR 269 (CA). See also *Bracewell v Appleby* [1975] Ch 408 (Ch) 416; *Shaw v Applegate* [1977] 1 WLR 970 (CA) 979 (breach of covenant); *Patel v WH Smith (Eziot) Ltd* [1987] 1 WLR 853 (CA).
[33] *Jaggard v Sawyer* (n 32) 279 (Bingham MR), 288 (Millett LJ).
[34] ibid 288.
[35] *Pirtek (UK) Limited v Robert Jackson* [2017] EWHC 2834 (QB).

defendant from further publishing the comments complained of and comments to the same effect. Importantly, however, Warby J declined to grant a mandatory injunction requiring the defendant to remove the offending comments from his social media accounts, as such action 'would be a necessary consequence of the negative injunction'.[36]

Finally, there are many prohibitory quia timet injunctions that require a defendant to take positive action. As we shall see below, a prohibitory quia timet injunction restrains a defendant from committing a tort *before* it has occurred. Generally, a prohibitory quia timet injunction requires a defendant not to do a specific act, which does not impose any cost or burden on the defendant. However, this is certainly not the case in respect of all prohibitory quia timet injunctions. A good example is the injunction granted but later discharged in *Lloyd v Symonds*.[37] In that case, an interim quia timet injunction was granted, restraining the defendant dog breeders from keeping any dogs on their premises on the basis that the dogs' barking would cause a private nuisance to the claimants who lived next door. After the trial, Hall J granted a final injunction restraining the defendants from, inter alia, keeping more than 30 dogs on their premises. Although the injunction was discharged by the Court of Appeal, the effect of the final prohibitory quia timet injunction was to require the defendants to take positive steps to remove their dogs from their premises and find alternative locations in which to keep them (and presumably incur significant costs in doing so).

Taken together, what the above examples demonstrate is that many prohibitory injunctions have the direct effect of requiring a defendant to take positive action and to incur significant expenses. As Hoffmann J remarked in *Films Rover International Ltd v Cannon Film Sales Ltd*:

> It is easy to construct other counter examples by way of exception to the proposition that mandatory injunctions are more drastic and irreversible in effect and involve greater expense and inconvenience if wrongly granted than prohibitory injunctions.[38]

For these reasons, it is implausible to maintain that there is a rigid dichotomy between prohibitory and desisting mandatory injunctions. While the specific *consequences* of each individual injunction may differ, both final prohibitory and desisting mandatory injunctions (irrespective of whether they are in ordinary or quia timet form) operate for the same underlying purpose: to prevent a future tort. Even though the form of the words used in the injunctions differ, they are identical as a matter of substance. This is a particularly important point, as a well-established equitable principle is that equity looks to substance rather than form.[39]

[36] ibid [65].

[37] *Lloyd v Symonds* [1998] EWCA Civ 511.

[38] *Films Rover International Ltd v Cannon Film Sales Ltd* [1987] 1 WLR 670 (Ch) 682. See also *Businessworld Computers Pty Ltd v Australian Telecommunications Commission* [1998] FCA 127, (1988) 82 ALR 499, 503.

[39] *Parkin v Thorold* (1852) 16 Beav 59, 66–67; *Wolverhampton City Council v London Gypsies and Travellers* [2023] UKSC 47, [2024] AC 983 [151].

The implications for the analysis of these injunctions are explained in chapters 4 and 5.

There is also a subtle feature of these injunctions that must not be overlooked. When a desisting mandatory injunction or a prohibitory injunction is granted requiring a defendant to take positive action, the court makes only one order. However, the order has *two* effects. The first effect, which is explicit in a desisting mandatory injunction and implicit in a prohibitory injunction, is to compel the defendant to take positive action to stop his tort from continuing. The second effect, which is explicit in a prohibitory injunction and implicit in a desisting mandatory injunction, is to restrain the defendant from repeating the same act that amounted to the tort in the future.

For example, consider a prohibitory injunction that restrains a defendant 'from causing or permitting roots from any tree on the defendant's land to encroach on to the [claimants'] land so as to cause a nuisance'.[40] This order first requires the defendant to take positive action to stop his ongoing nuisance. The second effect of the order is to restrain the defendant from allowing the tree roots to encroach onto the claimant's land at any point again in the future. Although a desisting mandatory injunction does not contain the same express words, it goes without saying that after a court orders a defendant to do a positive act to stop a tort from continuing, the defendant is not permitted to repeat the same tortious act in the future.[41] A court would clearly not be impressed with a defendant who, after being ordered to knock down his building that was causing a nuisance, built it back up again on the basis that the injunction did not prevent him from doing so. Thus, although a desisting mandatory injunction and a prohibitory injunction (requiring positive action) are awarded in the form of one order, they have two effects.

D. The Effects of the Distinction

Even though the extant literature is of the view that there is a clear distinction between mandatory and prohibitory injunctions, it is accepted in the literature that the principles governing the award of mandatory injunctions are the same as those governing the award of prohibitory injunctions.[42] Nevertheless, the distinction is said to have two effects.

First, it is asserted frequently that the consideration of undue hardship is easier to engage when a court is assessing whether to grant a mandatory injunction. For example, although cautioning that mandatory injunctions will not always give rise to undue hardship, Heydon, Leeming and Turner contend that 'it is

[40] *King v Taylor* (n 4) 133.

[41] The author was unable to locate any case in which a defendant committed the same tort in the future after a desisting mandatory injunction had been awarded.

[42] Heydon, Leeming and Turner (n 1) [21-440], [21-460]; Sharpe (n 11) [1.10], [1.520]; Glister and Lee (n 11) [28-018]; Davies (n 1) [18-011]; Spry (n 1) 557–58. cf Burrows (n 1) 463.

easier to establish a defence of hardship in the case of a mandatory injunction'.[43] Burrows holds a similar view, stating that hardship 'is a very wide restriction' in the context of a final mandatory injunction.[44] The validity of this view is examined in chapter 5.

Second, some authors take a wider view and suggest that in practice the discretionary considerations countervailing against the award of injunctive relief have more weight when a court is considering whether a mandatory injunction should be awarded, as such injunctions have more drastic effects.[45] This sentiment is reflected in some of the case law, as there is a body of older decisions holding that mandatory injunctions are to be granted 'sparingly and with caution'.[46]

The better view of the positive law is that judges must always be cautious when granting injunctions, and that the discretionary considerations operate in the same way irrespective of whether the injunction sought is prohibitory or mandatory. Consider the reasoning of the Privy Council in *National Commercial Bank Jamaica Ltd v Olint Corp Ltd*.[47] In that case, the lower courts in Jamaica could not agree on whether an injunction that was sought to restrain the defendant from closing the claimant's bank accounts was prohibitory or mandatory. This was important, as the Court of Appeal of Jamaica held that for an interlocutory mandatory injunction to be awarded a litigant must prove a 'high degree of assurance that at the trial it will appear that the injunction was rightly granted', while in the case of an interlocutory prohibitory injunction it need only be proved that there was a 'serious issue to be tried'. Lord Hoffmann, giving the advice on behalf of the Board, explicitly rejected the reasoning of the Court of Appeal of Jamaica. After laying down the principles that govern the award of interlocutory injunctions set out in *American Cyanamid Co v Ethicon Ltd*,[48] Lord Hoffmann reasoned:

> There is however no reason to suppose that, in stating these principles, Lord Diplock was intending to confine them to injunctions which could be described as prohibitory rather than mandatory. In both cases, the underlying principle is the same, namely, that the court should take whichever course seems likely to cause the least irremediable prejudice to one party or the other … What is true is that the features which ordinarily justify describing an injunction as mandatory are often more likely to cause irremediable prejudice than in cases in which a defendant is merely prevented from taking or continuing with some course of action: see *Films Rover International Ltd v Cannon Film Sales Ltd* [1987] 1 WLR 670, 680. *But this is no more than a generalisation. What*

[43] Heydon, Leeming and Turner (n 1) [21-460].

[44] Burrows (n 1) 463.

[45] Glister and Lee (n 11) [21-018], stating, 'problems of enforcement, supervision and hardship may be more acute'; Davies (n 1) [18-011], stating '[the] factors may carry different weight according to the type of injunction sought'.

[46] *Redland Bricks v Morris* [1970] AC 652 (HL), 665 (Lord Upjohn). See also *Shepherd Homes Ltd v Sandham* [1971] Ch 340 (Ch), 349.

[47] *National Commercial Bank Jamaica Ltd v Olint Corp Ltd* [2009] UKPC 16, [2009] 1 WLR 1405. See also *Smith v Smith* (n 21) 504.

[48] *American Cyanamid Co v Ethicon Ltd* [1975] AC 396 (HL).

> *is required in each case is to examine what on the particular facts of the case the consequences of granting or withholding of the injunction is* [sic] *likely to be.*[49]

The point that Lord Hoffmann is making is that when considering whether to grant an injunction, courts should not base their decisions on generalisations that arise from the classification of an injunction as prohibitory or mandatory. Rather, courts must focus on what the direct consequences of complying with the injunction will be on the particular facts of the case and, with these consequences in mind, conduct the usual discretionary analysis of whether it is appropriate to award an injunction. Although Lord Hoffmann made his point in the context of a case concerning an interlocutory injunction, there is no reason to think that his point does not hold in the context of the discretionary analysis of whether to award a final injunction. Accordingly, following Lord Hoffmann's reasoning, the discretionary considerations governing whether injunctions should be awarded operate in precisely the same way, irrespective of whether an injunction is prohibitory or mandatory.

Thus, the suggestion in the existing literature that the discretionary considerations countervailing against the grant of injunctive relief somehow have more weight in the analysis when a mandatory injunction is being sought is erroneous. Importantly, however, there is one caveat that needs to be made when discussing Lord Hoffmann's analysis in *Olint*. With respect, it would be unwise to go as far as Lord Hoffmann did in his penultimate paragraph, suggesting that on a wider scale 'arguments over whether the injunction should be classified as prohibitive or mandatory are barren'.[50] Although there is no substantive difference between a prohibitory injunction and a desisting mandatory injunction, it was explained above there is a meaningful distinction between a prohibitory injunction and a restorative mandatory injunction. As we shall see in chapter 5, this distinction directly affects the legal analysis that is conducted if an injunction is classified as a restorative mandatory injunction.

III. The Distinction between Ordinary and Quia Timet Injunctions

The extant literature indicates that a quia timet injunction is an injunction that is granted to prevent a defendant from committing a wrong *before* it has occurred.[51] It is widely accepted that a quia timet injunction can take mandatory or prohibitory, as well as interim or final, form. In the discussion that follows, the distinction

[49] *National Commercial Bank v Olint* (n 47) [19] (emphasis added). See also Capper (n 1) [4.07].

[50] *National Commercial Bank v Olint* (n 47) [20].

[51] Spry (n 1) 390–91; Heydon, Leeming and Turner (n 1) 700; Burrows (n 1) 467; Tettenborn (n 1) [29-20]; Glister and Lee (n 11) [28-007]; Davies (n 1) [18-029]; Bean, Parry and Burns (n 1) [1-01]; Oliphant (ed) (n 1) [8-29].

between quia timet and prohibitory and mandatory injunctions is clarified. Section III.A examines the distinction (or lack thereof) between a prohibitory quia timet injunction and a prohibitory injunction. Section III.B considers the distinction between a mandatory quia timet injunction and a desisting or restorative mandatory injunction.

A. Prohibitory Injunctions and Prohibitory Quia Timet Injunctions

i. The Distinction

Existing literature indicates that a quia timet injunction operates to prevent a wrong that has not yet occurred.[52] Consider the case of *In Re C*,[53] where an injunction was granted restraining a defendant hospital authority from committing a battery by amputating the claimant's leg without his consent.[54] The injunction is clearly quia timet, because the defendant had not yet committed a battery and was restrained from doing so by the injunction. Prohibitory quia timet injunctions operate in this way: they simply restrain the defendant from doing an act that amounts to a wrong before it has occurred.

Importantly, however, there is one minor exception. Courts have granted quia timet injunctions against unknown persons, even though the torts that were the subject of the injunctions had already been committed against the claimant by unknown persons.[55] Although not stated explicitly, in these cases courts seem to have taken the (sound) view that because it is not known whether the persons who may commit torts against the claimant in the future also committed the same torts against the claimant in the past, it is best to classify the injunction as being quia timet.

As a matter of form, it is therefore simple to distinguish a prohibitory injunction from a prohibitory quia timet injunction. The former is awarded where the defendant has previously committed a wrong against the claimant, while the latter is granted where the defendant has yet to commit a wrong against the claimant. However, what has been overlooked by most of the extant literature is how prohibitory injunctions and quia timet injunctions operate identically as a matter of *substance*.

The purpose of a prohibitory injunction is to restrain a defendant from committing a wrong against the claimant in the future, in circumstances where the defendant has already committed the same wrong against the claimant. Unlike

[52] See the works cited in n 51.
[53] *In Re C* [1994] 1 WLR 290 (Fam).
[54] ibid 295–96.
[55] See, eg, *Bromley LBC v Persons Unknown* [2019] EWHC 1675 (QB) [42]; *Vastint Leeds BV v Persons Unknown* [2018] EWHC 2456 (Ch) [33].

damages or a restorative mandatory injunction, a prohibitory injunction does not remedy the prior wrong that has been committed. As Channell J explained in *Carlton Illustrators v Coleman & Co Ltd*, 'an injunction is not a remedy for the past breach, but is a means for preventing further breaches'.[56] The tort previously committed against the claimant is therefore relevant only to the extent that it evidences that there is a real and imminent risk that the defendant will commit the same tort in the future, which an injunction must be granted to guard against. Although in most cases the previous tort will be sufficient to prove this risk, this is certainly not always the case. There are numerous cases in which prohibitory injunctions have been refused for failure to prove a real risk of a future tort, even though the defendant had already committed the same tort against the claimant.[57] Hence, as explained above, the operative purpose of a prohibitory injunction is to prevent *future* wrongs.

The purpose of a prohibitory quia timet injunction is to restrain a defendant from committing a wrong against the claimant in the future, in circumstances where the defendant has not yet committed the wrong against the claimant. As will be seen in chapter 6, once a court is satisfied that there is a real (and, in most cases, imminent) risk that the defendant will commit a tort against the claimant, a quia timet injunction is generally awarded to prevent the defendant from committing the tort. As Jolowicz[58] and Smith[59] have explained, the operative purpose of a prohibitory quia timet injunction is therefore identical to that of a prohibitory injunction. Both injunctions are granted to prevent *future* wrongs, upon the claimant's satisfying the court that there is a real and imminent risk that the defendant will commit a tort against her. Indeed, this explains why damages in lieu of an injunction are awarded in respect of the future damage or loss the claimant would suffer if the injunction were refused. As Viscount Finlay stated in *Leeds Industrial Cooperative Society v Slack* (the House of Lords decision that confirmed the power to grant damages in lieu of a quia timet injunction):

> Injunctions are given to prevent wrongs which are threatened, and the power to give damages in lieu of an injunction must in all reason import the power to give an

[56] *Carlton Illustrators v Coleman & Co Ltd* [1911] 1 KB 771 (KB) 782. See also: *British Railway Traffic & Electric Co Ltd v CRC Co Ltd* [1922] 2 KB 260 (KB), 272; *Attrill v Richmond River Shire Council* (1993) 30 NSWLR 122, 127; *Coventry v Lawrence* (n 5) [101]; *Ranger v Pycraft* [2021] EWHC 502 (QB) [60].

[57] *Barber v Penley* [1893] 2 Ch 447 (Ch) (private nuisance); *League Against Cruel Sports Ltd v Scott* [1986] QB 240 (QB) (trespass to land); *Anslow v Norton Aluminium Ltd* [2012] EWHC 2610 (QB) (private nuisance); *Levi v Bates* [2015] EWCA Civ 206 (harassment); *Rush v Nationwide News Pty Ltd (No 9)* [2019] FCA 1383 [88] (defamation). 'The instances to be found in the books of refusal of an injunction are all cases in which it was clear that the nuisance complained of had ceased after the institution of the suit and that there was no apparent likelihood of its repetition': *Attorney-General (Ex rel Hornsby Shire Council) v Farley And Lewers Ltd* (1962) 8 LGRA 186, 205.

[58] J Jolowicz, 'Damages in Equity – A Study of Lord Cairns' Act' (1975) 34 *CLJ* 224, 244.

[59] Smith (n 10) 135, 147.

> equivalent for what is lost by the refusal of the injunction; for this purpose compensation only for what has passed would be futile.[60]

Thus, although a quia timet injunction restrains a defendant from committing a wrong that he has not previously committed against the claimant, in substance a prohibitory quia timet injunction operates for the same purpose as a prohibitory injunction: to prevent a future wrong.

ii. The Effects of the Distinction

Even though as a matter of substance prohibitory injunctions and prohibitory quia timet injunctions operate in an identical manner, the formal distinction between the two injunctions is said to have two effects.

First, it has been alleged that there is a wider range of circumstances in which courts will refuse an injunction for hardship where the injunction sought is classified as quia timet. In the House of Lords case of *Redland Bricks v Morris*,[61] Lord Upjohn contended that although the cost a defendant would face when having to comply with an injunction granted to 'prevent the continuance or recurrence of a wrongful act' is to be disregarded by the court, the 'question of cost to the defendant to prevent or lessen the likelihood of a *future apprehended wrong* must be an element to be taken into account'.[62] Although Lord Upjohn did not give reasons for this view, his reasoning is to the effect that the discretionary factor of hardship is wider when applied in the context of quia timet injunctions. The validity of this statement is analysed in chapter 6.

Second, it is implicit in the case law concerning the award of quia timet injunctions that the claimant's evidential onus of proving that there is a real and imminent risk of a defendant's committing a tort is a heavy one where the injunction sought is classified as being quia timet. This position must be accepted. In circumstances where the defendant has not yet committed any wrong against the claimant, courts will justifiably be slow to accept that a defendant is about to commit a tort against the claimant.[63] By contrast, it is obviously much easier for a court to be persuaded that there is a real and imminent risk of a defendant committing a tort where the claimant seeks a prohibitory injunction to restrain a tort that has already been committed by the defendant against the claimant.

[60] *Leeds Industrial Cooperative Society v Slack* [1924] AC 851 (HL) 859.
[61] *Redland Bricks v Morris* (n 46).
[62] ibid 666 (emphasis added).
[63] See *Briginshaw v Briginshaw* (1938) 60 CLR 336, 361; cited with approval in *Blyth v Blyth* [1966] AC 643 (HL) 668. See also Hodge Malek (ed), *Phipson on Evidence* (20th edn, Sweet & Maxwell 2020) [6-02]–[6-03].

B. Mandatory Injunctions and Mandatory Quia Timet Injunctions

i. Mandatory Quia Timet Injunctions

There is disagreement in the case law as to when a mandatory injunction will be classified as quia timet. Before analysing the relevant distinction between an ordinary mandatory injunction and a mandatory quia timet injunction, it is therefore necessary to clarify when quia timet injunctions can be awarded in mandatory form.

Existing literature is of the view that a mandatory quia timet injunction orders a defendant to take positive action to prevent a tort that has not yet occurred.[64] A good example is found in *Islington LBC v Elliott*,[65] where the claimants sought a mandatory injunction ordering the defendant to cut down the ash trees on its property before the tree roots entered the claimant's land and caused a private nuisance. As the nuisance had not yet occurred, the injunction sought was quia timet.

However, in *Redland Bricks v Morris*,[66] the House of Lords maintained that there is a second type of mandatory quia timet injunction. The facts of the case were that the defendants carried out excavations on their land that caused the claimants' neighbouring land to subside on several occasions. It was accepted at the trial that further subsidence was likely to occur in the future, even though the defendants had stopped their operations. In proceedings in the County Court, the claimants obtained damages for the past subsidence (on the basis that it amounted to a private nuisance), a prohibitory injunction restraining further excavations by the defendants and a mandatory injunction ordering the defendants to refill their land so as to restore the natural support to the claimants' land. The Court of Appeal dismissed an appeal by the defendants in respect of the grant of the mandatory injunction.

In the House of Lords, Lord Upjohn gave the leading speech (with which the other Law Lords agreed). Although a reading of the Court of Appeal's judgment suggests that both the County Court and the Court of Appeal had assumed the mandatory injunction to be an ordinary one, Lord Upjohn conceptualised the injunction to be quia timet. He reasoned that quia timet injunctions are 'broadly applicable to two types of case'.[67] First, where the defendant has 'as yet done no hurt to the [claimant]'. This accords with the first category of mandatory quia timet injunctions described above. Second, where the claimant has been 'fully recompensed both at law and in equity for the damage he has suffered but where he alleges that the earlier actions of the defendant may lead to future causes of action'. It is this second category of case that Lord Upjohn applied to the facts. According

[64] See Jolowicz (n 58) 244; Burrows (n 1) 467.
[65] *Islington LBC v Elliott* [2012] EWCA Civ 56.
[66] *Redland Bricks v Morris* (n 46).
[67] ibid 665.

to his Lordship, because the claimants had been awarded damages in respect of the private nuisance that had already occurred, the mandatory injunction was sought to prevent further damage arising from that same private nuisance (which would also amount to a fresh, future wrong) and should therefore be classified as quia timet. Lord Upjohn's reasoning therefore indicates that a mandatory injunction will be classified as quia timet where it orders a defendant to take positive action to prevent a wrong, which he has already committed, from recurring and causing further damage.

With respect, there is a serious problem with Lord Upjohn's reasoning. Consistently with prior authority,[68] it seems that Lord Upjohn understood that an unreasonable interference with the claimants' use and enjoyment of their land occurred not when there was a withdrawal of support from the claimants' land, but when subsidence occurred and physical damage was sustained. Therefore, the defendants had committed a private nuisance when the withdrawal of support from the claimants' land had caused it to subside, and the claimants were seeking an injunction that would require the defendants to take positive action to prevent the same nuisance from being repeated when future subsidence occurred. As both Jolowicz[69] and Burrows[70] have pointed out, it follows that by classifying the injunction sought as quia timet, Lord Upjohn's analysis is contrary to the established body of case law that an injunction that restrains a wrong from being repeated should be classified as an ordinary injunction. To take one example that was well established at the time *Redland Bricks* was decided, courts grant ordinary prohibitory injunctions that restrain a defendant from repeatedly making noise on certain days, and at certain times, that amounts to a nuisance.[71] As Jolowciz has explained, if Lord Upjohn was correct to classify the injunction as quia timet, 'then so must also be almost every other claim for a mandatory or, indeed, for a prohibitory injunction' that is granted to prevent a wrong from being repeated.[72] Thus, if Lord Upjohn's analysis is accepted, one would have to adopt the untenable position that his Lordship intended not to follow every single prior decision involving a prohibitory and mandatory injunction that had previously been granted to prevent a wrong from being repeated.

It should be noted, however, that Smith has defended Lord Upjohn's classification of the injunction as being quia timet on the basis that ordinary injunctions are granted only in respect of wrongs that are 'ongoing', and the private nuisance in the case could not be defined as such.[73] Smith's argument is unconvincing because he does not cite any authorities that dictate that prohibitory injunctions can only

[68] *Darley Main Colliery v Mitchell* (1886) 11 App Cas 127. See also: *Midland Bank Plc v Bardgrove Property Services* (1993) 65 P & CR 153 (CA); Tettenborn (n 1) [19-142].

[69] Jolowicz (n 58) 244–45.

[70] Burrows (n 1) 442–43. See also Heydon, Leeming and Turner (n 1) [24-155].

[71] See, eg, *Christie v Davey* [1893] 1 Ch 316 (Ch); *Vanderpant v Mayfair Hotel Co Ltd* [1930] 1 Ch 138 (Ch); *Halsey v Esso Petroleum Co Ltd* [1961] 1 WLR 683 (QB).

[72] Jolowicz (n 58) 244.

[73] Smith (n 10) 149.

be granted in respect of ongoing wrongs, as distinct from recurring wrongs. With respect, his view is clearly contrary to existing authority: as this chapter has shown, and as will be explained further in chapter 4, it is well established that prohibitory injunctions can be granted to restrain recurring wrongs.

Thus, Lord Upjohn's statement that there exists a secondary category of mandatory quia timet injunction is inconsistent with the authorities and, as Jolowicz and Burrows have each suggested, is therefore an incorrect statement of principle. The better way to classify the injunction in *Redland Bricks* is as an ordinary (and not quia timet) desisting mandatory injunction, as it required the defendants to take positive action to stop their private nuisance from being repeated in the future. It follows that there is only one type of mandatory quia timet injunction: an injunction that orders a defendant to take positive action to prevent a wrong *before* it has been committed.

ii. The Distinction and its Effects

As already explained, a restorative mandatory injunction is an injunction that orders a defendant to take positive action to undo the consequence(s) of a tort already committed. Given that a quia timet injunction is granted before a wrong has been committed, it is impossible for a quia timet injunction to take a restorative, mandatory form. Mandatory quia timet injunctions and restorative mandatory injunctions are therefore entirely distinct types of injunction.

A desisting mandatory injunction is an injunction that orders a defendant to take positive action to stop a tort from continuing. By contrast, a mandatory quia timet injunction orders a defendant to take positive action to prevent a tort from being committed at all. The formal distinction between the two injunctions is therefore a simple one. The former is awarded where the defendant has previously committed the wrong in question against the claimant, while the latter is granted where the defendant has yet to commit the wrong against the claimant.

However, like prohibitory and prohibitory quia timet injunctions, desisting mandatory and mandatory quia timet injunctions operate for the same substantive purpose. The purpose of a desisting mandatory injunction is to order a defendant to do a particular positive act so that the defendant stops his wrong from continuing in the future. The purpose of a mandatory quia timet injunction is to order a defendant to do a particular positive act so that the defendant will not commit a wrong in the future. Both injunctions are therefore solely concerned with ensuring that a defendant takes positive action to prevent the defendant from committing a tort in the future.

It naturally follows that the formal distinction between the two injunctions has the same two effects as were identified in section III.A in respect of prohibitory and prohibitory quia timet injunctions. According to the reasoning of Lord Upjohn in *Redland Bricks*, there is supposedly a wider range of circumstances in which courts will refuse mandatory quia timet injunctions for hardship. Additionally, the evidential onus of proving that there is a real and imminent risk of the defendant's commission of a tort in the future will obviously be heavier when the claimant seeks a mandatory quia timet injunction as compared to a desisting mandatory injunction.

IV. Conclusion

At first sight, the formal distinctions between prohibitory, mandatory and quia timet injunctions are simple. However, this chapter has shown that the distinctions are more nuanced than they are made out to be. In summary, three core claims have been advanced in this chapter.

The first is that two types of mandatory injunctions are granted to restrain or remedy torts: desisting and restorative mandatory injunctions. The desisting mandatory injunction orders a defendant to do a positive act to stop his tort from continuing. By contrast, the restorative mandatory injunction orders a defendant to do a positive act to remedy damage or loss that was caused by the defendant's commission of a tort.

The second claim is that prohibitory injunctions and desisting mandatory injunctions are identical as a matter of substance. Both injunctions operate to prevent a defendant from committing a tort in the future. By contrast, restorative mandatory injunctions are distinct from these injunctions, as they are granted to rectify the past damage or loss that a claimant has suffered as a result of the defendant's tort.

The third claim of this chapter is that prohibitory and desisting mandatory injunctions, and quia timet injunctions, are also identical as a matter of substance. These injunctions operate to prevent a defendant from committing a tort in the future. Additionally, for the same reason as was outlined above, restorative mandatory injunctions are distinct from these injunctions.

We shall see in the remainder of the book that the conclusions drawn in this chapter have major practical implications for the law governing different types of injunctions. As we have seen, the distinctions between prohibitory, mandatory and quia timet injunctions have numerous effects. Having clarified the distinctions (or lack thereof) between prohibitory, mandatory and quia timet injunctions, we can now proceed to examine:

(a) in chapter 4, the law governing when a prohibitory injunction can be granted to restrain a future tort;
(b) in chapter 5, the law governing when a desisting mandatory injunction can be granted to restrain a future tort and when a restorative mandatory injunction can be granted to remedy a completed tort; and
(c) in chapter 6, the law governing when a quia timet injunction can be granted to restrain a future tort.

4

Prohibitory Injunctions

I. Introduction

The prohibitory injunction is a general remedy in tort law. As this chapter will show, many different torts have been restrained by prohibitory injunction. To give some flavour from just a handful of the cases, consider the decisions in which courts have restrained a defendant from: singing, shouting and whistling while drunk at late hours;[1] throwing mud at, and verbally assaulting, the claimant on the basis of his race;[2] unlawfully gaining access to the claimant's gaming website in order to cheat the system and steal money;[3] defaming the claimant on Twitter and LinkedIn;[4] and sending harassing emails and making threatening telephone calls to staff members employed by the claimant.[5]

The purpose of this chapter is to provide a comprehensive account of the positive law governing when a final prohibitory injunction can be awarded to restrain a future tort. Specifically, this chapter will clarify the conditions for the award of prohibitory injunctive relief in tort law, and provide an account of the nature of the discretion that courts exercise when granting prohibitory injunctions. Furthermore, as it has been established in chapter 3 that prohibitory and desisting mandatory injunctions are identical as a matter of substance, this chapter will analyse the general discretionary considerations relevant to whether injunctions should be granted by analysing the cases concerning both prohibitory *and* desisting mandatory injunctions. Many different claims are advanced in respect of the numerous issues that are analysed in this chapter. Rather than listing them here, the claims are brought to the reader's attention as each issue is considered.

The leading modern authority governing the award of prohibitory injunctions to restrain future torts in England and Wales is the judgment of Lord Neuberger in *Coventry v Lawrence*.[6] In that case, the claimants owned a house that was situated close to a stadium and moto-cross track owned and operated by the defendants. The claimants contended that the noise generated by motor sports conducted on

[1] *Vincent v Peacock* (1973) 1 NSWLR 466 (NSWCA).
[2] *Liburd v Cork* [1981] Lexis Citation 511 (CA) (interim).
[3] *Midasplayer.com Ltd v Watkins* [2006] EWHC 1551 (Ch).
[4] *Davies v Carter* [2021] EWHC 3021 (QB).
[5] *CSC Computer Sciences Ltd v Price* [2018] EWHC 3990 (QB).
[6] *Coventry v Lawrence* [2014] UKSC 13, [2014] AC 822.

the defendants' premises interfered with the quiet enjoyment of their land. At first instance, Judge Seymour QC held that the defendants' actions amounted to a private nuisance and granted a prohibitory injunction restraining the defendants from carrying on activities at the stadium or at the track that emitted more than a specified level of noise. This decision was overturned by the Court of Appeal on the basis that the defendants' activities did not constitute a nuisance. On appeal to the Supreme Court, Lord Neuberger gave the leading judgment, in which he held that the defendants had committed the tort of private nuisance. Lord Neuberger also reasoned that Judge Seymour QC was correct to find that he had jurisdiction to grant an injunction, but ordered that the defendants were to be given permission to make an application before the Judge asking for damages to be awarded in lieu of the injunction.[7]

In his judgment, Lord Neuberger laid down two statements of principle in respect of when it is appropriate to grant a prohibitory injunction to restrain a private nuisance. First, his Lordship accepted that where a claimant had established that the defendant's activities constitute a nuisance, 'prima facie the remedy to which she is entitled (in addition to damages for past nuisance) is an injunction to restrain the defendant from committing such nuisance in the future'.[8] Second, his Lordship stated that once it is proved that a nuisance is continuing, 'I would accept that the prima facie position is that an injunction should be granted, so the legal burden is on the defendant to show why it should not'.[9]

According to Lord Neuberger's reasoning, the claimant bears the onus of proving that a continuing tort is being committed against her (that is, the necessary condition), following which the onus is reversed onto the defendant to show why the injunction should not be awarded due to an applicable discretionary consideration (that is, the discretionary analysis). The analytical process that was adopted by Lord Neuberger to determine whether a final injunction should be granted to restrain a continuing tort is therefore the same as that employed by the Chancery in the eighteenth and nineteenth centuries. As explained in chapter 2, the Chancery would first consider whether it was satisfied that it had jurisdiction to interpose, after which the Court would then go on to conduct a discretionary analysis that weighed its reason for interposing against any countervailing discretionary factors to ultimately determine whether an injunction *should* be awarded on the facts of the case. This analytical approach is therefore still employed by the courts today.

Consistently with this approach, this chapter is split into six main sections. Section II focuses on the conditions that are necessary before it can be said that a court has jurisdiction to award a prohibitory injunction to prevent a future tort. Section III analyses the nature and limits of the discretion that courts exercise when granting prohibitory injunctions. Section IV examines the discretionary considerations that militate against the award of a prohibitory and mandatory

[7] ibid [149]–[152].
[8] ibid [101].
[9] ibid [121].

desisting injunction, and section V examines the discretionary considerations that militate in favour of such an award. Finally, section VI considers the discretion that courts exercise to determine whether an injunction should be suspended. Section VII concludes.

II. The Necessary Conditions

Pursuant to the reasoning of Lord Neuberger in *Coventry*, to be granted a prohibitory injunction to restrain a future tort a claimant must prove that the defendant is continuing to commit a tort against her. However, it is important to recognise that in *Coventry*, Lord Sumption and Lord Clarke stated that an injunction can be granted only where damages would *also* be an inadequate remedy.[10] Interestingly, we shall see below that this latter view is the position taken in most of the equity scholarship, as it accords with the oft-cited dictum of Lindley LJ in *London and Blackwell Ry v Cross* that '[t]he *very first* principle of injunction law is that prima facie you do not obtain injunctions to restrain actionable wrongs, for which damages are the proper remedy'.[11] For this reason, the validity of Lord Sumption and Lord Clarke's statement of law will be analysed at the outset, following which Lord Neuberger's position will be considered. It is argued that the view of Lord Sumption and Lord Clarke is incorrect and that the position adopted by Lord Neuberger (with whom Lord Mance and Lord Carnwath agreed) is a correct statement of the positive law.

A. Must Damages be Inadequate?

According to Lord Sumption and Lord Clarke in *Coventry*, an injunction will be granted to restrain a continuing tort only where damages would be an inadequate remedy (the 'inadequacy requirement'). What their Lordships meant by this requirement was that a claimant must prove that a monetary award would not adequately remedy her future damage or loss. As authority for their proposition, both Lord Sumption and Lord Clarke expressly relied on the dissenting judgment of Millett LJ in *Co-operative Insurance Society Ltd v Argyll Stores (Holdings) Ltd*,[12] which was said by both Lord Sumption and Lord Clarke to be 'subsequently upheld' on appeal to the House of Lords.[13] In *Argyll Stores*, Millett LJ stated that 'the leading principle' in English law is that 'where damages are an adequate remedy it is inappropriate to grant [any form of] equitable relief'.[14]

[10] ibid [159]–[160] (Lord Sumption), [171] (Lord Clarke).
[11] *London and Blackwell Ry v Cross* (1886) 31 Ch D 354 (CA) 369 (emphasis added).
[12] *Co-operative Insurance Society Ltd v Argyll Stores (Holdings) Ltd* [1996] Ch 286 (CA).
[13] *Co-operative Insurance Society Ltd v Argyll Stores (Holdings) Ltd* [1998] AC 1 (HL).
[14] *Argyll Stores* (CA) (n 12) 304.

Interestingly, the existing literature is in conflict over whether Lord Sumption and Lord Clarke's statements are an accurate account of the positive law. Three different approaches have been taken.

Davies,[15] Glister and Lee,[16] and Bean, Parry and Burns[17] state that for an injunction to be awarded, the claimant must prove that damages would be an inadequate remedy. However, they accept that once it is proved that a wrong is being repeatedly committed against the claimant, this will mean that damages are inadequate. With respect, this analysis is misconceived. As explained in chapter 2, courts have long recognised the distinction between the irreparable harm doctrine (that is, that damages would be an inadequate remedy) and the multiplicity of suits doctrine (that is, that a defendant should not be permitted to continuously invade a claimant's legal rights). Indeed, the central point of Lord Sumption and Lord Clarke's reasoning is that a continuing nuisance is not in and of itself sufficient to justify the award of an injunction; something more must be proved to demonstrate that damages are inadequate.

Heydon, Leeming and Turner contend that the inadequacy requirement correctly states the positive law.[18] However, these authors adopt the view of Laycock (who examines American cases)[19] that in recent years the meaning of 'damages must be inadequate' has become so wide that there is a 'tendency of the courts to view almost any damage as irreparable'.[20]

By contrast, while noting the influence of the irreparable harm doctrine, Spry states that 'it must be accepted as settled' that once a claimant has established the invasion of a common law right and that there are grounds for believing it will be repeated in the future, 'the claimant is, in the absence of special circumstances, entitled to an injunction against such repetition'.[21] Oliphant also recognises that proof of a continuing wrong will mean that a prohibitory injunction will be granted as of course.[22] He states that whether or not damages are an inadequate remedy is simply a discretionary consideration to be taken into account.[23] Burrows,[24] McBride and Bagshaw,[25] and Tettenborn[26] emphasise the importance of a claimant's proving

[15] P Davies, 'Injunctions' in J McGhee and S Elliott (eds), *Snell's Equity* (34th edn, Sweet & Maxwell 2021) [18-033]–[18-034].

[16] J Glister and J Lee, *Hanbury on Modern Equity* (22nd edn, Sweet & Maxwell 2021) [28-017].

[17] D Bean, I Parry and A Burns, *Injunctions* (14th edn, Sweet & Maxwell 2022) [2-09].

[18] JD Heydon, MJ Leeming and PG Turner, *Meagher, Gummow & Lehane's Equity: Doctrines & Remedies* (5th edn, LexisNexis 2015) [21-040].

[19] See generally D Laycock, *The Death of the Irreparable Injury Rule* (Oxford University Press 1991); D Laycock, 'Injunctions and the Irreparable Injury Rule' (1979) 57 *Texas Law Review* 1065.

[20] Heydon, Leeming and Turner (n 18) [21-040].

[21] I Spry, *Equitable Remedies* (9th edn, Thomson Reuters 2014) 397.

[22] K Oliphant (ed), *The Law of Tort* (3rd edn, LexisNexis 2015) [8.18].

[23] ibid [8.12].

[24] A Burrows, *Remedies for Torts, Breach of Contract, and Equitable Wrongs* (4th edn, Oxford University Press 2019) 443–44.

[25] N McBride and R Bagshaw, *Tort Law* (6th edn, Pearson Education 2018) 802–03.

[26] A Tettenborn, 'Injunctions' in M Jones and A Dugdale (eds), *Clerk & Lindsell on Torts* (23rd edn, Sweet & Maxwell 2020) [28-06].

that a tort is continuing to be committed against her, but are otherwise silent on the issue of whether damages must be inadequate. These authors therefore also seem to suggest that the fact that damages would be an inadequate remedy is not a necessary condition for prohibitory injunctive relief.

For the following reasons, the position adopted by Spry, Oliphant, Burrows, McBride and Bagshaw, and Tettenborn should be accepted as providing the best account of the positive law.

i. Inconsistency with the Prior Case Law

Lord Sumption and Lord Clarke's reliance on the remarks of Millett LJ in *Argyll Stores* is misplaced. In that case, Lord Hoffmann gave the leading speech, in which he came to the same result as that of Millett LJ in the Court of Appeal. However, contrary to what is stated by Lord Sumption and Lord Clarke in *Coventry*, Lord Hoffmann did not explicitly adopt or approve Millett LJ's judgment. In fact, Lord Hoffmann explicitly disagreed with Millett LJ's judgment in certain respects.[27] There is therefore nothing to suggest that the House of Lords approved of or 'upheld' Millett LJ's sweeping statement that 'where damages are an adequate remedy it is inappropriate to grant [any form of] equitable relief'.[28] Lord Hoffmann simply accepted, in the context of a dispute involving whether it was appropriate to order the *specific performance* of a 35-year lease, that 'the general principle [is] that specific performance will not be ordered when damages are an adequate remedy'.[29] There is no evidence that his Lordship intended that this principle should limit the circumstances in which prohibitory injunctions could be granted to restrain future torts.

Furthermore, contrary to the remarks of Lord Sumption and Lord Clarke, the inadequacy requirement is in fact inconsistent with the long-established principle in equity that a continuing wrong (in itself) gives rise to jurisdiction to award a final injunction. As explained in chapter 2, the Chancery was prepared to award a final prohibitory injunction to restrain a continuing wrong on the basis that an injunction was necessary to prevent a multiplicity of suits (and not because a monetary award would not adequately remedy the claimant's future damage or loss). This remains the law.[30] Three cases can be highlighted.

Consider first *Shelfer v City of London Electric Lighting Company (No 1)*.[31] In that case, before laying down his 'working rule' governing when it is appropriate to award damages in lieu of an injunction, AL Smith LJ reasoned that it

[27] *Argyll Stores* (HL) (n 13) 16.
[28] *Argyll Stores* (CA) (n 12) 304.
[29] *Argyll Stores* (HL) (n 13) 11.
[30] In addition to the cases discussed below, see: *Beswicke v Alner* [1926] VLR 72; *Patel v WH Smith (Eziot) Ltd* [1987] 1 WLR 853 (CA) 863 (interim); *Anchor Brewhouse Developments Ltd v Berkley House Docklands Developments Ltd* [1987] 2 EGLR 173 (Ch), 177–78 (interim); *Bendal Pty Ltd v Mirvac Project Pty Ltd* (1991) 23 NSWLR 464.
[31] *Shelfer v City of London Electric Lighting Company (No 1)* [1895] 1 Ch 287 (CA).

was the defendant's continuing nuisance that gave the court jurisdiction to award an injunction.[32] There was no mention of a requirement that the claimant prove that damages were an inadequate remedy. Indeed, AL Smith LJ explicitly stated in the third limb of his working rule that damages in lieu would be an appropriate remedy in cases where the injury to the claimant's legal rights is 'one which can be adequately compensated by a small money payment'.[33] If the claimant was *also* required to prove that damages were an inadequate remedy for jurisdiction to arise, then plainly it would not make sense for the court to consider, after jurisdiction had been established, whether damages would adequately compensate the claimant's future damage or loss in order to determine whether to award damages in lieu of an injunction. Although a strict application of AL Smith LJ's working rule was disapproved of by Lord Neuberger in *Coventry*, Lord Neuberger still applied the same analytical approach as AL Smith LJ by accepting that once a continuing nuisance has been proved by the claimant, 'prima facie the remedy to which she is entitled … is an injunction to restrain the defendant from committing such nuisance in the future'.[34] This part of AL Smith LJ's reasoning therefore remains good law.

The second case worth highlighting is *Wood v Conway*.[35] There, the claimant owned land that adjoined the defendants' gasworks. After smoke and fumes from the gasworks had poisoned trees on the claimant's land, he sought an injunction restraining the defendants from carrying on their gasworks, which was granted by Joyce J at first instance. The defendants appealed, arguing that no injunction should have been granted because a small money payment would be ample compensation for the claimant's damage. The Court of Appeal dismissed the appeal on the basis that damages were an inadequate remedy because it was impossible to determine in advance how much damage would be done by the defendants' nuisance in the future.[36] However, what is important to note is the analytical process that the Court employed to assess whether the injunction should have been awarded. Cozens-Hardy MR, giving the leading judgment, analysed the facts found by Joyce J and stated that the defendants 'are now committing that which is a legal wrong and they are threatening and intending to continue it'.[37] Immediately after making this finding, Cozens-Hardy MR stated:

> Then, that being so, the case seems to me to resolve itself into the question whether this Court ought to *exercise the discretion* given to it by Lord Cairns' Act … or whether the Court ought to *apply the settled principle* of the Court before Lord Cairns' Act, that where there is a legal wrong which it is threatened to continue, the Court ought as a matter of course to grant an injunction.[38]

[32] ibid 319, 322.
[33] ibid 322.
[34] *Coventry* (n 6) [101].
[35] *Wood v Conway* [1914] 2 Ch 47 (CA).
[36] ibid 57, 60.
[37] ibid 56.
[38] ibid (emphasis added).

It was only *after* he made this statement, in the context of assessing whether it was appropriate for Joyce J to have exercised his discretion to grant the injunction, that Cozens Hardy MR analysed whether damages were an inadequate remedy on the facts of the case.[39] What this reasoning therefore indicates is that Cozens Hardy MR did not believe that the claimant was required to establish that damages were an inadequate remedy. Rather, the 'settled principle' was that where a legal wrong is continuing, a court must ordinarily grant an injunction, and the fact that damages may be an adequate remedy was relevant only to the discretionary analysis.

The final noteworthy case is that of *Pride of Derby and Derbyshire Angling Association Ltd v British Celanese Ltd*.[40] As explained in chapter 3, in that case the claimants sought injunctions to compel the defendants to stop polluting two rivers. Giving the leading judgment, Evershed MR stated:

> It is, I think, well settled that if A proves that his proprietary rights are being wrongfully interfered with by B, and that B intends to continue his wrong, then A is prima facie entitled to an injunction, and he will be deprived of that remedy only if special circumstances exist, including the circumstance that damages are an adequate remedy for the wrong that he has suffered.[41]

Lord Evershed MR's reasoning is to the effect that a court has jurisdiction to grant an injunction simply upon a claimant's proving that a defendant is continuing to infringe the claimant's legal right.[42] It seems, therefore, that Evershed MR believed the burden of proof then shifts to the defendant to show that an injunction should not be awarded because 'special circumstances' exist, such as the fact that damages are an adequate remedy.

A counter argument that could be made here is that because Evershed MR did not describe the 'special circumstances' as being discretionary, what he meant was that it is a principle of law that if damages are adequate then a claimant will be 'deprived' of an injunction. However, this view is unconvincing, because it is unclear what else Evershed MR could have meant by the words 'special circumstances' other than the relevant discretionary considerations. Indeed, it is notable that Romer LJ, who agreed with Evershed MR on this point, stated in similar terms:

> Anyone who creates an actionable nuisance is a wrongdoer, and the court will prima facie restrain him from persisting in his activities. If special circumstances be shown, the court *may* leave the injured party to his remedy in damages …[43]

Romer LJ's use of the word 'may' indicates that he considered the 'special circumstances' to be discretionary, as they did not require the court to leave the claimant to his remedy in damages. Thus, the better understanding of

[39] ibid 57.

[40] *Pride of Derby and Derbyshire Angling Association Ltd v British Celanese Ltd* [1953] Ch 149 (CA).

[41] ibid 181. See also *Mayfair Trading Co Pty Ltd v Dreyer* (1958) 101 CLR 428, 451.

[42] Although Evershed MR refers specifically to 'proprietary rights', he does not suggest that the principle he laid down was confined to such rights. It seems he made reference to property rights because they were what the claimants were seeking to protect by the injunctions on the facts of the case.

[43] *Pride of Derby* (n 40) 194 (emphasis added).

Evershed MR's statement in *Pride of Derby* is that he considered that once a claimant has proved that the defendant is continuing to commit a tort against him, injunctive relief can be awarded. Whether damages would be an adequate remedy is only a discretionary consideration.

With the reasoning of *Shelfer*, *Wood v Conway* and *Pride of Derby* in mind, there is good reason to doubt the validity of Lord Sumption and Lord Clarke's inadequacy requirement. However, it must be recognised that there is an alternative interpretation of the cases.

ii. The Alternative Interpretation

Heydon, Leeming and Turner contend that the inadequacy requirement correctly states the law.[44] They cite *Imperial Gas and Coke Company v Broadbent*[45] as authority for the proposition that traditionally, injunctions would not be granted unless damages were an inadequate remedy. As was shown in chapter 2, *Imperial v Broadbent* is not authority for this proposition. Heydon, Leeming and Turner do, however, go on to make what seems like a convincing argument by focusing on two categories of case.

First, they argue that the inadequacy requirement is the basis for the 'rule' that 'normally' injunctions will not be granted to restrain a trespass to goods or conversion.[46] At first sight, this argument seems compelling. However, it is problematic when it is recognised that there is a dearth of case law concerning whether final injunctions can be granted to restrain trespass to goods or conversion. It is well established that courts will refuse to award *specific delivery* in respect of goods that are not unique or sentimental.[47] Although specific delivery is a form of specific relief, it is a remedy that is distinct from an injunction.[48] Hence, a non sequitur arises: the cases concerning specific delivery cannot ground a rule that normally injunctions will not be granted to restrain these causes of action because it is a precondition for injunctive relief that damages are an inadequate remedy. Thus, the 'rule' that Heydon, Leeming and Turner refer to does not seem to be supported by the authorities.

Additionally, it is important to recognise that, although no case law could be found in respect of the issue, there is a strong case to be made that courts would be prepared to award final injunctive relief to stop a repeated conversion or trespass to goods even though damages would adequately remedy the claimant. Consider the following scenario:[49] C is the owner of a bike purchased from Woolworths. D,

[44] Heydon, Leeming and Turner (n 18) [21-040].

[45] *Imperial Gas and Coke Company v Broadbent* (1859) 7 HLC 600, 11 ER 239.

[46] Heydon, Leeming and Turner (n 18) [21-040].

[47] See, eg, *Whiteley v Hilt* [1918] 2 KB 808 (CA) 819; *Blue Sky One Ltd v Blue Airways LLC* [2009] EWHC 3314 (Comm) [314]–[316].

[48] See Heydon, Leeming and Turner (n 18) [22-010].

[49] Note that the Torts (Interference with Goods) Act 1977 provides no specific provisions concerned with *final* injunctive relief. The usual position at common law therefore still applies.

who lives on the same street as C, notices C's bike and steals it by breaking C's bike lock. At this point, as the bike is not unique, C's remedy will be limited to damages for the cost of a replacement bike: he clearly has no entitlement to specific delivery. However, assume that after obtaining his damages award C purchases another bike from Woolworths. D decides he is going to continue to steal C's bike each time C purchases a new one and in fact does so. Each time conversion is committed, damages are an adequate remedy for the wrong, as they enable C to purchase a replacement bike. However, because the wrong is being repeatedly committed against C, this gives rise to a multiplicity of suits. Courts therefore have a good reason to grant a final injunction restraining D from stealing C's bike. This is not to say that final injunctions will be granted in all cases of repeated conversions or trespass to goods. The important point is that once a claimant has satisfied a court that a repeated conversion or trespass to goods is giving rise to a multiplicity of suits, courts will have jurisdiction to grant final injunctive relief.

The second category of case relied on by Heydon, Leeming and Turner concerns those cases in which injunctions to restrain repeated trespasses to land have been refused.[50] There are a number of late nineteenth- and early twentieth-century cases in which first-instance courts refused to award injunctions to restrain trifling trespasses. For example, in *Llandudno Urban Distinct Council v Woods*,[51] Cozens-Hardy J refused to grant an injunction restraining a clergyman of the Church of England from holding services and delivering sermons on a beach that was owned by the claimant council, without the council's consent. Additionally, in *Behrens v Richards*,[52] Buckley J refused to grant an injunction restraining members of the public from using walking tracks on the claimant's land without his consent.

At first sight, it seems as though these cases can be explained on the basis that because the future trespasses would not cause damage to the claimant's land, damages were an adequate remedy. However, this is not evident in the reasoning of the courts in these two cases. The courts did not state that the injunctions were refused because the claimants failed to prove that damages were an inadequate remedy, or that this was a necessary condition for the award of an injunction. Rather, the courts emphasised the fact that the public would be seriously disadvantaged if the injunction was granted to restrain such a trifling trespass. For example, in *Llandudno*, Cozens Hardy J stated:

> There are persons who derive satisfaction from listening to the addresses of the defendant … I cannot conceive why they should be deprived of this innocent pleasure. Nobody is obliged to listen. Nobody is molested. This action is an attempt to assert

[50] Heydon, Leeming and Turner (n 18) [21-110]. In addition to the cases discussed below, Heydon, Leeming and Turner also cite *Cooper v Crabtree* (1882) 20 Ch D 589 (CA). However, in that case, the injunction was refused by the Court of Appeal because a trespass to land had not been committed: see ibid 592–93.

[51] *Llandudno Urban Distinct Council v Woods* [1899] 2 Ch 705 (Ch).

[52] *Behrens v Richards* [1905] 2 Ch 614 (Ch). See also *Fielden v Cox* (1906) 22 TLR 411 (Ch).

> rights which the Crown would never have thought of putting forward, and which are in no way necessary.[53]

Similarly, in *Behrens*, Buckley J reasoned:

> It would, in my judgment, be a disastrous thing, not for the public only, but for the landowners also, if this Court, at the caprice of the landowner, … entertained every trivial application to restrain persons by injunction from using paths which, though not public highways, have in fact been used by the permission of the owners for many generations, and whose user is no injury to the owner of the land.[54]

The better view of these cases, therefore, is that the courts believed they had jurisdiction to grant an injunction, but that they refused to exercise their discretion and award an injunction for public-interest reasons.

Furthermore, even if it is accepted that these cases indicate that a claimant must prove that damages are inadequate before an injunction can be granted, they have not been followed. There is now a body of modern case law granting injunctions to restrain trifling trespasses to land.[55] In some of these cases, it was reasoned that a factor that militated in favour of the grant of the injunction was that damages were inadequate because the trespasses were continuing in circumstances where the claimants could obtain only nominal damages against the defendants.[56] However, this fact was only a *consideration*. The core justification for the grant of the injunctions in these cases was the fact that the defendant was continuing to trespass on the claimant's land. As Lord Neuberger stated in *Secretary of State for the Environment, Food and Rural Affairs v Meier*, in the context of the Supreme Court's upholding the grant of a prohibitory injunction to restrain a continuing trespass to land:

> [W]here a trespass to the claimant's property is threatened, and particularly where a trespass is being committed, and has been committed in the past, by the defendant, an injunction to restrain the threatened trespass would, in the absence of good reasons to the contrary, appear to be appropriate.[57]

Thus, the better view is that the trivial trespass to land cases do not assist Heydon, Leeming and Turner in establishing that the inadequacy requirement is a correct statement of the positive law.

53 *Llandudno* (n 51) 709.

54 *Behrens* (n 52) 622.

55 *Woollerton & Wilson Ltd v Richard Costain Ltd* [1970] 1 WLR 411 (Ch) (interim); *Graham v KD Morris and Sons Pty Ltd* [1974] Qd R 1 (interim); *John Trenberth Ltd v National Westminster Bank Ltd* (1980) 39 P&CR 104 (Ch) (interim); *League Against Cruel Sports Ltd v Scott* [1986] QB 240 (QB); *Patel v WH Smith* (n 30); *Anchor Brewhouse* (n 30); *Secretary of State for the Environment, Food and Rural Affairs v Meier* [2009] UKSC 11, [2009] 1 WLR 2780 (final). See also *Beswicke v Alner* [1926] VLR 72; *Madden v Coy* [1944] VLR 88.

56 *Woollerton* (n 55) 413; *Trenberth* (n 55) 107; *Patel v WH Smith* (n 30) 861; *Anchor Brewhouse* (n 30) 177–78. Note, however, that this reasoning is problematic, because the courts did not recognise that mesne profits or user fee damages are available for trifling trespasses that cause no damage. Hence, damages would have been an adequate remedy in these cases.

57 *Meier* (n 55) [79]. See also *Beswicke v Alner* [1926] VLR 72, 76–77; *Reliance Finance Corporation Pty Ltd v Orwin Walshe & Ward* [1964-5] NSWR 970, 976; *Jessica Estates v Lennard* [2007] NSWSC 1434 [28].

It must also be recognised here that Heydon, Leeming and Turner have overlooked an important category of case in which final injunctions have been granted. Courts have awarded final injunctions to restrain defendants from repeatedly committing economic torts like inducing a breach of contract,[58] deceit,[59] causing loss by unlawful means[60] and passing off.[61] In these cases, claimants generally seek an injunction to prevent a defendant from continuing to cause them *economic* loss.[62] Subject to what is said in section IV.B.i on adequacy of damages, it therefore seems as though a damages award will generally adequately remedy the claimant. Yet this fact has not persuaded courts to bar final injunctive relief altogether in respect of economic torts. In fact, in the relevant cases cited above, in which final injunctions were granted, in their reasoning the courts focused on the fact that the defendants intended to continue to commit the relevant torts against the claimants, rather than on whether a monetary sum would be an inadequate remedy for those future torts. These cases are therefore compelling evidence that the inadequacy requirement is not a necessary condition for the award of a final prohibitory injunction to restrain a future tort.

As a final point, it is worth emphasising the irrationality that would result if a claimant were required to prove that damages were an inadequate remedy for the award of prohibitive injunctive relief in tort law. It is well established that when damages are awarded in lieu of an injunction, such damages are 'awarded in substitution for an injunction'.[63] Accordingly, damages can be awarded in lieu of an injunction only where the court has jurisdiction to grant an injunction. In this context, 'jurisdiction' does not simply mean that the court has the power to hear the dispute. As Millett LJ stated in *Jaggard v Sawyer*, it means that 'the [claimant] must first establish a case for equitable relief … by proving his legal right and an

[58] eg, *National Phonographic Co Ltd v Edison Bell Consolidated Phonographic Co Ltd* [1908] 1 Ch 335 (CA); *Woolley v Dunford* (1972) SASR 243. See also the reasoning of the Court of Appeal in *Bowen v Hall* (1881) 6 QBD 333. For cases in which interim injunctions have been granted to restrain this tort, see, eg: *Keogh v Australian Workers Union* (1902) 2 SR (NSW) Eq 265; *JT Stratford & Son v Lindley* [1965] AC 269 (HL); *Union Traffic Ltd v Transport and General Workers Union* [1989] ICR 98 (CA); *East Midlands Trains Ltd v National Union of Rail, Maritime & Transport Workers* [2013] EWCA Civ 1072; *Govia Thameslink Railway Ltd v Associated Society of Locomotive Engineers and Firemen* [2016] EWHC 1320 (QB).

[59] eg, *Fullwood v Fullwood* (1878) 9 Ch D 176 (Ch) (although this case would now be analysed as one concerning passing off).

[60] eg, *Midasplayer.com Ltd* (n 3). For cases in which interim injunctions have been granted to restrain this tort, see: *Keogh* (n 58); *JT Stratford* (n 58); *Domestic & General Group Ltd v Premier Protect Holdings Ltd* [2021] EWHC 135 (QB); *AAA Plc v Persons Unknown* [2021] EWHC 2529 (QB).

[61] eg, *Reddaway v Banham* [1896] AC 199 (HL); *Erven Warnink BV v J Townend & Sons (Hull) Ltd* [1979] AC 731 (HL); *Reckitt & Colman Products Ltd v Borden* [1990] 1 WLR 491 (HL) (quia timet); *First Conferences Services Ltd v Bracchi* [2009] EWHC 2176 (Ch). See also *R Johnston & Co v Archibald Orr Ewing & Co* (1882) 7 App Cas 219, 229.

[62] Importantly, however, it should not be thought that the 'economic' torts are actionable only upon proof of economic loss. There are cases indicating that they are also actionable upon proof of personal injury or property damage, see: J Goudkamp and D Nolan, *Winfield & Jolowicz on Tort* (20th edn, Sweet & Maxwell 2020) [12-020]; McBride and Bagshaw (n 25) 669–73.

[63] *Leeds Industrial Co-operative Society Ltd v Slack* [1924] AC 851 (HL), 859; *One Step (Support) Ltd v Morris-Garner* [2018] UKSC 20, [2019] AC 649 [44].

actual or threatened infringement by the defendant'.[64] Consider what would occur if it were a necessary condition for the award of final injunctive relief that damages would be an inadequate remedy. It would lead to the odd conclusion that damages could be awarded in lieu of an injunction only where a court had already made a finding that damages would inadequately remedy the claimant. With respect, it would be paradoxical if this were the correct position of the law.[65] Indeed, this irrationality explains why, pursuant to AL Smith LJ's four-step test in *Shelfer*, it is only *after* jurisdiction to grant an injunction has been established that it is relevant to consider whether damages would adequately remedy the claimant.

For these reasons, Lord Sumption and Lord Clarke's inadequacy requirement is an incorrect statement of the positive law. The fact that damages would, or would not, adequately remedy the claimant is only a discretionary consideration.

B. The Tort must be Continuing

The better view of the positive law, which is evident in Lord Neuberger's leading judgment in *Coventry*, is that the necessary conditions for the award of a prohibitory injunction to restrain a future tort are that the claimant must prove that the defendant has committed a tort against her and is continuing to do so. As was explained in chapter 3, the word 'continuing' has two meanings in this context. First, it means that the tort is ongoing, in the sense that it is being committed every day and therefore likely at the very moment that the claimant seeks injunctive relief before the court. Second, it means that the tort is recurring (that is, it is being committed repeatedly but not on a daily basis).

Irrespective of whether a tort can be described as ongoing or recurring,[66] what the claimant must prove is that the defendant has previously committed a tort against her and that there is a real and imminent risk that the same tort (that is, all of its elements)[67] will be committed in the future.[68] This is a question of fact to be determined in accordance with the ordinary laws of evidence. What constitutes a 'real' and 'imminent' risk is not often discussed by the courts in the context of granting prohibitory injunctions, as it is simply presumed that these risks are established where it is proved that a wrong is continuing.[69] Where these

[64] *Jaggard v Sawyer* [1995] 1 WLR 269 (CA), 287. See also *One Step* (n 63) [45]; M Bryan, 'Injunctions and Damages: Taking *Shelfer* off the Shelf' (2016) 28 SAcLJ 921, 927–28.

[65] Heydon, Leeming and Turner do not recognise this paradox but identify a different paradox in respect of the principles governing when damages can be awarded in lieu of an injunction: Heydon, Leeming and Turner (n 18) [24-040].

[66] 'For this purpose there is no distinction between continuance and repetition': *Mayfair Trading Co Pty Ltd v Dreyer* (1958) 101 CLR 428, 451 (Dixon CJ).

[67] See *White v Mellin* [1895] AC 154 (HL), 163–64.

[68] For cases in which injunctions have been refused because there was no 'real' risk of the tort being committed, see ch 3.

[69] See Burrows (n 24) 467; *Proctor v Bayley* (1889) 42 Ch D 390 (CA), 398; *Race Relations Board v Applin* [1973] QB 815 (CA), 829.

terms are frequently considered, however, is in the context of granting quia timet injunctions before a tort has been committed at all. The precise meaning of a 'real' and 'imminent' risk is therefore examined in detail in chapter 6.

Subject to one exception, the effect of the above analysis is that the necessary conditions for the award of prohibitory injunctive relief do not change depending on the tort sought to be restrained. Provided a claimant can prove that a tort has been committed against her, and that there is a real and imminent risk that the same tort will be committed in the future, the prima facie position is that an injunction should be granted, and the burden is on the defendant to satisfy the court otherwise. Importantly, although property torts like trespass to land and private nuisance are frequently the subject of injunction claims due to the fact that these wrongs are often repeated by defendants, there is nothing in the reasoning of the cases to suggest that prohibitory injunctive relief is limited to, or favours, protecting property rights. Indeed, the torts of trespass to the person,[70] libel and slander,[71] malicious falsehood,[72] misuse of private information,[73] harassment,[74] inducing a breach of contract,[75] deceit,[76] causing loss by unlawful means,[77] intimidation,[78]

[70] eg, *Stevens v Stevens* (1907) 24 TLR 20 (interim); *Egan v Egan* [1975] Ch 218 (Ch) (interim); *Zimitat v Douglas* [1979] Qd R 454 (interlocutory); *Parry v Crooks* (1981) 27 SASR 1; *Corvisy v Corvisy* [1982] 2 NSWLR 557 (interlocutory); *Daley v Martin (No 1)* [1982] Qd R 23 (interlocutory); *Liburd* (n 2) (interim); *Patel v Patel* [1988] 2 FLR 179 (CA) (interim); *Burnett v George* [1992] 1 FLR 525 (CA) (interim); *Pidduck v Molloy* [1992] 2 FLR 202 (CA) (interim); *Burris v Azadani* [1995] 1 WLR 1372 (CA) (interim). See also *Parry v Crooks* (1981) 27 SASR 1 (as a matter of principle).

[71] '[P]erpetual injunctions to restrain publication of a libel are commonly granted, either after a trial, or after judgment is entered in default of defence': *Law Society v Kordowski* [2011] EWHC 3185 (QB) [3]. See, eg, *John v MGN Ltd* [1997] QB 586 (CA); *Brett Wilson LLP v Persons Unknown* [2015] EWHC 2628 (QB); *Zahawi v Press TV* [2017] EWHC 1010 (QB); *Burgon v News Group Newspapers Ltd* [2019] EWHC 195 (QB); *Glenn v Kline* [2020] EWHC 3182 (QB); *Mirza v Ali* [2021] EWHC 1494 (QB); *Dudley v Phillips* [2022] EWHC 930 (QB). See also *Grobbelaar v News Group Newspapers Ltd* [2002] 1 WLR 3024 (HL); R Parkes et al, *Gatley on Libel and Slander* (13th edn, Sweet & Maxwell 2022) [10-040]. In Australia, see *Zaia v Eshow* [2017] NSWSC 1540; *Rush v Nationwide News Pty Ltd (No 9)* [2019] FCA 1383; *Harbour Radio Pty Ltd v Wagner* [2019] 2 Qd R 468; *Capilano Honey Ltd v Dowling (No 4)* [2021] NSWSC 264; *Tribe v Simmons (No 2)* [2021] FCA 1164.

[72] eg, *University of Southampton v Mohtasham* [2012] EWHC 1630 (QB). See also *Al-Ko Kober Ltd v Sambhi* [2017] EWHC 2474 (QB) (interim); *Taher v Cumberland* [2019] EWHC 524 (QB) (interim). In Australia, see *Omega Plumbing Pty Ltd v Harbour Radio Pty Ltd t/as 2GB and 2GB 873* [2019] NSWSC 1576 (interlocutory); *Capilano Honey Ltd v Dowling (No 4)* [2021] NSWSC 264.

[73] eg, *WXY v Gewanter* [2012] EWHC 496 (QB) (interim); *BUQ v HRE* [2015] EWHC 1272 (QB); *Weller v Associated Newspapers Ltd* [2015] EWCA Civ 1176; *AXB v BXA* [2018] EWHC 588 (QB); *Bull v Desporte* [2019] EWHC 1650 (QB); *Hayden v Duckworth* [2020] EWHC 1033 (QB); *Duchess of Sussex v Associated Newspapers Ltd* [2021] EWHC 669 (Ch); *COS v PER* [2022] 5 WLUK 235 (QB).

[74] Cases in which final injunctions have been granted to restrain harassment are not wanting. See, eg, *Norwich City Council v Famuyiwa* [2004] EWCA Civ 1770; *Mitton v Benefield* [2011] EWHC 2098 (QB); *SKA v CRH* [2012] EWHC 2236 (QB); *Nursing and Midwifery Council v Nowak* [2014] EWHC 2945 (QB); *Brand v Berki* [2015] EWHC 3373 (QB); *GYH v Persons Unknown* [2018] EWHC 121 (QB); *Oliver v Shaikh* [2019] EWHC 3389 (QB); *Hodson v Person Unknown A* [2022] EWHC 1960 (QB).

[75] See n 58.

[76] See n 59.

[77] See n 60.

[78] eg, *Mohtasham* (n 72). In Australia, see *Dollar Sweets Pty Ltd v Federated Confectioners Association of Australia* [1986] VR 383 (interlocutory); *AS v Murray* [2013] NSWSC 733; *Uber BV v Howarth* (2017) 94 NSWLR 636; *Adani Mining Pty Ltd v Pennings* [2020] QSC 275 (interlocutory).

passing off[79] and breach of statutory duty[80] have all been restrained by prohibitory injunction. Additionally, it should be noted that some torts, like misfeasance in public office or malicious prosecution,[81] are not suited to being restrained by prohibitory injunction because it is highly unlikely that they would ever be committed repeatedly.[82] However, it should not be thought that this means courts can *never* award a prohibitory injunction in respect of these torts. The Privy Council recently quoted with approval Spry's statement that '[t]he powers of courts with equitable jurisdiction to grant injunctions are, subject to any relevant statutory restrictions, unlimited'.[83] Whether an injunction can be granted in respect of the tort of negligence is examined in detail in chapter 7.

What the above analysis demonstrates is that the multiplicity of suits doctrine is still what justifies the grant of prohibitory injunctions in tort law today. The default position is that courts will ordinarily restrain any continuing tort by a prohibitory injunction. That is because the courts are motivated to prevent the injustice that a claimant would suffer if a defendant was permitted to continuously commit a tort against the claimant, irrespective of whether a monetary payment would adequately remedy the claimant's future damage or loss. It is in this broader sense that the intervention of equity is triggered.

i. *The Exception*

There is, however, one notable exception to the general rule. The exception is in respect of 'torts' (or perhaps the better label is 'causes of action') that do not impose duties on defendants but instead generate primary liabilities (otherwise known as 'free-standing liabilities').[84] To fully understand this point, it is necessary to consider the distinction between torts that contain elements that are governed by a strict liability standard, and causes of action that generate primary liabilities.

As Goudkamp has explained, the correct meaning of strict liability is liability that 'is imposed regardless of whether the defendant was at fault in a technical legal sense'[85] ('that is to say, as meaning negligence or a relevant state of mind'[86]). A tort that contains strict liability elements (such as, for example, private nuisance,

[79] See n 61.

[80] eg, *Cooper v Whittingham* (1880) 15 Ch D 501 (Ch); *Attorney-General v Ashborne Recreation Ground Co* [1903] 1 Ch 101 (Ch); *Carlton Illustrators* [1911] 1 KB 771 (KB) (undertaking in lieu).

[81] The torts of malicious prosecution and abuse of process have been restrained by prohibitory injunction in Australia: *National Australia Bank Ltd v McFarlane* [2005] VSC 438 [67]–[69].

[82] Debate about the availability of injunctive relief in respect of the tort of negligence is examined in ch 7.

[83] Spry (n 21) 333, expressly approved in *Convoy Collateral Ltd v Broad Idea International Ltd* [2021] UKPC 24, [2023] AC 389 [57]–[58]; *Wolverhampton City Council v London Gypsies and Travellers* [2023] UKSC 47, [2024] AC 983 [17].

[84] Nicholas McBride, *The Humanity of Private Law: Part I* (Hart Publishing 2018) 55.

[85] James Goudkamp, 'Rethinking Fault Liability and Strict Liability in the Law of Torts' (2023) 139 LQR 269, 272.

[86] ibid 288.

conversion or libel)[87] therefore does not require the claimant to prove that the defendant has acted with fault in respect of the particular element(s) of the tort governed by a strict liability standard. Importantly, however, for liability to be made out, the claimant is still required to prove that the defendant, by his conduct, has breached the primary duty generated by the relevant tort. A prohibitory injunction can therefore be granted in respect of torts that contain elements of strict liability, as the injunction prohibits the defendant from doing an act that amounts to a breach of a primary duty.

By contrast, a primary liability is a cause of action pursuant to which a claimant acquires a claim against a defendant if a certain contingency materialises.[88] The liability does not exist to support an existing legal duty but is 'free-standing'.[89] As Nolan and Robertson have put it, in such cases 'the defendant is not susceptible to legal action because he or she has violated a right of the claimant, but simply because the law has laid down that in circumstances *x*, *y* has a claim against *z*'.[90] Primary liabilities are created to allocate a particular risk as between the claimant and the defendant. As Jaffey has explained, a primary liability

> imposes on D a risk relating to a certain contingency, *which may or may not involve an act by D*. D bears the risk of the contingency in the sense that he is responsible for remedying its effects on C, but *he does not have a duty to prevent the contingency from materializing*.[91]

A cause of action that generates a primary liability may therefore stipulate that the contingency for which a defendant bears the risk is made up of certain conduct and fault elements related to the defendant, as well as elements that may be governed by a strict liability standard. Importantly, however, what makes the cause of action a primary liability is that it does not proscribe the defendant from doing a particular act that amounts to, or may lead to, the materialisation of the contingency.[92] Hence, the claimant must prove only that the relevant contingency has materialised; there is no need for the claimant to prove that the defendant has breached a pre-existing duty.

Three (contestable) examples of primary liabilities that fall under the banner of 'tort law' are worthy of mention. First, consider the 'rule' (and notably not the 'tort') in *Rylands v Fletcher*,[93] which imposes liability on a defendant for property damage caused to a claimant as a result of the defendant's bringing onto (or keeping on) his land an exceptionally dangerous thing in unusual circumstances,

[87] As Goudkamp has argued persuasively, these torts are made up of both fault and strict liability elements.

[88] Peter Jaffey, 'Duties and Liabilities in Private Law' (2006) 12 *Legal Theory* 137, 146.

[89] McBride, *Humanity* (n 84) 55.

[90] D Nolan and A Robertson, 'Rights and Private Law' in D Nolan and A Robertson (eds), *Rights and Private Law* (Hart Publishing 2012) 1, 16.

[91] Jaffey (n 88) 150 (emphasis added).

[92] ibid 146, 150; Nolan and Robertson (n 90) 16–17.

[93] *Rylands v Fletcher* (1868) LR 3 HL 330.

which escapes.[94] Goudkamp has quite rightly observed that this rule is made up of elements that are governed by fault *and* strict liability standards.[95] Importantly, however, it has generally been accepted that the rule in *Rylands v Fletcher* does not impose any duty on the defendant not to do something (such as, for example, not to allow a dangerous thing on his land to escape).[96] The rule simply imposes a liability on the defendant when its elements are made out by the claimant. Second, consider the liability that arises under the Consumer Protection Act 1987 where damage is caused by a defective product. Section 2(1) of that Act provides that

> where any damage is caused wholly or partly by a defect in a product, every person to whom subsection (2) below applies shall be liable for the damage.

As numerous authors have observed, this provision imposes no duty on the defendant, only a liability.[97] Finally, the doctrine of vicarious liability imposes liability on a defendant as a result of a tort committed by a third party where: (i) there is a relationship between the defendant and the third party that attracts vicarious liability; and (ii) the third party committed the tort in the course of that relationship.[98] Again, the doctrine of vicarious liability does not impose any duty on the defendant, it simply imposes a liability on him when the two elements outlined above are made out by the claimant.

Irrespective of whether one agrees with whether these causes of action generate primary liabilities, it is necessary to distinguish torts that have elements of strict liability from causes of action that generate primary liabilities, as it is only the latter that cannot be restrained by a prohibitory injunction (or any other type of injunction). As Oliphant has observed briefly,[99] if an injunction were to be awarded in respect of primary liabilities, the injunction's effect would be to prohibit a contingency (that is, an event) rather than conduct that amounts to a breach of a duty by the defendant. The terms of the injunction would therefore have to provide that 'X must not occur' (rather than 'D must not do X'). Such an order is unacceptable for two reasons.

First, the order would be inconsistent with the structure of the cause of action. Causes of action that impose primary liabilities on defendants do not proscribe the events they are concerned with. They simply hold the defendant liable for the particular event. For example, if a defendant earns income, he must pay tax.

[94] *Transco Plc v Stockport MBC* [2004] 2 AC 1 (HL) [11].

[95] Goudkamp (n 85) 277–79.

[96] See, eg, OW Holmes, 'The Theory of Torts' (1873) 7 *American Law Review* 652, 653; J Smith, 'Tort and Absolute Liability – Suggested Changes in Classification' (1916-17) 30 *Harvard Law Review* 241; CK Allen, *Legal Duties and Other Essays in Jurisprudence* (Clarendon Press 1931) 193–94; C Wright, 'The English Law of Torts – A Criticism' (1961) 11 *University of Toronto Law Journal* 84, 86; Nolan and Robertson (n 90) 16–17; McBride and Bagshaw (n 25) 445. cf A Ripstein, *Private Wrongs* (Harvard University Press 2016) ch 5.

[97] See, eg, Nolan and Robertson (n 90) 16; McBride and Bagshaw (n 25) 362; Goudkamp and Nolan (n 62) [11-018], [11-027].

[98] *Barclays Bank Plc v Various Claimants* [2020] UKSC 13, (2020) AC 973 [1].

[99] Oliphant (ed) (n 22) [1.28].

Awarding an injunction that proscribes the relevant event would therefore hold the defendant liable for something that is not prohibited by the relevant cause of action, thereby unjustifiably constraining the defendant's liberties. Second, an order that proscribes an event would undermine a fundamental principle of injunction law: an 'injunction must define precisely what *acts* [by the defendant] are prohibited'.[100] For these reasons, prohibitory injunctions cannot be awarded in respect of causes of action that hold defendants liable for contingencies. This conclusion also explains why, and is consistent with the fact that, injunctions are not recognised to be available remedies in respect of unjust enrichments, as the latter are generally accepted to be causes of action that are primary liabilities and are therefore not classified as wrongs.[101]

Thus, except for causes of action that generate primary liabilities, the general rule is that *any* tort that is continuing to be committed against a claimant will prima facie justify the award of a final prohibitory injunction. Once the claimant has established that a continuing tort is being committed against her, the legal burden shifts to the defendant to show why a prohibitory injunction should not be granted. It is this discretionary exercise that will now be considered.

III. The Nature and Limits of the Discretion

Before analysing the discretionary considerations relevant to the award of a final injunction, it is necessary to examine what it means to say that a court exercises a discretion when deciding whether to grant an injunction to restrain a future tort. It is also necessary to identify the precise limits of that discretion. This is all the more important given that in the existing literature little attention is devoted to this issue.[102]

As was explained in chapter 2, historically, once it was proved that a defendant was infringing a claimant's rights, it was only in exceptional circumstances that courts would refuse to act. Modern courts adopt the same position. Once a court is satisfied that a tort was committed against the claimant and that there is a real and

[100] *Attorney-General v Punch Ltd* [2003] 1 AC 1046 (HL) [35] (emphasis added).

[101] See P Birks, 'The Concept of a Civil Wrong' in D Owen (ed), *Philosophical Foundations of Tort Law* (Oxford University Press 1997) 31, 48–49 (although Birks still described unjust enrichments as giving rise to a 'primary obligation' on the defendant); S Smith, 'A Duty to Make Restitution?' (2013) 26 *Canadian Journal of Law and Jurisprudence* 157, 160–65.

[102] A brief discussion of the discretion involved when courts grant an equitable remedy is found in: P Loughlan, 'No Right to the Remedy? An Analysis of Judicial Discretion in the Imposition of Equitable Remedies' (1989) 17 *Melbourne University Law Reivew* 132; S Waddams, 'Judicial Discretion' (2001) 1 *Oxford University Commonwealth Law Journal* 59; S Waddams, *Dimensions of Private Law: Categories and Concepts in Anglo-American Legal Reasoning* (Cambridge University Press 2003) 179–81; R Zakrzewski, *Remedies Reclassified* (Oxford University Press 2009) 91–94. More general literature concerned with discretion in the jurisprudence context is available: see, eg, R Dworkin, 'The Model of Rules' (1967) 35 *University of Chicago Law Review* 14.

imminent risk that the defendant will commit the same tort again in the future, a court has no discretion to refuse prohibitory injunctive relief unless a countervailing discretionary consideration is engaged by the defendant. It is only in circumstances that fall within the confines of the discretionary considerations that a court has a discretion to refuse injunctive relief. This observation is supported by the fact that there are numerous cases in which, upon its having been proved that the defendant is committing a continuing tort, a prohibitory injunction has been awarded as of course because the defendant did not plead any countervailing discretionary considerations.[103] Moreover, there are numerous cases where a prohibitory injunction has been awarded as of course after a court found that a defendant failed to make out a countervailing discretionary consideration that he or she had pleaded, or failed to persuade the court that the injunction should be refused because of the consideration.[104]

Suppose, however, that a countervailing discretionary consideration can be established by the defendant. In these circumstances, what does it mean to say that a court has a 'discretion' to decide whether an injunction is granted? In *Coventry*,[105] Lord Neuberger explicitly approved the statement of Millett LJ in *Jaggard v Sawyer*,[106] where he stated, in the context of deciding whether to award damages in lieu of an injunction, that:

> [r]eported cases are merely illustrations of circumstances in which particular judges have exercised their discretion, in some cases by granting an injunction, and in others by awarding damages instead. Since they are all cases on the exercise of a discretion, none of them is a binding authority on how the discretion should be exercised. The most that any of them can demonstrate is that in similar circumstances it would not be wrong to exercise the discretion in the same way. But it does not follow that it would be wrong to exercise it differently.[107]

What Millett LJ's remarks indicate is that a court is not bound to follow previous decisions when exercising a discretion as to whether an injunction should be granted. This should be accepted. If it were otherwise, and courts were bound to exercise their discretion in accordance with previous decisions, as if the exercise of a discretion was simply the application of a legal principle, it would be meaningless to state that a court has a 'discretion' to award an injunction. Thus, it seems that

[103] eg, *Bone v Seale* [1975] 1 WLR 797 (CA) (private nuisance); *Midasplayer.com* (n 3) (causing loss by unlawful means); *Jockey Club Racecourses Ltd v Persons Unknown* [2019] EWHC 1026 (Ch) (trespass to land); *Triad Group Plc v Makar* [2019] EWHC 423 (QB) (defamation, harassment); *COS v PER* (n 73) (misuse of private information).

[104] eg, *Martin v Price* [1894] 1 Ch 276 (CA); *Shelfer* (n 31); *Wood v Conway* (n 35); *Kennaway v Thompson* [1981] QB 88 (CA); *Anchor Brewhouse* (n 30); *Elliott v Islington LBC* [1991] 1 EGLR 167 (CA); *Grobbelaar* (n 71); *Mortimer v Bailey* [2004] EWCA Civ 1514; *ZAM v CFW* [2013] EWHC 662 (QB); *Rogers v Humphrey* [2017] EWHC 3681 (QB).

[105] *Coventry* (n 6) [120].

[106] *Jaggard v Sawyer* (n 64).

[107] ibid 288.

when it is said a court has a discretion to award an injunction, it means that where a defendant has engaged a countervailing discretionary consideration, the court has a free choice to decide whether to grant an injunction, irrespective of what was decided in prior cases.

However, it would be premature to conclude the analysis here. In *Beddow v Beddow*, Sir George Jessel MR stated, in the context of considering the discretion that is exercised by courts to grant an injunction, that 'what is right or just must be decided, not by the caprice of the judge, but according to sufficient legal reasons or on settled legal principles'.[108] Indeed, Lord Bingham stated extra-judicially in his seminal work on the rule of law that 'no discretion should be unconstrained so as to be potentially arbitrary. No discretion may be legally unfettered.'[109] An accurate account of what it means to say that a court has a discretion to award an injunction therefore requires the precise legal limits on that discretion to be identified. Those limits are most clearly expressed in the context of appellate courts dictating when it is appropriate for the exercise of a discretion to be set aside. The leading statement of principle on this issue was laid down by Griffiths LJ in *Alltrans Express Ltd v CVA Holdings Ltd*,[110] in the context of an appeal of a trial judge's decision to exercise his discretion to award costs to the claimants. Griffiths LJ, intending to lay down a general principle that guided appellate review of any kind of discretionary decision, stated:

> Before a court can interfere it must be shown that the judge has either erred in principle in his approach, or has left out of account, or taken into account, some [discretionary factor] that he should, or should not, have considered, or that his decision is wholly wrong, because the court is forced to the conclusion that he has not balanced the various factors fairly in the scale.[111]

Applied in the context of the discretion to award an injunction, Griffith LJ's statement indicates that the discretion is limited in three ways.

First, a court will err if it has made an error of law (or, to adopt Griffiths LJ's words, 'erred in principle'). This point is perhaps the most important. It means that courts are strictly bound by previous cases that dictate the legal principles that govern when a particular discretionary consideration (for example, undue hardship) is engaged. Accordingly, the usual rules of precedent apply when a court

[108] *Beddow v Beddow* (1878) 9 Ch D 89 (Ch) 93. Explicitly approved by the Privy Council in 2021: *Convoy v Broad* (n 83) [52]. See also *Doherty v Allman* (1878) 3 App Cas 709, 728–29; *Goodson v Richardson* (1873–74) LR 9 Ch App 221, 223; *Shelfer* (n 31) 316–17; *South Bucks DC v Porter* [2003] 2 AC 558 (HL) [29]; Davies (n 15) [18-036].

[109] Lord Bingham, *The Rule of Law* (Penguin 2010) 35. See also *Wolverhampton City Council v London Gypsies and Travellers* (n 83) [19] (in relation to the 'power' to award an injunction).

[110] *Alltrans Express Ltd v CVA Holdings Ltd* [1984] 1 WLR 394 (CA).

[111] ibid 403. Applied with approval in *AEI Ltd v PPL* [1999] 1 WLR 1507 (CA), 1523; *University of Oxford v Broughton* [2006] EWCA Civ 1305 [20]; *Grizzly Business Ltd v Stena Drilling Ltd* [2017] EWCA Civ 94 [57]; *Lejonvarn v Burgess* [2020] EWCA Civ 114 [49]. See also *Jackson v Murray* [2015] UKSC 5 [35].

states what must be proved by a defendant or a claimant for a particular discretionary consideration to be engaged so that the court can validly consider it in the court's discretionary exercise. Millett LJ's statement above should therefore not be interpreted as giving judges a mandate to discard standard precedent-based legal reasoning by analogy.

Second, a court will err if it takes into account an irrelevant consideration or fails to take into account a discretionary consideration that was engaged by the defendant or the claimant. This reaffirms the point made above, that courts are bound to consider only those discretionary considerations that have been developed by previous courts or that develop in the future pursuant to precedent-based legal reasoning by analogy. They cannot, for example, refuse to grant an injunction because the claimant was wearing green socks or because it was particularly gloomy weather outside. Conversely, courts cannot choose to ignore relevant discretionary considerations that have been engaged by the defendant or the claimant. As the Supreme Court explained in *Wolverhampton City Council v London Gypsies and Travellers*, 'it is certainly not the case that judges can grant or withhold injunctions purely on their own subjective perception of the justice and convenience of doing so in a particular case'.[112]

Third, a court will err if it has come to a decision that is 'wholly wrong … because the court is forced to the conclusion that [the judge] has not balanced the various factors fairly in the scale'. This means that courts cannot exercise their discretion by balancing the competing factors in a way that is plainly wrong.

In the light of these three points, as well as the statement of Millett LJ in *Jaggard v Sawyer*, what it means to say that a court has a 'discretion' to award a final injunction is as follows. Once the necessary conditions have been proved by the claimant, and the defendant has engaged one or more countervailing discretionary considerations (irrespective of whether the claimant has also established a consideration that militates in favour of injunctive relief), a court can make a free choice unconstrained by prior cases about where the balance lies as to whether an injunction should be granted. However, that free choice is subject to three qualifications: first, that the court applies the correct legal principles to determine which discretionary considerations are engaged; second, that the court does not take into account an irrelevant consideration or fail to take into account a relevant consideration; and, third, that the final decision reached is not plainly wrong. As we shall see in later chapters, the discretion is the same irrespective of whether a prohibitory, desisting or restorative mandatory, or quia timet injunction is sought by the claimant.

With the nature of the discretion that judges exercise when granting final injunctive relief in mind, the equitable discretionary considerations can now be examined.

[112] *Wolverhampton City Council v London Gypsies and Travellers* (n 83) [145].

IV. Discretionary Considerations Militating Against Relief

Numerous discretionary considerations have been developed by the courts that militate against the award of a final injunction. These considerations are central to this book, as they denote when courts will refuse to protect a claimant's legal right from being continuously infringed. As was explained in chapter 3, desisting mandatory injunctions are virtually identical to prohibitory injunctions, except for the form of the words used in the court's order. As a result, the analysis of the discretionary considerations will include cases involving desisting mandatory injunctions, except for the considerations of undue hardship and constant supervision, which are considered in chapter 5, because there are opposing views in the literature in respect of how these considerations are to be applied specifically in the context of deciding whether to grant a mandatory injunction.

Section IV.A will focus on the considerations that concern the defendant, namely: undue hardship, the public interest, constant supervision and human rights considerations. Section IV.B will focus on the considerations that concern the claimant, namely: the adequacy of damages, unclean hands, acquiescence and laches. The discretionary considerations are split into these two categories to give some structure to this area of the law. In the current texts on equitable remedies, authors simply lay out the variety of discretionary considerations without rhyme or reason. Analysing the considerations by reference to claimant-sided factors and defendant-sided factors sharpens our thinking. It reminds us that, in private law, the juristic reasons for generating a right and awarding a remedy are concerned with the parties to the action.

Before examining the discretionary considerations listed above, it is necessary to address two points. The first is a semantic point. In the existing literature, numerous authors describe the discretionary considerations that militate against injunctive relief as 'defences'. For example, it is often said that defendants can rely on the 'defence' of undue hardship. Except for the defence of acquiescence, this language should be avoided because the discretionary considerations are merely *considerations*. Contrary to what has been suggested by some, it was explained in section III of this chapter that once a consideration is engaged by a defendant, this does not mean that the court is bound to refuse injunctive relief.

The second point is a classificatory one. It could be argued that the public interest consideration is policy based and is therefore related neither to the defendant nor to the claimant. The difficulty with this view, however, is that when the public interest consideration is relied on by a defendant, the defendant is making the argument that *his tortious activity* benefits the public. Conversely, when the public interest consideration is relied on by a claimant, the claimant is making the argument that *enforcing her legal right* benefits the public. In this sense, although the public interest consideration is a policy consideration, the consideration can still be classified as being 'defendant-related' or 'claimant-related'. Additionally, the discretionary considerations of the public interest, and the adequacy of damages, cut both ways. Depending on the facts of the case, they can be relied on as factors that militate against the award of injunctive relief *or* in favour of injunctive relief. Accordingly, these considerations are examined in both section IV and section V.

A. Defendant-Related Considerations

i. Undue Hardship

Perhaps the most well-known discretionary consideration relevant to the award of a final injunction is undue hardship. In respect of prohibitory injunctions, there is little contention surrounding the application of this consideration. It is well established that a final prohibitory injunction cannot be refused simply because the defendant will suffer hardship if the injunction is granted.[113] Courts can only consider hardship that is undue. Specifically, the defendant must establish that the hardship he would suffer by the grant of the injunction is so out of proportion to the injunction's value to the claimant that it would be oppressive to grant the injunction.[114] Additionally, as will be explained in section V.A.i, a defendant can rely on the consideration of undue hardship only where he inadvertently committed his tort against the claimant.[115]

Although there are no limits on the types of consequences that could amount to undue hardship, it is extremely difficult to make out. As Lord Sumner stated in the Privy Council case of *Stollmeyer v Trinidad Lake Petroleum Co Ltd* (in the context of rejecting a defendant polluter's plea of hardship):

> There can be no doubt that if the respondents have … violated the appellants' rights, they cannot excuse or defend their wrong by showing how disproportionate is the loss which they will suffer by being restrained to any loss which the appellants have suffered or are likely to suffer by their wrongful acts, or by dwelling on the general importance of the enterprises … These considerations may be relevant to the form of the remedy, especially to the time and opportunities which should be given them, for finding some way out of their difficulty, but they cannot operate to deprive the appellants of their right to have their wrong redressed, if wrong has been done [to] them.[116]

[113] See, eg, Spry (n 21) 414; Davies (n 15) [18-040]; Glister and Lee (n 16) [28-046]; Oliphant (ed) (n 22) [8.11]; Burrows (n 24) 447; S Smith, *Rights, Wrongs and Injustices: The Structure of Remedial Law* (Oxford University Press 2019) 316.

[114] *Jaggard v Sawyer* (n 64) 283; *Watson v Promo-Sport Ltd* [2009] EWCA Civ 15 [45].

[115] Note that a defendant will have acted inadvertently even where the defendant reasonably, but mistakenly, believed that his tortious act was consented to by the claimant: see *Tollemache and Cobbold Breweries Ltd v Reynolds* [1983] 2 EGLR 158 (CA) 161.

[116] *Stollmeyer v Trinidad Lake Petroleum Co Ltd* [1918] AC 485 (PC) 494.

Consistently with this approach, courts have not hesitated to grant prohibitory injunctions that allegedly had the effect of: preventing a hotel from using a kitchen;[117] requiring a fish and chip shop to move locations if it wanted to continue trading;[118] severely limiting the profitability of a poultry farm;[119] causing building works to be delayed by nine weeks, which resulted in an increased cost of $4.5 million;[120] shutting off the sewerage system of a township;[121] and shutting down or limiting the profitability of gas works and other enterprises that employ numerous people.[122] Making out undue hardship is therefore an arduous task.

As Stephen Smith has recognised,[123] it necessarily follows that cases in which final injunctions are refused for undue hardship are rare. In *Bracewell v Appleby*[124] and *Jaggard v Sawyer*,[125] injunctions were refused for undue hardship (and damages were awarded in lieu) because they would have had the effect of rendering the defendants' houses uninhabitable. These cases seem to suggest that only the most serious of consequences will give rise to undue hardship. However, there are cases that indicate that where the claimant is seeking an injunction to protect her rights solely for economic reasons, a serious economic consequence suffered by the defendant is more likely to amount to undue hardship. Consider the decision in the 2017 case of *Brothers Enterprises Ltd v New World Hospital UK Ltd*.[126] There, the claimant operated a restaurant situated next door to the defendant's hotel and held a right of way over part of the hotel's premises so that its customers could use the hotel's toilets. To facilitate refurbishments to the hotel, the defendant blocked the claimant's right of way and intended to continue to do so for 10 weeks, meaning that the claimant could not operate its restaurant. As a result, the claimant brought proceedings for an interim injunction restraining the defendant from blocking its right of way. The defendant admitted that it had infringed the claimant's property right and was continuing to do so. However, Roth J held that in circumstances where the claimant was using its property right solely to gain an economic benefit, it would be oppressive to grant the injunction. This was because the effect of granting the injunction would be to prevent the defendant from engaging in building works to refurbish its hotel for as long as the right of way existed. The economic consequences that would flow to the defendant therefore

[117] *Reinhardt v Mentasti* (1889) 42 Ch D 685 (CA); *Vanderpant v Mayfair Hotel Co Ltd* [1930] 1 Ch 138 (Ch).
[118] *Adams v Ursell* [1913] 1 Ch 269 (Ch).
[119] *Leeman v Montagu* [1936] 2 All ER 1677 (KB). See also *Baulkham Hills Shire Council v AV Walsh Pty Ltd* (1968) 15 LGRA 338.
[120] *Bendal* (n 30) 476–77.
[121] See, eg, *Jones v Llanrwst* [1911] 1 Ch 393 (Ch); *Haigh v Deudraeth RDC* [1945] 2 All ER 661 (Ch); *Pride of Derby* (n 40).
[122] *Pennington v Brinsop Hall Coal Co* (1877) 5 Ch D 769 (Ch); *Wood v Conway* (n 35); *Stollmeyer* (n 116).
[123] Smith (n 113) 316.
[124] *Bracewell v Appleby* [1975] Ch 408 (Ch).
[125] *Jaggard v Sawyer* (n 64).
[126] *Brothers Enterprises Ltd v New World Hospital UK Ltd* [2017] EWHC 2455 (Ch). See also *Goode v Owen & Four Ashes Golf Centre Ltd* [2001] EWCA Civ 2101; *Greenmanor Ltd v Laurence Pilford* [2012] EWCA Civ 756.

far outweighed the economic consequences that would be suffered by the claimant (which the defendant was still liable to pay for) due to the temporary interference with the right of way.[127]

The decision in *Brothers Enterprises* is sound. It reflects the fact that the undue hardship test is one of proportionality and hence that it is highly relevant if the claimant is enforcing her rights solely for economic reasons. However, it should be borne in mind that even in such cases, a court cannot employ a balance-of-convenience test and refuse to grant an injunction for undue hardship simply because the economic consequences to the defendant outweigh those to the claimant. As the facts of *Brothers Enterprises* indicate, the consequences to the defendant must be so disproportionate that it would be oppressive to grant the injunction.

As numerous authors have noted,[128] the reason why the courts have adopted a demanding test to make out undue hardship is because once it is accepted that there is jurisdiction to grant final injunctive relief, the defendant is regarded as a wrongdoer. Courts will therefore only rarely and reluctantly permit a rights violation to continue. Moreover, consistently with the 1859 House of Lords decision in *Imperial v Broadbent*,[129] modern courts have recognised that it is not appropriate to adopt a balance-of-convenience test, as it would mean that the courts would permit a rights violation to continue where it would be more convenient for the defendant, as against the claimant, to do so.[130] If such a test were adopted, it would raise the question of whether it would be correct to describe common law rights as 'rights' at all.

ii. The Public Interest

In *Coventry v Lawrence*, Lord Neuberger (with whom Lord Carnwath explicitly agreed on this issue) stated that as a matter of principle he 'found it hard to see how there could be any circumstances in which [the public interest] arose and could not, as a matter of law, be a relevant factor [going to whether a final injunction should be granted]'.[131] Although this statement was expressed as obiter dicta, it strongly suggests that where the grant of an injunction may not be in the public interest (or would adversely affect a particular third person)[132] because the tortious activity of the defendant is beneficial to the public or a third person, this is a consideration

[127] *Brothers Enterprises* (n 126) [22], [41], [42].

[128] Spry (n 21) 413; Davies (n 15) [18-040]; Glister and Lee (n 16) [28-046].

[129] *Imperial v Broadbent* (n 45).

[130] See, eg, *Smith v Smith* (1875) LR 20 Eq 500, 505; *Krehl v Burrell* (1879) 11 Ch D 146 (CA), 148; *Shelfer* (n 31) 322; *Cowper v Laidler* [1903] 2 Ch 337 (Ch), 341; *Leeds* (n 63) 861; *Halsey v Esso Petroleum Co Ltd* [1961] 1 WLR 683 (QB), 703; *Elliott* (n 104) 168; *Jaggard v Sawyer* (n 64) 283, 286.

[131] *Coventry* (n 6) [124]. See also ibid [239] (Lord Carnwath).

[132] A third person may apply to have an injunction discharged: *Cretanor Maritime Co Ltd v Irish Marine Management Ltd* [1978] 1 WLR 966 (CA); *Silktone Pty Ltd v Devreal Capital Pty Ltd* (1990) 21 NSWLR 317.

that militates against the grant of an injunction and which must be considered by a court when exercising its discretion.

Most authors adopt Lord Neuberger's dictum uncritically or simply state that the public interest is a relevant factor.[133] However, Pontin,[134] Davies,[135] Bryan[136] and Nolan[137] have suggested that Lord Neuberger's dictum oversimplifies the law on this issue. Building on the two reasons given by these authors, their analysis should be accepted.

(a) Inconsistency with the Prior Case Law

In his judgment, Lord Neuberger did not cite an authority for his proposition. It seems that he believed his dictum was so obvious that it went without saying. However, when one analyses the prior authorities, it is evident that Lord Neuberger's dictum is inconsistent with them.

Traditionally, courts were circumspect about refusing injunctions on the basis of what was supposedly in the best interests of the public or a class of third persons. Examples of such cases are not wanting.[138] In *Shelfer*,[139] the defendants argued that the injunction should be refused because the defendant's electricity works benefited the public by providing electricity in London. This contention was rejected by the Court of Appeal. Lindley LJ stated:

> [E]ver since Lord Cairns' Act was passed the Court of Chancery has repudiated the notion that the legislature intended to turn that court into a tribunal for legalising wrongful acts … Expropriation, even for a money consideration, is only justifiable when Parliament has sanctioned it. Courts of Justice are not like Parliament, which considers whether proposed works will be so beneficial to the public as to justify exceptional legislation, and the deprivation of people of their rights with or without compensation.[140]

Identical reasoning is found in the complex 1930 House of Lords decision in *Manchester Corporation v Farnworth*.[141] In that case, the claimant farmer brought

[133] Oliphant (ed) (n 22) [8.11]; Burrows (n 24) 454; Spry (n 21) 416; Heydon, Leeming and Turner (n 18) [21-460]; Glister and Lee (n 16) [28-049]; Smith (n 113) 318–19; Bean, Parry and Burns (n 17) [2-12].

[134] B Pontin, 'Private Nuisance in the Balance: *Coventry v Lawrence (No 1)* and *(No 2)*' (2015) 27 *Journal of Environmental Law* 119.

[135] P Davies, 'Injunctions in Tort and Contract' in G Virgo and S Worthington (eds), *Commercial Remedies: Resolving Controversies* (Cambridge University Press 2017) 127, 132–35; Davies (n 15) [18-042].

[136] Bryan (n 63) 943–45.

[137] D Nolan, 'Injunctions' in W Day and S Worthington (eds), *Challenging Private Law: Lord Sumption on the Supreme Court* (Hart Publishing 2020) 155, 167–72.

[138] In addition to the below cases, see: *Attorney-General v Birmingham* (1858) 4 K&J 528; *Goodson v Richardson* (n 108) 223–24; *Raphael v Thames Valley Railway Co* (1866-67) LR 2 Ch App 147 (award of specific performance).

[139] *Shelfer* (n 31).

[140] ibid 315–16.

[141] *Manchester Corporation v Farnworth* [1930] AC 171 (HL). See also B Pontin, *Nuisance Law and Environmental Protection: A Study of Nuisance Injunctions in Practice* (Lawtext Publishing 2013) ch 4.

a private nuisance claim against the defendant corporation after sulphuric acid and other chemicals were emitted into the atmosphere from its power station and caused damage to the claimant's farmlands. At first instance, Talbot J found that a nuisance had been committed but declined to grant an injunction. On appeal, the Court of Appeal allowed the claimant's appeal and granted an injunction. On appeal to the House of Lords, the majority held that the defendant had statutory authority to operate its power station, provided it did so with reasonable care. Nevertheless, the majority upheld the grant of the injunction, but modified its terms to reflect the changed standard of care. It was argued by the defendant that its power station was beneficial to the public and that the effect of the injunction would be to increase the price of electricity in Manchester. Viscount Sumner, writing the leading judgment for the majority, seemed to reject this argument by stating:

> The nature and degree of the plaintiff's suffering and the cost, trouble and inconvenience to the defendant Corporation of saving him from it are elements on the two sides of the case, which must be considered in deciding what is reasonable, but I cannot see that either on principle or on authority it is a sufficient answer to a criticism, otherwise sound, to say that, if so, Manchester's electricity would cost it more. … I do not know by what authority, short of the express direction of the Legislature, the interests of the public are thus summarily to override the rights of the individual.[142]

It is important to recognise, however, that as Viscount Sumner's remarks were given in the context of assessing whether the defendant's actions were reasonable, to the extent that his remarks were intended to apply to the appropriateness of the grant of the injunction, they were obiter dicta.

Finally, even in *Attorney-General v Acton Local Board*,[143] where the mandatory injunction sought by the claimants would have required the defendant authority to disconnect the drains and sewers attached to every house in Acton in the previous six years, Fry J refused to grant the injunction only because of the public interest considerations *and* the claimants' laches.[144] The position in the late nineteenth century and early twentieth century therefore seemed to be that that unless an additional countervailing discretionary consideration was engaged by the defendant, courts would not refuse injunctive relief on public interest considerations alone. As Cozens-Hardy MR put it in *Price's Patent Candle Co v London CC*, '[c]onsiderations of public welfare may justify the suspension of an injunction upon terms, but they do not justify the denial of relief to the private person whose rights have been affected'.[145]

[142] ibid 194–95.

[143] *Attorney-General v Acton Local Board* (1882) 22 Ch D 221 (Ch). See also *Lillywhite v Trimmer* (1867) 36 LJ Ch 525.

[144] *Attorney-General v Acton Local Board* (n 143) 231–32.

[145] *Price's Patent Candle Co v London CC* [1908] 1 Ch 526 (CA), 544. See also *Pride of Derby* (n 40) 192.

The positive law today, while cognisant of the traditional approach, is more nuanced. Four cases can be highlighted.

The first two cases are decisions of the Court of Appeal: *Kennaway v Thompson*[146] and *Elliott v Islington LBC*.[147] In *Kennaway*, the claimant alleged that noise generated by water-sports activities conducted on a lake by the defendants (who were members of a motorboat racing club) amounted to a private nuisance, and sought a prohibitory injunction. At first instance, Mais J refused to grant an injunction because, inter alia, permitting the defendants' water-sports activities to continue benefited that section of the public that was interested in motor-boat racing.[148] On appeal, the Court of Appeal allowed the claimant's appeal and granted a prohibitory injunction. It was reasoned that the decision in *Shelfer* was binding on the Court, and that courts are generally not permitted to refuse to enforce a claimant's rights for public-interest reasons.[149] Similar reasoning is found in *Elliott*. In that case, Rice J granted a mandatory injunction ordering the defendant to remove an ancient chestnut tree that was growing into the wall of the claimant's house. On appeal, the defendant local authority argued that damages should be awarded in lieu because the removal of the tree would be 'oppressive' to the public. The Court dismissed the appeal. Lord Donaldson MR stated:

> [I]t is not generally appropriate that specific private rights should be denied in order to give rise to indefinite advantages to the general public. Were it otherwise, the court would, as I see it, be legislating to deprive people of their rights.[150]

What the decisions in *Kennaway* and *Elliott* demonstrate is that modern courts have applied what was held by the Court of Appeal in *Shelfer*, and later stated obiter in *Farnworth*. The general position, therefore, is that ordinarily it is not appropriate for courts to determine that a tortious act committed by a defendant is so beneficial to the public that it justifies the expropriation of a claimant's legal rights.

It is the third noteworthy case, however, that exhibits the subtlety in the law that has since developed. The case is *Dennis v Ministry of Defence*.[151] Here, Buckley J refused to grant a declaration (treated as being equivalent to an injunction for the reasons explained in chapter 1)[152] in respect of a private nuisance created by the noise of RAF aircraft flying over the first claimant's land, because of the strong public interest in the continued training of RAF pilots in England. The decision therefore indicates that public-interest arguments can persuade a court to refuse injunctive relief. However, it is important to recognise that Buckley J accepted that 'the cases indicate [that] very often the private interest will prevail

[146] *Kennaway v Thompson* (n 104).
[147] *Elliott v Islington LBC* (n 104).
[148] *Kennaway v Thompson* (n 104) 92.
[149] ibid 92–93.
[150] *Elliott v Islington LBC* (n 104) 169.
[151] *Dennis v Ministry of Defence* [2003] EWHC 793 (QB). See also *Harold Stephen & Co v Post Office* [1977] 1 WLR 1172 (CA), 1180 (obiter).
[152] *Dennis v Ministry of Defence* (n 151) [80].

[over the public interest]'.[153] It seems that three factors persuaded Buckley J to refuse to grant the declaration for public interest reasons. First, it was possible for Buckley J to make a finding of fact on the available evidence that there would be 'enormous inconvenience and cost [in] uprooting RAF Wittering and RAF Cottesmore to another location'.[154] Second, Buckley J accepted the submission of counsel (which has also been accepted by other courts in the tort law context)[155] that the public interest in defending the realm is of 'a different and greater order altogether from commerce and other interests' that were beneficial to the public.[156] Finally, Buckley J emphasised that the claimant had delayed bringing proceedings for a declaration.[157] The decision in *Dennis* is therefore a nuanced one. It confirms that the general position is that courts are not permitted to refuse injunctive relief in aid of a private legal right for public-interest reasons. However, the decision also demonstrates that courts are prepared to accept that in exceptional circumstances where the defendant's tortious act is overwhelmingly in the public interest, it is permissible for them to refuse to award an injunction.

The final important case is *Watson v Croft Promo Sport Ltd*.[158] There, the defendant operated and managed a motor-racing circuit that was situated next door to houses owned and occupied by the claimants. The claimants brought proceedings against the defendant, alleging that the activities conducted on the circuit caused excessive noise that amounted to a private nuisance. Simon J found that a nuisance had been committed but refused to grant an injunction. The claimants appealed against the latter finding, but the defendant argued that because motor racing was enjoyed by members of the public, the Court of Appeal was required to take into account the fact that awarding an injunction would be detrimental to the public interest. The Court rejected this argument, allowed the claimants' appeal and awarded an injunction. The Chancellor of the High Court reasoned:

> In a marginal case where the damage to the claimant is minimal I can accept that … the effect on the public of the grant of an injunction is properly to be taken into account. But the fact that the public benefit might be relevant in those circumstances does not mean that its existence can, alone, negate the requirement of exceptional circumstances or oppression of the defendant which both Shelfer and Jaggard clearly require. There was no evidence or finding of the judge as to the effect on the public interest of a restriction on the defendants' use of their circuit to their core activities. But even if there were I am unable to see how this could be regarded as a marginal case so as to let in consideration of the public interest.[159]

[153] ibid [44].
[154] ibid [48]. See also ibid [43].
[155] See, eg, *Mulcahy v Ministry of Defence* [1996] QB 732 (CA); *Smith v Ministry of Defence* [2013] UKSC 41, [2014] AC 52.
[156] *Dennis v Ministry of Defence* (n 151) [31(ii)], [45], [48].
[157] ibid [48].
[158] *Watson v Croft Promo Sport Ltd* (n 114).
[159] ibid [51].

The Chancellor is making two points in his remarks. The first is that the proportionality test that is employed to determine whether a defendant would suffer undue hardship is also employed when considering whether an injunction should be refused for public-interest reasons. Accordingly, it is only where the effects of the injunction would far outweigh the benefits of the injunction to the claimant that it will be a correct exercise of a court's discretion to refuse injunctive relief for public-interest reasons. The second point made by the Chancellor is that, in the context of applying a proportionality test, the public's interest can be *considered* as a factor that weighs against the award of an injunction only where the damage (or loss) suffered by the claimant due to the defendant's tort is minimal.

Thus, in the light of the decisions in *Kennaway*, *Elliott*, *Dennis* and *Watson*, the positive law is as follows. Even where a court can, on the available evidence, assess where the public interest lies, it will only be in a case where the damage or loss that would be suffered by the claimant is minimal that the public interest can be considered as a factor that militates against the grant of injunctive relief. Additionally, it is only in the most exceptional of cases, like *Dennis*, where the consequences of awarding an injunction are overwhelmingly inconsistent with the public interest and far outweigh the benefits of the injunction to the claimant, that it would be a correct exercise of a court's discretion to refuse injunctive relief. Otherwise, as we shall see below, public interest considerations are relevant only to whether an injunction should be suspended. It is important to recognise that this conception of the law is distinct from Lord Neuberger's dictum in *Coventry*, as clearly the above authorities do not suggest that public-interest considerations (regardless of their strength) are always relevant.

It must be accepted, however, that there is one case that supports Lord Neuberger's dictum: *Miller v Jackson*.[160] In that case, the claimant had moved into a house that was recently built as part of a new housing development situated adjacent to a cricket field. After numerous cricket balls landed in the claimant's garden, causing property damage and an apprehension of personal injury, the claimant brought proceedings against the defendant cricket club in private nuisance. Reeve J found that a nuisance had been committed and awarded a prohibitory injunction restraining the club from playing cricket except in accordance with particular conditions. On appeal, a majority in the Court of Appeal allowed the defendant's appeal and discharged the grant of an injunction. Cumming-Bruce LJ considered that the trial judge had not sufficiently considered 'the interest of the inhabitants of the village as a whole'.[161] Lord Denning MR, who believed that there was no actionable nuisance, also reasoned that the public interest 'in protecting the environment by preserving our playing fields in the face of mounting development' dictated that the injunction must be refused.[162] The decision therefore suggests

[160] *Miller v Jackson* [1977] QB 966 (CA).
[161] ibid 989.
[162] ibid 981.

that any level of public interest is always relevant to whether an injunction should be granted.

There are, however, major difficulties with the majority's reasoning. First, on the available evidence, it was entirely unclear whether it was in fact in the public interest for the injunction to be refused. To the contrary, particularly in the 1970s,[163] there was significant public interest in ensuring that adequate housing was developed in England (which therefore would have militated in favour of the grant of the injunction). The competing considerations of protecting the 'environment', on the one hand, and ensuring that there is sufficient housing, on the other hand, demonstrate how difficult it is (and how ill-suited courts are) to determine where the public interest lies. Lord Denning MR and Cumming-Bruce LJ simply did not have sufficient resources, or the expertise, to determine that the environmental reasons were so beneficial to the public that they justified the expropriation of the claimant's common law right. Second, as Geoffrey Lane LJ intimated in dissent,[164] and as the Court of Appeal later recognised in *Kennaway v Thompson*,[165] the reasoning of the majority is obviously inconsistent with the prior case law regarding when public-interest arguments could be taken into account. Indeed, Lord Denning MR's reasoning in *Miller* is directly contrary to his own reasoning in *Pride of Derby*, where he stated that the fact that an injunction would be contrary to the public interest is only relevant to whether the injunction should be suspended.[166] As other authors have intimated,[167] *Miller* should therefore be regarded as wrongly decided, such that the decision does not form part of the positive law. The dissent of Geoffrey Lane LJ should be accepted as stating the correct outcome: the injunction should have been granted but suspended for 12 months. Thus, the decision provides little support for Lord Neuberger's approach.

(b) Disregard for the Proper Function of the Courts

A further difficulty with Lord Neuberger's dictum is that it pays insufficient regard to the important reasons why courts are hesitant to accept public-interest arguments. As Lord Sumption specifically pointed out in *Coventry*,[168] as the above case law indicates, and as other authors have identified,[169] it is generally not appropriate for courts to assess where the public interest lies. Courts are not Law Commissions.[170] They do not have the resources, nor the democratic legitimacy, to determine what is in the public interest except in the clearest of cases. Even

[163] See *Southwark LBC v Williams* [1971] Ch 734 (CA).
[164] *Miller v Jackson* (n 160) 987.
[165] *Kennaway v Thompson* (n 104) 93.
[166] *Pride of Derby* (n 40) 192.
[167] Heydon, Leeming and Turner (n 18) [21-095].
[168] *Coventry* (n 6) [158].
[169] See, eg, Davies, 'Injunctions in Tort and Contract' (n 135) 133; Bryan (n 63) 944–45; Nolan, 'Injunctions' (n 137) 169; R Stevens, *Torts and Rights* (Oxford University Press 2007) 308.
[170] *Robinson v Chief Constable of West Yorkshire Police* [2018] UKSC 4, [2018] AC 736 [2].

Dworkin's 'Hercules J' was said not to have the authority to determine what was in the public interest.[171] Additionally, even if it is possible for courts to determine where the public interest lies, it is not appropriate for them to adopt a balance-of-convenience test. Consistently with the cases concerning undue hardship, the Court of Appeal has correctly stated that it would be unacceptable for courts to refuse to enforce a claimant's legal rights simply because, on balance, it is more convenient to the public or a class of third persons for the claimant's rights to be infringed. The above two considerations are ignored when a grand statement is made to the effect that the public interest is always relevant to whether a final injunction should be granted. The authors who seem to support such a grand statement by criticising the courts' reticence in relying on public interest arguments, also fail to acknowledge either of these considerations.[172]

In the light of the foregoing, Lord Neuberger's dictum should not be accepted as a correct statement of the positive law. The better view, which adequately captures the law's nuance, is that the public interest can only be considered as a factor that militates against the grant of an injunction where it is possible for a court to be satisfied on the available evidence that awarding the injunction would not be in the public interest *and* the damage or loss that would be suffered by the claimant would be minimal. Additionally, it is only in the most exceptional of cases, like that of *Dennis*, where the consequences of awarding an injunction are overwhelmingly inconsistent with the public interest and far outweigh the benefits of the injunction to the claimant, that it would be a correct exercise of a court's discretion to refuse injunctive relief. Otherwise, the mere fact that the award of an injunction would not be in the public interest is only relevant to whether an injunction should be suspended.

iii. Constant Supervision

If the terms of an injunction would require a court to constantly supervise the parties, this is a fact that will militate against the grant of an injunction. The constant supervision consideration is thought to apply differently to mandatory injunctions and is therefore examined in detail in chapter 5. However, contrary to what is intimated in the existing literature,[173] it should not be thought that the constant supervision consideration is irrelevant to the award of a prohibitory injunction.

[171] R Dworkin, 'Hard Cases' (1975) 88 *Harvard Law Review* 1057, 1061–62, 1087–88, 1092–93.

[172] See, HE Read, 'Equity and Public Wrongs' (1933) 11 *Canadian Bar Review* 73, 85; RA Buckley, 'Injunctions and the Public Interest' (1981) 44 *MLR* 212, 214; S Tromans, 'Nuisance – Prevention or Payment?' (1982) 41 *CLJ* 78, 90; M Lee, 'Tort Law and Regulation: Planning and Nuisance' [2011] *Journal of Planning and Environment Law* 986; M Wilde, 'Nuisance Law and Damages in Lieu of an Injunction: Challenging the Orthodoxy of the *Shelfer* Criteria' in SGA Pitel, JW Neyers and E Chamberlain (eds), *Tort Law: Challenging Orthodoxy* (Hart Publishing 2013) 356.

[173] The existing literature generally limits the discussion of constant supervision to the award of mandatory injunctions.

One of the ways in which a risk of constant supervision can arise is if the terms of an injunction do not state precisely what acts the defendant is prohibited from doing. The leading statement of principle is found in *Attorney-General v Punch Ltd*, where Lord Nicholls stated:

> An interlocutory injunction, like any other injunction, must be expressed in terms which are clear and certain. The injunction must define precisely what acts are prohibited. The court must ensure that the language of its order makes plain what is permitted and what is prohibited. This is a well established, soundly-based principle. A person should not be put at risk of being in contempt of court by an ambiguous prohibition, or a prohibition the scope of which is obviously open to dispute.[174]

In accordance with Lord Nicholls' remarks, when awarding prohibitory injunctions, courts cannot simply restrain a defendant from committing the general elements of a tort.[175] For example, it would be unfairly prejudicial and lead to constant supervision for a court to restrain a defendant from committing 'nuisance' or 'unlawful means conspiracy' without specifying the acts that, on the facts of the case, amount to such torts.[176]

Courts are therefore required to state exactly what acts are prohibited by the injunction. For example, defendants have been restrained from: making 'any threat to cause harm' to a defined group of individuals;[177] publishing 'the words complained of or any similar such words as are defamatory to each of the Claimants';[178] and creating noise that exceeded '85dBA$_{\text{Leq}}$ over any [one] minute period … measured at a position midway between the speakers and 1m from the dance floor [inside the defendant's restaurant]'.[179] These examples demonstrate that the terms of an injunction must reflect the scope and nature of the underlying duty that is being enforced by the injunction. They reflect the application of 'the cardinal principle of equity that the remedy must be fashioned to fit the nature of the case and the particular facts'.[180] So, for example, where an injunction is justified by proof of a continuing private nuisance, a court cannot grant an injunction

[174] *Attorney-General v Punch Ltd* (n 100) [35]. See also *Low v Innes* (1864) 4 De GJ & Sm 286, 295–96; *Hackett v Baiss* (1875) LR 20 Eq 494, 499; *Attorney-General v Staffordshire City Council* [1905] 1 Ch 336 (Ch), 342; *Australian Consolidated Press Ltd v Morgan* (1965) 112 CLR 483, 515; *ICI Australia Operations Pty Limited v Trade Practices Commission* (1992) 38 FCR 248, 259; *Optus Networks Pty Ltd v City of Boroondara* [1997] 2 VR 318, 336–37; *O v Rhodes* [2015] UKSC 32, [2016] AC 219 [79]; *Boyd v Ineos Upstream Ltd* [2019] EWCA Civ 515 [34(5)] (quia timet).

[175] Although note that courts do have the power to grant *interim* injunctions that restrain conduct that is lawful: see, eg, *Burris v Azadani* (n 70) 1377; *Cuadrilla Bowland Ltd v Persons Unknown* [2020] EWCA Civ 9 [50] (interim quia timet).

[176] See, eg, *Animal Liberation (Vic) Inc v Gasser* [1991] 1 VR 51, 57; *Jarosz v New South Wales* [2019] NSWSC 692 [65]. There are certainly many older cases that fall foul of this consideration. See, eg, *Hampstead and Suburban Properties v Diomedous* [1969] 1 Ch 248 (Ch), 257–58; *Shoreham-By-Sea UDC v Dolphin Canadian Proteins Ltd* (1972) 71 LGR 261 (QB), 268.

[177] *Albert Court (Westminster) Management Co Ltd v Fetaimia* [2022] EWHC 1657 (QB) annexure (harassment).

[178] *Mirza v Ali* (n 71) [44] (libel).

[179] *White v Lynch* [2011] EWHC 1664 (QB) [106], [112] (private nuisance).

[180] *Warman International Ltd v Dwyer* (1995) 182 CLR 544, 559.

restraining acts that do not amount to a private nuisance as well as the acts that constitute the private nuisance.[181]

Furthermore, the way in which the prohibited acts are expressed must not require the defendant to make a value judgement to determine what conduct could amount to a breach. For example, in *O v Rhodes*,[182] the Court of Appeal granted an interim injunction restraining the defendant from publishing information in a book which gave 'graphic' accounts of sexual abuse suffered by the defendant, on the basis that such a publication amounted to the tort of intentionally inflicting harm as laid down in *Wilkinson v Downton*.[183] On appeal, Baroness Hale and Lord Toulson (with whom Lord Clarke and Lord Wilson agreed) disapproved of the injunction on the basis that '[w]hat is sufficiently "graphic" to fall within the ban is a matter of impression'.[184] The majority intimated that terms that require defendants to make value judgements operate oppressively against a defendant and give rise to a risk of wasteful litigation over compliance.[185]

It follows that if a court is persuaded that it would be impossible for it to articulate sufficiently the acts the defendant is prohibited from doing, this will militate against the grant of injunctive relief. However, persuading a court that it would be impossible adequately to formulate the terms of an injunction is a demanding task. Consider the decision in *Kennaway v Thompson*,[186] the facts of which were outlined in section III.A.ii. At first instance, Mais J refused to grant an injunction against the defendants because, inter alia, he considered that an injunction that restrained them 'from using or permitting the use of the waters in such a way as to be a nuisance … would only lead to further litigation'.[187] It seemed that Mais J did not believe it was possible to stipulate what level of noise caused by the defendants' activities (and at which particular time periods) constituted a nuisance. The Court of Appeal rejected this reasoning and, in an excellent analysis of the facts of the case and the legal principles governing the tort of private nuisance, granted an injunction that restrained 'motor boat racing, water skiing and the use of boats creating a noise of more than 75 decibels on the club's water', on the condition that the club was allowed to host particular racing events each season.[188] What the decision in *Kennaway* demonstrates is that courts cannot refuse to award an injunction where it is possible on the available evidence and the existing law to state precisely what conduct amounts to the wrong that is to be prohibited by the

[181] eg, *Barloworld Coatings Pty Ltd v Australian Liquor, Hospitality and Miscellaneous Workers' Union* (2001) 108 IR 107 [23]; *Frost v Northern Beaches Council* (2022) 110 NSWLR 265 (quia timet).

[182] *O v Rhodes* (n 174).

[183] *Wilkinson v Downton* [1897] 2 QB 57.

[184] *O v Rhodes* (n 174) [79].

[185] The Australian authorities seem to take a different position, see: *Maggbury Pty Ltd v Hafele Australia Pty Ltd* (2001) 210 CLR 181, 220; *Bankstown City Council v Alamdo Holdings Pty Ltd* (2004) 135 LGERA 312 (NSWCA), 331–32.

[186] *Kennaway v Thompson* (n 104). See also: *Microsoft Corporation v Marks (No 1)* (1996) 69 FCR 117, 143; *Kirkpatrick v Kotis* (2004) 62 NSWLR 567 [57]–[58].

[187] *Kennaway v Thompson* (n 104) 91–92.

[188] ibid 94–95.

injunction. It necessarily follows that the constant supervision consideration rarely operates as a reason to refuse injunctive relief. Rather, it is better characterised as a safety check that reminds courts that injunctions must be ordered in sufficiently precise terms.

iv. Human Rights

Pursuant to section 12(1) and (4) of the Human Rights Act ('HRA') 1998, a court considering whether to grant any 'relief' that might affect the exercise of the right to freedom of expression under the European Convention on Human Rights (ECHR or 'the Convention') must have particular regard to that right. Additionally, where the proceedings relate to material that appears to be journalistic, literary or artistic in nature, the court must consider the extent to which the material has become, or is about to become, available to the public, or the extent to which it is, or would be, in the public interest for the material to be published.

Section 12 of the HRA 1998 is therefore relevant to courts considering whether to grant an injunction that may affect a defendant's right to freedom of expression.[189] The relevance of the provision has been raised in cases where the claimant seeks to restrain the defendant from committing libel and slander,[190] harassment,[191] misuse of private information[192] and public nuisance.[193] Importantly, however, the general view seems to be that once a claimant has proved that the defendant is continuing to commit a wrong against him the claimant is 'normally entitled to a permanent injunction to vindicate the right that he has proved that he has'.[194]

Additionally, pursuant to section 6 of the HRA 1998, the other remaining Convention rights will also be relevant to whether an injunction should be granted. Other than the right to freedom of expression (Article 10), and the right to freedom of assembly and association (Article 11), the cases do not indicate that any other Convention right is particularly relevant in respect of final prohibitory or desisting mandatory injunctions. The cases do, however, indicate that Article 8 (the right to respect for private and family life), often weighs in favour of granting a final injunction in respect of defamation, harassment or misuse of private information.[195]

[189] Davies (n 15) [18-021]; Tettenborn (n 26) [28-12]; Oliphant (ed) (n 22) [8.4].

[190] eg, *Grobbelaar* (n 71) [40] (Lord Steyn (in dissent on this point)); *ZAM v CFW* (n 104); *Davies v Carter* (n 4); *Rafique v Association of Community Organisation for Reform Now Ltd* [2022] EWHC 414 (QB); *Unite the Union v Freitas* [2022] EWHC 666 (QB).

[191] eg, *ZAM v CFW* (n 104); *SKA v CRH* (n 74); *AXB v BXA* (n 73); *Rafique* (n 189).

[192] *SKA v CRH* (n 74); *AXB v BXA* (n 73); *Duchess of Sussex* (n 73).

[193] eg, *Birmingham City Council v Afsar* [2019] EWHC 3217 (QB) (where protesting amounted to a public nuisance).

[194] *ZAM v CFW* (n 104) [22]. See also *Kordowski* (n 71) [178]; *Davies v Carter* (n 4) [109]; *Unite v Freitas* (n 189) [22]; Tettenborn (n 26) [28-12].

[195] See, eg, *Oliver v Shaikh* (n 74); *Zahawi* (n 71); *AXB v BXA* (n 73).

B. Claimant-Related Considerations

i. Damages would be an Adequate Remedy

As was explained in chapter 2, courts have traditionally considered that whether a claimant would suffer irreparable harm as a result of a defendant's future wrongdoing is a discretionary factor to consider. The meaning of 'irreparable harm' was that the damage could be described as substantial *and* would not be remedied properly by a pecuniary payment. Importantly, however, as Gummow and Spry have observed, in the late twentieth century, English courts extended the availability of injunctions to protect legal rights by diluting the irreparable harm test.[196] Instead of asking whether the harm is irreparable, courts now favour a test that asks whether it is 'just, in all the circumstances, that a [claimant] should be confined to his remedy in damages?'.[197] Hence, the courts do not require the damage or loss to be substantial but instead focus on the extent to which a pecuniary payment will not remedy the claimant.

It follows that where a court is satisfied that damages would adequately remedy the claimant for the future damage or loss that would be suffered if the tort were permitted to continue, this weighs against the grant of an injunction (the 'adequacy consideration'). Although the existing literature unanimously confirms the relevance of the adequacy consideration,[198] authors often criticise it as 'elusive',[199] and it has been said that there is a 'tendency of the courts to view almost any damage as [being inadequately remedied by a pecuniary payment]'.[200] It seems that the existing literature has therefore given up on identifying the parameters of the adequacy consideration. The problem with the existing analysis is that authors focus on the numerous different cases, across a variety of legal contexts, in which courts have held that damages would be an *inadequate* remedy. As we shall see, the better way to analyse the concept is to consider the small number of cases, specifically in the context of a court determining whether to grant a final injunction, in which courts have accepted that damages would be an adequate remedy.

In the final injunction context, the only cases the author could locate in which courts have accepted that damages would adequately remedy the claimant's future damage or loss concern the infringement of property rights. This finding is consistent with the claim of Burrows that it is only in relation to ongoing or repeated private nuisances and trespasses to land that there has been debate over

[196] Justice William Gummow, 'The Injunction in Aid of Legal Rights – An Australian Perspective' (1993) 56 *Law & Contemporary Problems* 83, 94–96; Spry (n 21) 396.

[197] *Evans Marshall & Co v Bertola SA* [1973] 1 WLR 349 (CA), 379. Approved and applied in *Tullett Prebon (Australia) Pty Ltd v Purcell* [2008] NSWSC 852 [97]; *B v D* [2014] EWCA Civ 229 [32].

[198] See, eg, Oliphant (ed) (n 22) [8-12]; Tettenborn (n 26) [28-08]; Glister and Lee (n 16) [28-017]; Smith (n 113) 304-07; Davies (n 15) [18-034]; Spry (n 21) 396–402.

[199] Burrows (n 24) 472.

[200] Heydon, Leeming and Turner (n 18) [21-040].

whether the presumption should be that prima facie an injunction is available as of course.[201] The relevant cases can be divided into two categories:

1. *Cases concerning minor trespasses to land.* For example, damages have been held to be an adequate remedy for repeated trespasses on a private road,[202] the building of a sewer on a small part of the claimant's land,[203] the building of a bathroom that encroached onto the claimant's land by 1'6"[204] and the building of an extension to a house that encroached onto a wall owned by the claimant.[205]
2. *Cases concerning trivial private nuisances.* Although most cases concern a reduction in the light coming into the claimant's property,[206] damages have also been held to be adequate where a defendant allowed its customers to continually hit golf balls into the claimant's paddocks, which prevented the claimant from selling hay,[207] where a defendant obstructed the claimant's right of way[208] and where a defendant caused excessive noise that interfered with the claimant's enjoyment of his home.[209]

With these cases in mind, four preconditions can be identified that clarify when damages will adequately remedy a claimant's future damage or loss.

First, the right that is being infringed by the defendant must be alienable or relate to an economic interest. This precondition reflects the fact that only economic loss and certain property rights can be adequately replaced with a monetary sum. Clearly, a claimant cannot buy her lost reputation, leg or privacy with a damages award. It necessarily follows that damages will always be an inadequate remedy where a defendant is continuing to commit a tort that is not classified as a property tort or an economic tort. This explains why injunctions in respect of a continuing battery, assault, harassment, libel, slander, malicious falsehood or misuse of private information are restrained by injunction virtually as of right.[210] Indeed, the rights that are protected by these torts are obviously incommensurate with money. In this

[201] Burrows (n 24) 443–44.

[202] *Jaggard v Sawyer* (n 64); *Greenmanor* (n 126). See also *Rashid v Sharif* [2014] EWCA Civ 377.

[203] *Armstrong v Sheppard and Short Ltd* [1959] 2 QB 384 (CA) (implicit ruling).

[204] *Griffiths v Kingsley-Stubbs* [1986] Lexis Citation 1584 (CA). See also *Pettey v Parsons* [1914] 1 Ch 704.

[205] *Seeff v Ho* [2011] EWCA Civ 186; *Jones v Ruth* [2011] EWCA Civ 804.

[206] See, eg, *Kine v Jolly* [1905] 1 Ch 480 (CA); *Price v Hilditch* [1930] 1 Ch 500 (Ch); *Midtown Ltd v City of London Real Property Co Ltd* [2005] EWHC 33 (Ch); *Tamares (Vincent Square) Ltd v Fairpoint Properties (Vincent Square) Ltd* [2006] EWHC 3589 (Ch). See also C Rotherham, 'Remedies for Breaches of Rights to Light: Averting a Tragedy of the Anticommons' in B McFarlane and S Agnew (eds), *Modern Studies in Property Law* (Hart Publishing 2019) 154.

[207] *Goode v Owen* (n 126). See also *Bracewell v Appleby* (n 124) (infringement of easement).

[208] *Jacklin v Chief Constable of West Yorkshire* [2007] EWCA Civ 181; *Lea v Ward* [2017] EWHC 2231 (Ch). See also *AD Astra Property Pty Ltd v David's Ltd* [1998] VSC 59 [35], [44].

[209] *Sampson v Hodson-Pressinger* [1981] 3 All ER 710 (CA). In this case the claimant did not seek an injunction but damages in lieu of an injunction.

[210] See the cases cited in nn 70–74.

sense, property rights are given slightly less protection than other rights protected in tort law.[211]

Second, the future damage or loss must be able to be quantified in advance for the period the defendant wishes to commit the tort (which in some cases may be forever). Notably, none of the cases in which damages were held to be adequate concern nuisances that involve physical interferences, noise[212] or smells that vary on each day. Only in cases where the nuisance will cause the same amount of damage each day in the future (for example, a loss of an amount of light forever) has it been held that damages would adequately remedy the claimant. This is because if the damage varies, it is impossible to calculate the claimant's damages in advance. Indeed, in the seminal case of *Imperial v Broadbent*, Lord Campbell LC stated that the reason why damages were inadequate was because the gas works were damaging the claimant's crops to differing extents on each day.[213] By contrast, trespass-to-land cases generally satisfy this requirement. If the future trespass is for a temporary period then damages can be awarded on a user-fee or mesne profits basis. If the trespass is permanent then damages can be awarded according to the market value for which the right being infringed could be sold. A contentious question that has never been considered in the case law is whether damages could be determined in advance in respect of the continued commission of an economic tort. Without meaning to suggest that it would *never* be possible, it seems unlikely.[214] As was explained in chapter 2, the Chancery reasoned that damages would be an inadequate remedy for continuous copyright and patent infringements because the economic loss that the claimant might suffer in the future is incalculable. The same reasoning has force in the context of the economic torts: could it really be said that a court can determine accurately in advance how much loss a claimant would suffer when the defendant proposes to repeat, for example, the unlawful means tort?

Third, the claimant must not value her right for more than economic reasons. For example, in *Allen v Greenwood*, Goff LJ held that damages were an inadequate remedy for a continued loss of light caused by the defendants' neighbouring fence and caravan, which prevented the claimants from being able to use the greenhouse on their land.[215] Goff LJ's decision reflects Lord Sumner's astute observation in *Leeds Industrial Co-operative Society Ltd v Slack*:

> I doubt … whether it is complete justice to allow the big man, with his big building and his enhanced rateable value and his improvement of the neighbourhood, to have his

[211] This point is elaborated on in ch 7.

[212] The *Sampson* case cited in n 209 is not particularly illuminating, as damages in lieu were specifically sought by the claimant.

[213] *Imperial v Broadbent* (n 45) 610. See also *Wood v Conway* (n 35) 57, 60; *Redland Bricks v Morris* [1970] AC 652 (HL) 667.

[214] cf *Shell UK Oil Products Ltd v Persons Unknown* [2022] EWHC 1215 (QB) [33] (interim injunction restraining unlawful means conspiracy).

[215] *Allen v Greenwood* [1980] Ch 119 (CA) 134. See also *Deakins v Hookings* [1994] 1 EGLR 190 (CC) 195; *Rogers v Humphrey* (n 104) [64].

> way, and to solace the little man for his darkened and stuffy little house by giving him a cheque that he does not ask for.[216]

Indeed, as Dixon and Davies have both observed,[217] it has long been recognised that individuals hold property rights for more than simply economic reasons.

A further point related to this precondition is that it is relevant that there is evidence suggesting that the claimant was willing to accept a monetary payment from the defendant. Courts are motivated to guard against the risk that a claimant may be seeking an injunction to demand an extortionate price from the defendant for the injunction to be discharged. For example, in numerous cases concerning the infringement of rights to light, courts were persuaded to refuse an injunction because, inter alia, the claimant had in previous negotiations with the defendant indicated that he or she would be prepared to accept a monetary sum for the loss of light.[218] Importantly, however, courts do not readily infer that a claimant will act in this way. For example, in *Watson v Croft Promo Sport*,[219] the Court of Appeal held that it was incorrect for the primary judge to reason that because the claimants were prepared to accept monetary compensation up to a certain level of inconvenience caused by the defendant's nuisance, they were also willing to be compensated with money for inconvenience suffered in excess of that level.[220] The courts' hesitation to refuse injunctive relief in these circumstances is for good reason. Even if a claimant does go on to use her injunction to extort money from the defendant, it is likely that the defendant can later seek damages from the claimant for committing the tort of abuse of process.[221] By contrast, if the court incorrectly refuses to grant injunctive relief and instead awards damages in lieu, the defendant will be permitted to continue to infringe the claimant's right forever. There is therefore much less risk of injustice if injunctive relief is granted.

The final precondition for damages to be an adequate remedy is that the defendant must have the means to pay the damages award.[222] Such an award will be meaningless if the defendant does not have assets against which the award can be enforced.

When the above four preconditions are satisfied, this will mean that damages would adequately remedy the claimant's future damage or loss, and this will militate against the grant of an injunction. Importantly, however, it must not be

[216] *Leeds Industrial Co-operative Society Ltd v Slack* (n 63) 872.

[217] M Dixon, 'The Sound of Silence' [2014] *Conveyancer & Property Lawyer* 79, 84; Davies, 'Injunctions in Tort and Contract' (n 135) 128. See also E Peñalver, 'Land Virtues' (2009) 94 *Cornell Law Review* 821.

[218] See, eg, *Isenberg v East House India Estate Co* (1863) 3 De GJ&S 263; *Aynsley v Glover* (1874) LR 18 Eq 544 (interim); *Senior v Pawson* (1866-67) LR 3 Eq 330. See also *Midtown* (n 206).

[219] *Watson v Croft Promo Sport* (n 114). See also *Jordeson v Sutton Southcoates and Drypool Gas Co* [1899] 2 Ch 217 (CA); *Cowper v Laidler* (n 130). In the context of trespass, see *Graham v K D Morris and Sons Pty Ltd* [1974] Qd R 1.

[220] *Watson v Croft Promo Sport* (n 114) [48].

[221] There are good grounds to believe that the claimant will have committed such a tort: see, generally, E Hynard and A Lerch, 'The Tort of Collateral Abuse of Process' (2021) 44 *UNSW Law Journal* 714.

[222] See, eg, *Hodgson v Duce* (1856) 2 Jur (NS) 1014; *Shell UK Oil* (n 214) [34]. See also Davies (n 15) [18-034].

forgotten that the fact that damages would adequately remedy a claimant is only a discretionary *consideration*. Even if damages are adequate, a court still has a discretion to award an injunction. Indeed, courts have granted injunctions even though damages were adequate where the defendant knowingly committed the tort against the claimant,[223] and where no other discretionary considerations were made out.[224] If the above four preconditions are not met, however, it will mean that damages will be an *inadequate* remedy, and this fact will weigh in favour of the grant of an injunction.

ii. Clean Hands

It is well established that a court may refuse equitable relief to a claimant who has unclean hands.[225] Two elements, considered in a multifactorial assessment, must be satisfied for this consideration to come into operation. First, the claimant must have engaged in conduct that was not necessarily unlawful but was 'in some way immoral and deliberate and not trivial'.[226] Second, the misconduct must have an 'immediate and necessary relation to the equity sued for'.[227]

Although there appear to be few cases in which the clean-hands doctrine operated to persuade a court to refuse a final injunction in respect of a continuing tort, an example is *Armstrong v Sheppard and Short Ltd*.[228] There, the defendants sought to build a sewerage system on a small strip of the claimant's land. As a result, they telephoned the claimant and asked for his permission to build the sewer. The claimant was not aware that he owned the land and told the defendants that he had no objection to the construction of the sewer. After the sewer was built and the claimant became aware that he was the owner of the land, the claimant sought an injunction restraining the defendants from discharging effluent through the sewer, on the basis that it amounted to a continuing trespass. In his evidence, however, the claimant lied to the Court by stating that he had never given consent to the defendants to build the sewer and had no knowledge that it was to be built. Thus, although Hargreaves J awarded damages for the past trespass to land, he refused to

[223] See *Goodson v Richardson* (n 108) 224–25; *Harrow LBC v Donohoe* [1995] 1 EGLR 257 (CA), 259; *HKRUK II (CHC) Ltd v Heaney* [2010] EWHC 2245 (Ch) [85]–[86].

[224] See *Jacklin* (n 208) [29], [52].

[225] *Dering v Earl of Winchelsea* (1787) 1 Cox 318, 319; *Royal Bank of Scotland v Highland Financial Partners* [2013] EWCA Civ 328 [158]–[159]. See also: *Black Uhlans Inc v New South Wales Crime Commission* [2002] NSWSC 1060 [160]; Davies (n 15) [18-039]; Burrows (n 24) 487; Bean, Parry and Burns (n 17) [2-05]; Glister and Lee (n 16) [28-047]; Oliphant (ed) (n 22) [8.15]; Smith (n 113) 315; Heydon, Leeming and Turner (n 18) [3-090]; Spry (n 21) 423.

[226] *Fiona Trust & Holding Corp v Privalov* [2008] EWHC 1748 (Comm) [19]. See also *CF Partners (UK) LLP v Barclays Bank Plc* [2014] EWHC 3049 (Ch) [1122]. See also RP Meagher, WMC Gummow and JRF Lehane, *Equity: Doctrines and Remedies* (Butterworths 1975) 67. cf A Burrows, 'Remedial Coherence and Punitive Damages in Equity' in S Degeling and J Edelman (eds), *Equity in Commercial Law* (Thomson Reuters 2005) 386.

[227] *Dering* (n 225) 319; *Grobbelaar* (n 71) [70].

[228] *Armstrong v Sheppard and Short Ltd* (n 203). See also *Grobbelaar* (n 71) (clean-hands consideration not engaged).

grant the injunction (and damages in lieu were not awarded for the future trespass that would continue)[229] on the basis that the claimant had unclean hands. The Court of Appeal upheld this decision.[230]

In the light of the above analysis, it seems as though the clean-hands doctrine is a straightforward discretionary consideration. However, in the case law and existing literature there is little discussion of *why* this consideration should operate to give judges discretion to refuse specifically to enforce legal rights, other than simply for the sake of following precedent, which derives from the fact that the Chancery was a court of 'conscience'. There are two good reasons to question the continued validity of the clean-hands doctrine.

First, the doctrine requires courts to determine whether a claimant's conduct is 'immoral'. Although there are clear-cut cases, such as where the claimant has acted illegally, committed a civil wrong or acted in contempt of court, there are also cases where a claimant has committed no unlawful act and judges are required to assert their *moral* judgement. For example, in *Hubbard v Vosper*, the Court of Appeal overturned Kilner Brown J's decision to grant an interim injunction restraining copyright infringement and breach of confidence because, inter alia, the religious beliefs of the Scientologist claimants, which would have been protected by the injunction, were said to be 'deplorable'.[231] It is well established that courts can determine whether a claimant's conduct is *unconscionable* in the context of enforcing their legal rights.[232] However, unconscionability is judged according to principles that have been developed by the courts over time. The problem with the clean-hands doctrine is that it gives judges the ability to judge a claimant's conduct not according to developed principles, but according to their own personal views on what is 'immoral'. Indeed, in *Hubbard v Vosper*, Megaw LJ did not rely on any principle to determine that the claimants' religious views were deplorable.[233] Administering justice according to law (whether in England and Wales or in another common law jurisdiction) requires courts to apply ascertained legal principles pursuant to 'a standard of reasoning which is not personal to the judges themselves'.[234] Simply because the clean-hands doctrine is an 'equitable' consideration does not mean that courts should be permitted to act outside their judicial function and judge conduct according to their personal beliefs on morality.

[229] In the Court of Appeal, Evershed MR (erroneously) stated at 397–98 that because such damages were not specifically sought by the claimant, Hargreaves J was not required to consider whether they should be awarded.

[230] *Armstrong v Sheppard and Short Ltd* (n 203) 397.

[231] *Hubbard v Vosper* [1972] 2 QB 84 (CA) 101.

[232] See, generally, *Royal Bank of Scotland v Etridge (No 2)* [2002] 2 AC 773 (HL); D Capper, 'Undue Influence and Unconscionability: A Rationalisation' (1998) 114 *LQR* 479.

[233] It is my view that the claimants' conduct in this case was deplorable. The central point, however, is that without guiding principles, such a determination can only be predicated on one's own personal beliefs.

[234] Sir Owen Dixon, 'Concerning Judicial Method' (1956) 29 *Australian Law Journal* 468, 470.

A counter argument that could be made here is that the clean-hands doctrine is necessary to guard against undesirable behaviour that is not technically unlawful. But the problem with this view is that if a court believes that a second-order response is required because of a particular type of *conduct*, the court can develop a principled exception that is predicated on that conduct to enable the court to refuse relief (as has been done where an opportunistic claimant attempts to seek an injunction to extract an extortionate payment from the defendant). There is no need for a 'catch-all' clean-hands doctrine that judges a claimant's morals rather than her conduct.

The second reason why the clean-hands doctrine is problematic relates to a point made by McBride. He has argued that because the clean-hands doctrine does not operate as a defence at common law to defeat a claimant's legal rights,[235] it cannot operate to enable a court to refuse injunctive relief to a claimant whose rights are continuously being infringed by the defendant.[236] However, this is exactly how the doctrine operated in the case of *Armstrong*, discussed above. There, the court refused to grant an injunction to stop the claimant's property right from being invaded because of his unclean hands, and damages were not awarded in lieu of the injunction.[237] This meant that the claimant would be required to bring repeated actions at common law for damages to enforce his property right.[238] The major difficulty with the clean-hands doctrine operating in this way is that, as McBride has explained, it undermines the law's legitimacy.[239] The reason for this is as follows.

If the claimant can still enforce her legal right at law irrespective of her unclean hands (that is, the defences of acquiescence or illegality do not apply) then the courts straightforwardly have a good reason to stop the defendant from continuing to infringe the claimant's right. A doctrine that instead requires the claimant to return to court, day after day or year after year, to claim damages for a wrong that could have been prevented by an injunction, indicates that courts are indifferent to enforcing the legal rights of a particular class of claimants. This is certainly not the mark of a sophisticated legal system. By refusing an injunction *and* damages in lieu, the courts would be giving permission to the defendant to continue to commit his tort against the claimant for so long as he pleases, provided he pays damages after the fact. As McBride has put it, such an outcome 'make[s] the law seem uncaring'.[240] Moreover, if a claimant were required to return to court year

[235] *Hurley v Mustoe (No 2)* [1983] ICR 422 (EAT), 426.

[236] N McBride, 'The Future of Clean Hands' in P Davies, S Douglas and J Goudkamp (eds), *Defences in Equity* (Hart Publishing 2018) 267, 273. See also N Tiverios, 'Preventing the Infinite Regress: Discretion, Bars to Relief and the Structure of Equity' [2023] *CLJ* 1, 7–9.

[237] In *Jaggard v Sawyer* (n 64), Millett LJ stated obiter that 'all equitable defences' apply when considering whether to award damages in lieu: ibid 287.

[238] Oddly, however, in the case itself Lord Evershed MR found that the defendants had lawful justification to commit the trespass because of an oral licence given by the claimant, even though the claimant was not aware that he owned the land.

[239] McBride (n 236) 273, 283, 288.

[240] ibid 283.

after year to pursue a legitimate and fresh tort claim, this would not amount to an abuse of process. However, it would certainly be a waste of judicial resources. Such an outcome is therefore contrary to the courts' overriding aim, when controlling their own processes, to ensure that 'judicial and court resources are appropriately and proportionately used in accordance with the requirements of justice'.[241]

In summary, as a matter of positive law, the clean-hands doctrine can operate as a consideration that militates against the award of injunctive relief. However, its operation to defeat legal rights in this context should be questioned.

iii. Acquiescence and Laches

Acquiescence is a form of estoppel.[242] It is established where a claimant makes a *prior* representation (often implied from conduct) encouraging or allowing the defendant to commit his or her wrong, and the defendant relies on the representation such that it would be dishonest or unconscionable for the claimant to seek to enforce her legal or equitable rights.[243] The test is a 'flexible and very fact-specific' one.[244] So, for example, in *Armstrong v Sheppard and Short Ltd*, even though the claimant gave the defendant permission to build the sewer, acquiescence was not made out because at the time such permission was given the claimant was not aware that he owned the land on which the sewer was to be built.[245] The effect of a finding of acquiescence is that the claimant is estopped from enforcing her rights. In this sense, acquiescence is a *defence*: it will extinguish the defendant's past *and* future liability, as the claimant is estopped from relying on her underlying legal rights to make out the relevant cause of action.[246] It is therefore incorrect to describe acquiescence as a discretionary consideration.

By contrast, laches is a discretionary consideration that can bar the grant of injunctive relief when the claimant has been guilty of unreasonable delay in asserting her rights *after* the defendant has committed his wrong, such that it would be unjust to grant the specific relief in question (whether absolutely or on specific terms).[247] It has been said that delay, in itself, is usually not sufficient to deprive a claimant of her rights.[248] Courts are more willing to consider the claimant's delay in bringing proceedings as a factor that militates against granting injunctive relief

[241] *Jameel v Dow Jones and Co* [2005] EWCA Civ 75 [54]; AAS Zuckerman, *Zuckerman on Civil Procedure: Principles and Practice* (4th edn, Sweet & Maxwell 2021) [11.230].

[242] *Lester v Woodgate* [2010] EWCA Civ 199 [25]; Burrows (n 24) 434, 487–88.

[243] *Shaw v Applegate* [1977] 1 WLR 970 (CA), 978, 978; *Jones v Stones* [1999] 1 WLR 1739 (CA), 1745. See also Oliphant (ed) (n 22) [8.13]; Spry (n 21) 429, 454–60; Davies (n 15) [18-041]; Glister and Lee (n 16) [28-045].

[244] *Lester v Woodgate* (n 242) [39].

[245] *Armstrong v Sheppard and Short Ltd* (n 203) 396.

[246] *Shaw v Applegate* (n 243) 978; *Bulmer v Bollinger* [1977] 2 CMLR 625 (CA), 681.

[247] *Lindsay Petroleum Company v Hurd* (1874) LR 5 PC 221, 239. Approved by the House of Lords in *Fisher v Brooker* [2009] UKHL 41 [64]. See also: Burrows (n 24) 489; Oliphant (ed) (n 22) [8.14]; Spry (n 21) 429, 446; Davies (n 15) [18-041]; Glister and Lee (n 16) [28-043]; Smith (n 113) 384–85.

[248] *Fullwood* (n 59) 179; *Fisher v Brooker* (n 247) [64].

where the delay is relied upon by the defendant to his detriment. For example, in *Senior v Pawson*,[249] seven months after being told by the defendants that they were commencing construction on their neighbouring property, the claimant threatened legal proceedings and later sought a desisting mandatory injunction ordering the defendants to pull down their buildings to their original height. Wood VC reasoned that because the claimant had delayed bringing proceedings, which in turn caused the defendants to incur greater costs on constructing the buildings, injunctive relief should be refused and damages were awarded in lieu.[250] Similar sentiments can be found in in *Wrotham Park Estate Co Ltd v Parkside*,[251] where the fact that the claimants had decided not to apply for an interim injunction and the defendants kept building houses in breach of a negative covenant, was a factor that weighed against the grant of a final injunction.

Taking into account the claimant's delay in bringing proceedings is warranted. Where the delay demonstrates that the claimant could have prevented the defendant from incurring substantial costs when having to comply with the injunction, it is obviously a relevant factor to consider. However, it is important to appreciate that claimants should not be subjected to overbearing standards. There may be good reasons for a claimant not to seek interim relief.[252] Moreover, in some cases, although a claimant will become aware of the defendant's actions that give rise to the claim, there may be no reason for the claimant to believe that the defendant is infringing her rights. For example, in *Smith v Smith*,[253] the claimant's delay in bringing proceedings after becoming aware that the defendant had begun construction work on his property was held to be irrelevant because the claimant had no reason to believe that the work would cause a nuisance. As Jessel MR stated, 'where a man has a right to do a thing, and appears to be doing what he has a right to do, you must not assume that he is going to use his right for an unlawful purpose'.[254] It follows that laches is established only where the claimant's delay can be described as *unreasonable*.

V. Discretionary Considerations Militating in Favour of Relief

Even after a defendant has made out a countervailing discretionary consideration militating against the grant of injunctive relief, the analysis does not stop there. There remains a discretion in the court to award injunctive relief, even though a

[249] *Senior v Pawson* (n 218). In addition to the cases discussed below, see *Attorney-General v Grand Junction Canal Company* [1909] 2 Ch 505 (Ch); *Gafford v Graham* (1999) 77 P & CR 73 (CA).

[250] *Senior v Pawson* (n 218) 335.

[251] *Wrotham Park Estate Co Ltd v Parkside* [1974] 1 WLR 798 (Ch) 810–11.

[252] *Deakins v Hookings* (n 215) 194–95; *Mortimer v Bailey* (n 104) [30].

[253] *Smith v Smith* (n 130).

[254] ibid 503. See also *Mortimer v Bailey* (n 104) [30], [35]–[37].

defendant has made out the countervailing consideration. Moreover, it may be that the claimant can show that there are further reasons why injunctive relief should be granted beyond the fact that a tort is continuing to be committed against her.

There are four discretionary considerations that militate in favour of the grant of injunctive relief: that the defendant knew he was committing a wrong; that damages would be an inadequate remedy; that the claimant would suffer grave damage if an injunction is not awarded; and that the public interest is in favour of the grant of the injunction. Each of these considerations will be analysed below according to whether the consideration can be classified as defendant-related or claimant-related.

A. Defendant-Related Considerations

i. *The Defendant's Knowledge of His Wrongdoing*

In *Winter Garden Theatre (London)* v *Millennium Productions*, Lord Uthwatt observed that '[i]n a court of equity, wrongful acts are no passport to favour'.[255] This statement is particularly relevant when assessing whether it is appropriate to award a final injunction. There are two ways in which a defendant's 'wrongful' acts will mean that such injunctive relief should be awarded.

(a) The Defendant Knowingly or Recklessly Committed a Tort against the Claimant

If a defendant commits a tort with actual knowledge that his conduct will infringe the claimant's rights, or with a reckless disregard for the claimant's rights, this will weigh in favour of granting an injunction *and* the defendant will also be barred from relying on the consideration of undue hardship. Numerous authors point this out,[256] and the cases in which this consideration has been engaged are not wanting.[257] Consider the 1879 decision of *Krehl v Burrell*,[258] where the defendant

[255] *Winter Garden Theatre (London)* v *Millennium Productions* [1948] AC 173 (HL), 203.

[256] D Sawtell, 'Injunctions, Land and the Cynical Breach' (2022) 42 *Legal Studies* 649, 658–60; Burrows (n 24) 464; Heydon, Leeming and Turner (n 18) [21-460]; Oliphant (ed) (n 22) [8.24]; R Sharpe, *Injunctions and Specific Performance* (4th edn, Thomson Reuters 2012) [1.590]–[1.620]; Tettenborn (n 26) [28-18].

[257] In addition to the cases discussed below, see *Smith v Smith* (n 130) 503; *Attorney-General v PYA Quarries Ltd* [1957] 2 QB 169 (CA), 189; *Graham v KD Morris and Sons Pty Ltd* [1974] Qd R 1, 5; *Trenberth* (n 55) 106; *Harrow* (n 223) 259; *Jessica Estates v Lennard* [2007] NSWSC 1434 [58] (breach of covenant); *Charlie Properties Ltd v Risetall Ltd* [2014] 11 WLUK 267 (Ch) [10]; *HKRUK* (n 223) [85]; *Ottercroft Ltd v Scandia Care Ltd* [2016] EWCA Civ 867 [13]–[14]. For cases in which the consideration is discussed favourably in obiter dicta, see *Shelfer* (n 31) 323; *Colls v Home and Colonial Stores Ltd* [1904] AC 179 (HL), 193; *Brickmore v Dimmer* [1903] 1 Ch 158 (CA), 168 (breach of covenant); *Redland* (n 213) 666; *Coventry* (n 6) [121].

[258] (n 130). See also *Woodhouse v Newry Navigation Co* [1898] 1 IR 161 (CA).

began to construct a building on land over which the claimant had a right of way. After the claimant gave notice to the defendant of its right of way, the defendant disregarded him and simply continued with construction. At first instance, Jessel MR awarded a perpetual mandatory injunction ordering the defendant to pull down the completed building. The defendant appealed on the basis that damages should have been awarded in lieu because an injunction 'to pull down the expensive structure which has been erected would be very oppressive'.[259] The Court of Appeal dismissed the appeal. James LJ reasoned:

> The Plaintiff brought his action complaining of the obstruction in due time, but the Defendant went on with the obstruction, relying upon the defence that the Plaintiff had no such right of way as he claimed. Having taken upon himself to do this he must take the consequences.[260]

A similar result was reached in the 1984 decision of *Pugh v Howells*.[261] In that case, the defendants had received a report from their architect that the proposed extension to their house would reduce the amount of light coming into the kitchen of the claimants' neighbouring property. Nevertheless, and despite the claimants' objections, the defendants decided to build the extension. At first instance, Francis J refused to award a mandatory injunction ordering the defendant to pull down the extension. The Court of Appeal allowed the claimants' appeal and granted the mandatory injunction. In the words of Waller LJ:

> [W]hen the defendants have been warned more than once that what they were doing would be resisted by an application to the County Court; and where the defendants, in spite of that warning and in spite of the advice from their own expert which indicated that it would be an interference with the rights of light to the house next door, and in spite of a further letter warning them about continuing, by carrying on and taking a risk, the defendants cannot complain if such risk is one which should not have been taken and results in their being ordered to pull down that which they have put up.[262]

Finally, consider the 1981 decision in *Wakeham v Wood*.[263] In that case, the defendant bought a property with actual knowledge that his title was subject to a restrictive covenant that no building could be erected over a particular height. The defendant then started constructing a building in breach of the restrictive covenant, and ignored the protests of the claimant (the owner of the dominant tenement) and his solicitor. At first instance, Chope J refused to award a mandatory injunction ordering the defendant to pull down the building on the basis that the defendant would suffer undue hardship and awarded damages in lieu. On appeal to the Court of Appeal, the claimant's appeal was allowed and the mandatory injunction was granted. Waller LJ stated 'It no doubt will be oppressive to the defendant if a

[259] ibid 147.
[260] ibid.
[261] *Pugh v Howells* (1984) 48 P&CR 298 (CA).
[262] ibid 304.
[263] *Wakeham v Wood* (1981) 43 P&CR 40 (CA).

mandatory injunction is granted against him, but that is entirely his own fault for proceeding with the construction in breach of the covenant after warning.'[264]

Taking stock of the above cases, the authorities seem to *require* that when a defendant knowingly or recklessly commits a tort against the claimant that is continuing, a court cannot permit the defendant to rely on the consideration of undue hardship. However, there are two important caveats to this proposition.

First, a court is still permitted to take account of any undue hardship that may be suffered by third parties or the public if the public-interest consideration is engaged. This is evident from the decision in *Wrotham Park*.[265] In that case, a developer built a number of houses, knowing that it was in breach of a restrictive covenant restraining it from building on the land unless in accordance with a lay-out plan approved by the claimants. Although the claimants issued proceedings seeking a final mandatory injunction to demolish the buildings shortly after the building work began, they did not seek interim relief, and by the date of the trial the houses had been sold by the developer to third parties (who were in fact joined as defendants). Although the developer had clearly acted in deliberate breach of the claimants' contractual rights, Brightman J still gave consideration to the fact that the houses had become people's homes and that it would be an 'unpardonable waste of much needed houses to direct that they now be pulled down'.[266] This factor was extremely relevant to why injunctive relief was refused and damages were awarded in lieu.

Second, where a defendant knowingly commits a wrong but the claimant unreasonably fails to seek interim injunctive relief despite knowing that she has a genuine claim, the court can still take into account any hardship that would be suffered by the defendant. Consider the decision of the Court of Appeal in *Gafford v Graham*.[267] There, the defendant constructed an indoor horse-riding school on his land, knowing that such a building was in breach of restrictive covenant. Although the claimants objected to the construction of the school, they chose not to seek interim relief. Nourse LJ reasoned that because it was unreasonable for the claimant to decide not to seek interim relief, it was appropriate to take into account the hardship the defendant would suffer if a mandatory injunction was granted.[268] This approach is justified. A claimant who makes an unreasonable decision to not seek interim relief has knowingly taken the risk that the defendant will incur more costs and could suffer undue hardship. As such, even though the defendant knowingly or recklessly committed the tort against the claimant, it is appropriate to allow the defendant to rely on the consideration of undue hardship where he has incurred greater expenditure that the claimant could have prevented.

[264] ibid 45.
[265] *Wrotham Park* (n 251).
[266] ibid 811.
[267] *Gafford v Graham* (n 249). See also *Ketley v Gordon* (1997) 73 P&CR 305 (CA). cf *HKRUK* (n 223) [84]–[85].
[268] *Gafford v Graham* (n 249) 82–84.

(b) The Defendant Tries to 'Steal a March' on the Claimant

If the defendant attempts to dilute the effectiveness of a prohibitory injunction after being made aware that his actions may be infringing the claimant's rights, the courts will have no sympathy. In such circumstances, the courts are prepared to award a *mandatory* injunction that orders the defendant to reverse action taken after he obtained actual knowledge, regardless of the amount of actual damage or loss suffered by the claimant or the hardship that would be suffered by the defendant. So, in *Daniel v Ferguson*,[269] where the defendant doubled his efforts to construct a wall after he was made aware that it would cause a nuisance to the claimant and that the claimant was seeking a prohibitory injunction, an interim mandatory injunction (affirmed on appeal) was granted ordering the defendant to pull down the wall. In *Von Joel v Hornsey*,[270] a similar interim mandatory injunction (affirmed on appeal) was awarded after the defendant purposefully evaded being served with the claimant's writ through which the claimant sought interim prohibitory injunctive relief. This seemingly punitive response of the courts is appropriate. If it were otherwise, defendants would be able to take advantage of their conscious decision to hurry on work so as to evade the effectiveness of prohibitory injunctions.

B. Claimant-Related Considerations

i. Damages would be an Inadequate Remedy

If damages would *not* adequately remedy the claimant, this fact will militate in favour of the grant of an injunction. Where the four preconditions for a finding that damages would be an adequate remedy (as outlined in section IV.B.i) are not satisfied, this will mean that damages would be inadequate.

ii. Grave Damage

If the claimant would suffer grave damage as a result of the defendant's continuing tort, this will generally outweigh any other factors militating against the grant of injunctive relief to such an extent that it would be a 'wholly wrong' exercise of the court's discretion to refuse to grant an injunction. The leading case on this issue (albeit in the context of enforcing a positive covenant) is *Parker v Camden LBC*.[271] In that case, three housing estates were owned by the defendant council, which included sheltered homes for the elderly, the infirm and families with

[269] *Daniel v Ferguson* [1891] 2 Ch 27 (CA), 29–30. See also *Wimbledon Local Board v Croydon Rural Sanitary Authority* (1886) 32 Ch D 421 (CA), 428–29; *Price v Hilditch* (n 206) 509–10.
[270] *Von Joel v Hornsey* [1895] 2 Ch 774 (CA), 776–77.
[271] *Parker v Camden LBC* [1986] Ch 162 (CA).

children. The tenants had signed a lease in which the council undertook to keep in repair the services for space heating and water heating. During a strike by boilermen employed by the council, the boilers on the estates broke down, which deprived the tenants of heating and hot water. Even though the event occurred during the middle of winter, the council refused to engage outside contractors to repair the boilers as the council feared that this would intensify the industrial dispute. Three tenants (in two actions) sought a mandatory (interim) injunction ordering the council to repair the boilers and restore the supply of heating and hot water.[272]

At first instance, both Scott J and Walton J refused to award injunctive relief because the defendant had established that such relief would not be in the public interest, as it would have the effect of aggravating and extending an industrial dispute. On appeal, Donaldson MR, and Browne-Wilkinson and Mustill LJJ, allowed the appeals and granted the mandatory injunctions. Giving the leading judgment, Donaldson MR accepted that there was a risk that the injunctions would extend the industrial dispute and that this would not be in the public interest. However, Donaldson MR intimated that this consideration was outweighed by the risk of grave personal injury to the tenants. He stated:

> We are faced with old people suffering very grave privations – the old and the very young are being exposed to a real risk of damage to health and even a very far from fanciful risk of death. In those circumstances, I would be extremely sorry to conclude that the courts could do nothing for them. … Inconvenience is what we are being asked to weigh against the desperate situation which the evidence shows to be afflicting these old people …[273]

What Donaldson MR's reasoning demonstrates is that where a claimant is at risk of suffering grave damage unless injunctive relief is awarded, this factor (particularly if the damage is personal injury) will almost always outweigh any other discretionary considerations that militate against injunctive relief. This is for good reason. As the case of *Parker v Camden LBC* exemplifies, the graver the risk of damage, the more unreasonable it becomes for the *courts* to sacrifice the common law rights of individuals for the interests of defendants or the public.

iii. The Public Interest

The relevance of public interest cuts both ways. In *Coventry v Lawrence*, Lord Neuberger stated that the public interest may also weigh in favour of the granting of an injunction.[274] Therefore, consistently with what has been stated so far, where

[272] It is important to appreciate here that specific performance was not an available remedy because it can only be awarded as a final, and not an interim, remedy: Burrows (n 24) 401–02.

[273] *Parker v Camden LBC* (n 271) 174.

[274] *Coventry* (n 6) [124].

there is sufficient evidence for a court to be able to determine that it would be in the public's interest to grant an injunction, this should be taken into account.[275]

The most important decision on this issue is *Abingdon Corporation v James*.[276] In that case, the claimant corporation obtained consent to lay a water main in A's land that supplied water to the Abingdon area. The claimant was also granted an easement over A's land to maintain and repair the water main in accordance with the claimant's statutory duties. A subsequently sold part of the land to L, who took the land with notice of the water main and the easement. Without the knowledge of the claimant, L then built two houses directly on top of the water main and sold them to the defendants (without giving the defendants notice of the water main or the easement). After becoming aware of this fact, the claimant brought proceedings for a desisting mandatory injunction ordering the defendants to demolish the houses, on the basis that the defendants were continuing to substantially interfere with the easement. Simonds J granted the injunction (although it was suspended for one year). He reasoned that even though the effect of the order would be to require the defendants' homes to be demolished, 'It would not be right to leave matters as they are with a mere declaration of rights. The claimants have duties the neglect of which might have serious [consequences] for a number of people.'[277]

Although Simonds J did not state that the award of the injunction would cause the defendants undue hardship (remarkably, this was not argued by the defendants), there is no doubt that this was the case. However, it was necessary to weigh this undue hardship against the fact that if the injunction were not granted, the claimant's employees would be unable to access the water main to maintain and repair it, and this could lead to disruption of the entire water supply of Abingdon. The pellucid public interest in awarding the injunction justifiably outweighed the undue hardship that would be suffered by the defendants. What this case demonstrates is that even where it is certain that the defendant would be oppressed by the award of an injunction, where it is clearly in the public interest for the injunction to be granted the court still has a discretion to award injunctive relief.

VI. Suspension of the Injunction

If any discretionary considerations are engaged, a court will decide whether to award an injunction in accordance with the discretion given to it, as outlined in section III. If the court ultimately decides that an injunction should be granted, it also has a discretion to suspend the injunction. The final step in the analysis therefore requires a consideration of the principles governing when it is appropriate for an injunction to be suspended.

[275] See, eg, *NSW Harness Racing Club Ltd v Leichhardt Municipal Council* (1997) 97 LGERA 256, 263 (interlocutory); *CG v Facebook Ireland Ltd* [2015] NIQB 11; *Greenwich RLBC v Ogbuka Housing Ltd* [2015] EWHC 2707 (QB).

[276] *Abingdon Corporation v James* [1940] Ch 287 (Ch).

[277] ibid 299.

Although considerations of hardship and the public interest may not persuade a court to refuse an injunction, they are relevant to whether a court should exercise its discretion to suspend the operation of an injunction and fashion a remedy that achieves more complete justice.[278] As Lord Sumner stated in *Stollmeyer*:

> [C]onsiderations [of hardship] may be relevant to the form of the remedy, especially to the time and opportunities which should be given them, for finding some way out of their difficulty, but they cannot operate to deprive the appellants of their right to have their wrong redressed, if wrong has been done [to] them.[279]

It is appropriate for hardship and the public interest (where it can be determined on the available evidence) to be taken into account at this stage of the analysis, because suspending an injunction does not ultimately expropriate the rights of the claimant. Rather, the technique simply permits the defendant to continue his tortious activities for a limited time, during which he can attempt to change the way he conducts his activities so that they do not infringe the claimant's rights. If that time expires and the defendant is continuing to infringe the claimant's rights, an injunction will be granted and the claimant's rights will prevail.

The onus is on the defendant to persuade the court that it should suspend an injunction. Injunctions are often suspended to give defendants time to take certain steps, so that when the injunction does come into force, the defendant (or the public or a class of third persons) will not suffer any hardship or substantially less hardship than if the injunction had been granted immediately.[280] For example, injunctions restraining public bodies from discharging sewage into rivers have been suspended so that the drainage service can continue to be provided to the public while the defendant is given an opportunity to implement a sewerage system that does not cause a nuisance.[281] Suspension has also been ordered to give the defendant an opportunity to find the best way to proceed,[282] to find alternative accommodation before the injunction required demolition of the defendants' houses,[283] and to permit the defendants to continue with their activities that made excessive noise while the claimants were not occupying their property.[284]

In some of these cases, suspension is granted on the condition that the defendant compensate the claimant for any damage or loss caused by the tortious activity during the period of the suspension.[285] Surprisingly, there is no principle in the

[278] Oliphant (ed) (n 22) [8.9]; Spry (n 21) 417; Davies (n 15) [18-096]; Glister and Lee (n 16) [28-021].

[279] *Stollmeyer* (n 116) 494.

[280] In addition to the cases discussed below, see: *Pennington* (n 122); *Great Central Railway Co v Doncaster Rural Council* (1917) 87 LJ Ch 80; *Frost v King Edward VII Welsh, etc, Association* [1918] 2 Ch 180 (Ch); *Don Brass Foundry Pty Ltd v Stead* (1948) 48 SR (NSW) 482; *Leeman v Montagu* (n 119); *Halsey* (n 130).

[281] See, eg, *Jones v Llanrwst* (n 121); *Haigh* (n 121); *Pride of Derby* (n 40).

[282] For example, in *Reinhardt v Mentasti* (n 117) the injunction was suspended for three months so the defendants could be given the opportunity to find an alternative location to operate a stove in the kitchen of their hotel without having to close the kitchen immediately.

[283] *Abingdon Corporation v James* (n 276).

[284] *Coventry v Lawrence (No 2)* [2014] UKSC 46, [2015] AC 106.

[285] eg, *Pennington* (n 122); *Haigh* (n 121). In *Stollmeyer* (n 116), the defendant undertook to pay damages and suspension was ordered on this basis.

case law dictating when courts should require the defendant to pay such compensation. Courts seem to pick and choose when such a condition should be included. The existing literature is also silent on this issue. This lack of principle is unfortunate. As the effect of the suspension of the injunction is to permit the defendant to inflict more damage or loss to the claimant, it should go without saying that the payment of damages should be an ordinary term of suspension. Indeed, the claimant is entitled as of *right* to such damages.

Suspension of an injunction is an effective balancing technique, as it encourages defendants to invest in ensuring that their activities can continue without infringing the claimant's rights. Suspension therefore often leads to added benefits for the public, particularly in nuisance cases. For example, as Pontin has explained, the courts' decisions to grant but suspend injunctions against local authorities that discharged raw sewage into waterways ultimately led to beneficial investment in modern systems of sewage purification in the nineteenth century.[286]

However, it is important to recognise that courts do not have an unlimited discretion to suspend an injunction so as to enable the defendant to achieve the state of affairs the injunction is designed to prevent.[287] This was decided by the Court of Appeal in *Charrington v Simons & Co Ltd*,[288] although in the context of enforcing a negative covenant. In that case, the defendant knowingly raised a farm track above a certain height in breach of negative covenant, and so the claimant sought a mandatory injunction requiring the defendant to lower the track to its original height. The defendant objected on the basis that it would be required to pay an unspecified (but possibly exorbitant) amount to comply with the injunction. At first instance, Buckley J granted the injunction. However, to reduce the defendant's costs, he suspended the injunction's operation for three years to enable the defendant to carry out other ameliorative works that Buckley J believed would solve the problem without its being necessary to reduce the height of the track. The Court of Appeal allowed the claimant's appeal and discharged the term of the injunction requiring it to be suspended. The Court reasoned:

> In our judgment the judge, in adopting the course which he did, travelled beyond the bounds within which discretion may be judicially exercised; for in effect he sought to force upon a reluctant plaintiff some thing very like a settlement involving operations by the defendant on the plaintiff's land which must lead to greatly increased harm to his business, as a condition or term of his obtaining a mandatory injunction should the works not prove a satisfactory solution.[289]

These remarks indicate that judges do not have an open-ended discretion in which they are free to award any type of injunctive relief, particularly if the terms of the injunction entirely undermine the claimant's rights. It was certainly not appropriate

[286] Pontin (n 141) 45–57.

[287] In addition to the cases discussed below, see the suspension in *Woollerton* (n 55), which was disapproved in *Trenberth* (n 55) 107 and *Jaggard v Sawyer* (n 64) 278.

[288] *Charrington v Simons & Co Ltd* [1971] 1 WLR 598 (CA).

[289] ibid 602–03 (Russell, Cross and Cairns LJJ).

to suspend the injunction for three years so that the defendant could engage in other ameliorative works and allow the track to remain at the same height in breach of the negative covenant. Indeed, as was explained in chapter 2, courts have consistently taken the position that if a defendant is proven to be a wrongdoer and is continuing to commit that same wrong, he must face the consequences of his actions and in most cases suffer the burdens of complying with an injunction. As the Court of Appeal stated in *Mid Bedfordshire District Council v Brown*, in the context of overturning a first-instance decision to suspend an injunction, too readily suspending an injunction 'would be to diminish respect for court orders, to undermine the authority of the court and to subvert the rule of law'.[290]

VII. Conclusion

As a matter of positive law, the analytical process by which courts consider whether to award a prohibitory injunction to prevent *any* future tort (other than a 'tort' that generates a primary liability) is best understood as follows.

Determination 1: The claimant must prove that a tort has been committed against her and that the tort is continuing. If the claimant fails to satisfy her burden of proof, no injunction can be awarded. If the claimant satisfies her burden of proof, the defendant bears the onus of proving that an injunction should *not* be awarded. See Figure 4.1.

Figure 4.1 Determination 1

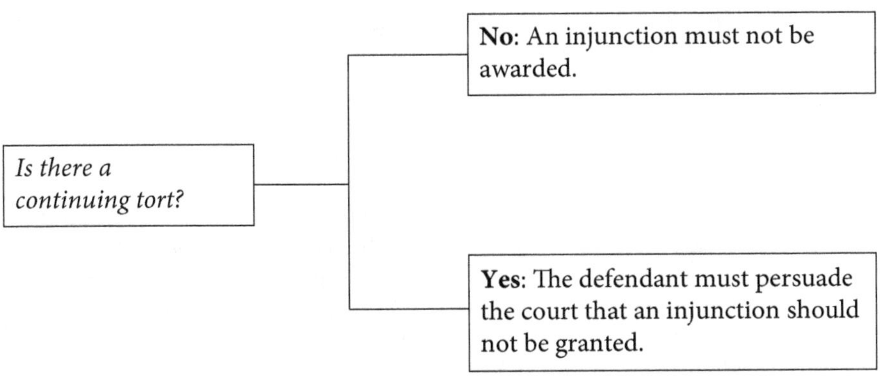

Determination 2: The defendant bears the onus of persuading the court that an injunction should not be awarded. He must therefore prove that a countervailing discretionary consideration has been engaged. If the defendant fails to engage such a consideration, the court *must* award injunctive relief. If the defendant engages

[290] *Mid Bedfordshire District Council v Brown* [2004] EWCA Civ 1709, [27]. See also Spry (n 21) 417.

a countervailing consideration, the court must then determine whether a discretionary consideration that militates in favour of relief has been engaged by the claimant. See Figure 4.2.

Figure 4.2 Determination 2

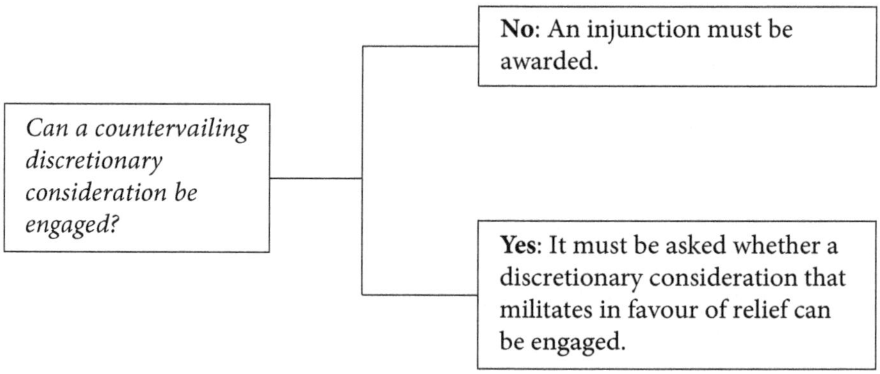

Determination 3: The claimant *may* prove that a discretionary consideration is engaged that militates in favour of relief. If the claimant fails to engage such a consideration, the court must decide whether to award an injunction by weighing the fact of the continuing tort against the countervailing consideration engaged by the defendant. If the claimant engages a consideration in favour of relief, the court must decide whether to award an injunction by weighing the fact of the continuing tort and the consideration in favour of relief, against the countervailing consideration engaged by the defendant. See Figure 4.3.

Figure 4.3 Determination 3

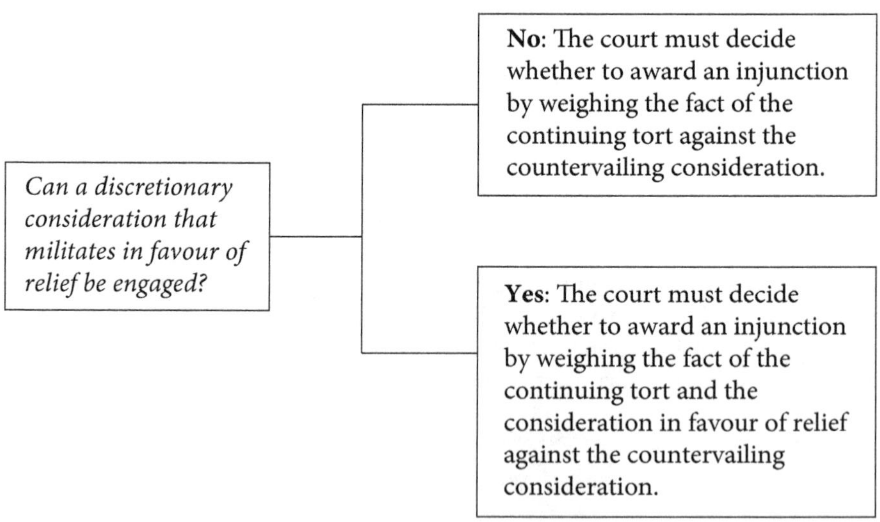

Determination 4: Finally, if the court decides to grant injunctive relief, it has a limited discretion to suspend the operation of the injunction for a specific time period, provided the defendant indemnifies the claimant for any damage or loss suffered by the defendant's continued wrongdoing during the period of the suspension.

5

Desisting and Restorative Mandatory Injunctions

I. Introduction

It was argued in chapter 3 that the existing literature has overlooked the fact that there are two different types of mandatory injunction that are granted in tort law: first, the desisting mandatory injunction, which compels the defendant to do a positive act to *stop* a tort from continuing to be committed; and, second, the restorative mandatory injunction, which compels the defendant to do a positive act to *remedy* a completed tort. For example, in some cases, defendants have been ordered by a desisting mandatory injunction to take action to remove pipes that were laid in the claimant's land without permission,[1] delete websites that were defamatory of the claimant[2] and delete a Facebook group in which the claimant's personal information was being misused.[3] In other cases, defendants have been ordered by a restorative mandatory injunction to delete a video they had posted on YouTube after trespassing on the claimant's land,[4] transfer title to land back to a third party who had been induced to breach their contract with the claimant by the defendant,[5] and immediately surrender a sub-lease that had been obtained by inducing a third party to breach its lease with the claimant.[6]

This chapter offers the first comprehensive account of the positive law governing when desisting and restorative mandatory injunctions can be awarded to restrain or remedy torts. The chapter is divided into two main sections. Section II examines the necessary conditions that must be proved by a claimant to be awarded a desisting mandatory injunction to restrain a future tort, as well as the discretionary considerations that are specifically relevant to whether such an injunction should be granted. Section III examines the necessary conditions that must be met before a restorative mandatory injunction will be granted to remedy a tort, as well as the discretionary considerations relevant to whether such an injunction should be granted. The chapter concludes by clarifying the critical differences between

[1] *Goodson v Richardson* (1873–74) LR 9 Ch App 221.
[2] *Brett Wilson LLP v Persons Unknown* [2015] EWHC 2628 (QB) [34].
[3] *CG v Facebook Ireland Ltd* [2015] NIQB 11.
[4] *Ansco Arena v Law* [2019] EWHC 835 (QB) (interim).
[5] *Esso Petroleum Co Ltd v Kingswood Motors (Addlestone) Ltd* [1974] QB 142 (interim).
[6] *Hemingway Securities Ltd v Dunraven Ltd* [1995] 1 EGLR 61 (Ch) (interim).

the principles governing the award of desisting and restorative mandatory injunctions in tort law.

For the avoidance of doubt, the cases analysed in this chapter are those in which courts have expressly recognised that the claimant seeks a mandatory injunction or an injunction that has mandatory effect. As the courts have not explicitly labelled mandatory injunctions as desisting or restorative, the author has categorised the cases according to the definitions of the two types of injunction given in chapter 3.

II. Desisting Mandatory Injunctions

The leading authority on the general principles governing the award of desisting mandatory injunctions in England and Wales is *Redland Bricks v Morris*.[7] In that case, the defendants conducted a brickmaking business on a property in Swanwick. The claimants owned the neighbouring piece of land, which they used to carry on a strawberry farm. After the defendants had quarried down to considerable depths to extract clay from their property, this withdrew the natural support from the claimants' land and caused the land to subside. There was also a significant risk that further subsidence would occur. In the County Court, Talbot J awarded the claimants damages for the property damage caused to their land by the subsidence, and a mandatory injunction ordering the defendants to take all necessary steps to restore the support to the claimants' land to prevent a future nuisance. This decision was affirmed by the Court of Appeal. On appeal to the House of Lords, their Lordships discharged the mandatory injunction on the basis that its terms would give rise to an unacceptable risk of constant supervision.

In his leading speech, Lord Upjohn conceptualised the mandatory injunction in the case as being quia timet. His discussion of the authorities was therefore, in some respects, limited to principles governing the award of mandatory quia timet injunctions. However, Lord Upjohn also laid down three general principles that were said to guide the exercise of a court's discretion when deciding whether to award a (desisting) mandatory injunction more generally.[8] In summary, they were as follows. First, the claimant must show 'a very strong probability upon the facts that grave damage will accrue to him in the future'. Second, damages must 'not be a sufficient or adequate remedy if such damage does happen'. And third, if mandatory injunctive relief is appropriate, 'the court must be careful to see that the defendant knows exactly in fact what he has to do'.

It follows from the way in which these three principles were expressed that the first two principles are necessary conditions, as they *must* be met for mandatory injunctive relief to be awarded, while the third principle is a discretionary consideration that need be considered by the court only when deciding whether

[7] *Redland Bricks v Morris* [1970] AC 652 (HL).
[8] ibid 665–66.

it *should* award such an injunction in the particular circumstances of the case. Lord Upjohn's approach therefore reflects the analytical process undertaken by the Chancery when it awarded injunctions in the eighteenth and nineteenth centuries, as found in chapter 2: the claimant must prove certain conditions to satisfy the court that it can award injunctive relief, following which the court has a discretion to refuse relief if a countervailing consideration is established by the defendant.

Consistently with this approach, this section is split into five main subsections. Section II.A focuses on the conditions that are necessary before it can be said that a court has jurisdiction to award a desisting mandatory injunction. Section II.B examines the nature and limits of the discretion that courts exercise when determining whether to award a desisting mandatory injunction. Sections II.C and II.D examine the discretionary considerations that are said to operate differently when employed by the courts to determine whether a mandatory injunction should be awarded. And section II.E clarifies the analytical process by which courts consider whether to award a desisting mandatory injunction to prevent a future tort.

A. The Necessary Conditions

Lord Upjohn held in *Redland Bricks* that to be awarded a mandatory injunction, a claimant must establish that she is suffering grave damage as a result of the defendant's tort and that damages would be an inadequate remedy. With respect, it is argued below that both statements of principle are inconsistent with prior authority and are not correct statements of the positive law.

i. Grave Damage?

According to Lord Upjohn in *Redland Bricks*, the first necessary condition that a claimant must prove is a 'very strong probability upon the facts that grave damage will accrue to him in the future' (the 'grave damage requirement').[9] There seem to be two reasons why Lord Upjohn believed that proof of grave damage was a necessary condition for mandatory injunctive relief. The first was that this was stated in the nineteenth-century Court of Appeal decision of *Durell v Pritchard*,[10] which was cited by Lord Upjohn immediately before he set out his three general principles. In *Durell*, the Court of Appeal upheld the decision of the Master of the Rolls refusing to grant a mandatory injunction requiring the defendant to pull down a building that was substantially interfering with the claimants' light. Turner LJ (with whom Knight Bruce LJ agreed) reasoned that although the defendants had committed a nuisance, the claimants had not suffered 'extreme, or at all events very serious, damage', which was said to be a condition of the award of a

[9] ibid 665.
[10] *Durell v Pritchard* (1865–66) LR 1 Ch App 244.

mandatory injunction.[11] Second, as the facts of *Redland Bricks* involved a slippage of land, when Lord Upjohn laid down the grave harm requirement he presumably had in mind the cases in which mandatory injunctions were granted to remedy nuisances that were causing serious damage to property[12] or pollution.[13] Indeed, according to the reported version of the decision, these were the only kinds of cases that were brought to the House of Lords' attention.[14]

The existing literature is split over whether the grave-harm requirement is a correct statement of the positive law. On the one hand, Tettenborn, and Oliphant adopt Lord Upjohn's statement uncritically.[15] On the other hand, Heydon, Leeming and Turner, Glister and Lee, and Spry are of the view that the grave-harm requirement is mistaken because, to quote Heydon, Leeming and Turner, 'mandatory injunctions still lie to compel defendants to remove trespassory hoardings, although no question of grave damage to the claimant could arise'.[16]

The latter view is to be preferred. However, a further reason why the grave-damage requirement does not accurately represent the positive law is that it is inconsistent with prior authorities that Lord Upjohn could not have intended to overrule.

Although Lord Upjohn considered the cases mentioned above, the list of cases cited to the House of Lords in the law report indicates that there were two critical components of the pre-existing case law to which the House of Lords was not referred. These were an obiter dictum of Lord Macnaghten in the 1904 decision of the House of Lords in *Colls v Home & Colonial Stores Ltd*,[17] in which his Lordship stated that mandatory injunctions could be awarded where there was a continuing infringement of the claimant's rights, and the numerous cases upon which Lord Macnaghten's dictum was based.

In *Colls*, the defendant proposed to construct a building opposite office premises that were leased by the claimants. The claimants alleged that the defendant's building already had interfered, and would further substantially interfere, with the natural light that came into their premises, and sought a prohibitory injunction to restrain the defendant from building any further and a mandatory injunction ordering the defendant to pull down what had already been built. The primary question for the House of Lords was whether the defendant had committed a

[11] ibid 250–51.

[12] eg, *Attorney-General v Roe* [1915] 1 Ch 235 (Ch); *Kennard v Cory Bros & Co Ltd (No 2)* [1922] 1 Ch 1 (CA).

[13] eg, *Pride of Derby and Derbyshire Angling Association Ltd v British Celanese Ltd* [1953] Ch 149 (CA).

[14] *Redland* (n 7) 653.

[15] A Tettenborn, 'Injunctions' in M Jones and A Dugdale (eds), *Clerk & Lindsell on Torts* (23rd edn, Sweet & Maxwell 2020) [28-15]; K Oliphant (ed), *The Law of Tort* (3rd edn, LexisNexis 2015) [8.22].

[16] JD Heydon, MJ Leeming and PG Turner, *Meagher, Gummow & Lehane's Equity: Doctrines & Remedies* (5th edn, LexisNexis 2015) [21-465]. See also J Glister and J Lee, *Hanbury on Modern Equity* (22nd edn, Sweet & Maxwell 2021) [28-109]; I Spry, *Equitable Remedies* (9th edn, Thomson Reuters 2014) 567–68.

[17] *Colls v Home & Colonial Stores Ltd* [1904] AC 179 (HL).

nuisance, which was answered in the negative. However, Lord Macnaghten went on to provide considered obiter remarks on when it was appropriate to award a mandatory injunction to remedy a continuing nuisance caused by a reduction of light. He stated:

> It has been said that an injunction ought to be granted [only] when *substantial damages* would be given at law. I have some difficulty in following out this rule ... *the recovery of damages, whatever the amount may be, indicates a violation of right, and in former times, unless there were something special in the case, would have entitled the plaintiff as of course to an injunction in equity.* I rather doubt whether the amount of the damages which may be supposed to be recoverable at law affords a satisfactory test.[18]

Lord Macnaghten's remarks were in response to a suggestion in the earlier case law that a mandatory injunction requiring a defendant to pull down a building could be granted only where the claimant was entitled to 'substantial damages',[19] and hence where the nuisance had caused substantial damage or loss. Such a rule is akin to a grave-damage requirement. And yet Lord Macnaghten casts doubt on it, indicating to the contrary that a mandatory injunction is available as of course where there is a '[continuing] violation of right'.

As Lord Macnaghten's remarks were obiter, they were not strictly binding on the House of Lords in *Redland Bricks*. Therefore, it could be said that the grave-damage requirement is still in accordance with prior authority. However, the difficulty with this view is that it overlooks the fact that Lord Macnaghten's remarks were supported by a body of decisions that were not discussed by Lord Upjohn in his speech in *Redland Bricks* and which he cannot have meant to overrule. There are two relevant categories of case.

The first category is those cases in which mandatory injunctions were granted to stop the defendant from continuing to commit a trespass to land that was not necessarily causing the claimant any substantial damage.[20] For example, take the 1873 case of *Goodson v Richardson*.[21] After the defendant had committed a trespass to land by laying down water pipes in the claimant's land, Jessel MR granted a mandatory injunction ordering the defendant to remove the pipes, even though, as the defendant pointed out, the pipes were not causing the claimant any damage. On appeal, the Court of Appeal dismissed the defendant's appeal and affirmed the injunction. Lord Selborne LC stated 'it is enough to say that ... no interference of this kind can lawfully take place without [the claimant's] consent'.[22] A similar view

[18] ibid 192–93 (emphasis added).

[19] See *Aynsley v Glover* (1874) LR 18 Eq 544, 551–53.

[20] In addition to the cases discussed below, see also: *Williamson v Friend* (1901) 1 SR (NSW) Eq 23; *Westminster Corp v London & North Western Railway Co* [1902] 1 Ch 269 (Ch); *Andrews v Abertillery Urban District Council* [1911] 2 Ch 398 (CA); *Schweder v Worthing Gas Light & Coke Co (No 1)* [1912] 1 Ch 83 (Ch).

[21] *Goodson v Richardson* (n 1).

[22] ibid 224.

was taken in the later and oft-cited decision of *Kelsen v Imperial Tobacco Co.*[23] In that case, although he accepted that the 'injury to the claimant's legal rights … is small', McNair J granted a mandatory injunction that ordered the defendant to remove an advertising board that trespassed into the claimant's airspace.[24]

The second category of case is those decisions in which mandatory injunctions were granted to remedy continuing nuisances even though the damage being caused to the claimant was not 'grave' or 'very serious'. For example, mandatory injunctions have been awarded where a defendant has tried to steal a march on the claimant by constructing a building quickly to avoid having to comply with a prohibitory injunction.[25] In these cases, the injunctions were granted regardless of the extent of the damage said to have been caused by the defendant's conduct. In *Daniel v Ferguson*,[26] after the claimant served the defendant with a notice of motion seeking a prohibitory injunction, the defendant instructed a number of additional workmen to work through the night and construct a 39-foot wall so as to undermine the effectiveness of any future prohibitory injunction. The Court of Appeal affirmed the decision of Stirling J granting an interim injunction ordering the defendant to demolish the entirety of the wall (regardless of the height at which the wall would have caused a nuisance). As Lindley LJ explained, '[i]t is right that buildings thus run up should be pulled down at once, without regard to what the result of the trial may be'.[27]

In *Redland Bricks*, neither of the above two categories of case was brought to the attention of the House of Lords. The result is that Lord Upjohn's grave-damage requirement is not only inconsistent with a considered dictum of a member of the House of Lords, but it is also impossible to reconcile with a body of case law that Lord Upjohn could not have intended to overrule. Thus, with respect, the grave-damage requirement set down by his Lordship is not a correct statement of law.

As a final point, it should be noted that the foregoing conclusion is further supported by the fact that since *Redland Bricks* was decided, the lower courts have seemingly ignored the grave-harm requirement and awarded mandatory injunctions in circumstances where the damage that was being suffered by the claimant was certainly not grave. Such cases are not wanting.[28] In *Pugh v Howells*,[29] for example, the Court of Appeal allowed an appeal and awarded a mandatory injunction that ordered the defendant to pull down a building extension made

[23] *Kelsen v Imperial Tobacco Co* [1957] 2 QB 334 (QB). In Australia, see *Lawlor v Johnston* [1905] VLR 714; *LJP Investments Pty Ltd v Howard Chia Investments Pty Ltd* (1989) 24 NSWLR 490; *Motor Group Australia Pty Ltd v Owners Corporation Strata Plan 64622* [2004] NSWSC 633; *Centrepoint Group Pty Ltd v Dewsbery* [2004] TASSC 64.

[24] *Kelsen* (n 23) 346–47.

[25] In addition to the case discussed below, see *Von Joel v Hornsey* [1895] 2 Ch 774 (CA).

[26] *Daniel v Ferguson* [1891] 2 Ch 27 (CA).

[27] ibid 30.

[28] In addition to the cases discussed below, see *John Trenberth Ltd v National Westminster Bank Ltd* (1980) 39 P&CR 104 (Ch) (scaffolding not causing any damage); *Nelson v Nicholson* [2000] 12 WLUK 10 (CA) (hedge not causing any damage).

[29] *Pugh v Howells* (1984) 48 P & CR 298 (CA).

to its house because it interfered with light coming into only two windows of the claimant's house. Furthermore, in *Jones v Stones*,[30] the Court of Appeal allowed an appeal and awarded a mandatory injunction that ordered the defendant to remove flowerpots placed on, and an oil tank supported by, a wall owned by the claimants. This was so even though the flowerpots and the oil tank were not causing any property damage to the claimants. In these cases, no attention was paid to the decision in *Redland Bricks*.

ii. Must Damages be Inadequate?

The second necessary condition laid down by Lord Upjohn is that damages (that is, a monetary award) must 'not be a sufficient or adequate remedy if such [grave] damage does happen'.[31] Immediately after stating this, Lord Upjohn explained that the inadequacy requirement 'is only the application of a general principle of equity'.[32] He seems to be referring here to the oft-cited (but, as we saw in chapter 4, problematic) dictum of Lindley LJ in *London and Blackwell Ry v Cross* that '[t]he very first principle of injunction law is that prima facie you do not obtain injunctions to restrain actionable wrongs, for which damages are the proper remedy'.[33]

The existing literature is not in agreement over whether the inadequacy requirement is a correct statement of the positive law. Some of the leading texts adopt it as a valid statement.[34] However, Spry, and McBride and Bagshaw are of the view that the question of whether damages are an inadequate remedy is a discretionary consideration to be taken into account rather than a necessary requirement that must be proved by the claimant.[35] Although McBride and Bagshaw do not give reasons for this, Spry posits that regardless of whether a prohibitory or a mandatory injunction is sought, 'it is well established that the court does not refuse to consider whether it should exercise its discretion merely because the injury in question is minor or because as a matter of calculation the amount of damages can be readily ascertained'.[36]

The view of Spry, and McBride and Bagshaw should be accepted. It was explained in chapter 3 that desisting mandatory injunctions and prohibitory injunctions are identical as a matter of substance: both types of injunction operate to stop a defendant from continuing to commit a tort. It follows that the reasons

[30] *Jones v Stones* [1999] 1 WLR 1739 (CA). See also *Nelson v Nicholson* [2000] 12 WLUK 10 (CA).

[31] *Redland Bricks* (n 7) 665.

[32] ibid.

[33] *London and Blackwell Ry v Cross* (1886) 31 Ch D 354 (CA) 369.

[34] Tettenborn (n 15) [28-16]; Oliphant (ed) (n 15) [8.23]; P Davies, 'Injunctions' in J McGhee and S Elliott (eds), *Snell's Equity* (34th edn, Sweet & Maxwell 2021) [18-033]–[18-034]. Heydon, Leeming and Turner treat the principle as a requirement for injunctive relief at one part of their text, but as a discretionary consideration at another: (n 16) [21-040], [21-465].

[35] Spry (n 16) 562–63; N McBride and R Bagshaw, *Tort Law* (6th edn, Pearson Education 2018) 803.

[36] Spry (n 16) 562.

that were given in chapter 4 explaining why the inadequacy requirement is an incorrect statement of principle, apply equally here. Furthermore, it has been recognised implicitly in the case law that a claimant is not required to prove that damages would be an inadequate remedy before a court can award a desisting mandatory injunction. Two cases can be highlighted.

First, in *Shelfer v City of London Electric Lighting Co*, before laying down his 'working rule' governing when it was appropriate to award damages in lieu of an injunction, AL Smith LJ stated that it was the defendant's continuing nuisance that gave the court jurisdiction to award an injunction.[37] Importantly, however, he went on to state that his working rule applied irrespective of 'whether the case be for a *mandatory* injunction or to restrain a continuing nuisance'.[38] AL Smith LJ's reasoning therefore indicates that he assumed that it was only *after* a claimant had proved that he was prima facie entitled to a mandatory injunction that it was necessary for a court to ask whether damages would be an adequate remedy.

The second noteworthy decision is that of *Pride of Derby*.[39] As we have seen (in chapter 4), in that case Evershed MR stated that it was 'well settled that if A proves that his proprietary rights are being wrongfully interfered with by B, and that B intends to continue his wrong, then A is prima facie entitled to an injunction'. Lord Evershed MR also indicated that the fact that damages would be an adequate remedy is only a discretionary consideration.[40] It is important to recognise that Evershed MR made these statements after he had accepted that the injunction sought by the claimants against the second defendant was 'mandatory in substance'.[41] His reasoning therefore indicates that he did not believe that damages must be shown to be inadequate before a mandatory injunction ordering a defendant to stop a continuing wrong could be awarded.

When the considerations outlined in chapter 4, along with *Shelfer* and *Pride of Derby*, are borne in mind, there is no doubt that Lord Upjohn's inadequacy requirement is contrary to the long-established principle that a continuing wrong (in itself) gives rise to jurisdiction to award final injunctive relief. With respect, Lord Upjohn's inadequacy requirement is therefore not a correct statement of the positive law.

iii. *The Tort must be Continuing*

The first necessary condition for the award of a *desisting* mandatory injunction is that the claimant must prove that the defendant has committed a tort against her that is continuing. As was explained in chapter 3, the word 'continuing' has two meanings in this context.

[37] *Shelfer v City of London Electric Lighting Co* [1895] 1 Ch 287 (CA) 319.
[38] ibid 322 (emphasis added).
[39] *Pride of Derby* (n 13).
[40] ibid 181.
[41] ibid 162.

First, it means that the tort is ongoing in the sense that it is occurring day after day. There are numerous examples of this in the case law. Consider where: the defendant's pipes remain in the claimant's land;[42] roots that emanate from trees on the defendant's land are continuing to interfere with the plaintiff's land;[43] the defendant's building is interfering with the amount of natural light coming onto the claimant's neighbouring property;[44] the sewerage system operated by the defendant is discharging effluent into a river;[45] the defendant's building has been constructed on part of the claimant's land;[46] and where the defendant created and refuses to delete a Facebook group in which he revealed the claimant's personal information.[47] In all these cases, the tort is continuing each day, including at the time the claimant is before the court seeking desisting mandatory injunctive relief.

The second meaning of the word 'continuing' is that a tort is recurring (that is, it is being committed repeatedly but not on a daily basis). So, if the claimant can prove that the defendant has previously committed a tort against her and that there is a real and imminent risk that the same tort will be committed against the claimant in the future, this will also suffice. For example, it was explained in chapter 3 that in *Redland Bricks* the defendants had caused the claimants' land to subside (which amounted to a private nuisance) and that there was a real risk that further subsidence would occur. Thus, the desisting mandatory injunction awarded by the County Court (and affirmed by the Court of Appeal but discharged by the House of Lords) was granted to stop the nuisance from being repeated.

Irrespective of whether a tort can be described as ongoing or recurring, what the claimant must prove is that the defendant has previously committed a tort against her and that there is a real and imminent risk that the same tort (that is, all of its elements) will be committed in the future. Accordingly, like the law governing the grant of a prohibitory injunction to restrain a future tort, the effect of the above analysis is that the necessary conditions for the award of desisting mandatory injunctive relief do not change depending on the tort sought to be restrained (except, as was explained in chapter 4, if the 'tort' generates a primary liability). Although, for the most part, desisting mandatory injunctions have been granted to enforce a property right, there is nothing in the reasoning of the cases to

[42] *Goodson v Richardson* (n 1). See also the cases cited in n 20 and *Bockenfield Aerodrome Ltd v Clarehugh* [2021] EWHC 848 (Ch) [157].

[43] *Morgan v Khyatt* [1964] 1 WLR 475 (PC); *Malliate v Sharpe* [2001] NSWSC 1057; *Michos v Council of the City of Botany Bay* [2012] NSWSC 625.

[44] See, eg, *Staight v Burn* (1869–70) LR 5 Ch App 163; *Smith v Smith* (1875) LR 20 Eq 500; *Daniel v Ferguson* [1891] 2 Ch 27 (CA); *Allen v Greenwood* [1980] Ch 119 (CA); *Pugh v Howells* (1984) 48 P&CR 298 (CA); *Regan v Paul Properties Ltd* [2006] EWCA Civ 1391.

[45] *Pride of Derby* (n 13). See also *Stollmeyer v Trinidad Lake Petroleum Co Ltd* [1918] AC 485 (PC).

[46] *Harrow LBC v Donohoe* [1995] 1 EGLR 257 (CA).

[47] *CG* (n 3).

suggest that such relief is limited to the protection of property rights.[48] It is simply because the torts of nuisance and trespass to land are often the types of wrongs that are continued by defendants that desisting mandatory injunctions are frequently granted to stop these torts. Indeed, the torts of inducing a breach of contract,[49] unlawful means conspiracy,[50] libel,[51] passing off,[52] misuse of private information[53] and breach of statutory duty[54] have also been restrained by a desisting mandatory injunction.

To prove the point further, consider a hypothetical scenario where a defendant prison authority refuses to remove a monitor from the claimant's ankle after he has finished a period of home detention. Although there is some debate in the case law over whether a battery can be committed by omission,[55] presume that a court holds that the defendant has committed a battery by failing to remove the monitor. That battery will continue until the monitor is removed by the defendant. There is clearly no basis whatsoever to assert that a desisting mandatory injunction ordering the defendant to remove the ankle monitor should be refused simply because the claimant is seeking to stop a battery and protect his personal, rather than proprietary, right.

iv. It must be Necessary and Possible for the Defendant to do a Positive Act to Stop His Continuing Tort

Just because a claimant can prove that the defendant is continuing to commit a tort against her does not mean that she is entitled to a desisting mandatory injunction. For example, a desisting mandatory injunction will not be granted to a claimant who has proved that a defendant is trespassing repeatedly on her land by continuously and intentionally landing hot air balloons on the claimant's property without permission. The natural and proper remedy in this case is a prohibitory injunction. Accordingly, to obtain a desisting mandatory injunction the claimant must also

[48] In *Pride of Derby* (n 13), Evershed MR refers specifically to 'proprietary rights'. However, he does not suggest that the principle he laid down was confined to such rights. It seems he simply made reference to property rights because they were what the claimants were seeking to enforce by the injunctions.

[49] In Australia, see *Woolley v Dunford* (1972) 3 SASR 243.

[50] eg, *Acrow (Automation) Ltd v Rex Chainbelt Inc* [1971] 1 WLR 1676 (CA) (interim).

[51] eg, *Smith v Unknown Defendants* [2016] EWHC 1775 (QB); *Brett Wilson* (n 2) [34]; *Hayden v Duckworth* [2020] EWHC 1033 (QB) [6] (on the presumption that every day defamatory material is permitted to remain on a website may give rise to a separate cause of action: see *Sellman v Slater* [2017] 2 NZLR 218 [36]–[40]). Interestingly, it has been held that a prohibitory injunction restraining further defamatory publication compels a defendant to remove defamatory material that has already been published on websites or social media: *Pirtek (UK) Ltd v Jackson* [2017] EWHC 2834 (QB) [65]. In Australia, see *Al Muderis v Duncan (No 3)* [2017] NSWSC 726; *Doe v Dowling* [2019] NSWSC 1222.

[52] eg, *Fletcher Challenge Ltd v Fletcher Challenge Pty Ltd* [1981] NSWLR 196 (interlocutory); *Derrimut Health and Fitness Pty Ltd v Revival 24:7 Gym Pty Ltd* [2019] FCA 1988 (interlocutory).

[53] eg, *CG* (n 3) [105].

[54] In Australia, see *Thoo v The Owners Strata Plan No 50276 (No 2)* [2012] NSWSC 1313 (although overturned on appeal on the basis that there had been no breach of statutory duty).

[55] See *Iqbal v Prison Officers Association* [2009] EWCA Civ 1312.

persuade the court that it is necessary and possible for the defendant to do a positive act to stop his tort from continuing.

In the cases where desisting mandatory injunctions have been granted, this element is not usually discussed.[56] In the courts' reasoning, it went without saying that the defendants were required to do a positive act to stop their torts from continuing, which is why the claimant sought a desisting mandatory injunction in the first place. Where there are different acts that a defendant could undertake to stop his tort from continuing, the defendant will usually retain the choice as to which act he would like to undertake.[57] However, as explained in respect of the constant supervision consideration in section II.C.ii, courts will favour the course of conduct that is most consistent with the principle that the consequences (financial or otherwise) a defendant would suffer as a result of doing the act(s) must be reasonably proportionate to the benefits of the injunction to the claimant in the light of the threatened, continuing or completed wrong.

This element is therefore not a particularly contentious one. However, there is one point in respect of this element that seems to be misunderstood in the existing literature. It is well established that a court will refuse to grant a mandatory injunction that requires the defendant to do an act which is impossible or unlawful.[58] The extant literature conceptualises impossibility as being a sub-topic that falls within the discretionary consideration of undue hardship.[59] With respect, this is misconceived. Impossibility is not merely a discretionary consideration. As a matter of fact, it is either possible or impossible for someone to do a positive act. Accordingly, if a court is not satisfied that it would be possible for the defendant to do the positive act required by the injunction, the court *must* refuse to grant that relief. Impossibility is therefore better conceptualised as a precondition for relief. Importantly, however, it is a defendant-sided element. It is for the defendant to raise the issue of whether it would be possible for him to comply with the terms of the injunction.

B. The Nature and Limits of the Discretion

Once the claimant has established that a continuing tort is being committed against her and that it is necessary and possible for the defendant to do a positive act to restrain his future tort, the legal burden shifts to the defendant to

[56] A notable exception is *Malliate v Sharpe* (n 43) [60]–[62].

[57] ibid [60]–[62]; *Alamdo Holdings Pty Ltd v Bankstown City Council* (2003) 134 LGERA 114, 127 [89].

[58] *Attorney-General v Colney Hatch Lunatic Asylum* (1868–69) LR 4 Ch App 146, 154; *Earl of Harrington v Derby Corp* [1905] 1 Ch 205 (Ch), 220; *Pride of Derby* (n 13) 181; *Roberts v Rodier* [2006] NSWSC 282 [169].

[59] *Harold Stephen & Co v Post Office* [1977] 1 WLR 1172 (CA); *Bargain Pages Ltd v Midland Independent Newspapers Ltd* [2003] EWHC 1887 (Ch) [46] (contract claim); Oliphant (ed) (n 15) [8.16]; Spry (n 16) 419; Tettenborn (n 15) [28-09].

show why a desisting mandatory injunction should not be granted. The court's discretion to award a desisting mandatory injunction is therefore identical to the discretion that is applied in the context of a court's deciding whether to award a prohibitory injunction. This observation is supported by the fact that there are numerous cases in which, upon its being proved that the defendant was committing a continuing tort, a desisting mandatory injunction was awarded as of course because the defendant did not plead any countervailing discretionary factors.[60] Moreover, there are numerous cases where a desisting mandatory injunction has been awarded after a court found that a defendant failed to make out a countervailing discretionary consideration that he or she had pleaded, or failed to persuade the court that the injunction should be refused (and damages should be awarded in lieu) because of the consideration.[61] Thus, the conclusions reached in chapter 4 in respect of the nature and limits of the discretion to award prohibitory injunctive relief apply equally here. It is to the relevant discretionary considerations that we will now turn.

C. Discretionary Considerations Militating Against Relief

It was explained in chapter 3 that desisting mandatory injunctions operate identically to prohibitory injunctions, except for the form of the words used in the court's order. As a result, chapter 4 analysed the discretionary considerations relevant to whether an injunction should be granted by reference to the cases involving both prohibitory injunctions and desisting mandatory injunctions. The primary focus of this section is to explore the two considerations that arise frequently when courts are asked to award desisting mandatory injunctions, and which some scholars suggest operate differently in this context compared to when the same considerations are employed to determine whether a prohibitory injunction should be awarded. Those considerations are undue hardship and constant supervision.

i. Undue Hardship

Undue hardship is perhaps the discretionary consideration that defendants most frequently rely on when arguing that a desisting mandatory injunction should not be awarded. It is also the discretionary consideration that attracts the most

[60] eg, *Martyr v Lawrence* (1864) 2 De GJ & S 261, 379; *Goodson v Richardson* (n 1) 224–25; *Westminster Corp* (n 20) 281; *Andrews* (n 20) 414, 417; *Schweder* (n 60) 90; *Kynoch Ltd v Rowlands* [1912] 1 Ch 527 (CA), 534.

[61] eg, *Kelsen* (n 23) 347; *Elliott v Islington LBC* [1991] 1 EGLR 167 (CA), 169; *Jones v Stones* (n 30) 1746; *Harrow* (n 46) 259; *Jacklin v Chief Constable of West Yorkshire* [2007] EWCA Civ 181 [52]; *HKRUK II (CHC) Ltd v Heaney* [2010] EWHC 2245 (Ch) [85]–[86]; *Higson v Guenault* [2014] EWCA Civ 703 [51].

attention in the existing literature when the positive law on mandatory injunctions is discussed.[62]

From the outset of any discussion of this consideration, it is necessary to bear two things in mind. First, as was explained in chapter 4, undue hardship can only be relied on by a defendant who *inadvertently* commits a tort against the claimant. Second, 'hardship' is not a readily definable concept. There are no limits on what will amount to undue hardship, as it will ultimately depend on the unique factual circumstances in which the parties find themselves. For example, final mandatory injunctive relief has been refused for undue hardship because the injunction would: require the defendant to continue running a business at a loss;[63] require the defendant to engage in extremely costly works in circumstances where the claimant did not bring its claim for 60 years;[64] require the defendant to spend an exorbitant sum of public funds.[65]

The most contentious issue that has arisen in respect of this discretionary factor is the question of how courts assess whether undue hardship has been made out, specifically when deciding whether to award a mandatory, rather than a prohibitory, injunction.

(a) The Oppression Test

Spry and Davies are of the view that, just as in the context of a final prohibitory injunction, courts will refuse to award a final mandatory injunction for undue hardship only where the grant of the injunction 'is so disproportionate that that course is unjust in all the circumstances'.[66] As Davies explains, once it has been proved that the defendant is continuing to commit a wrong against the claimant, 'the fact that an injunction would pose considerable difficulties to the defendant is not a reason to refuse equitable relief'.[67] On this approach, courts are not entitled to apply a balance-of-convenience test that weighs the burden that would be suffered by the defendant against the benefit that would be gained by the claimant. So, a desisting mandatory injunction that would require the defendant to engage in positive action and incur significant costs can only be refused where the interference with the defendant's freedoms and the subsequent costs are so disproportionate that the award of the injunction would be oppressive (the 'oppression test').

[62] See Davies (n 34) [18-010]; Heydon, Leeming and Turner (n 16) [21-460]–[21-465]; Oliphant (ed) (n 15) [8.24]; Spry (n 16) 569-72; A Burrows, *Remedies for Torts, Breach of Contract, and Equitable Wrongs* (4th edn, Oxford University Press 2019) 463–64.
[63] *Attorney-General v Colchester Corporation* [1955] 2 QB 207.
[64] *Attorney-General v Grand Junction Canal Company* [1909] 2 Ch 505 (Ch).
[65] *Rileys v Halifax Corporation* (1907) 97 LT 278.
[66] Spry (n 16) 568. See also Davies (n 34) [18-040].
[67] Davies (n 34) [18-040].

This approach finds significant support in the case law. Two cases can be highlighted. First, consider the decision of the Court of Appeal in *Pride of Derby*.[68] In that case, the defendants appealed to the Court of Appeal after injunctions (which both Evershed MR and counsel conceptualised as mandatory) were awarded restraining them from discharging effluent into the Rivers Derwent and Trent. The second defendant, being the local authority that operated a sewerage system for the city of Derby, argued that because the injunction would cause it 'peculiar' difficulties, damages should have been awarded in lieu of an injunction. Specifically, the injunction required the sewerage system to be reconstructed, which in turn required the local authority: (i) to apply for and obtain a licence for building operations; and (ii) to expend funds that could only be borrowed with the consent of the relevant government minister (as the second defendant was acting pursuant to statutory powers).[69] Lord Evershed MR (with whom Denning and Romer LJJ agreed) explicitly rejected this argument and dismissed the appeal, stating:

> I venture to think that the fallacy which underlies this part of the corporation's argument is based on the statement made on their part that an injunction is purely discretionary – if by that [it] is meant that in a case where a person's rights, such as the plaintiffs' rights, are being damaged, and there is a threat of continuing damage, the question whether an injunction will be granted is determined by the court upon balance of convenience on one side or the other. In my judgment, that is not a correct statement of the position.[70]

Lord Evershed MR's remarks clearly indicate that when determining whether to award an injunction to stop a continuing wrong after the defendant has been proved to be a wrongdoer, courts do not have the discretion to weigh the conveniences of the parties so that an injunction can be refused merely because that course would be more convenient to the defendant.

The reasoning of the Court of Appeal in *Jaggard v Sawyer* is to similar effect.[71] In that case, the facts of which were outlined in chapter 3, Jack J refused to grant a prohibitory injunction restraining the defendants from using the private road to access Property B and awarded damages in lieu because, inter alia, 'it would be oppressive to the defendants to grant the injunctions sought'.[72] The claimant appealed on the basis that Jack J had been wrong to award damages in lieu. One of the primary issues for the Court of Appeal, therefore, was whether the judge had been correct to find that the award of an injunction would have been oppressive

[68] *Pride of Derby* (n 13). See also the decision of the Court of Appeal in *Harrow*, where the injunction issued despite the 'very considerable cost' that would be involved for the defendants: (n 46) 259. See also *Jacklin* (n 61) [16], [33], [46].

[69] *Pride of Derby* (n 13) 161.

[70] ibid 181.

[71] *Jaggard v Sawyer* [1995] 1 WLR 269 (CA). See also *Break Fast Investments Pty Ltd v PCH Melbourne Pty Ltd* (2007) 20 VR 311, 321 [47].

[72] *Jaggard v Sawyer* (n 71) 283.

to the defendants. In line with Lord Hoffmann's analysis in *National Commercial Bank Jamaica Ltd v Olint Corp Ltd*,[73] Bingham MR and Millett LJ accepted that the direct effect of the injunction would be the same as a mandatory injunction ordering the defendants to demolish their house.[74] Having made this pertinent observation, Bingham MR (with whom Kennedy LJ agreed, and with whom Millett LJ concurred on this point) said that it was 'important to bear in mind that the test is one of oppression, and the court should not slide into application of a general balance of convenience test'.[75] The Court's acceptance that the injunction was mandatory in effect therefore did not mean that it adopted a different approach when assessing undue hardship. Like Evershed MR in *Pride of Derby*, Bingham MR was of the view that because the defendants were proved to be wrongdoers, it was necessary for them to establish that the injunction would oppress them to make out undue hardship (which they ultimately did prove).

(b) The Balancing Test

In the light of the decision in *Pride of Derby*, and the reasoning in *Jaggard*, there is strong authoritative support for the oppression test adopted by Spry and Davies. However, as was explained in chapter 3, there is an alternative interpretation of the cases. According to Burrows and Oliphant, undue hardship 'is a very wide restriction' in the context of a final mandatory injunction,[76] and when assessing whether to award such an injunction a court is required to 'weigh the burden to [the defendant], against the benefit to the claimant'.[77] On this analysis, if the burden of the injunction outweighs its benefits, it should be refused (the 'balancing test'). Such an approach is therefore very similar (if not identical) to the balance-of-convenience test adopted in the context of interim injunctions, and is entirely distinct from how hardship is considered in the context of a final prohibitory injunction.

Both Burrows and Oliphant cite *Redland Bricks* as the primary authority for the proposition that a balancing test is adopted in the context of *all* mandatory injunctions. However, with respect, the decision in *Redland Bricks* is not authority for this proposition. In that case, Lord Upjohn reasoned that a mandatory quia timet injunction should not be granted because, inter alia, the cost of complying with the injunction would be £30,000 but the claimants' land was worth only £12,000.[78] Prima facie, Lord Upjohn's weighing of the cost to the defendant against the benefit to be gained by the claimants seems to suggest that a balancing test is

[73] *National Commercial Bank Jamaica Ltd v Olint Corp Ltd* [2009] UKPC 16, [2009] 1 WLR 1405.
[74] *Jaggard v Sawyer* (n 71) 279 (Bingham MR), 288 (Millett LJ).
[75] ibid 283.
[76] Burrows (n 62) 463. See also Oliphant (ed) (n 15) [8.24]. Note that Heydon, Leeming and Turner put it slightly differently, stating that hardship is 'easier' to engage in the case of a mandatory injunction: (n 16) [21-460].
[77] Burrows (n 62) 464.
[78] *Redland Bricks* (n 7) 667.

adopted in cases involving mandatory injunctions. Importantly, however, before applying the consideration of hardship to the facts of the case, Lord Upjohn stated:

> Unlike the case where a negative injunction is granted to *prevent the continuance or recurrence of a wrongful act* the question of the cost to the defendant to do works to prevent or lessen the likelihood of *a future apprehended wrong* must be an element to be taken into account …[79]

Lord Upjohn's specific reference to a 'negative' injunction suggests that he appreciated that in the context of a final prohibitory injunction where a wrong is continuing, the cost to the defendant of complying with such an injunction is not a relevant factor unless it is oppressive. His Lordship then went on to state:

> So the amount to be expended under a mandatory order by the defendant must be balanced with these considerations in mind against the anticipated possible damage to the plaintiff and if, on such balance, it seems unreasonable to inflict such expenditure upon one who for this purpose is *no more than a potential wrongdoer* then the court must exercise its jurisdiction accordingly.[80]

Lord Upjohn's discussion of hardship is clearly limited to the case where a claimant seeks a mandatory quia timet injunction. In the situation where an injunction is sought to prevent a wrong that has not yet occurred, it could be argued that a court should give more weight to the costs that a defendant would have to expend to comply with the injunction. But this argument has little force (if any) in the very different situation where a claimant seeks a *desisting* mandatory injunction after the defendant is proved to have committed a tort and is continuing to do so. Indeed, as Lord Upjohn himself recognised, the cost of complying with an injunction is not a factor to be considered where an injunction is granted to 'prevent the continuance or recurrence of a wrongful act'.[81] It necessarily follows that Burrows and Oliphant can rely on the decision in *Redland Bricks* only to make the claim that a balancing test represents the positive law governing when a quia timet, and not a *desisting*, mandatory injunction should be refused for undue hardship.

In addition to *Redland Bricks*, Burrows and Oliphant cite five other cases in support of the balancing test.[82] It would be superfluous to analyse each of these cases in detail, as four of them are first-instance decisions that, on a close reading, either do not support the balancing test[83] or contain faulty reasoning.[84] Perhaps the best evidence in support of a balancing test is the reasoning of the Court of

[79] ibid 666 (emphasis added).

[80] ibid (emphasis added).

[81] ibid.

[82] *Kelk v Pearson* (1870–1) LR 6 Ch App 809; *National Provincial Plate Glass Insurance Co v Prudential Assurance Co* (1877) 6 Ch D 757; *Rileys* (n 65); *Sharp v Harrison* [1922] 1 Ch 502 (Ch) (breach of covenant); *Jordan v Norfolk County Council* [1994] 1 WLR 1353 (Ch).

[83] Because the reasoning adopts the oppression test (*Rileys* (n 65); *Sharp v Harrison* (n 82) 515) or the decision involved a restorative mandatory injunction (*Jordan v Norfolk CC* (n 82) 1358–59).

[84] *National Provincial* (n 82) 768–69.

Appeal in the 1871 decision of *Kelk v Pearson*.[85] In that case, the claimant sought a mandatory injunction ordering the defendants to pull down a neighbouring building that they had constructed that interfered with the light in the claimant's scullery, kitchen and dining room. Bacon VC granted the injunction, and the Court of Appeal dismissed the defendant's appeal. However, in his reasoning James LJ stated:

> I think it is very fit for this Court, taking into consideration all the surrounding circumstances, to consider whether the interference of the Court will be productive of more or less inconvenience to the parties … [I]n this case I cannot help noticing that to the Defendants it is the mere loss of a piece of building-land, the site of one house …; whereas on the part of the Plaintiff it is a very serious de-privation of the comfort of his house, and a very serious diminution of the lettable value of his house as a residence.[86]

There is no doubt that James LJ adopts a balance-of-convenience approach. However, with respect, he was wrong to do so. As the numerous authorities set out above have indicated, in circumstances where a defendant is proved to be a wrongdoer, and is continuing to commit his or her wrong, it is not justifiable to deny injunctive relief simply because it is more convenient to the defendant to do so. Accordingly, the reasoning of James LJ in *Kelk v Pearson* is incorrect and should not be followed.

For the above reasons, it is difficult to find much support for Burrows' and Oliphant's view in the case law. The better view of the positive law is that put forward by Spry and Davies. Just as in the case of prohibitory injunctions, a desisting mandatory injunction will be refused for undue hardship only where the consequences that would be suffered by the defendant would be so disproportionate that it would be oppressive to grant the injunction.

This conclusion aligns with the fact that, as was demonstrated in chapter 3, prohibitory injunctions are identical to desisting mandatory injunctions. However, it should not be thought that an application of the oppression test means that it is irrelevant that a desisting mandatory injunction requires a defendant to do a positive act that may impinge on the defendant's freedoms and causes the incurring of expenses. On the contrary, the specific consequences the grant of the injunction would have for the defendant are always germane to assessing undue hardship. The point is simply that the same threshold test governs whether a prohibitory or desisting mandatory injunction should be refused for undue hardship, because both injunctions operate for the same purpose.

As a final point, it is worth emphasising that there is a good reason for preferring the oppression test over the balancing test. It is that there is no justifiable basis for adopting a balancing test when deciding whether to award a desisting mandatory injunction. The test is premised on the assumption that because 'mandatory' injunctions are ordinarily more coercive than 'prohibitory' injunctions, the

[85] *Kelk v Pearson* (n 82).
[86] ibid 812.

burdens of complying with an injunction should be given greater weight. However, as was explained in chapter 3, this assumption is misconceived. Hence, greater weight should not be given to the burdens of complying with a desisting mandatory injunction as opposed to a prohibitory injunction. As Sharpe has observed:

> It is not suggested that consideration of cost or burden is inappropriate but merely that undue attention to this factor in mandatory cases is uncalled for as significantly higher costs are often imposed by prohibitive injunctions when considerably less concern is expressed.[87]

By contrast, the oppression approach ensures that the burden that would be placed on a defendant as a result of complying with an injunction is always assessed, regardless of whether the injunction sought is prohibitory or mandatory in form. This is advantageous, as the analysis draws the court's attention to the specific consequences of the injunction sought rather than to the way in which it is expressed (and therefore accords with the guidance given by Lord Hoffmann in *Olint*).

ii. Constant Supervision

It was explained in chapter 4 that the constant-supervision consideration requires courts to ensure that injunctions are ordered in sufficiently precise terms. Accordingly, if the terms of a mandatory injunction do not specifically state what acts the defendant is required to do (for example, by requiring the defendant to achieve a result), this will give rise to a risk of constant supervision.[88] It should be noted, however, that in the context of a mandatory injunction, this risk does not arise where the result to be achieved by the order is simple. So, in *Redland Bricks*, Lord Upjohn specifically stated that an order requiring a defendant to 'restore the right of way to its former condition' would suffice.[89]

Importantly, however, where an injunction requires a defendant to do a positive act (whether directly in the case of a desisting mandatory injunction, or indirectly in the case of a prohibitory injunction which has a mandatory effect), a risk of constant supervision can arise in another way. Such a risk will arise where the terms of the order require the defendant to carry on a business or some other activity over a long period of time.[90] Giving the leading speech in *Co-operative Insurance Society Ltd v Argyll Stores (Holdings) Ltd*,[91] Lord Hoffmann stated that if there is a possibility that a court will have to 'give an indefinite series of rulings in order to ensure the execution of the order', that is a discretionary matter to

[87] R Sharpe, *Injunctions and Specific Performance* (4th edn, Thomson Reuters 2012) [1.540].

[88] *Attorney-General v Staffordshire City Council* [1905] 1 Ch 336 (Ch), 342; *Redland Bricks* (n 7) 666–67; *Co-operative Insurance Society Ltd v Argyll Stores (Holdings) Ltd* [1998] AC 1 (HL), 13–14. cf *Fawcett v Phoenix Inns Ltd* [2003] EWCA Civ 128 [37]–[39].

[89] *Redland Bricks* (n 7) 667. See also *Argyll Stores* (n 88) 14.

[90] *Dowty Boulton Paul Ltd v Wolverhampton Corporation* [1971] 1 WLR 204 (Ch), 211; *Braddon Towers Ltd v International Stores Ltd* [1987] 1 EGLR 209 (Ch), 213.

[91] *Argyll Stores* (n 88).

be taken into account.[92] Although this statement of principle was given in the context of upholding Maddock J's decision to refuse specific performance of a lease, Lord Hoffmann intimated that it was equally applicable when a court was assessing whether to award a mandatory injunction.[93] This should be accepted, as there are cases in which mandatory injunctions have been refused on this basis. For example, in *Powell Duffryn Steam Co v Taff Vale Railway Co*, a mandatory injunction was refused that would have required the defendant railway company to employ people to work the points and signals of a railway indefinitely in the future.[94]

However, this does not mean that courts can *never* grant mandatory injunctions that impose ongoing obligations on defendants. The leading case is *Kennard v Cory Bros & Co Ltd (No 2)*.[95] The claimants owned a piece of land on a mountain slope. They leased the upper part of the land to the defendants, and the defendants were given a licence to use part of the land as a tip for waste from their coal mine. After the defendants' tip caused a landslide that damaged the claimants' buildings on the lower part of their land, they sought, *inter alia*, a mandatory injunction ordering the defendants to restore and maintain a drainage system on the land. At first instance, Sargant J granted the injunction. The Court of Appeal dismissed the defendants' appeal. As Scrutton LJ explained, 'if the works can be exactly specified and are of such a character that the maintenance or repair is slight, the Court will in some cases make an order which involves future maintenance'.[96] The effect of this reasoning is that where the positive act to be undertaken by the defendant is not particularly burdensome and the defendant knows exactly what it is required to do, the courts will be more willing to order the defendant to do that act over a long period of time.[97]

For the most part, existing literature is of the view that the constant supervision consideration is justified.[98] However, Burrows argues that the requirement that orders must specify exactly what the defendant must do (rather than a result that the defendant must achieve) is unjustified. In *Argyll Stores*, Lord Hoffmann stated that *one* of the reasons why this rule must be followed is that otherwise parties would be repeatedly coming to courts for guidance or for contempt applications, and that this would amount to a waste of judicial resources.[99] Yet Burrows contends that 'in almost all cases defendants do obey … orders [that

[92] ibid 12.

[93] ibid 11, 14.

[94] *Powell Duffryn Steam Co v Taff Vale Railway Co* (1873–4) LR 8 Ch App 331.

[95] *Kennard* (n 12). See also *Gravesham Borough Council v British Railways Board* [1978] Ch 379, 405.

[96] *Kennard* (n 12) 21.

[97] Presumably the injunction would be discharged if the defendant's property was sold to a third party, and the claimant would be required to seek a new injunction against the third-party purchaser.

[98] Spry (n 16) 564–66; Glister and Lee (n 16) [28-018]; Oliphant (ed) (n 15) [8.25]–[8.26]; Tettenborn (n 15) [28-19].

[99] *Argyll Stores* (n 88) 13–14.

specify results]', such that 'it is unsatisfactory to deny justice on an unsubstantiated hunch about the costs of specific performance'.[100] This contention is sound when courts refuse specific remedies solely because they do not state exactly what the defendant must do (as clearly, there is no reason for a court to refuse relief when it has the capacity to amend the order to make it more precise). However, Burrows' argument does not justify a total abandonment of the constant-supervision consideration. That is because he does not acknowledge that the primary reason for the constant-supervision objection is that simply, as a matter of fairness, a person should not be put at risk of being held in contempt of court because of an ambiguous order. As was explained in chapter 4, it is well established that the terms of an injunction must be precise so as not to put the defendant at risk of being in contempt of court. As Lord Hoffmann said in *Argyll Stores*, '[t]he less precise the order, the fewer the signposts to the forensic minefield which [the defendant] has to traverse'.[101]

The constant supervision consideration is therefore justified to the extent that it ensures that courts give due consideration to the fact that injunctive relief (regardless of whether it is in prohibitory or mandatory form) must be ordered in sufficiently precise terms. Thus, although it may be easier for a court to make a positive order specifying the result the defendant must achieve, to ensure fairness to the defendant the court must specify the acts the defendant must do to comply with the order (and achieve the relevant result).

As a final point, it is worth highlighting here that in some cases there may be a dispute over which act(s) should be undertaken because a range of different steps could be taken to stop the relevant tort from continuing. This issue arose in *Jordan v Norfolk County Council*,[102] albeit in the context of the award of a restorative mandatory injunction. In that case, the council had knowingly trespassed onto the claimant's land, removed fences, cut down over 250 trees and installed a sewer. After the trial, Mr Andrew Park QC granted a final restorative mandatory injunction ordering the council to restore the claimant's land to its original condition by doing acts stipulated in a schedule to be drawn up by the claimant's expert. It later turned out that the acts proposed by the expert would cost between £230,000 and £300,000. As a result, the council brought a motion before Nicholls VC asking for the order to be amended in accordance with a revised schedule drawn up by the council's expert, which would cost, at most, £25,000 to implement. Nicholls VC granted the motion on the basis that the cost of complying with the injunction would be 'altogether disproportionate to the benefit it would confer on Mr Jordan'.[103] However, he ordered that a new expert should be appointed to draw up a revised schedule of works, bearing

[100] Burrows (n 62) 418–19.
[101] *Argyll Stores* (n 88) 13–14.
[102] *Jordan v Norfolk CC* (n 82). See also *Malliate v Sharpe* (n 43) [60]–[62].
[103] *Jordan v Norfolk CC* (n 82) 1358.

in mind that 'the remedy must be reasonably proportionate to the [benefits of remedying the] wrong'.[104] The decision in *Jordan v Norfolk County Council* therefore demonstrates two points. First, that courts can leave it to an expert to determine the specific acts that a defendant is required to carry out to achieve a result. And, second, that where there is a dispute over what acts should be undertaken, courts will favour the course of conduct that is most consistent with the principle that the consequences (financial or otherwise) a defendant would suffer as a result of doing the act(s) must be reasonably proportionate to the benefits of the injunction to the claimant in the light of the threatened, continuing or completed wrong. In complex cases, this will require the court to hear submissions from the parties and their experts.

D. Discretionary Considerations Militating in Favour of Relief

If the claimant can show that there are further reasons why injunctive relief should be granted, there remains a discretion in the court to award injunctive relief irrespective of the fact that the defendant has made out a countervailing discretionary consideration. Although there are numerous discretionary factors that have been relied on by claimants to persuade the court to grant desisting mandatory injunctive relief, they have not been applied more frequently or analysed differently simply because the injunction sought was mandatory. Accordingly, the relevant cases have already been analysed in chapter 4.

E. Overview

As a matter of positive law, the analytical process by which courts consider whether to award a desisting mandatory injunction to restrain *any* future tort (other than a 'tort' that generates a primary liability) is virtually identical to the analytical process the courts employ when deciding whether to award a prohibitory injunction to restrain a future tort. The only difference is that an additional necessary condition for desisting mandatory relief is that it must be necessary and possible for the defendant to do a positive act (rather than simply refrain from acting) to stop his tort from continuing.

Accordingly, *Determination 1* asks whether there is a continuing tort, and whether it is necessary and possible for the defendant to do a positive act to stop that tort (see Figure 5.1). The remaining determinations outlined in respect of prohibitory injunctions in chapter 4 otherwise apply.

[104] ibid 1358–59.

Figure 5.1 Determination 1 (Desisting Mandatory Injunctions)

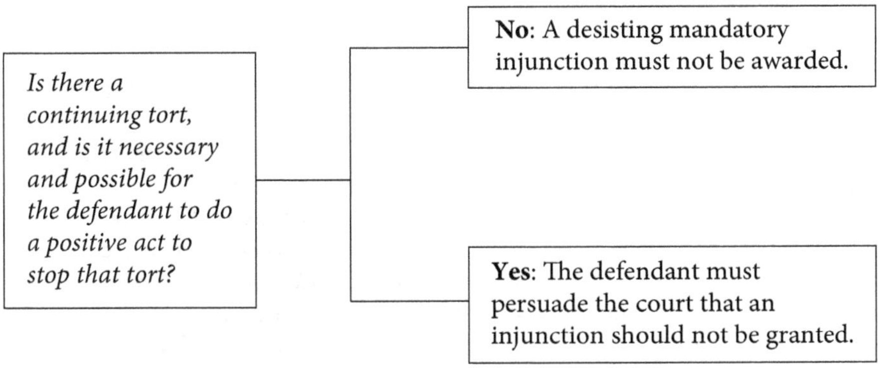

III. Restorative Mandatory Injunctions

The restorative mandatory injunction differs from the desisting mandatory injunction because it does not operate to stop a tort from continuing. Rather, it remedies the damage or loss caused by a tort that has been completed. It is therefore backward looking: like damages, the injunction has the effect of putting the claimant in the same position as if the tort had not occurred. However, the restorative injunction is much less frequently granted to remedy torts than the desisting mandatory injunction. The author was able to find only seven cases in England and Wales where such an injunction was granted,[105] and two cases in which such an injunction was sought but refused.[106]

This section is split into four main subsections. Section III.A clarifies why the courts have the power to develop and award restorative mandatory injunctions. Section III.B focuses on the conditions that are necessary before it can be said that a court has jurisdiction to award a restorative mandatory injunction. Section III.C examines the nature and limits of the discretion that courts exercise when determining whether to award a mandatory injunction, as well as the relevant discretionary considerations. And section III.D clarifies the analytical process

[105] *Luganda v Service Hotels Ltd* [1969] 2 Ch 209 (Ch) (breach of statutory duty); *Warder v Cooper* [1970] Ch 495 (Ch) (breach of statutory duty); *Esso Petroleum* (n 5) (inducing a breach of contract); *Jordan v Norfolk CC* (n 82) (trespass to land); *Hemingway* (n 6) (inducing a breach of contract); *Crestford Ltd v Tesco Stores Ltd* [2005] EWHC 805 (Ch) (inducing a breach of contract); *Ansco* (n 4) (trespass to land). In Australia, see *Clifford v Doe* [2003] NSWSC 938 (mandatory injunction ordering the defendant to reinstate cattle yards).

[106] *Perlman v Rayden* [2004] EWHC 2192 (Ch) (trespass to land); *Richmond v Selecta Systems* [2018] EWHC 1446 (Ch) (negligence). See also *Smethurst v Commissioner of Police* (2020) 272 CLR 177 (High Court of Australia).

by which the courts consider whether to award a restorative mandatory injunction to remedy torts.

A. The Power to Grant Restorative Mandatory Injunctions

Unlike desisting mandatory injunctions, which were awarded to remedy continuing torts during the latter half of the nineteenth century, the restorative mandatory injunction is quite a new equitable remedy. The first time that a court analysed whether it had the power to grant a mandatory injunction to remedy a completed tort was in the 1974 decision of *Esso Petroleum Co Ltd v Kingswood Motors (Addlestone) Ltd.*[107] Given how recent this development is, the legal basis on which courts have the power to award such injunctions should be clarified.

In *Esso Petroleum*, Bridge J recognised explicitly that the court has power to grant a restorative mandatory injunction to remedy a tort. The primary authority on which Bridge J relied was the decision of the Court of Appeal in *Torquay Hotel Co Ltd v Cousins.*[108] In that case, an interim quia timet injunction was granted to prevent the defendant from committing the tort of inducing a breach of contract. After stating that the broader principle laid down by Lord Denning MR in *Torquay* was that a court is entitled to intervene by injunction if the tort of inducing a breach of contract has been (or is going to be) committed, Bridge J stated:

> I am asked to enforce the personal liability incurred by a tortfeasor to undo the consequences of his tort which could have been restrained before it was committed. In a proper case, I ask myself: what reason can there be in principle why the tortfeasor should not be ordered to undo that which he has done?[109]

What Bridge J's remarks seem to indicate is that because a court clearly has the power to restrain a defendant from doing a particular act that would amount to a tort *before* it has occurred (that is, on a quia timet basis), it would be irrational to hold that courts do not have the power to grant an injunction that reverses the consequences of a tort *after* it has occurred. Therefore, courts must have the power to award restorative mandatory injunctions to remedy completed torts.

In addition to the justification given by Bridge J, there is a further reason why English courts should have the power to award restorative mandatory injunctions to remedy torts. As was explained in chapter 1, the courts' jurisdiction to award injunctions is confirmed in section 37(1) of the Senior Courts Act 1981, which provides:

> The High Court may by order (whether interlocutory or final) grant an injunction or appoint a receiver in all cases in which it appears to the court to be just and convenient to do so.

[107] *Esso Petroleum* (n 5).
[108] *Torquay Hotel Co Ltd v Cousins* [1969] 2 Ch 106 (CA).
[109] *Esso Petroleum* (n 5) 156.

This provision confirms that the wide jurisdiction to grant injunctions that was exercised by the Chancery before 1875 has been transferred to the modern courts. As Lord Nicholls stated in the landmark decision of the Privy Council in *Mercedes Benz AG v Leiduck*, when assessing whether the courts of Hong Kong have jurisdiction to award *Mareva* injunctions pursuant to section 21L of the Supreme Court Ordinance in Hong Kong (which is the equivalent to section 37 of the 1981 Act):

> [T]he jurisdiction to grant an injunction, unfettered by statute, should not be rigidly confined to exclusive categories by judicial decision. The court may grant an injunction against a party properly before it where this is required to avoid injustice, just as the statute provides and just as the Court of Chancery did before 1875. The court habitually grants injunctions in respect of certain types of conduct. But that does not mean that the situations in which injunctions may be granted are now set in stone for all time.[110]

As Lord Nicholls' reasoning makes clear, it does not follow from the fact that an injunction has not previously been awarded in a particular situation that the courts do not have the power to award an injunction. Spry similarly explains, with the recent endorsement of the Supreme Court in *Wolverhampton City Council v London Gypsies and Travellers*:[111]

> The preferable analysis involves a recognition of the great width of equitable powers, an historical appraisal of the categories of injunctions that have been established and an acceptance that pursuant to general equitable principles injunctions may issue in new categories when this course appears appropriate.[112]

This statement rings true in the present context. Claimants seek a restorative mandatory injunction to remedy a tort when the damage or loss caused by the tort cannot be adequately repaired by a monetary award. The purpose of the injunction, therefore, is to supplement the common law remedy of damages (and any other applicable legal remedies) by restoring the claimant to his or her previous position, insofar as compliance with an in personam order directing a defendant to do a positive act can do so. The situation in response to which the injunction is granted therefore falls squarely within the ambit of the Chancery's jurisdiction to award injunctions during the eighteenth and nineteenth centuries. Just as the interlocutory injunction was (as was shown in chapter 2) awarded by the Chancery upon proof of a *risk* of irreparable harm, the restorative injunction is awarded upon proof of *actual* irreparable harm. Both injunctions are therefore granted to supplement the common law and achieve more complete justice. Accordingly, in line with the reasoning of Lord Nicholls in *Mercedes*, and the Privy Council in *Convoy v Broad*, it would be wrong to deny that courts have jurisdiction to award

[110] *Mercedes Benz AG v Leiduck* [1996] AC 284 (PC), 308. See also *South Carolina Insurance Co v Assurantie Maatschappij 'De Zeven Provincien' NV* [1987] AC 24, 44; *Wolverhampton City Council v London Gypsies and Travellers* [2023] UKSC 47, [2024] AC 983 [22].

[111] *Wolverhampton City Council v London Gypsies and Travellers* (n 110) [112]. See also *Convoy Collateral Ltd v Broad Idea International Ltd* [2021] UKPC 24, [2023] AC 389 [56]–[58] (Lord Leggatt).

[112] Spry (n 16) 333.

restorative mandatory injunctions simply because, prior to 1974, such an injunction had not been awarded to remedy a tort.

Having clarified that there is a sound legal basis for the courts to award restorative mandatory injunctions to remedy torts, this section will now explore the necessary conditions for the award of such relief.

B. The Necessary Conditions

This subsection argues that two conditions are necessary for a restorative mandatory injunction to be granted to remedy a tort. First, the defendant's tort must have caused damage or loss that cannot be adequately remedied by an award of damages (or any other legal remedy). Second, it must be possible for the defendant to rectify that damage or loss by doing the positive act that the claimant seeks. As we shall see, the fact that a defendant knowingly commits a tort with an intention to profit or benefit in some other way is only a discretionary factor that strongly militates in favour of the award of such an injunction.

i. Damages must be Inadequate

The first necessary condition for the award of a restorative mandatory injunction is that the defendant's tort must have caused damage or loss that an award of damages (or any other legal remedy) would not adequately remedy. As previously explained, this condition reflects the underlying reason why the injunction is necessary in the first place. So, in all but one case in which a restorative mandatory injunction was granted to remedy a tort, an award of damages would not have adequately remedied the damage or loss caused by the defendant's tort. Three examples will suffice.

First, as was explained in chapter 3, in *Esso Petroleum* the effect of the third defendant's acts, which (allegedly) induced the first defendant to breach its solus tie agreement with the claimant, was that the claimant was unable to enforce the solus tie agreement effectively against the first or third defendant, and the third defendant was therefore free to make a significant profit as a result. As Bridge J explained, 'damages in a case of this kind would be a wholly inadequate remedy to protect the plaintiffs from the consequences of this sort of tie-breaking'.[113]

The second example is *Crestford Ltd v Tesco Stores Ltd*.[114] In that case, Tesco was the lessee of a warehouse that was owned by the claimant landlords. In breach of clause 4 of the lease, which stipulated that the lessee was not to sub-let the premises without the consent of the lessor and without the intended assignee's

[113] *Esso Petroleum* (n 5) 157.

[114] *Crestford v Tesco* (n 105). See also *Hemingway* (n 6), where a final restorative mandatory injunction was also awarded ordering the second defendant to immediately surrender the sub-lease after it had induced a breach of the head lease by entering into a sub-lease without the claimant's consent.

having first covenanted directly with the lessor by deed, Tesco knowingly entered a sub-lease with Magspeed Ltd (the second defendant), without the claimants' consent and without Magspeed's directly covenanting with the claimants. The purpose of the sub-lease was to reduce Tesco's liabilities under the head lease for having to comply with a covenant to repair the premises. Lightman J held that when Magspeed entered the sub-lease knowing that Tesco would be in breach of the head lease, it committed the tort of inducing a breach of contract.[115] The consequences of the tort were that Magspeed had factual possession of the leased premises without the claimants' consent, and the claimants would be unable to enforce the original covenant to repair against Magspeed.[116] Damages would not adequately remedy these consequences, as a monetary award would still leave the claimants unable to enforce the head lease against Magspeed. Therefore, 'because the grant of any lesser relief would be inadequate', Lightman J granted a restorative mandatory injunction ordering Magspeed to surrender the sub-lease.[117]

The final, and most vivid, example is *Ansco Arena Ltd v Law*.[118] Here, the claimants were the owners of the O2 Arena in London. The three named defendants were 'urban explorers', who had trespassed onto the roof of the Arena so that they could post videos on their social media accounts to make a profit. The claimants subsequently brought proceedings against the defendants, seeking not only an interim prohibitory injunction restraining them from committing any further trespasses in the future, but also an interim mandatory restorative injunction ordering them to remove from their social media accounts (and any other websites) any videos that they had taken of the Arena while they were trespassing. Hugh Mercer QC granted the injunction. He reasoned that by taking videos during their trespass and uploading them on social media, a consequence of the defendants' trespass was that they had encouraged, and were continuing to encourage, other people to trespass on O2 Arena. Given that damages would not be able to undo this consequence, the injunction was granted.

In the light of the above cases, it would seem quite obvious that a claimant must prove that damages are an inadequate remedy before a restorative mandatory injunction will be awarded. However, the decision in *Jordan v Norfolk County Council*[119] casts doubt on this view of the positive law.

In *Jordan*, Norfolk County Council and the second defendant wanted to build a major supermarket in the Norfolk area but needed to install a sewerage system for the development to take place. The claimant owned a stretch of disused railway embankment that was a suitable place for the sewer. However, he strongly objected to the laying of a sewer, as he had obtained planning permission for

[115] *Crestford v Tesco* (n 105) [66]–[68].

[116] As the sub-lease provided that Magspeed's liability to repair the premises would be limited to 'maintaining the premises in no worse state of repair, then [*sic*] in their present condition': ibid [14].

[117] ibid [70]. See also ibid [71].

[118] *Ansco Arena Ltd v Law* (n 4).

[119] *Jordan v Norfolk CC* (n 82).

residential development and wished to sell his land. In complete disregard of the claimant's rights, the council trespassed on his land, removed the fences, cut down over 250 trees and installed the sewer. At trial, Andrew Park QC granted a mandatory injunction ordering the council to remove the sewerage system from the claimant's land (to stop the continuing trespass) *and* to 'reinstate the land as far as is reasonably practicable in the circumstances to its state before [the trespass]' by performing certain acts listed in the court's order (which were recommended by the claimant's expert).[120] The difficulty with this second limb of the injunction was that it required the council to plant about 250 trees (ranging in maturity) and build new fences on the claimant's land. Clearly, an award of damages would adequately remedy the claimant's property damage, as the claimant could engage a third party to install new fences and plant new trees – the council's expertise was not necessary to do this. Indeed, the claimant had in fact sought damages for the costs of replacing the fences and the trees.[121] Despite this, the judge refused to award damages and granted the injunction instead. On an application by the council to amend the injunction's terms after it had been granted, Sir Donald Nicholls VC approved of the injunction and amended its terms so that the cost of complying with the second limb of the injunction would be limited to approximately £25,000. The reason why the injunction was granted was that, in the words of Sir Donald Nicholls VC:

> Mr Jordan has been severely wronged by his local county council, a powerful body. It rode roughshod over his rights. But for his tenacity it would have got away with this. The remedy afforded to Mr. Jordan ought fairly to reflect this and his justified sense of outrage. The local authority can have no complaint on this score.[122]

What Sir Donald Nicholls VC seems to be suggesting is that from the claimant's perspective, an award of compensatory damages would not be adequate because it would not impose a punishment on the council sufficient to mark the fact that it had 'rode roughshod' over the claimant's rights. The problem with this reasoning is that it is likely that exemplary damages could have been awarded alongside compensatory damages to punish the council for its flagrant disregard of the claimant's rights. Indeed, it is at least arguable that the oppressive and unconstitutional conduct limb of the *Rookes v Barnard* test for the award of exemplary damages would have been satisfied.[123] The available remedies at law were therefore adequate.

Hence, the decision in *Jordan v Norfolk CC* indicates that perhaps, as a matter of positive law, it is not necessary for the claimant to prove that damages would be an inadequate remedy to be awarded a restorative mandatory injunction. There is,

[120] ibid 1356. Note that the decision of Andrew Park QC is not physically or electronically available and so only the reasoning of Sir Donald Nicholls VC can be analysed.

[121] ibid.

[122] ibid 1358.

[123] *Rookes v Barnard* [1964] AC 1129 (HL). See also J Goudkamp and D Nolan, *Winfield & Jolowicz on Tort* (20th edn, Sweet & Maxwell 2020) [23-014].

however, a problem adopting this position. As was explained in section III.A the reason why courts have jurisdiction to award restorative mandatory injunctions to remedy torts is that the injunction is needed to supplement the available common law remedies in order to achieve more complete justice. It follows that there is no need for a court to award a restorative injunction to remedy a tort in circumstances where there is an available and adequate legal remedy.

Furthermore, if restorative mandatory injunctions are awarded in circumstances where a monetary award would adequately remedy a claimant, this would make such injunctions a readily available remedy for the commission of a tort and thereby severely restrict individual freedoms. By way of example, consider a defendant who negligently drives his vehicle into the parked car of the claimant. If the courts were permitted to grant a restorative mandatory injunction ordering the defendant to repair the damage to the claimant's car himself, this would prevent the defendant from contributing to society in his usual way (for example, through employment) as he would, in effect, have to become a smash repairer.[124] To protect the defendant's freedom of action, the law recognises that in such a case damages are the primary remedy and so a restorative mandatory injunction cannot be awarded. As Edelman J explained in the decision of the High Court of Australia in *Smethurst v Commissioner of Police*:

> A libertarian principle of the common law is that it is usually easier to justify ordering a wrongdoer to pay money to ameliorate the consequences of wrongdoing than to justify ordering a wrongdoer personally to act to ameliorate those consequences.[125]

Thus, it is only when damages are an inadequate remedy that courts are justified in ordering wrongdoers to act personally to remedy the consequences of their torts. Accordingly, with respect, Andrew Park QC and Sir Donald Nicholls VC were wrong to grant the second limb of the injunction, and the decision in *Jordan*, to this extent, should be regarded as contrary to established principle.

It follows that the first necessary condition for a claimant to be awarded a restorative mandatory injunction to remedy a tort is that damages (and any other legal remedies) must be inadequate.

ii. It must be Possible for the Defendant to do a Positive Act to Rectify the Relevant Consequence

Just because a claimant can prove that damages are an inadequate remedy does not mean that the claimant is entitled to a restorative mandatory injunction. Consider a situation where the defendant's negligence has severed the claimant's leg. Damages are clearly an inadequate remedy, as no matter how much monetary

[124] We would also have to put aside the problem that the defendant would have to take possession of the claimant's car to repair it.

[125] *Smethurst v Commissioner of Police* (n 106) [250].

compensation is awarded, it will not regrow the claimant's leg and put the claimant in the same position she would have been in had the tort not occurred. Yet neither will an injunction: it is impossible for the defendant, or anyone else, to regrow the claimant's leg.

Accordingly, the second condition for the award of a restorative mandatory injunction to remedy a tort is that it must be possible (and, of course, lawful) for the defendant to do a positive act to rectify the relevant consequence sought to be remedied. So, for example, in *Richmond v Selecta Systems Ltd*, Matthews J refused to award a restorative mandatory injunction ordering the defendant to restore the personal email, WhatsApp, iTunes and LinkedIn accounts of the claimant (which the defendant had negligently interfered with) because it was not possible for the defendant to do this act.[126]

iii. Must the Defendant Knowingly Commit the Tort with an Intention to Profit?

In all the cases in which a restorative mandatory injunction has been granted to remedy a tort, the defendant was not acting inadvertently but knowingly committed a tort against the claimant *and* intended by doing so to make a profit or otherwise gain some benefit. Interestingly, this factor is given much more emphasis in the reasoning of the courts than the requirement that damages must be inadequate.

In *Esso Petroleum*, Bridge J reasoned that there is 'as strong a case calling for the exercise of the [injunction] … as it is well possible to imagine', because:

> The very history of this case strongly suggests that tie-breaking, by acquiring petrol stations the subject of solus agreements, then disregarding those agreements and acting in breach of them, must be a profitable activity, if you can get away with it subject only to a liability to pay damages. That calculation has clearly motivated the defendants in this case, and if that is a correct calculation, it affords the strongest possible reason why others who may be tempted to make it, should be shown that it is a calculation based on a false premise, namely, the premise that the only liability the tie-breaker incurs is a liability to pay such damages as the supply company can eventually prove.[127]

In *Hemingway Securities Ltd v Dunraven Ltd*,[128] the second defendant induced the first defendant to breach its contract with the claimant landlords by sub-letting the leased premises to the second defendant. Jacob J granted an interim mandatory injunction ordering the second defendant to give up the premises immediately. Although as a matter of fact damages were clearly an inadequate remedy, Jacob J did not identify this in his reasoning. Rather, after quoting the remarks of Bridge J in *Esso Petroleum*, Jacob J stated that the injunction should be granted because:

[126] *Richmond v Selecta Systems Ltd* (n 106) [83].
[127] *Esso Petroleum* (n 5) 157.
[128] *Hemingway Securities Ltd v Dunraven* (n 6).

> it seems to me that it would be wrong in principle to allow the second defendants to stay on and in effect to get the benefit of their tort. True it is that they may find themselves in more difficulty having to make a sudden exit than they would have been in if they had not caused the restrictive covenant to be broken; but that is a problem they made for themselves.[129]

Similarly, in *Crestford v Tesco*, Lightman J reasoned that

> [i]n my judgment the Landlords in justice should be granted the mandatory order which they seek and the grant of any lesser relief would be inadequate, for interference with their rights was knowing and deliberate to serve the Defendants' financial interests.[130]

It could be argued that in the above cases, the reason why the courts focused on the defendant's intention to make a profit or achieve some other benefit is that this is what motivates all defendants when they commit the tort of inducing a breach of contract. The difficulty with this contention, however, is that it does not explain why restorative mandatory injunctions have been granted to remedy a trespass to land or a breach of statutory duty only where the defendant commits the tort to make a profit or gain some other benefit.[131] For example, in *Jordan v Norfolk CC*, Sir Donald Nicholls VC stated from the outset of his judgment that the reason why the council trespassed onto the claimant's land and installed a sewerage system was because it would then be able to continue with the development of a major supermarket in Norfolk (from which the council would benefit more broadly and presumably from which the second defendant would profit).[132] Although the judgment of Andrew Park QC is not publicly available, Sir Donald Nicholls VC implicitly relied on this fact when he explained why the injunction was an appropriate remedy in response to the defendants' wrongdoing (but amended its terms).[133] Similarly, in *Ansco Arena v Law*, Hugh Mercer QC had regard to the fact that:

> the primary purpose for [the defendants'] trespass in this case is to take videos which can be posted on the internet and which can then earn the defendants monies through their share of the advertising revenue from a variety of websites.[134]

Taking stock of the above cases, two conclusions can be drawn.

First, the reasoning of the courts indicates that one of the reasons why a restorative mandatory injunction is granted is to punish the defendant. It seems that just as the fact that a defendant sought to profit from his tort (regardless of any

[129] ibid 62.

[130] *Crestford v Tesco* (n 105) [70].

[131] It must be noted, however, that the author was unable to locate any cases in which a restorative mandatory injunction was refused simply because the defendant did not knowingly commit the tort with an intention to profit or otherwise benefit.

[132] *Jordan v Norfolk CC* (n 82) 1355.

[133] ibid 1358.

[134] *Ansco Arena v Law* (n 4) [13].

award of compensatory damages) justifies an award of exemplary damages,[135] it also justifies the award of a restorative mandatory injunction because it will, at least in some part, operate as a punishment. This observation therefore partially undermines Barker's contention that 'there is no evidence that [equity] regards itself as punishing when it issues an injunction'.[136]

Second, any future court that decides to grant a restorative mandatory injunction where the defendant has *not* knowingly committed a tort to make a profit or benefit will need to justify why it has departed from the confines of the existing case law. This finding raises the question: should knowledge on the part of the defendant that it is committing a tort, combined with an intention to profit or benefit in some way, be a necessary condition for the award of a restorative mandatory injunction?

The better view is that such an injunction should be available to remedy the consequences of a tort even where it has been committed inadvertently. This is because the presence of actual knowledge on the part of the defendant is not the underlying justification for the award of the injunction. The fact that a defendant knowingly commits a tort shows that there is level of moral opprobrium on his part, such that there is *more* reason for the injunction to be awarded. However, this does not mean that it is *the* reason why the injunction should be granted. As was explained in section III.A, and as was recognised by Edelman J in *Smethurst v Commissioner of Police*:

> The central rationale for a mandatory injunction in cases where there is no anticipated or continuing unlawful action is that the interference with the liberty of the defendant by ordering the defendant to take action where inaction would be lawful is justified by the extent of the inadequacy of damages to ameliorate the consequences of the wrongdoing.[137]

Accordingly, a claimant can still be left without a remedy and suffer an 'injustice' even without the defendant's knowing commission of a tort against the claimant. This is best understood by considering a hypothetical example based on the facts of *Ansco Arena v Law*.[138] Consider a situation where D decides to go bushwalking on the outskirts of a national park. Without realising that he has crossed the boundary of the park onto C's land, D comes across a spectacular waterfall. He decides to film the waterfall on his mobile phone. Afterwards, D posts the video on YouTube. The consequence is that the video goes viral, such that numerous people are encouraged to (and in fact, do) trespass on C's land to gain access to the waterfall. On these facts, it would be difficult to justify a decision to refuse to award C a restorative mandatory injunction ordering D to delete the video from YouTube

[135] *Rookes v Barnard* (n 123) 1226.

[136] K Barker, 'Punishment in Private Law – No Such Thing (Any More)' in E Bant et al (eds), *Punishment and Private Law* (Bloomsbury Publishing 2021) 35, 52.

[137] *Smethurst v Commissioner of Police* (n 106) [252].

[138] *Ansco Arena v Law* (n 4).

solely because when D trespassed on C's land he did so unknowingly. D's tort has caused more individuals to trespass on C's land. An award of damages obviously will not adequately remedy this consequence; however, an injunction ordering D to delete the video will go some way towards remedying it. Accordingly, without the establishment by the defendant of any other countervailing factors militating against relief, there is no good reason why the claimant should be denied the injunction.

For the above reasons, a claimant should not be required to prove that a defendant knowingly committed a tort against them with an intention to profit or benefit to be awarded a restorative mandatory injunction. This should instead be treated as a discretionary factor that weighs in favour of granting such an injunction.

C. The Discretionary Analysis

Once the claimant has proved the necessary conditions, the court *must* award a restorative mandatory injunction unless a countervailing consideration can be established by the defendant. This was explicitly recognised by Lightman J in *Crestford v Tesco*, when he stated:

> [I]n the absence of any equitable defence and any plea that its grant would be oppressive (and there is none pleaded, established or maintained) the Landlords are prima facie entitled to mandatory orders for surrender of the Underlease and should not be required to accept damages in its place.[139]

The discretion that a court exercises to determine whether to award a restorative mandatory injunction is therefore identical to that for a desisting mandatory injunction and a prohibitory injunction. Additionally, the discretionary considerations, which by their nature are general and apply across many different areas of equity, also seem to operate in the same way when applied to consider whether a restorative mandatory injunction should be awarded.[140]

There is, however, one exception. When considering whether a restorative mandatory injunction should be refused for undue hardship, a balancing test is adopted. Although this has never been decided by an English court, it was accepted by two justices in the High Court of Australia in *Smethurst v Commissioner of Police*.[141] In that case, Ms Smethurst sought a restorative mandatory injunction pursuant to section 75(v) of the Constitution of Australia, ordering the Commissioner of the Australian Federal Police to destroy or return personal data that had been taken from her mobile phone as a consequence of

[139] *Crestford v Tesco* (n 105) [69].

[140] For example, in *Hemingway*, Jacob J explicitly stated that the second defendant was unable to rely on the consideration of undue hardship because it knowingly committed the tort against the claimant: (n 6) 62.

[141] *Smethurst v Commissioner of Police* (n 106).

Australian Federal Police officers' commission of a trespass to land and a trespass to goods against her. The injunction was refused by the majority (made up of Kiefel CJ, Bell and Keane JJ, and Nettle J) for a variety of reasons. However, Nettle J and Edelman J (the latter in dissent) each accepted that when deciding whether to award a restorative mandatory injunction, a court must balance the reasons for awarding the injunction against the extent to which ordering the defendant to do a positive act would interfere with the defendant's liberty.[142] As Edelman J said, 'the greater the intrusion into a defendant's liberty arising from the injunction the more that the decision to make the order must be "attended with the greatest possible caution"'.[143]

It follows that the extent to which damages are inadequate, and the extent to which ordering the defendant to act personally will interfere with his or her liberty, are weighed against each other to determine whether a restorative mandatory injunction should ultimately be granted. As Edelman J explained:

> A mandatory injunction is most easily justified where the consequences are ongoing and serious, the interference with the defendant's liberty is trivial and, compared with an injunction, damages are an inadequate means to 'undo the consequences of a wrong'.[144]

Hence, the balancing test endorsed by Burrows and Oliphant *is* applied in the context of *restorative* mandatory injunctions. But this raises the question: why is a balancing test justified when determining whether to refuse a restorative, but not a desisting, mandatory injunction for undue hardship?

As previously explained, it is a libertarian principle of the common law that wrongdoers are generally only ordered to pay money to ameliorate the consequences of their wrongdoing, rather than ordered to act personally. And there is good reason for this principle: it is necessary to protect individual liberty. However, the libertarian principle does not have application where an injunction is awarded to stop a continuing tort. This is because, in such a situation, the injunction is preventing a *future* infringement of the claimant's rights, rather than rectifying the consequences of a *prior* infringement. Consider the facts of, and decision in, *Pride of Derby*.[145] In that case, it was justifiable to order the defendants to take positive steps to stop effluent from continuing to flow into the rivers, even though the injunctions would place significant (but not oppressive) burdens on the defendants. There was no need to give effect to the libertarian principle because the defendants intended to continue their wrong and cause future damage.

However, imagine if in *Pride of Derby* the defendants had stopped discharging effluent into the rivers and the claimants had instead sought injunctions ordering the defendants to take positive steps to remove the effluent that had

[142] ibid [156] (Nettle J), [250]–[254] (Edelman J).
[143] ibid [252] (footnotes omitted).
[144] ibid [253] (footnotes omitted).
[145] *Pride of Derby* (n 13).

already flowed into the rivers (so as to restore them to their previous state). If the oppression test were applied, the courts would be almost entirely disregarding the libertarian principle, as it would only be when an injunction would oppress the defendant that a restorative mandatory injunction could be refused for hardship. By contrast, by applying a balancing test, courts can weigh the extent to which the injunction would curtail the defendant's freedoms against the extent to which the injunction would adequately remedy the claimant. The approach is therefore much better attuned to the libertarian principle. Accordingly, the use of the balancing test to assess whether a *restorative* mandatory injunction should be refused for hardship is justified, as it is necessary to give practical effect to the libertarian principle.

As a final point, it must be borne in mind that in the case law concerning prohibitory, desisting mandatory and quia timet injunctions, it is well established that the consideration of hardship cannot be relied on by a defendant who knowingly or recklessly committed his wrong against the claimant. There seems to be no reason why the same principle should not also be applied here.

D. Overview

As a matter of positive law, the analytical process by which courts consider whether to award a *restorative* mandatory injunction to remedy any completed tort is best understood as follows.

Determination 1: The claimant must prove that: (i) a tort has been committed against her and that certain damage or loss (the 'consequence') she has suffered would not adequately be remedied by an award of damages; and (ii) it is possible for the defendant to do a positive act to rectify that consequence. If the claimant satisfies her burden of proof, the defendant bears the onus of proving that an injunction should *not* be awarded. See Figure 5.2. The remaining determinations outlined in respect of prohibitory injunctions in chapter 4 otherwise apply.

Figure 5.2 Determination 1 (Restorative Mandatory Injunctions)

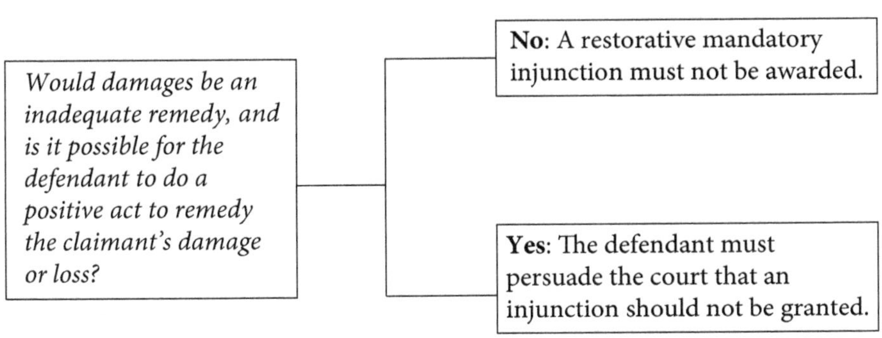

IV. Conclusion

Like the prohibitory injunction, desisting and restorative mandatory injunctions are general remedies in tort law. As the foregoing analysis has demonstrated, both injunctions have been granted to restrain many different torts. However, because desisting and restorative mandatory injunctions have different purposes, there are two central distinctions between the positive law that governs their award.

First, distinct conditions are necessary for the award of these injunctions. If a claimant seeks a desisting mandatory injunction, she must prove that the defendant is continuing to commit a tort against her, and it must be necessary and possible for the defendant to do a positive act to stop his tort from continuing. By contrast, if a claimant seeks a restorative mandatory injunction, she must prove that: (i) a tort has been committed against her and that certain damage or loss (the 'consequence') she has suffered would not be adequately remedied by an award of damages; and (ii) it is possible for the defendant to do a positive act to rectify that consequence. The necessary conditions reflect the distinctive purpose of each injunction.

The second distinction is more subtle and concerns the discretionary consideration of hardship. Once a court is satisfied that the necessary conditions for the award of a desisting mandatory injunction have been made out, the court can refuse to award such an injunction for hardship only if the defendant can prove that the injunction's consequences would be oppressive. By contrast, once a court is satisfied that the necessary conditions for the award of a restorative mandatory injunction have been made out, the court can refuse to award such an injunction for hardship if the defendant can prove that, on balance, the injunction's consequences to the defendant outweigh the benefits of the injunction to the claimant.

6

Quia Timet Injunctions

I. Introduction

The quia timet injunction is a powerful weapon in the armoury of judicial remedies because its function is to prevent a wrong before it has occurred. It operates on the assumption that preventing a wrong is better than a cure or, as Sir Edward Coke put it, 'preventing justice excelleth punishing justice'.[1] Quia timet injunctions have been granted to restrain many different torts. To give some colour to the case law, consider the cases in which quia timet injunctions have been awarded to: prevent gypsy travellers from camping on public land;[2] prevent unknown persons from gathering in public parks in breach of COVID-19 restrictions;[3] prevent unknown persons from 'car cruising' on public roads;[4] prevent a hospital authority from amputating the claimant's leg without his consent;[5] prevent protestors from conspiring to engage in unlawful acts to obstruct the free passage of a public highway with the intention of causing economic loss to a fracking company;[6] and prevent urban explorers from trespassing on the roof of the O2 Arena.[7]

Quia timet injunctions are also increasingly being granted against unknown persons. Indeed, in the recent decision of *Wolverhampton City Council v London Gypsies and Travellers*, the United Kingdom Supreme Court held that courts have the power to grant *final* quia timet injunctions against unknown persons who are likely to commit torts in the future.[8]

This chapter offers the first in-depth account of the positive law governing when quia timet injunctions can be awarded to restrain future torts. Specifically,

[1] Coke made this oft-cited statement in the context of discussing the common law writ of prohibition that issued to restrain legal wrongs in the 13th to 17th centuries: E Coke, *The Second Part of the Institutes of the Lawes of England* (M Flesher 1644) 299.

[2] As of January 2020, 38 of these injunctions were in force in England and Wales: *Bromley LBC v Persons Unknown* [2020] EWCA Civ 12 [11].

[3] *Hackney LBC v Persons Unknown* [2020] EWHC 1900 (QB) (interim).

[4] *Wolverhampton City Council v Persons Unknown* [2020] EWHC 759 (QB) ('*Wolverhampton* 2020').

[5] *In Re C* [1994] 1 WLR 290 (Fam).

[6] *Cuadrilla Bowland Ltd v Persons Unknown* [2020] EWCA Civ 9 (interim, considered in the context of an appeal over sentence pursuant to committal).

[7] *Ansco Arena v Law* [2019] EWHC 835 (QB).

[8] *Wolverhampton City Council v London Gypsies and Travellers* [2023] UKSC 47, [2024] AC 983. For cases involving such interim injunctions, see: *Boyd v Ineos Upstream Ltd* [2019] EWCA Civ 515; *Bromley* (n 2); *Canada Goose UK Retail Ltd v Persons Unknown* [2020] EWCA Civ 12, [2020] 1 WLR 2802 (CA).

the chapter will clarify the necessary conditions for the award of quia timet injunctions and analyse the general discretionary considerations relevant to whether such injunctions should be granted. For the avoidance of doubt, prohibitory and mandatory quia timet injunctions are not analysed separately in this chapter. That is because, as was explained in chapter 3, prohibitory and mandatory quia timet injunctions are identical as a matter of substance.

The chapter also explores the historical origins of quia timet injunctions. The reason why this topic is considered here (instead of in chapter 2) is that, as we shall see, the first cases that could be located in which the courts articulated what conditions were necessary for the award of quia timet injunctions in aid of tort law rights were decided *after* the passing of the Judicature Act reforms of 1873–75.

The leading authority governing the award of quia timet injunctions to restrain future torts in England and Wales is the Court of Appeal decision in *Bromley LBC v Persons Unknown*.[9] In that case, members of the Gypsy and Traveller community had set up unauthorised camps in a number of different public spaces in Bromley. Those camps amounted to a trespass to land and, at times, caused a public nuisance. As a result, the local council[10] brought proceedings seeking a quia timet injunction, which amounted to a 'de facto boroughwide prohibition of encampment and upon entry/occupation … in relation to all accessible public spaces in Bromley except cemeteries and highways'.[11] At first instance, Judge Mulcahy QC held that although the necessary conditions for the injunction had been made out, it must be refused on the basis that it would infringe Article 8 ECHR.[12] On appeal, Coulson LJ (with whom Haddon-Cave LJ and the Senior President of Tribunals agreed) dismissed the Council's appeal and confirmed the decision and reasoning of Judge Mulcahy QC. Notably, Coulson LJ set out (and approved of) the reasoning process of Judge Mulcahy QC as follows:

> Accordingly, the judge found that all the necessary ingredients for a quia timet injunction against unknown persons were in place, and that what remained was the discretionary exercise of weighing up whether or not it was proportionate to grant such an injunction in all the circumstances of the case.[13]

Although Coulson LJ also refers to the principles concerning the grant of injunctions against unknown persons, his reasoning indicates that when courts analyse whether a quia timet injunction should be awarded, they undertake a two-stage process.[14] First, certain threshold conditions ('necessary conditions') must be

[9] *Bromley* (n 2). In Australia, see *Bendigo & Country Districts Trustees & Executors Co Ltd v Sandhurst & Northern District Trustees Executors & Agency Co Ltd* (1909) 9 CLR 474.

[10] Using its statutory power to institute civil proceedings for the protection of the interests of the inhabitants in their area under the Local Government Act 1972, s 222.

[11] *Bromley* (n 2) [1].

[12] *Bromley LBC v Persons Unknown* [2019] EWHC 1675 (QB) [57], [72] ('*Bromley* (HC)').

[13] *Bromley* (n 2) [21].

[14] Coulson LJ's reasoning process is also reflected in numerous first-instance decisions: see, eg, *Cambridge City Council v Traditional Cambridge Tours* [2018] EWHC 1304 (QB) [81]; *Mace Ltd v Persons Unknown* [2021] EWHC 726 (QB) [25]–[28]; *UK Oil and Gas Plc v Persons Unknown* [2021]

established to satisfy a court that a quia timet injunction *can* be awarded. Second, there are supplemental, discretionary considerations that, if engaged, a court must consider when determining whether an injunction *should* be granted in the circumstances of the particular case. Coulson LJ's approach therefore reflects the analytical process undertaken by the Chancery when it awarded injunctions in the eighteenth and nineteenth centuries, as found in chapter 2: the claimant must prove certain conditions to satisfy the court that it can award injunctive relief, following which the court has a discretion to refuse relief if a countervailing consideration is established by the defendant.

Consistently with this approach, this chapter is split into four main sections. Section II explores the origins of the quia timet injunction, both generally and in tort law specifically. This is important, as extant literature has yet to provide an account of the historical development of the quia timet injunction and to consider how the history of the remedy can assist in understanding the modern law. Section III examines the first set of necessary conditions for the award of a quia timet injunction. Section IV contends that there is a second set of necessary conditions that can also justify the award of quia timet relief. Section V examines the nature and limits of the discretion courts exercise when determining whether to award a quia timet injunction, as well as the relevant discretionary considerations.

II. The Origins of Quia Timet Injunctions

The quia timet injunction derives from six common law writs. In 1633, Sir Edward Coke identified 'that there be six writs in Law that may be maintained, quia timet, before any molestation, distress, or impleading'.[15] Coke classified them as '[b]revia anticipantia, writs of prevention'.[16] Both Story and Hazeltine observed that it was in place of the common law writs that fell into disuse, and motivated 'to accomplish the ends of precautionary justice',[17] that the Chancery founded the quia timet injunction.[18]

It was by bringing a 'Bill quia timet' in Chancery that plaintiffs could seek an injunction to prevent future wrongs.[19] Story explained that '[t]he party seeks the

EWHC 599 (Ch) [49]–[50]; *City of London Corp v Persons Unknown* [2021] EWHC 1378 (QB) [53]; *National Highways Ltd v Persons Unknown* [2021] EWHC 3081 (QB) [25].

[15] E Coke, *The Fourth Part of the Institutes of the Lawes of England* (M Flesher 1644) 100.

[16] ibid. 'This is a bill quia timet, and the jurisdiction of this Court exercised upon it is only an expansion of that common law jurisdiction, which in ancient times was exercised upon preventive writs, then called Brevia Anticipatia': *Fisher v Hughes* (1820) 1 Coop t Cott 329, 329–30.

[17] J Story, *Commentaries on Equity Jurisprudence: As Administered in England and America* (Maxwell & Sons 1836) vol 2, 130.

[18] ibid 129–31; HD Hazeltine, 'The Early History of English Equity' in P Vinogradoff (ed), *Essays in Legal History* (Oxford University Press 1913) 285. It is not explained why the common law writs became disused.

[19] Story (n 17) 130.

aid of a Court of Equity, because he fears (quia timet) some future probable injury to his rights or interests'.[20] The injunction was therefore available to prevent any wrong, irrespective of whether it was classified as legal or equitable. As Jessel MR stated in the 1878 decision of *Frearson v Loe*:

> No part of the jurisdiction of the old Court of Chancery was considered more valuable than that exercise of jurisdiction which prevented material injury being inflicted, and no subject was more frequently the cause for bills for injunction than the class of cases which were brought to restrain threatened injury as distinguished from injury which was already accomplished.[21]

A close analysis of the cases reveals that the Chancery did not impose a single, overarching test for the award of a quia timet injunction; rather, there were multiple tests, which were developed according to the type of wrong at hand. To explain briefly, the Chancery awarded interlocutory quia timet injunctions to prevent waste upon proof of a threat or an intention to commit future waste.[22] By contrast, in cases involving the expected misapplication of funds by an executor of a testamentary trust, the Chancery would grant an injunction upon the claimant's proof of *any* risk that the trust property might be converted to other purposes.[23] The test was different again for surety bonds. If a surety could show any delay on the part of a principal debtor to pay the relevant debt after it had become due, the surety was prima facie entitled to an injunction compelling the debtor to discharge the debt.[24]

At the time, tort law did not exist as a holistic body of law. However, the Chancery 'from a very ancient date'[25] developed requirements specific to when a quia timet injunction should be awarded to prevent a future *nuisance*. In the early cases, without expressly using the label 'quia timet', the Chancery interposed on an *interlocutory* basis to stop a defendant from constructing a building until it was determined at trial whether allowing the defendant to continue construction would lead to a nuisance in the form of a wrongful interference with the claimant's right to light.[26] In this context, the Chancery was concerned to ensure that the threatened tort was immediate such that the matter could go to trial,[27] and that the predicted interference with the claimant's right to light would amount to irreparable harm.[28] A number of cases followed in which these requirements were applied in radically different contexts, including whether to restrain a defendant

[20] ibid.

[21] *Frearson v Loe* (1878) 9 Ch D 48 (Ch), 65.

[22] *Gibson v Smith* (1741) 2 Atk 182, 183; *Robinson v Litton* (1744) 3 Atk 209, 210; *Coffin v Coffin* (1821) Jac 70, 71–72.

[23] *Taylor v Allen* (1741) 2 Atk 213, 213; *Rogers v Rogers* (1793) 1 Anst 174, 174–75. See also Story (n 17) 130-31.

[24] *Comes Ranelaugh v Hayes* (1683) 1 Vern 189, 190; *Wooldridge v Norris* (1868) LR 6 Eq 410, 413–14; *Ascherson v Tredegar Dry Dock and Wharf Co* [1909] 2 Ch 401, 407–09.

[25] Story (n 17) 201.

[26] *Ryder v Bentham* (1750) 1 Ves Sen 543; *Attorney-General v Bentham* (1755) Dick 277.

[27] *Fishmongers' Company v East India Company* (1752) Dick 163.

[28] *Attorney-General v Nichol* (1809) 16 Ves Jun 338, 342–43.

from: constructing a building to store gun powder next to the claimant's paper mills;[29] pulling down a wall that protected travellers on a public highway from falling into a river;[30] and draining water from a river.[31] In these cases, the plaintiffs sought interlocutory quia timet relief. Accordingly, consistently with the findings in chapter 2, the central issue in dispute was whether the plaintiff would suffer irreparable harm such that the Chancery had jurisdiction to grant injunctive relief.

Interestingly, it seems that it was not until after the passing of the Judicature Act reforms that the necessary conditions for *final* quia timet relief were considered.[32] In the 1885 case of *Fletcher v Bealey*, Pearson J laid down two overarching tests for determining when a final quia timet injunction could be awarded to prevent a future nuisance.[33] It is this case that has since been employed by modern courts to found the quia timet injunction as an available remedy to prevent future torts.[34] Extant literature similarly relies upon the decision when analysing the modern law on quia timet relief.[35] Yet neither the cases nor the scholarship provide a detailed analysis of the decision in *Fletcher*. Moreover, the centrality of the decision to the modern law has gone unremarked, as the scholarship has not emphasised how frequently the decision is relied upon by courts today when stating the preconditions for quia timet relief. It is therefore necessary to investigate this case in detail.

A. The Decision in *Fletcher*

The story in *Fletcher* began in 1884, when the defendant alkali manufacturers leased a piece of land on the bank of the River Irwell in Manchester to store 'vat waste'. The claimant, Fletcher, owned a paper mill situated on the bank of the river one mile below the defendants' land. He used a large quantity of the river water to manufacture paper, and the mill depended on clean water to ensure that the paper it produced was white. Although it had not been proved that any vat waste had entered the river, Fletcher sought a quia timet injunction restraining

[29] *Crowder v Tinkler* (1816) 19 Ves Jr 617. See also *Haines v Taylor* (1847) 2 Ph 209.

[30] *Attorney-General v Johnson* (1819) 2 Wils Ch 87. See also *Attorney-General v Forbes* (1836) 2 My & Cr 123.

[31] *Earl of Ripon v Hobart* (1834) 3 My & K 169. See also *Dawson v Paver* (1847) 5 Hare 415.

[32] In addition to the analysis below, see *Pattinson v Gilford* (1874) LR 18 Eq 259; *Goodhart v Hyatt* (1883) 25 Ch D 182 (Ch).

[33] *Fletcher v Bealey* (1885) 28 Ch D 688 (Ch), 698.

[34] See, eg, *Hooper v Rogers* [1975] 1 Ch 43 (CA), 49–50; *Islington LBC v Elliott* [2012] EWCA Civ 56 [30]–[34] ('*Islington* 2012'); *Bromley* (n 2) [35]. The decision was also cited in *Network Rail Infrastructure Ltd v Williams* [2019] QB 601 (CA) [71].

[35] A Tettenborn, 'Injunctions' in M Jones and A Dugdale (eds), *Clerk & Lindsell on Torts* (23rd edn, Sweet & Maxwell 2020) [28.21]; A Burrows, *Remedies for Torts, Breach of Contract, and Equitable Wrongs* (4th edn, Oxford University Press 2019) 468; I Spry, *Equitable Remedies* (9th edn, Thomson Reuters 2014) 392; J Murphy, 'Rethinking Injunctions in Tort Law' (2007) 27 *OJLS* 509, 510.

the defendants from causing any vat waste to flow into the river, on the basis that it would amount to a private nuisance.

The sole issue before Pearson J, in the Chancery Division of the High Court, was whether a quia timet injunction should be awarded. After setting out the facts, Pearson J analysed the existing legal principles. He examined only three decisions, in two of which an interlocutory quia timet injunction to restrain a future nuisance had been refused,[36] and in the third of which an ordinary prohibitory injunction to restrain a continuing nuisance had been refused.[37] In the cases concerning quia timet injunctions, two different standards were applied to determine whether relief should be given. In the first case, the claimant was required to prove 'risks which are so imminent … although they do not amount to absolute certainty of damage' or 'a somewhat less imminent probability in cases where the mischief, should it be done, would be vast and overwhelming'.[38] By contrast, in the second case it was held that a claimant must simply establish 'an actual immediate nuisance'.[39]

After summarising these differing approaches, Pearson J laid down his oft-cited general statement of principle:

> [T]here are at least two necessary ingredients for a *quia timet* action. There must, if no actual damage is proved, be proof of imminent danger, and there must also be proof that the apprehended damage will, if it comes, be very substantial. I should almost say it must be proved that it will be irreparable, because, if the danger is not proved to be so imminent that no one can doubt that, if the remedy is delayed, the damage will be suffered, I think it must be shewn that, if the damage does occur at any time, it will come in such a way and under such circumstances that it will be impossible for the Plaintiff to protect himself against it if relief is denied to him in a *quia timet* action.[40]

In the above extract, Pearson J seems to have intended to set out two tests.[41] They require that:

1. '*There must … be proof of imminent danger*' and the apprehended damage must '*be very substantial*' if not irreparable (the 'First Test'); or
2. '*[I]f the danger is not … imminent*', the future irreparable harm must occur in circumstances where it would '*be impossible for the [claimant] to protect himself against it*' without quia timet relief (the 'Second Test').

[36] *Fletcher* (n 33) 696–98. See *Earl of Ripon* (n 31); *Attorney-General v Corp of Kingston* (1865) 13 WR 888.

[37] *Salvin v North Brancepeth Coal Co* (1873-74) LR 9 Ch App 705.

[38] *Earl of Ripon* (n 31) 176.

[39] *Kingston* (n 36) 891.

[40] *Fletcher* (n 33) 698.

[41] This is evident from a previous paragraph in the judgment, in which Pearson J stated (ibid 696): '[P]roceeding upon practical views of human affairs, the law will guard against risks which are so imminent that no prudent person would incur them, although they do not amount to absolute certainty of damage. Nay, it will go further, according to the same practical and rational view, and, balancing the magnitude of the evil against the chances of its occurrence, it will even provide against a somewhat less imminent probability in cases where the mischief, should it be done, would be vast and overwhelming.'

The First Test is clearly predicated upon the authorities analysed above. However, it is unclear how Pearson J came to articulate its precise formulation; he gives no reasons for this. As to the Second Test, the closest to an earlier statement of this principle was made by Brougham LC in *Earl of Ripon v Hobart*, where he explained, in the context of deciding whether to award an interlocutory quia timet injunction, that the law 'will even provide against a somewhat less imminent probability in cases where the mischief, should it be done, would be vast and overwhelming'.[42]

Turning to the application on the facts, Pearson J found that the danger to the claimant was not imminent because on the evidence it would be some years before the vat waste leaked into the river.[43] Therefore, the case turned on whether the Second Test was satisfied. The essence of Fletcher's argument was that because the expert evidence proved that it was 'certain' that if the vat waste entered the river this would cause his business irreparable harm, quia timet relief should be granted.[44]

Pearson J rejected this argument and denied relief.[45] He held that Fletcher could protect himself against the damage without a quia timet injunction for three reasons. First, because, 'in ten years time it is highly probable that science … may have discovered some reasons for rendering this green liquid innocuous'.[46] Second, because the defendant was willing to use tanks and pumps to prevent the liquid from entering the river.[47] And third, because even if the liquid did get into the river, Fletcher would be able to discover it and then re-apply to the Court for relief.[48]

Putting to one side the faith in scientific discovery, the reasoning indicates that what Pearson J meant by his Second Test was that quia timet relief will be awarded only where it is probable that the risk of irreparable harm will materialise and there are no reasonable and lawful actions that the claimant or a (willing) defendant could take to reduce the risk.

B. Analysis of the Decision

Pearson J's reasoning is influential because it placed two clear limits on when quia timet relief should be granted to restrain a future nuisance. First, although Pearson J was not required to identify the jurisdictional basis for the court's power to grant final quia timet injunctive relief (because the decision was after the passing of the

[42] *Earl of Ripon* (n 31) 68.

[43] He made this finding after applying the Second Test: *Fletcher* (n 33) 700.

[44] ibid 698–99.

[45] Note that Pearson J expressly stated that the claimant could bring a new action if circumstances changed: ibid 704.

[46] ibid 700.

[47] ibid.

[48] ibid.

Judicature Acts), he nevertheless required proof of a risk of irreparable harm for quia timet relief to be awarded. Accordingly, it seems that Pearson J believed that it was the irreparable-harm doctrine that justified such relief.

Second, even though it was certain that if the vat waste entered the river it would cause irreparable harm to the claimant, this was held not to be sufficient. As Pearson J stated, what must also be proved is that either the tort is going to be committed imminently *or* that a quia timet injunction is the only remaining method by which the claimant can protect herself from the irreparable harm that will be caused in years to come. Thus, from an early stage, and consistently with equity's desire to maintain flexibility to achieve complete justice, it was recognised that quia timet injunctions could be awarded in circumstances where a tort was not going to be committed imminently. However, it has never expressly been said in the modern case law that Pearson J laid down *two* tests governing when quia timet relief can be granted to restrain a future tort.[49] The case is instead cited for the proposition that a tort must be imminent, and risk causing the claimant irreparable harm, before relief is granted.[50] Similarly, in the scholarship, the case is cited for the claim that imminency is a necessary condition for (or relevant to) the award of a quia timet injunction,[51] even though Pearson J stated that quia timet relief could still be granted where a future tort was not going to be committed imminently.

With the historical development of the quia timet injunction in mind, the necessary conditions for the award of such an injunction can now be considered.

III. The Necessary Conditions: The First Test

The conditions that are required for the grant of quia timet relief have been stated in a variety of conflicting ways. For example, it has been said that a quia timet injunction will be granted only where: there is 'a sufficiently real and imminent risk of a tort being committed';[52] 'the risk of actual damage occurring is both imminent and real';[53] there is 'a very strong probability upon the facts that grave damage will accrue to [the claimant] in the future';[54] and there is 'a strong probability that, unless restrained by an injunction, the defendant will act in breach of the claimant's rights … [and] the harm resulting would be so grave and irreparable that … a remedy of damages would be inadequate'.[55]

[49] Counsel for the claimant in *Hooper* identified that there were two tests in *Fletcher*: see *Hooper* (n 34) 45. However, in its reasons, the Court of Appeal did not direct attention to this submission.

[50] See *Hooper* (n 34).

[51] See the works cited in n 35.

[52] *Boyd* (n 8) [34].

[53] *Islington* 2012 (n 34) [29].

[54] *Redland Bricks v Morris* [1970] AC 652 (HL), 665.

[55] *Vastint Leeds BV v Persons Unknown* [2018] EWHC 2456 (Ch) [31(3)].

In *Bromley LBC v Persons Unknown*, Coulson LJ, relying on the decision in *Fletcher*, clarified the position by stating that a quia timet injunction can be awarded to prevent a future tort only where it is proved that there is a 'sufficiently real and imminent risk'[56] that a tort will be committed, which would cause the claimant 'irreparable harm'.[57] Interestingly, there is division in the literature over whether this test is correct. Burrows states that 'the claimant must show that the tort is highly probable to occur and to occur imminently'.[58] He makes no mention of an irreparable-harm requirement. Davies, Bean, Parry and Burns, Glister and Lee, and Tettenborn also state that the claimant must prove a real and imminent risk that a tort will be committed, but they adopt uncritically the judicial claim that proof of a risk of 'substantial damage' or 'irreparable harm' is required.[59]

This section explores the meaning of the First Test and argues that Burrows' view of the law is correct: a risk of irreparable harm is not strictly a necessary condition for quia timet relief.

A. Real and Imminent Risk that a Tort will be Committed

The probability that a tort will be committed, and the point in time when it is anticipated to occur, is plainly relevant to assessing whether quia timet relief is justified. Therefore, no objection can be made to the employment of these considerations by the courts. The more contentious question is what exactly is meant by a sufficiently 'real' and 'imminent' risk, as courts have not expressly defined these terms and scholars have not explored them in detail.

i. Real Risk

In determining whether a risk is 'real', courts assess the size of the risk that a tort may be committed by considering the probability of its materialising. It is for this reason that some of the cases require the claimant to prove a 'strong probability' that the tort will occur.[60] The method is therefore analogous to the first step of

[56] *Bromley* (n 2) [29]. See also *Boyd* (n 8) [34]; *Canada Goose* (n 8) [82]; *Cambridge* (n 14) [80]–[81]; *Wolverhampton* 2020 (n 4) [7], [9]; *UK Oil* (n 14) [49]; *Mace* (n 14) [19]; *Barking and Dagenham LBC v Persons Unknown* [2021] EWHC 1201 (QB) [186]; *City of London* (n 14) [53]; *Hackney LBC v Grant* [2021] EWHC 2548 (QB) [62]; *National Highways* (n 14) [25].

[57] *Bromley* (n 2) [35], [95]. See also *Vastint* (n 55); *Sutton LBC v Persons Unknown* [2018] 11 WLUK 819 (QB) [28]; *Ansco* (n 7) [5]; *London Borough of Epsom and Ewell v Persons Unknown* [2019] EWHC 1690 (QB) [47]; *RGCM Ltd v Lockwood* [2019] EWHC 1937 (Ch) [8]; *Hertsmere BC v Persons Unknown* [2019] EWHC 3230 (QB) [22].

[58] Burrows (n 35) 467.

[59] P Davies, 'Injunctions' in J McGhee and S Elliott (eds), *Snell's Equity* (34th edn, Sweet & Maxwell 2021) [18-029]; J Glister and J Lee, *Hanbury on Modern Equity* (22nd edn, Sweet & Maxwell 2021) [28-042]; Tettenborn (n 35) [28-20]; D Bean, I Parry and A Burns, *Injunctions* (14th edn, Sweet & Maxwell 2022) [2-14].

[60] See *Redland Bricks* (n 54) 655; *Vastint* (n 55); *Bromley* (HC) (n 12) [20]–[21].

the 'negligence calculus' when assessing the standard of care a reasonable person would exercise, which requires a court to determine the size of the relevant risk of damage by assessing the probability of its occurring.[61] Where the two tests differ, however, is in respect of the kind of risk at issue. In the quia timet context, the focus is on the probability of the risk that *all elements of the relevant tort* will materialise. In this sense, although the test is expressed generally, the specific tort pleaded is central to its application.

It has been said that the degree of probability required to be proved is 'not an absolute standard'.[62] The Court of Appeal in *Hooper v Rogers* held that 'what is to be aimed at is justice between the parties, having regard to all the relevant circumstances'.[63] The guidance provided by the High Court of Australia in the negligence context is therefore similarly applicable: '[w]hat is involved … is not a calculation; it is a judgment'.[64] While these statements must be borne in mind, it is equally important to recognise that they do not grant courts a licence to award or refuse relief based on imprecise meanings of ambiguous terms. Simply pointing out that a remedy is equitable 'does not … operate as a green light to invent new general or specific rules to achieve what one judge might regard as a fair result'.[65] A comprehensive investigation of the 'real risk' test therefore poses two issues: (i) what is relevant to assessing whether a risk is real; and (ii) what size of risk is required by the term?

As to the first issue, all the circumstances of the case can be taken into account when assessing the size of the risk.[66] However, an analysis of the cases reveals that there are four factors that are most relevant to determining whether a risk is a 'real' one.

The first factor is evidence that the defendant has (or unknown persons have) committed *identical* tortious conduct in the past, irrespective of whether it was against the specific claimant or another person. Consider cases where urban explorers had previously trespassed on the claimant's property,[67] and gypsy travellers had already trespassed on other land owned by the claimant.[68] Or, even more curiously, where unknown protestors had committed similar acts of trespass not against the claimants but against other persons involved in the same line of business as the claimants.[69] In all of these cases, this evidence was sufficient, in itself, to make the risk of commission of a trespass to land 'real'. These conclusions are sound. As demonstrated by the tendency rule in the law of evidence, courts have

[61] J Goudkamp and D Nolan, *Winfield & Jolowicz on Tort* (20th edn, Sweet & Maxwell 2020) [6.019]–[6.020]; Tettenborn (n 35) [7.173], [7.176].

[62] *Hooper* (n 34) 50 (Russell LJ), quoted with approval in *Islington* 2012 (n 34) [33]. See also S Gee, *Commercial Injunctions* (7th edn, Sweet & Maxwell 2020) [2-045]; Spry (n 35) 393.

[63] *Hooper* (n 34) 50 (Russell LJ).

[64] *Mulligan v Coffs Harbour City Council* (2005) 223 CLR 486 [2] (Gleeson CJ).

[65] *Edlington Properties v JH Fenner & Co Ltd* [2006] 1 WLR 1583 (CA) [46] (Neuberger LJ).

[66] *Hooper* (n 34) 50; *Vastint* (n 55) [31].

[67] *Ansco* (n 7) [9], [17].

[68] *Bromley* (HC) (n 12) [51].

[69] *Ineos Upstream Ltd v Persons Unknown* [2017] EWHC 2945 (Ch) [93]–[96], [142] ('*Ineos* (HC)').

long inferred that past conduct is a strong indication that the same conduct will be committed again in the future.[70]

Second, and relatedly, where the claimant has shown that it took steps to attempt to reduce the risk of commission of a tort, but that these steps had failed, this will indicate that there is a real risk that a tort will occur in the future.[71] For example, in *Mace Ltd v Persons Unknown*, Stacey J acknowledged that the first claimant had already put in place security measures to prevent 'urban explorers' from trespassing on its property but that these were insufficient to deter them such that they were likely to occur again.[72] Additionally, in *Cambridge City Council v Traditional Cambridge Tours*, Whipple J noted that the council had tried 'many different strategies' to prevent unknown persons from punting without a licence on the River Cam, and that because they had failed it was reasonable to infer that such trespasses would occur in the future.[73]

Third, where the future tort is an intentional one, conduct on the part of the defendant that indicates that it has the requisite intention is required. For example, in *Torquay Hotel Co Ltd v Cousins*, the fact that the defendants had threatened to blacklist an oil supplier if it delivered oil to the claimant demonstrated that they intended to induce the supplier to breach its contract with the claimant, and quia timet relief was therefore granted.[74] Enquiring into whether the defendant has the requisite intention reinforces the point that while the test is expressed generally, it is heavily dependent on the specific tort pleaded.

Fourth, there will not be a real risk where the defendant undertakes to do, or refrain from doing, exactly what is required by the quia timet injunction. In *Bridlington Relay Ltd v Yorkshire Electricity Board*,[75] the claimant radio and television broadcaster sought an interim quia timet injunction restraining the defendant local electricity board from powering an electricity line that was within 250 yards of the claimant's broadcasting mast on the basis that this would interfere with the claimant's broadcasts and amount to a private nuisance. However, the claimant sought the injunction even though the defendant had already given an undertaking that it would not energise the power line until judgment or further order. Buckley J refused relief on the basis that:

> it would be wrong for this court in quia timet proceedings to grant relief by way of injunction to compel this defendant to do something which it appears to be willing to do without the imposition of an order of the court.[76]

[70] See *Hales v Kerr* [1908] 2 KB 601 (CA), 604–05 (a claim in negligence); R Munday, *Evidence* (10th edn, Oxford University Press 2019) [7.176].

[71] In addition to the cases discussed below, see also *Harlow DC v Stokes* [2015] EWHC 953 (QB) [11].

[72] *Mace* (n 14) [27].

[73] *Cambridge* (n 14) [81(ii)].

[74] *Torquay Hotel Co Ltd v Cousins* [1969] 2 Ch 106 (CA), 141. See also *Cuadrilla Bowland Ltd v Persons Unknown* [2018] 5 WLUK 628 (unlawful means conspiracy).

[75] *Bridlington Relay Ltd v Yorkshire Electricity Board* [1965] Ch 436 (Ch).

[76] ibid 445. cf *Attorney-General v Beck* [1980] 2 NSWLR 77, 94–95.

Buckley J's reasoning echoes sentiments akin to the maxim that equity will not act in vain. However, the better explanation for the decision is that the quia timet injunction was refused because there was not a real risk that a nuisance was going to be committed. If a defendant provides an undertaking to a court to do, or refrain from doing, precisely what a claimant requires by way of the injunction, it ordinarily cannot be said that there is a real risk that the relevant tort will be committed in the future.

The above factors indicate that it is quite a burdensome task to establish that there is a real risk that a tort will be committed. This observation gives rise to the second issue: what size of risk is required?

It has been held on numerous occasions that the claimant must show a 'strong case of probability',[77] a 'strong probability',[78] or a 'very strong probability upon the facts'[79] that the apprehended wrong *will* be committed. This is a question of fact and degree, and it is one on which opinions may well differ.[80] Nevertheless, the 'strong probability' standard is justified. As Burrows explains, if any non-fanciful and existing risk were capable of founding quia timet relief, this would too readily hamper defendants' freedoms.[81] Claimants have argued, however, that this rationale is overstated.[82] It is said that as tortious conduct is not permitted in any event, restraining a defendant from committing a tort in the future will not impinge on its freedoms. The difficulty with this argument is that it does not appreciate the serious consequences of awarding a quia timet injunction. This is best understood by considering the effects of the grant of an injunction more generally.

A prohibitory injunction will restrain a defendant from doing a particular act or acts and ensures 'immediate obedience on pain of imprisonment [or fine, or sequestration] for contempt of court'.[83] The effect of awarding such an injunction is that a claimant's private rights will not only restrict a defendant from doing an act (which he is already not permitted to do), but *also* subject the defendant to a risk of severe penalty if he does not comply with the injunction's terms. For example, if a defendant trespasses on a claimant's land in breach of an injunction, that defendant can be subjected to a punishment well beyond what is ordinarily imposed by tort law and (if applicable) the criminal law. The inevitable effect of any injunction, therefore, is that a defendant will be limited in the way he can act for fear, as Lord Hoffmann put it, of 'a sword of Damocles which may descend if the [defendant] … does not conform to the terms of the order'.[84]

[77] *Attorney-General v Corp of Manchester* [1893] 2 Ch 87 (Ch), 92; *Attorney-General v Corp of Nottingham* [1904] 1 Ch 673 (Ch), 677.

[78] *Vastint* (n 55); *RGCM* (n 57) [8].

[79] *Redland Bricks* (n 54) 655.

[80] This is not something to be critical of: see *Bolton v Stone* [1951] AC 850 (HL), 867.

[81] Burrows (n 35) 468.

[82] See *Paul (KS) (Printing Machinery) Ltd v Southern Instruments (Communications) Ltd* [1964] RPC 118 (CA), 123.

[83] St Waddams, *Dimensions of Private Law: Categories and Concepts in Anglo-American Legal Reasoning* (Cambridge University Press 2003) 179. A power of arrest can also be attached to an injunction, see Police and Justice Act 2006, s 27.

[84] *Co-operative Insurance Society Ltd v Argyll Stores (Holdings) Ltd* [1998] AC 1 (HL), 13.

With these consequences in mind, the problems with permitting a quia timet injunction to be awarded where there is less than a strong probability that a tort will be committed in the future become apparent. As McBride and Bagshaw point out, such an approach would have the effect of creating a 'two-tier' criminal law.[85] Claimants would have a basis to obtain an injunction and enforce their private law rights by way of a criminal penalty simply because they held those rights in the first place. All private rights would therefore be made quasi-public rights that could be enforced *privately* by civil contempt proceedings. Moreover, faced with the threat of possible criminal punishment, defendants would be extremely cautious to act, and their individual liberties would thereby be unnecessarily constricted. It is to guard against these consequences that courts require a claimant to prove that there is a strong probability that a tort will be committed before a quia timet injunction will be granted. It is only in the most clear-cut of cases, where the strong probability threshold is satisfied, that it is justified for the courts to limit the way in which a defendant can act by threatening him with the full force of the judiciary's powers of enforcement.

ii. Imminent Risk

The next step required by the case law is to assess whether the real risk is also imminent. The concept of imminency is a familiar one. Indeed, the tort (and crime) of assault requires proof of an act 'causing the victim to apprehend an imminent application of [unlawful] force upon her'.[86] The imminency requirement, more commonly termed 'immediacy',[87] focuses on the immediacy in time of the apprehended unlawful conduct, and therefore strictly requires that the defendant, at the time of making the relevant threat, had the capacity to commit a battery within a very short time.[88]

The 'imminency' test in the quia timet context similarly focuses on immediacy in time. However, the concept is clearly broader than in assault. Courts do not require that it be proved that the risk is capable of materialising within a very short time but only within a matter of weeks or months. For example, in the Australian case of *Plaintiff S99/2016 v Minister for Immigration and Border Protection*, evidence that the Minister's negligence would cause damage to the applicant in one or two weeks' time satisfied the imminency test.[89] Moreover, 'imminency' has been established in cases where a defendant is restrained from constructing a building that *months* later would interfere with the claimant's light.[90] However, in *Islington LBC*

[85] N McBride and R Bagshaw, *Tort Law* (6th edn, Pearson Education 2018) 807.

[86] *R v Ireland* [1998] AC 147 (HL), 161.

[87] The two terms were equated in *Mbasogo v Logo Ltd* [2007] 2 WLR 1062 (CA) [81].

[88] Goudkamp and Nolan (n 61) [4.018]; Tettenborn (n 35) [14.12].

[89] *Plaintiff S99/2016 v Minister for Immigration and Border Protection* (2016) 243 FCR 17, [492].

[90] *Dicker v Popham Radford & Co* (1890) 63 LT 379; *Slack v Leeds Industrial Co-operative Society Ltd* [1924] 2 Ch 475 (Ch) (damages awarded in lieu). In *Nair v Edwards* [2006] NSWSC 1310 (at [12]), six months was said to be sufficient.

v Elliott, the fact that the council's trees would not be capable of causing damage to the claimants' house for another three years meant that the risk of a nuisance was not imminent.[91] Furthermore, in *Fletcher* it was held that the danger that a nuisance would be committed was not imminent because the vat waste would not enter the river for 'some years'.[92] The test is therefore best described as requiring that the risk is capable of materialising in the *immediate future*.

On the above analysis, the assessment of imminency is clearly a question of fact. Either the risk is likely to materialise in the immediate future, or it is not. However, it is often stated by courts and scholars that what is meant by 'imminency' in the quia timet context is that 'the injunction must not be issued prematurely'.[93] The decision relied on as authority for this proposition is *Hooper v Rogers*.[94] In that case, the defendant had cut a track across a steep slope that provided the foundation of the claimant's farmhouse. This exposed the slope to soil erosion, and the evidence was that there was a 'long-term danger'[95] that this would cause the farmhouse to collapse, thereby resulting in a private nuisance. The defendant refused to take any steps to prevent the soil from eroding further, and so the claimant asked the court to exercise its discretion to award damages in lieu of a quia timet injunction for the costs of repairing the slope.[96] Chope J held that the circumstances justified the award of a mandatory quia timet injunction ordering the defendant to repair the soil erosion, and awarded the claimant damages in lieu of £750. On appeal, the defendant challenged the award on the basis that the risk that the tort would be committed was not imminent. Russell LJ (with whom Stamp and Scarman LJJ agreed) dismissed the appeal. After analysing the imminency requirement, Russell LJ stated:

> I take the use of the word to indicate that the injunction must not be granted prematurely. But here the operation has been performed, and there was no evidence that any other step would avoid the proven probability of damage to the farmhouse than the step sought by way of mandatory injunction: it could not be said to be premature.[97]

The effect of Russell LJ's reasoning was to hold that because the award of the injunction was not premature in the circumstances, the 'long-term'[98] risk of commission of a nuisance constituted an imminent one.

With respect, this reasoning is misguided. By widening the meaning of the term 'imminent' to focus on whether injunctive relief would not be

[91] *Islington* 2012 (n 34) [35]–[40].

[92] *Fletcher* (n 33) 700.

[93] *Islington* 2012 (n 34) [31]; *Ineos* (HC) (n 69) [89]; *UK Oil and Gas Investments Plc v Persons Unknown* [2018] EWHC 2252 (Ch) [156]; *Vastint* (n 55) [31(4)]; Burrows (n 35) 468; Tettenborn (n 35) [28.21].

[94] *Hooper* (n 34).

[95] The expert surveyor 'could not give a time when the erosion would reach the farmhouse': ibid 48.

[96] Pursuant to the Senior Courts Act 1981, s 50; *Leeds Industrial Co-operative Society Ltd v Slack* [1924] AC 851 (HL).

[97] *Hooper* (n 34) 49.

[98] ibid 48.

premature, Russell LJ conflated the imminency test with the further, secondary test, as outlined in *Fletcher*, which determines when quia timet relief is justified in circumstances where a risk is not imminent.[99] It is illogical to hold that because an injunction is the only means by which a *long-term* risk of commission of a tort can be prevented, this somehow transforms that risk into an *imminent* one. As reiterated above, the authorities (both in the quia timet context and in the assault context) hold that imminency means immediacy, and assessing whether a risk is immediate is plainly a question of fact. Accordingly, the decision in *Hooper* is best explained as falling into the second category of cases where quia timet relief is justified, as argued in section IV.

It should also be recognised that there is an analytical advantage to conceptualising imminency as immediacy. It will mean that in every case, a court must expressly decide whether the alleged tort will be committed in the immediate future. If this is established, the court can give adequate weight to this fact. If immediacy is not established, the court is then put on express notice that further factors must be proved before quia timet relief can be awarded. The approach therefore provides courts with a meaningful structure to guide their reasoning process.

Now that the meaning of a sufficiently 'real' and 'imminent' risk has been clarified, it is clear that courts have relied on the 'imminent danger' requirement in *Fletcher* to formulate the necessary conditions for quia timet relief. It must not be forgotten, however, that Pearson J also required a risk of irreparable harm to found quia relief under his First Test. Whether this is also the contemporary approach will now be explored.

B. A Risk of Irreparable Harm?

i. Bromley*: An Error?*

In *Bromley*, Coulson LJ (with whom Haddon-Cave LJ and the Senior President of Tribunals agreed) stated that the first-instance judge's conclusion that 'what was required was [a risk of] "irreparable harm", was in accordance with authority'.[100] Coulson LJ expressly relied on the decision in *Fletcher* to draw this conclusion. The problem with this reasoning, however, is that the irreparable harm requirement is no longer good law.

As was explained in chapter 2, courts have traditionally considered that whether a claimant would suffer irreparable harm as a result of a defendant's future wrongdoing is a discretionary factor to consider when determining whether to

[99] The Court did not direct attention to the Second Test in *Fletcher*, notwithstanding that counsel for the claimant argued that relief should be awarded pursuant to it: see ibid 46.

[100] *Bromley* (n 2) [35].

award a final prohibitory injunction.[101] On this analysis, the meaning of 'irreparable harm' was that the damage could be described as substantial *and* would not be remedied properly by a pecuniary payment. This is what Pearson J meant by the term 'irreparable' when laying down his requirements in *Fletcher*.

Importantly, however, it was explained in chapter 4 that in the late twentieth-century English courts extended the availability of injunctions to protect legal rights by diluting the irreparable-harm requirement.[102] Instead of asking whether the harm is irreparable, courts now favour a test that asks whether it is 'just, in all the circumstances, that a [claimant] should be confined to his remedy in damages' (the 'Inadequacy Test').[103] The courts therefore do not require the damage or loss to be substantial but instead focus on the extent to which a pecuniary payment will not adequately remedy the claimant.

Coulson LJ's reliance on the decision in *Fletcher* to hold that a risk of irreparable harm is a requirement for quia timet relief is therefore misplaced. As Lord Nicholls observed in *Mercedes Benz AG v Leiduck*, injunctions are to be granted 'in light of today's conditions and standards, not those of yester-year'.[104] However, it is important to recognise that *Fletcher* was not the only case on which Coulson LJ relied in his judgment. He also referred to the 1998 decision of the Court of Appeal in *Lloyd v Symonds*,[105] where the Court did not apply the Inadequacy Test and propounded what prima facie seems to be a different meaning of 'irreparable harm' from the traditional understanding. In that case, the defendants were dog breeders and kept numerous dogs on their property. At first instance, Hall J found that the barking of the dogs had caused a private nuisance from November 1995 to May 1996. However, Hall J also found that by the beginning of June 1996, the nuisance had ceased. Nevertheless, Hall J was satisfied that it was 'likely' that unless an injunction was awarded against them, the defendants would commit the same nuisance in the future.[106] Putting to one side the issue of whether it was correct to classify the injunction as being quia timet,[107] Hall J granted a final quia timet injunction ordering the defendants, inter alia, not to keep more than 30 dogs on their premises.

The Court of Appeal allowed the defendants' appeal and discharged the injunction. Giving the leading judgment, Chadwick LJ stated that Hall J had erred, because a quia timet injunction

> should not, ordinarily, be granted unless the plaintiff can show a strong probability that, unless restrained, the defendant will do something which will cause the plaintiff irreparable harm – that is to say, harm which, if it occurs, cannot be reversed or restrained by

[101] See also *Litchfield-Speer v Queen Anne's Gate Syndicate (No 2)* [1919] 1 Ch 407 (Ch), 411 (quia timet).

[102] See ch 4, section IV.B.i.

[103] *Evans Marshall & Co v Bertola SA* [1973] 1 WLR 349 (CA) 379.

[104] *Mercedes Benz* [1996] AC 284 (PC), 308.

[105] *Lloyd v Symonds* [1998] EWCA Civ 511.

[106] ibid (pinpoint unavailable as the judgment is not reported).

[107] See ch 3.

> an immediate interlocutory injunction and cannot be adequately compensated by an award for damages.[108]

Chadwick LJ's statement of principle means that a quia timet injunction can only be awarded where: (i) damages would be an inadequate remedy for the damage or loss that the claimant would suffer; and (ii) that damage or loss must not be able to be reversed or restrained by an immediate interim injunction when the tort occurs. This was the first time that the term 'irreparable harm' was defined in this way.[109]

When applying his definition of irreparable harm to the facts of the case, Chadwick LJ reasoned that the quia timet injunction should not have been granted because the future damage that the claimant would suffer (that is, unreasonable interference with the enjoyment of land due to the constant barking of dogs) could be restrained immediately by an interim injunction. In other words, as the claimant would not have suffered very substantial or grave damage the moment the nuisance occurred, the quia timet injunction should not have been granted.

Although it is expressed in different words, the effect of Chadwick LJ's statement of principle is simply to reintroduce the old (now extinct) irreparable-harm requirement. The only way that damage or loss cannot be reversed or restrained by an immediate interim injunction is if it is very substantial or grave. Indeed, in his judgment, Chadwick LJ went on to state that Hall J should have asked himself whether, if the nuisance did recur in the future, 'the damage suffered by the plaintiff would be so grave and irreparable that, notwithstanding the grant of an immediate interlocutory injunction (at that stage) to restrain further occurrence of the acts complained of, a remedy in damages would be inadequate'.[110]

Coulson LJ's approach in *Bromley* therefore derives little support from the decision in *Lloyd v Symonds*. *Lloyd* makes the same error as that in *Bromley*: it applies a requirement for injunctive relief that no longer exists. A retort that could be made here is that the Court of Appeal in both *Lloyd* and *Bromley* considered that the old irreparable-harm requirement deserves to be retained in the context of quia timet injunctions. However, not only is this not stated in the reasoning in these cases, but neither Chadwick LJ in *Lloyd* nor Coulson LJ in *Bromley* drew attention to the case law holding that an Inadequacy Test is to be applied. Moreover, as was explained in chapter 3, ordinary prohibitory and desisting mandatory injunctions operate for the same purpose as quia timet injunctions: they are awarded to prevent future torts. Hence, there is no good reason to retain the irreparable-harm requirement as a necessary condition solely for quia timet relief.

[108] *Lloyd v Symonds* (n 105), paragraph reference unavailable.

[109] Chadwick LJ cited the first-instance decision of Farwell J in *Attorney General v Corp of Nottingham* (n 77) to support his statement of principle. However, in that case, a quia timet injunction was refused because the claimant had not proved a real risk that a public nuisance would occur in the future. The decision therefore does not provide any authoritative support for Chadwick LJ's statement.

[110] *Lloyd v Symonds* (n 105), paragraph reference unavailable. The test was applied by Marcus Smith J in *Vastint* (n 55).

As a final point, it should be noted that in the more recent first-instance decisions applying the irreparable harm requirement endorsed in *Bromley*, the term has been given such a wide meaning that in reality the Inadequacy Test is being applied. For example, in *Sutton LBC v Persons Unknown*, the requirement seemed to be satisfied by the fact that a future trespass by gypsy travellers would prevent local residents from using public spaces.[111] And in *London Borough of Hackney v Powlesland*, the fact that future trespassers could possibly confront council workers or disturb the public by obstructing a highway was held to be sufficient.[112] In these cases, it is difficult to describe the future damage or loss that would be suffered by the claimants as 'very substantial' or 'grave'. These cases therefore give further support to the conclusion that the irreparable-harm requirement is now extinct.

ii. The Positive Law Explained

In the light of the foregoing, there was no persuasive basis for the Court of Appeal in *Bromley* to demand proof of a risk of irreparable harm instead of a risk that if the tort were committed, damages would be an inadequate remedy. But this raises the question: is it a necessary condition for quia timet relief that the claimant prove that there is a risk that damages would be an inadequate remedy?

On the one hand, the multiplicity of suits doctrine, as discussed in chapter 2, has no application in the context of a claimant seeking a quia timet injunction before a wrong has occurred. Accordingly, as reflected in Pearson J's judgment in *Fletcher*, it would seem that proof of a risk that damages would be an inadequate remedy is the underlying justification for the award of a quia timet injunction to restrain a future tort.

On the other hand, there are two categories of case in which quia timet injunctions have been awarded that suggest that no such necessary condition exists. First, courts have awarded quia timet injunctions in respect of economic torts, like inducing a breach of contract and unlawful means conspiracy, where the risk of pure economic loss is (arguably) capable of being adequately remedied by a damages award.[113] Moreover, quia timet injunctions restraining future trespasses to land have been granted even though there is little or no risk of damage to the claimant.[114] It is difficult to argue that in these cases damages would be an inadequate remedy if the future tort were committed.

Having considered the competing arguments, the better view is that the question of whether damages would be an adequate remedy is only a discretionary

[111] *Sutton* (n 57) [28], [35]–[36].

[112] *London Borough of Hackney v Powlesland* [2020] EWHC 2102 (Ch) [39].

[113] *Torquay Hotel Co* (n 74) (interim); *Express Newspapers plc v Mitchell* [1982] IRLR 465 (QB) (interim); *Cuadrilla* (n 6) (interim).

[114] *Cambridge* (n 14); *Fitzwilliam Land Co v Cheesman* [2018] EWHC 3139 (QB); *Ansco* (n 7).

factor to be taken into account. The reason for this view can be derived from two statements of principle.

First, consider the underlying purpose of the quia timet injunction, as explained by Lord Hanworth MR in *Graigola Merthyr Co Ltd v Swansea*:

> When the Court has before it evidence sufficient to establish that an injury will be done if there is no intervention by the Court – it will … supply the need of what has been termed protective justice. It is a very old principle. Sir E Coke … says that 'preventing justice excelleth punishing justice,' and quotes Bracton's advice: 'Et hoc faciat tempestive, ne per negligentiam damnum incurrat, quia melius est in tempore occurrere quam post causam vulneratam remedium quaerere'.[115]

The Latin translates as 'it is better to restrain in time than to seek a remedy after the injury has been inflicted'.[116]

Second, it is the prime duty of the courts to uphold the individual rights generated by the common law.[117] As remarked by Arden LJ in the context of awarding a prohibitory injunction restraining a future trespass to land:

> The grant of an injunction is undoubtedly discretionary but, in my judgment, in a society governed by the rule of law, the court should grant an injunction necessary to uphold legal rights against a threatened invasion unless there is some factor which is sufficiently weighty to displace this general rule.[118]

Taken together, these lines of reasoning strongly suggest that courts should not sit idly by and allow a claimant's rights to be infringed when they are satisfied that a defendant is about to commit a tort against the claimant. The significance of a finding by a court that there is a real and imminent risk that the defendant will commit a tort against the claimant, should not be underestimated. Once the claimant surmounts this high threshold, there is sufficient justification to award a quia timet injunction regardless of whether the future damage or loss is irreparable, or whether damages would be an inadequate remedy. This is because refusing quia timet relief (without an additional countervailing factor) would erode legal rights. Consider the following hypothetical example.

C is the consignee listed on a non-negotiable bill of lading providing for the carriage of £1m worth of bauxite from Jamaica to England. Ten days before the arrival of the vessel in England, C obtains strong evidence that the shipowner and his stevedores have hatched a plan to steal the bauxite upon the vessel's arrival in the UK. C, having title to the cargo, immediately brings proceedings in England

[115] *Graigola Merthyr Co Ltd v Swansea* [1928] Ch 235 (CA) 242. Approved in *Lloyd* (n 105); *Islington* 2012 (n 34) [31].

[116] *Plaintiff S99/2016* (2016) 243 FCR 17 [458].

[117] '[T]he High Court possesses the power, and bears the responsibility, to act so as to maintain the rule of law': *Wolverhampton* (n 8) [18]. See also R Stevens, 'Damages for Wrongdoing in the Absence of Loss' in J Varuhas and NA Moreham (eds), *Remedies for Breach of Privacy* (Hart Publishing 2018) 97, 105.

[118] *Secretary of State for Environment, Food and Rural Affairs v Meier* [2008] EWCA Civ 903 [53].

seeking a quia timet injunction against the shipowner and his agents to restrain them from committing the tort of conversion. However, bauxite is readily available on the commodities market and C could find an alternative cargo of bauxite to replace his cargo if it were stolen. Damages would therefore be an adequate remedy if the tort was committed.

In these circumstances, it would be odd if a court were to hold that although there is a real and imminent risk that the defendants are going to commit conversion against C, a quia timet injunction should be refused because damages would be an adequate remedy, and therefore C should simply wait until the tort has been committed against him and commence litigation afterwards. What this example demonstrates is that if courts automatically refused quia timet relief solely on the basis that, for example, pure economic loss could be remedied after the fact, or that a trespass to land or conversion of goods could be adequately remedied by damages, this would significantly diminish the rights that tort law generates, undermine public confidence in the administration of justice and risk destabilising judicial legitimacy. As Gaudron and McHugh JJ observed in the High Court of Australia in another context:

> If the courts ... do not uphold the rights of individuals by granting effective remedies, they invite anarchy, for nothing breeds social disorder as quickly as the sense of injustice which is apt to be generated by the unlawful invasion of a person's rights ...[119]

Lady Hale made a similar statement in the context of the Supreme Court's unanimous upholding of the award of an injunction to restrain a future trespass to land, where her Ladyship remarked '[t]he underlying principle is *ubi ius, ibi remedium*: where there is a right, there should be a remedy to fit the right'.[120] In the unique situation where a court is satisfied that the defendant is about to commit a tort against the claimant, in almost all cases the best 'remedy to fit the right' will be a quia timet injunction.

For these reasons, the best explanation of the positive law is that once a court is satisfied that there is a real and imminent risk of commission of a tort, the claimant's burden of proof is discharged, and the onus shifts to the defendant to show why an injunction should not be granted. The claimant does not have to prove a risk of irreparable harm or that damages would be an inadequate remedy: the question of whether damages would be an adequate remedy is only a discretionary factor.

Although this conclusion may at first sight seem to be quite controversial, it accords with the approach taken by the courts when awarding ordinary prohibitory injunctions and desisting mandatory injunctions that restrain continuing

[119] *Plenty v Dillon* (1991) 171 CLR 635, 655.

[120] *Secretary of State for the Environment, Food and Rural Affairs v Meier* [2009] UKSC 11, [2009] 1 WLR 2780 [25]. See also *Western Counties Manure Co v Lawes Chemical Manure Co* (1874) LR 9 Ex 218, 222; *Secretary of State for the Environment, Food and Rural Affairs v Drury* [2004] 1 WLR 1906 (CA) [20]; *Meier* (CA) (n 118) [53].

torts. As was explained in chapters 4 and 5, it is not a necessary condition for the award of a prohibitory injunction or a desisting mandatory injunction that damages would be an inadequate remedy. Rather, proof of a real and imminent risk of a tort's being committed is sufficient to justify the grant of injunctive relief. It is therefore unsurprising that the same position is taken in the context of quia timet injunctions, subject to the caveat that the claimant's evidential onus of proving that there is in fact a real and imminent risk of commission of a tort is much more difficult to satisfy in the quia timet context.[121]

iii. Overview

The effect of the foregoing analysis is that a quia timet injunction can be awarded where there is a real and imminent risk that the defendant will commit a tort against the claimant. Indeed, the torts of private nuisance,[122] public nuisance,[123] trespass to land,[124] battery,[125] assault,[126] harassment,[127] inducing a breach of contract,[128] unlawful means conspiracy,[129] intimidation,[130] passing off[131] and breach of statutory duty[132] have all been restrained quia timet pursuant to the First Test. The necessary conditions for the award of quia timet relief pursuant to the First Test therefore do not change depending on the tort sought to be restrained (except, for the reasons given in chapter 4, if the 'tort' generates a primary liability). It is also worth highlighting that unlike ordinary prohibitory and mandatory desisting injunctions, which are not suited to restraining torts that are unlikely to be repeated, a quia timet injunction can be granted to restrain any threatened tort before it has occurred. It therefore has greater scope to be deployed as a tort remedy.[133]

[121] As was explained in ch 3.

[122] eg, *Litchfield-Speer* (n 101) (declaration treated as an injunction); *High Speed Two (HS2) Ltd v Persons Unknown* [2022] EWHC 2360 (KB) (both private and public nuisance restrained). In Australia, see *Grasso v Love* [1980] VR 163; *Onus v Telstra Corporation Limited* [2011] NSWSC 33.

[123] eg, *Medcalf v R Strawbridge Ltd* [1937] 2 KB 102 (KB); *Hackney LBC v Persons Unknown* (n 3) (interim); *Wolverhampton* 2020 (n 4). In Australia, see *Kenthurst Investments Pty Ltd v Wyong Shire Council* (1964) 10 LGRA 307; *NSW Harness Racing Club Ltd v Leichhardt Municipal Council* (1997) 97 LGERA 256 (interlocutory).

[124] eg, *Vastint* (n 55); *Ansco* (n 7); *RGCM* (n 57).

[125] eg, *In Re C* (n 5).

[126] eg, *Khorasandjian v Bush* [1993] QB 727 (CA) (interim).

[127] eg, *AstraZeneca UK v Mathai* [2014] EWHC 2774 (QB).

[128] eg, *Torquay Hotel Co* (n 74) (interim); *Express Newspapers* (n 113) (interim). See also *Union Traffic Ltd v Transport and General Workers Union* [1989] ICR 98 (CA), 111; *Kestrel Coal Pty Ltd v Construction, Forestry, Mining and Energy Union* [2001] 1 Qd R 634.

[129] eg, *Cuadrilla* (n 6) (interim). See also *Mbasogo v Logo Ltd (No 1)* [2005] EWHC 2034 (QB) [97].

[130] eg, *News Group Newspapers Ltd v Society of Graphical and Allied Trades (No 2)* [1987] ICR 181 (QB) (interim).

[131] eg, *Ewing v Buttercup Margarine Co Ltd* [1917] 2 Ch 1 (CA); *Reckitt & Colman Products Ltd v Borden* [1990] 1 WLR 491 (HL).

[132] eg, *Attorney-General v Wellingborough UDC* (1974) 72 LGR 507 (CA) (note that the Attorney-General brought suit in this case).

[133] The implications of these findings for negligence law are discussed in ch 7.

A counter argument could be made here in respect of the torts of libel and slander. In order to protect a defendant's freedom of expression,[134] courts are reluctant to grant *interim* injunctions (whether ordinary or quia timet) restraining those torts. It could be argued that the same reluctance would arise when a court is considering whether to grant a final quia timet injunction to restrain libel or slander, as the claimant is seeking to restrain the torts before they have occurred. Therefore, the argument would run, a different test operates in respect of those torts.

The problem with this argument, however, is that it overlooks the distinction between an interim and final injunction. If a claimant were to seek a *final* quia timet injunction to restrain libel or slander, after the trial a court would have all the evidence adduced by the parties in order to rule on: (i) whether the words contained in the future publication (or oral statement) are defamatory; and (ii) and whether any defences apply (such as truth or qualified privilege). Accordingly, there is much less risk of stifling a defendant's freedom of expression. It follows that, although the author was unable to locate a case in which a final quia timet injunction was granted to restrain libel or slander,[135] these torts can be restrained upon proof (at trial) of a real and imminent risk of their commission.

There is a final point that can be derived from the above example, which must be considered here. The author was unable to locate a case in which a quia timet injunction was refused because a defendant was able to satisfy a court that at the time the tort would occur in the future, the defendant would be able to make out a defence at law. If a defence would be able to be made out by a defendant at the time of the alleged tort then a quia timet injunction must be refused.

IV. The Necessary Conditions: A Second Test?

The Court of Appeal has assumed that a quia timet injunction can be awarded only where the claimant has established that there is a real and imminent risk that a tort will be committed that will cause irreparable harm. The existing literature also seems to adopt this position,[136] in that no author has considered whether there could be other types of case in which justice would require quia timet relief to be granted to prevent a future tort.

This section contends that, as a matter of positive law, there is a second type of case in which courts can award a quia timet injunction to prevent a future tort. As

[134] See R Parkes et al, *Gatley on Libel and Slander* (13th edn, Sweet & Maxwell 2022) ch 27.

[135] Although see *Cartus Corporation v Siddell* [2014] EWHC 2266 (QB), where a quia timet injunction was refused only because of the claimant's failure to prove that there was a real risk that the defendant would commit libel.

[136] Bean, Parry and Burns (n 59) [2-14]; Davies (n 59) [18-029]; Burrows (n 35) 467; Tettenborn (n 35) [28-20]–[28-22].

explained in section II, although on the facts Fletcher failed to obtain an injunction, the ratio decidendi of the decision in *Fletcher* is that quia timet relief can be granted where the risk that a nuisance will be committed is not imminent but the circumstances are such that the claimant is unable to protect herself from irreparable harm. Despite quoting the Second Test in *Fletcher* on numerous occasions,[137] the modern courts have never expressly applied it. Nor has the scholarship identified the test's existence.[138] This section argues that it is the best explanation for two oft-cited Court of Appeal decisions and that there are compelling reasons for accepting it as a ground for quia timet relief.

A. The Law Explained

As already intimated, the decision in *Hooper v Rogers* is best understood as applying the Second Test in *Fletcher*. The reason for Russell LJ's decision was that the 'long-term danger' of commission of a nuisance was sufficient because it was not premature to award an injunction. As already explained, this reasoning is misconceived. However, the award of quia timet relief in the case is widely accepted by courts and scholars alike.[139] It is the author's contention that the result is correct for a different reason: that the claimant was unable to protect himself from irreparable harm that would be caused by the future nuisance. There are four features of the case that indicate this: first, there was a 'real probability'[140] that the damage (and therefore a nuisance) would materialise; second, the damage would be irreparable in the traditional sense: the nuisance was going to destroy the claimant's house; third, and unlike in *Fletcher*, where the defendants were willing to reduce the risk by way of tanks and pumps, Rogers wantonly refused to make any repairs to the land; fourth, the only remaining reasonable action that the claimant could take to reduce the risk was to repair the track himself, which is precisely what Rogers, as the co-owner of the land, ought to have done. Taken together, these four factors demonstrate that the claimant was unable to protect himself from the future nuisance causing irreparable harm, such that 'the remedy sought [was] not premature'.[141] It follows that the decision to grant quia timet relief, albeit in the form of damages in lieu, is better explained on this basis.

This conclusion also derives significant support from the decision in *Islington LBC v Elliott*.[142] In that case, the council owned a residential property that it let to short-term tenants. Over the years, ash trees began to grow unchecked. The

[137] *Hooper* (n 34) 49–50; *Islington* 2012 (n 34) [30]; *Vastint* (n 55) [30].

[138] Nolan has, however, identified that preventive damages can be awarded in circumstances where a tort is not imminent, see D Nolan, 'Preventive Damages' (2016) 132 *LQR* 68, 86.

[139] *Islington* 2012 (n 34) [31]; *Vastint* (n 55) [31(4)]; Spry (n 35) 392–93; Gee (n 43) [2-045]; Burrows (n 35) 468; Tettenborn (n 35) [28.21].

[140] *Hooper* (n 34) 48.

[141] ibid 50.

[142] *Islington* (n 34).

claimants, who owned the property next door, expressed concern to the council that the tree roots might enter their land and undermine the foundations of their house. For many years the council ignored the claimants' concerns until, immediately before the claimants commenced proceedings, it issued a 'works order' to remove the trees. Unaware of this, the claimants commenced proceedings for quia timet relief. The trees were later removed by the council and the question before the Court was who should bear the legal costs. In order to determine that question, the claim had to be tried, and the sole issue was whether the claimants were entitled to relief. The major hurdle for the claimants was that the risk could not be described as imminent, as the expert evidence was that the tree roots would not damage the claimants' house for another three years.

The trial judge found for the claimants and awarded costs in their favour.[143] On appeal, Patten LJ, giving the leading judgment, reversed the order on costs and held that the trial judge had been wrong to conclude that the claimants would have been entitled to quia timet relief.[144] As we shall see, this result is correct and Patten LJ's reasons for it are persuasive, bar one perplexing observation.

After setting out the real-and-imminent-risk test, Patten LJ quoted *Hooper* to explain that a court in this type of case is entitled to look beyond this test.[145] Moreover, he approved of the decision in *Hooper* and observed that:

> nothing short of [the track's] removal would cure the problem. It was therefore realistic for the judge in that case to have taken the view that an injunction should be granted as the only means of preventing that risk from materialising.[146]

Having made this accurate observation, Patten LJ was able to hold that the claimant 'has to show that an injunction is necessary in order to prevent the occurrence of the nuisance'.[147] He held that this was not satisfied on the facts of the instant case because, in contrast to the defendant in *Hooper*, the defendant council was willing to do precisely what the claimants sought: it was in the process of removing the ash trees.[148] Therefore it could not be said that an injunction was warranted. This is undoubtedly correct. Unfortunately, however, Patten LJ summed up his analysis of the law by stating that it is only in cases where 'the risk of damage is so imminent and the intransigence of the defendant so obvious that the court should ordinarily be prepared to grant an injunction in order to prevent a nuisance which does not yet exist'.[149]

This statement of principle is the major complication with the reasoning. It is anomalous to hold on the one hand that *Hooper* can be explained entirely on the

[143] The basis for the first-instance result is unclear, as no electronic or physical copy of the judgment can be located.
[144] *Islington* (n 34) [40].
[145] ibid [34], [36].
[146] ibid [37].
[147] ibid [38].
[148] ibid [39]–[40].
[149] ibid [38].

basis that the injunction was justified as the only means of preventing the long-term risk from materialising; and yet, on the other hand, to hold that imminency is always a requirement for quia timet relief. The better explanation is that injunctive relief was not merited in this case only because the defendant was willing to remove the trees, and therefore it could not be said that there was a real risk that a nuisance was going to be committed. It follows that Patten LJ applied the Second Test in *Fletcher*, but (as in *Fletcher*) it was not made out.

Although it was not expressly applied in the reasoning, the results in both *Hooper* and *Islington* are consistent with the Second Test in *Fletcher.* Indeed, in the more recent Court of Appeal decision of *Network Rail Infrastructure Ltd v Williams*, Sir Terence Etherton MR cited *Hooper* and *Islington* and observed briefly in an obiter dictum that the imminency requirement 'is too prescriptive and what matters is the probability and likely gravity of damage rather than simply its imminence'.[150] There is, therefore, a sound authoritative basis for the acceptance of the Second Test. Moreover, as we shall see below, there are good reasons for awarding quia timet relief in these circumstances.

B. Arguments Justifying the Test's Existence

On the preceding analysis, it is clear that four factors persuade courts to award relief pursuant to the Second Test: (i) there must be a real risk that a tort will be committed; (ii) if that risk materialised, the harm must be irreparable (that is, substantial and unable to be remedied by a damages award); (iii) the defendant must refuse to take reasonable steps to lessen the risk; and (iv) the claimant must be unable to take any further reasonable and lawful action to avoid the risk.

Although not stated in the cases, quia timet relief is justified in these circumstances because, in accordance with the principles of equity, it ensures that injustice is avoided by extending the protection of legal rights. This is best understood by considering what would occur if injunctive relief were refused.

In these types of cases, the reason why claimants cannot obtain relief on the First Test is that there is no *imminent* risk that the tort will be committed. The difficulty that this presents is that if quia timet relief is refused, the claimant will be left in anguish for a number of years over the fact that irreparable harm is likely to result and that there is nothing she can do until much closer to the time when the risk will materialise. Because the damage she would then suffer would be irreparable, the claimant will probably consider bringing further litigation or taking matters into her own hands. For example, a claimant may commit a wrong to reduce the risk of harm (like, for example, trespassing on the defendant's

[150] *Williams* (n 34) 621 (with whom Sharp and Leggatt LJJ agreed). This dictum accords with the approaches favoured by Murphy (n 35) 532–33 and Nolan (n 138) 86–87.

property to remove the trees that may undermine the foundations of her house), or re-ignite a legal or personal conflict with the defendant in an attempt to persuade him to take action. Allowing this to occur would be contrary to the courts' fundamental duty, based on public policy, to achieve finality in litigation; *interest rei publicae ut sit finis litium* ('it is for the common good that there should be an end to litigation').[151] Indeed, given that many of the quia timet cases involve nuisances between neighbours that create disputes that transcend legal conflicts, this consideration is crucial.

Furthermore, from a practical perspective, in most cases it will be *less* burdensome for a defendant to comply with a quia timet injunction before the relevant tort becomes imminent. As Nolan has observed in the context of analysing the law on preventive damages, 'a threatened tort may be more difficult or more expensive to avert when it has become imminent than when it first becomes apparent'.[152] This is another argument against a strict rule requiring proof of imminence before quia timet relief is awarded.

The award of quia timet relief recognises that legal rights generated by the law of tort must be enforced in exceptional circumstances. In doing so, it upholds social order by placating the claimant's valid anxieties with a remedy, while simultaneously demonstrating that the law will provide a proportionate response in justified circumstances. Such a response reflects the modern role of equity. As Lady Arden remarked in *Vauxhall Motors Ltd v Manchester Ship Canal Co Ltd*:

> Equity serves to finesse rules of law in deserving cases. It thus makes the system of law in England and Wales one which is more likely to produce a fair result than would be possible if equity did not exist.[153]

Three main objections could be made here. First, it could be said that the further availability of quia timet relief pursuant to the Second Test would interfere unduly with individual freedoms. This concern is a valid one if relief is awarded solely on the basis of there being a real, but not imminent, risk. However, it holds much less weight where not only is there a real risk that a tort will be committed, but the defendant also refuses to take any steps to reduce the risk, the claimant will suffer irreparable harm if the risk materialises, and there is no reasonable and lawful action that the claimant can take to avoid the risk. Such circumstances are exceptional and justify a degree of interference with the defendant's freedoms.

Second, it could be argued that the requirement of a risk of irreparable harm is subject to the same difficulties identified in section III.B; that is, the requirement is now extinct. This objection should be accepted. Given that the courts have now abandoned the irreparable-harm criterion and replaced it with the Inadequacy

[151] E Rock, 'Resolving Conflicts at the Interface of Public and Private Law' (2020) 94 *Australian Law Journal* 381, 392. See also *Murphy v Stone-Wallwork (Charlton) Ltd* [1969] 1 WLR 1023 (HL) 1035; *Rogers v The Queen* (1994) 181 CLR 251, 273 (although the maxim is applied in a different context in these cases).

[152] Nolan (n 138) 86.

[153] *Vauxhall Motors Ltd v Manchester Ship Canal Co Ltd* [2019] UKSC 46, [2020] AC 1161 [63].

Test, there is no reason why the former criterion should be retained when applying the Second Test. It will ultimately be for the courts to make this change. It is important to recognise, however, that in contrast with the First Test, where the fact that damages would be inadequate is a discretionary factor to consider, the Second Test *requires* that damages would be an inadequate remedy before relief can be granted.

Third, given that *Fletcher*, *Hooper* and *Islington* all concerned whether a nuisance should be prevented, it could be said that the Second Test does not apply to other torts. The problem with this conclusion is that there is no good reason for such a limitation. When the four limbs of the Second Test are made out, the adverse consequences of refusing relief will arise irrespective of whether the defendant's actions would amount to a nuisance, a trespass or any other actionable tort. Thus, the better view is that the Second Test is not so confined.

C. Broader Implications for the Positive Law in Respect of Ordinary Injunctions

It was explained in chapter 3, and it has been reiterated on numerous occasions throughout this chapter, that ordinary prohibitory injunctions and desisting mandatory injunctions operate for the same purpose as quia timet injunctions. It necessarily follows that if the Second Test represents the positive law in respect of when a quia timet injunction can be granted to restrain a future tort, that same test should also apply to the award of an ordinary prohibitory injunction or a desisting mandatory injunction.

The author was unable to locate a case that considers whether an ordinary injunction can be granted in circumstances where the future tort is not imminent. This dearth of case law is unremarkable, however. Where a prohibitory injunction or a desisting mandatory injunction is granted in circumstances in which a defendant has previously committed a tort against the claimant and intends to continue to do so in the future, the past tort and the future tort will generally be close in time. Therefore, the real-and-imminent-risk test is applied. However, it should not be thought that where the past tort and the future tort are not close in time, the automatic conclusion is that an injunction can never be granted.

Recall the case of *Redland Bricks v Morris*.[154] Assume for a moment that after the defendants had committed the private nuisance by causing the claimant's land to subside, expert evidence was put before the court that indicated that if the defendants failed to take positive action to fill in the excavations on their land, it was certain that the claimant's land would subside again in *three years' time*. The past nuisance and the future nuisance are therefore three years apart. For the same reasons that justify the existence of the Second Test in respect of the award of quia timet injunctions, a desisting mandatory injunction should be granted. Where no

[154] *Redland Bricks* (n 54).

countervailing discretionary considerations can be made out by the defendant, there is clearly no good reason to deny relief simply because the threat of the future tort's being committed is not imminent. As Nolan has explained in the preventive damages context, '[t]here is … no particular magic in the imminence of the threat'.[155]

Accordingly, although there is no case dealing with the issue, the better view is that ordinary prohibitory injunctions and desisting mandatory injunctions can also be granted to restrain future torts where the Second Test is satisfied.

V. The Discretionary Analysis

Once the claimant has proved the necessary conditions contained in either the First Test or the Second Test, the usual discretionary analysis follows. The discretion that a court exercises to determine whether to award a quia timet injunction is identical to the discretion that courts exercise when considering whether to grant ordinary prohibitory injunctions, as outlined in chapter 4. The discretionary considerations, which by their nature are general and apply across many different areas of equity, seem to operate in the same way in quia timet cases. For example, in *Redland Bricks*, the House of Lords discharged (what their Lordships incorrectly believed to be) a mandatory quia timet injunction on the ground that it imposed an unqualified obligation on the defendants (that is, it was contrary to the constant-supervision consideration).[156] A number of claims for quia timet injunctions have also been refused for the reason that the proposed injunction would infringe the defendants' rights under the ECHR – meaning that the injunction would fall foul of the maxim that equity follows the law and any relevant statutes.[157] This occurs frequently in cases in which claimants seek quia timet injunctions to prevent travellers and the Roma community or protesters (being unknown persons) from committing acts that may amount to torts. For example, in *Boyd v Ineos Upstream Ltd*, the Court of Appeal discharged two quia timet injunctions on the basis that they infringed the defendant anti-fracking protestors' right to freedom of peaceful assembly under Article 11 ECHR.[158]

These cases show that there is good reason to believe that the discretionary considerations analysed in chapter 4 operate in the same way when courts decide whether to award quia timet injunctions. As explained in chapter 3, however, there is said to be one exception: the consideration of undue hardship.

[155] Nolan (n 138) 86.

[156] *Redland Bricks* (n 54) 667.

[157] See *South Bucks DC v Porter* [2003] 2 AC 558 (HL); JD Heydon, MJ Leeming and PG Turner, *Meagher, Gummow & Lehane's Equity: Doctrines & Remedies* (5th edn, LexisNexis 2015) [3-030]–[3-040]. See also the discussion of human rights considerations in ch 4.

[158] *Boyd* (n 8) [42], [50]. See also *Canada Goose* (n 8) [93].

In *Redland Bricks*, Lord Upjohn stated that 'unlike the case where a negative injunction is granted to prevent the continuance or recurrence of a wrongful act', the cost that would be suffered by a defendant to prevent 'a future apprehended wrong' must be taken into account.[159] His Lordship then clarified this point by providing two further statements of principle.

First, Lord Upjohn stated that where the defendant 'has acted without regard to his neighbour's rights, or has tried to steal a march on him or has tried to evade the jurisdiction of the court', injunctive relief may be granted 'even if the expense to him is out of all proportion to the advantage thereby accruing to the plaintiff'.[160] This statement of principle is sound. As explained in chapter 4, it is well established in the case law concerning prohibitory and desisting mandatory injunctions that a defendant cannot rely on the consideration of undue hardship where he committed his tort with actual knowledge that his conduct would infringe the claimant's rights, or with a reckless disregard for the claimant's rights.

Second, Lord Upjohn stated that where the defendant has acted reasonably, any costs the defendant would suffer as a result of the granting of the quia timet injunction should be taken into account for two reasons:

> First, because no legal wrong has yet occurred (for which [the claimant] has not been recompensed at law and in equity) and, in spite of gloomy expert opinion, may never occur, or possibly only upon a much smaller scale than anticipated. Secondly, because if ultimately heavy damage does occur the plaintiff is in no way prejudiced for he has his action at law and all his consequential remedies in equity.[161]

The point that Lord Upjohn is making is that, for the above two reasons, a balancing test should be applied when assessing whether a quia timet injunction should be refused for hardship. It is important to bear in mind, however, that Lord Upjohn ultimately decided the case on the basis that the injunction should be refused because 'it imposed an unlimited and unqualified obligation upon the [defendants]'.[162] Nevertheless, he indicated that because the defendants had acted reasonably and the mandatory injunction could cause them to have to spend up to £30,000 in order to prevent future damage to the plaintiffs' market garden (which was valued at £1,600), the injunction also would have imposed unjustifiable hardship on the defendants.

With respect, Lord Upjohn's dictum should not be accepted. As explained in chapters 4 and 5, ordinary prohibitory injunctions and desisting mandatory injunctions are granted upon proof of a *real* risk of commission of a future tort by the defendant. Additionally, as Lord Upjohn accepted explicitly in *Redland Bricks*, such injunctions are granted irrespective of the cost that would be suffered by the defendant, unless it would be oppressive to grant the injunction. Pursuant

[159] *Redland Bricks* (n 54) 667.
[160] ibid.
[161] ibid.
[162] ibid.

to the First Test or the Second Test, quia timet injunctions are also granted upon proof of there being a *real* risk of a future tort being committed by the defendant. Accordingly, unless there are convincing reasons demanding otherwise, the rule of law (and specifically, the principle that like cases must be treated alike) demands that the same oppression test should be applied to determine whether a quia timet injunction should be refused for hardship. The major difficulty with accepting Lord Upjohn's dictum is that he does not articulate convincing reasons for adopting a balancing test in this context.

Lord Upjohn's first argument – that, in the quia timet context, cost is relevant because 'the tort may never occur, or possibly only upon a much smaller scale than anticipated' – is problematic. In circumstances where a repeated tort is restrained by an ordinary prohibitory injunction, it may also be the case that the tort will not be repeated or that the damage that will eventuate is much smaller than anticipated. Yet a balancing test is not adopted.

Lord Upjohn's second argument – that 'if ultimately heavy damage does occur the plaintiff is in no way prejudiced for he has his action at law' – is even less convincing. Lord Upjohn is in effect telling claimants who have established that there is a real (and, in most cases, imminent) risk that a tort will be committed against them that they need not worry if the defendant later causes them 'heavy damage', because they will be able to seek damages after the fact. For the reasons given in section III.B.ii, such an approach would diminish the rights that tort law generates and undermine public confidence in the administration of justice.

Thus, Lord Upjohn's dictum that a balancing test should be applied to assess hardship cannot be supported.[163] The better view is that a quia timet injunction can be refused for hardship only where the defendant proves that the consequences that would be suffered by him as a result of granting the injunction would be oppressive.

VI. Conclusion

As a matter of positive law, the analytical process by which courts consider whether to award a (prohibitory or mandatory[164]) quia timet injunction to restrain *any* future tort (other than a 'tort' that generates a primary liability) is as follows.

Determination 1.1: The claimant must prove that there is a real and imminent risk that the defendant will commit a tort against her. If the claimant fails to satisfy her burden of proof, the Second Test must be considered. If the claimant satisfies her

[163] It should be noted that the author was unable to locate any case in which Lord Upjohn's dictum on this point was considered.

[164] It is presumed that any form of mandatory injunctive relief requires proof that it is necessary and possible for the defendant to do a positive act to prevent his future tort, as explained in ch 5.

burden of proof, the defendant bears the onus of proving that an injunction should *not* be awarded.

Figure 6.1 Determination 1.1 (Quia Timet Injunction)

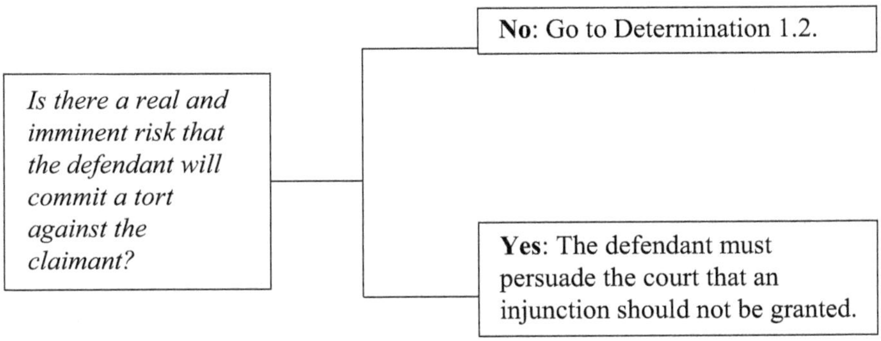

Determination 1.2: The claimant must prove that she is unable to protect herself from a real risk that the defendant will commit a tort against her that will cause irreparable harm. If the claimant fails to satisfy her burden of proof, no injunction can be awarded. If the claimant satisfies her burden of proof, the defendant bears the onus of proving that an injunction should *not* be awarded.

Figure 6.2 Determination 1.2 (Quia Timet Injunction)

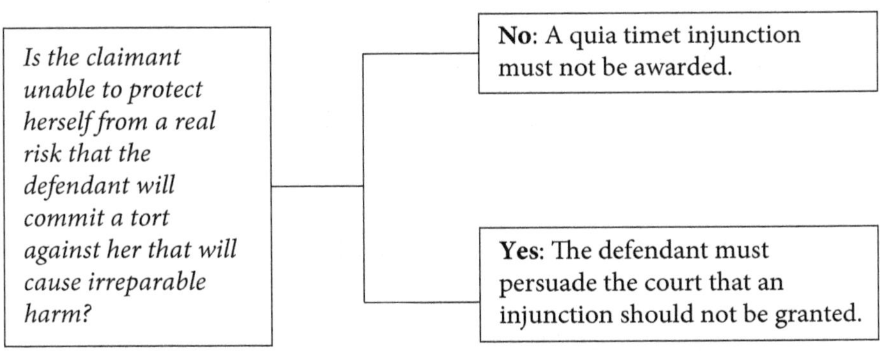

The remaining determinations outlined in respect of prohibitory injunctions in chapter 4 otherwise apply.

7

Implications for Tort Law

I. Introduction

The leading tort theorist Ernest Weinrib has said that '[a]n enquiry into the nature of tort law is not an exploration of uncharted territory, but a visit to the familiar landmarks of our legal world'.[1] This penultimate chapter challenges Weinrib's suggestion. Having set out the doctrinal findings as to when prohibitory, desisting and restorative mandatory injunctions and quia timet injunctions can be granted, this chapter considers what implications these findings have for understanding tort law more generally. As was explained in chapter 1, the final objective of this book is to understand what the availability of injunctive relief in tort indicates about tort law itself.

In chapters 3, 4, 5, and 6, the principles governing the award of injunctions in tort law were exposited and analysed in the light of the large body of contemporary and historical case law in England and Wales, and in other common law jurisdictions, in which injunctions have been granted to restrain or remedy many different torts. In showing exactly which torts have been restrained or remedied by which types of injunctions, we can see vividly the extent to which injunctive relief has been awarded in the modern law of torts. The analysis of the case law and the taxonomy of final injunctions that has been developed therefore provides a launching pad from which to test and develop claims that have been made about the law of tort and about particular issues in tort law.

In order to identify what implications the earlier findings of this book have for tort law, this chapter evaluates tort scholarship that has used the availability (or otherwise) of injunctive relief to make claims about tort law itself. The chapter tests such claims by comparing them against the doctrinal findings in chapters 3, 4, 5, and 6. This technique enables the chapter to go beyond the claims made in the existing scholarship in order to provide further, original insights about how tort law operates.

For the avoidance of doubt, the implications of the doctrinal findings for general theories of tort law are not considered in this chapter. That is because, for the reasons explained in chapter 1, this book is confined to engaging in doctrinal research. An identification of the theoretical implications that arise from the

[1] E Weinrib, 'Understanding Tort Law' (1989) 23 *Valparaiso University Law Review* 485, 490.

doctrinal findings therefore falls outside the scope of the book. Furthermore, as we shall see below, a number of more general doctrinal issues have not yet been addressed and it is necessary that these issues be given exclusive focus in this chapter.

This chapter is split into three main sections, with separate claims being made in each one. Section II evaluates John Gardner's contention that damages are tort law's 'primary' remedy.[2] It is argued that Gardner's contention is overstated, as the injunction has an essential function in tort: it enables courts to directly enforce the ex ante duties created by tort law. The modern law of tort is not simply, as Gardner would have it, a law of repair in the form of common law damages, with 'equitable additions' thrown in for good measure.

In section III, Calabresi and Melamed's classic account of the relationship between property law and tort law is critically analysed.[3] The claim that is advanced is that tort law and property law cannot be distinguished on the basis that property rights are generally protected by injunctive relief, while other rights in tort law are generally protected by liability rules.

Section IV considers the claims that have been made in existing tort scholarship about the availability (or lack thereof) of injunctive relief in negligence law and related claims about the duty of care. It is argued that the tort of negligence can be restrained by an injunction; however, one should not conclude from this finding that the duty of care in negligence is a primary duty.

II. Injunctions and Damages in Tort Law

Since the inception of tort law as a distinct legal category, an issue that has plagued tort scholars is whether tort law can truly be said to contain a thread that unifies the disparate causes of action that are known as 'torts'. Indeed, when Pollock published his pioneering treatise on the subject, he stated that it was his aim to 'show that there really is a Law of Torts, not merely a number of rules of law about various kinds of torts … a true living branch of the Common Law, not a collection of heterogeneous instances'.[4]

One argument that scholars have deployed in support of the view that tort law is a unified body of law is that an award of reparative damages is universally available in all tort cases and is therefore tort law's 'primary' remedy. This argument has been advanced most clearly by John Gardner.[5] Gardner argues that the expression 'default remedy' is 'too weak to capture the special place of reparative

[2] J Gardner, 'Torts and Other Wrongs' (2011) 39 *Florida State University Law Review* 43, 52–57.

[3] G Calabresi and AD Melamed, 'Property Rules, Liability Rules, and Inalienability: One View of the Cathedral' (1972) 85 *Harvard Law Review* 1089.

[4] F Pollock, *The Law of Torts: A Treatise on the Principles of Obligations Arising from Civil Wrongs in the Common Law* (Stevens & Sons 1887) vi.

[5] Gardner (n 2) 52–57.

damages in the law of torts'.[6] He contends that reparative damages are in fact one of the 'defining features of the law of torts', as '[t]ort law cannot be understood without understanding the primacy of the reparative'.[7] According to Gardner, in 'all tort litigation' reparative damages are 'the only remedy … [that] the successful plaintiff enjoys *as of right*'.[8] The assured availability of damages after a tort occurs, the argument runs, demonstrates that 'torts are characterized by the primacy of reparation'.[9]

It is necessary to pause for a moment here and clarify what Gardner meant by the word 'primary'. Gardner was not making the claim that an award of damages, compared to other remedies, is the remedy that is awarded most frequently in tort cases.[10] Rather, Gardner meant that an award of damages is the most important remedy for the purpose of understanding tort law, as the fact that damages can be awarded in every tort case indicates that 'torts are characterized by the primacy of reparation'.[11] In the analysis that follows, it is argued that Gardner's argument is overstated, and some of the implications that this has for understanding the law of tort are teased out.

A. The Difficulties for Gardner's Claim

The doctrinal findings of this book present two main difficulties for Gardner's claim. First, a point that is crucial to Gardner's argument is that injunctive relief, compared to damages, is of lesser importance in tort law because it is discretionary. Gardner reasons that because injunctions are discretionary, the court 'is not legally bound to issue an injunction of any kind'.[12] By contrast, when a court is deciding to award damages, ultimately the court must always award damages, even if they are nominal.[13] However, in the light of the findings in chapters 4, 5, and 6, Gardner's point is overstated for two reasons.

First, when one closely analyses the discretion to award final injunctive relief to restrain tortious conduct, it can be determined that the discretion is much more limited than Gardner makes it out to be. As was explained in detail in chapters 4, 5 and 6, where the necessary conditions for the grant of a prohibitory, desisting mandatory or quia timet injunction are established, a court *must* award an injunction unless a countervailing discretionary consideration is engaged by the defendant. As was explained in chapter 2, since 1859 it has been trite law that

[6] ibid 52.
[7] ibid 61.
[8] ibid 53 (emphasis added).
[9] ibid 53.
[10] This assumption is supported by empirical research in P Cane and J Goudkamp, *Atiyah's Accidents: Compensation and the Law* (9th edn, Cambridge University Press 2018) 184–85.
[11] Gardner (n 2) 53.
[12] ibid 55.
[13] ibid 56.

'unless there be something special in the case, [a claimant] is entitled as of course to an injunction to prevent the recurrence of [a rights] violation'.[14] In this sense, contrary to what Gardner suggests, the default position is that injunctive relief must be awarded in cases where a claimant has proved a threatened infringement of her rights.

Second, even though (because of the limited discretion that is retained by the courts) it may be that in some cases injunctive relief is refused outright or damages are awarded in lieu of an injunction, this discretion should not be used to make the claim that injunctions are 'secondary' tort remedies. The discretion is an effective technique employed by the courts to avoid the undesirable consequences that would arise if injunctive relief were available as of right in tort law. The discretion therefore exists to ensure that courts can achieve more sophisticated justice in hard cases, not because courts believe that cases involving a threat to the claimant's rights are somehow secondary to rights-infringement cases. In fact, the opposite could be argued. As was explained in chapter 6, Sir Edward Coke's statement that 'preventing justice excelleth punishing justice' has long been accepted by the courts.[15] Indeed, the highest courts in England and Wales have said more recently, in cases involving the award of final injunctions, that 'in a society governed by the rule of law, the court should grant an injunction necessary to uphold legal rights against a threatened invasion unless there is some factor which is sufficiently weighty to displace this general rule'[16] and that 'the High Court possesses the power, and bears the responsibility, to act so as to maintain the rule of law'.[17] It is therefore too glib to assert that because injunctions are not always available in respect of rights threats (whether in a prohibitory, desisting mandatory or quia timet injunction context), this relegates them to being a secondary tort remedy.

The second difficulty for Gardner's claim relates to his point that damages are awarded to a successful claimant in 'all tort litigation'. John Murphy, in a persuasive article demonstrating why tort law lacks homogeneity, has observed that a problem with Gardner's contention is that 'there are certain types of tort case in which no damages at all are available'.[18] One such category of case that Murphy identifies is where a quia timet injunction is awarded. He argues that because quia timet injunctions are granted *before* a defendant has infringed the claimant's rights, it follows that 'no injustice requires correction' and 'such cases consequently clash' with Gardner's argument.[19]

[14] *Imperial Gas and Coke Company v Broadbent* (1859) 7 HLC 600, 11 ER 239, 612. See also *Crestford Ltd v Tesco Stores Ltd* [2005] EWHC 805 (Ch) [69]; *Coventry v Lawrence* [2014] UKSC 13, [2014] AC 822 [121].

[15] Edward Coke, *The Second Part of the Institutes of the Lawes of England* (M Flesher 1644) 299. This statement was approved in: *Graigola Merthyr Co Ltd v Swansea* [1928] Ch 235 (CA), 242; *Lloyd v Symonds* [1998] EWCA Civ 511 (no pinpoint available); *Islington LBC v Elliott* [2012] EWCA Civ 56 [31]. See further, ch 6.

[16] *Secretary of State for Environment, Food and Rural Affairs v Meier* [2008] EWCA Civ 903 [53].

[17] *Wolverhampton City Council v London Gypsies and Travellers* [2023] UKSC 47, [2024] AC 983 [18].

[18] J Murphy, 'The Heterogeneity of Tort Law' (2019) 39 *OJLS* 455, 476.

[19] ibid 479.

The findings of this book support Murphy's view. As was explained in chapter 6, quia timet injunctions can be granted to restrain the commission of *any* future tort. And (unless they are awarded in lieu of the injunction) damages are not an available remedy in this category of case.

Furthermore, the doctrinal findings in chapters 3, 4 and 5 can be used to extend Murphy's argument. As was explained in chapter 3, ordinary prohibitory injunctions and desisting mandatory injunctions are not granted in response to a prior wrong. Rather, they are granted to prevent the commission of a *future* wrong. As Channell J explained in *Carlton Illustrators v Coleman & Co Ltd*, 'an injunction is not a remedy for the past breach, but is a means for preventing further breaches'.[20] The fact that a defendant has committed the same tort against the claimant in the past is therefore only relevant to whether there is a real and imminent risk that the defendant will commit the same tort in the future. Accordingly, each time a prohibitory or desisting mandatory injunction is awarded (whether or not alongside a damages award for a past wrong), a remedy is being granted in respect of a tort law right for which damages are not awarded. Moreover, as was explained in chapters 4 and 5, prohibitory injunctions and desisting mandatory injunctions can be granted to restrain the commission of *any* future tort. It necessarily follows that each time an ordinary prohibitory or desisting mandatory injunction is granted (for example, in a classic trespass-to-land or nuisance case), damages are not the primary remedy. Rather, an award of damages remedies the past wrong, but the injunction is the means by which the defendant's duty in tort law is enforced directly so as to prevent him from breaching it again in the future. Accordingly, consistently with what Murphy has argued, it cannot be said that the award of damages is what constitutes tort law's unifying thread. The findings in chapters 3, 4, 5, and 6 demonstrate that there are many tort cases in which a damages award is not the claimant's primary remedy.

In the light of the foregoing, there is good reason to doubt Gardner's contention that damages are tort law's primary remedy. It would, however, be premature to conclude here. By building on the above analysis, much more can be derived from the doctrinal findings to assist in understanding tort law's structure and the function of the injunction in tort. Specifically, three further implications can be drawn, discussed in section II.B–II.D.

B. There are Two Forms of Tort Actions

The first implication is that in tort law there exist only two categories of case. The first is the classic case where a claimant seeks a remedy (such as damages or a restorative mandatory injunction) in response to a wrong that has been committed

[20] *Carlton Illustrators v Coleman & Co Ltd* [1911] 1 KB 771 (KB), 782. See also: *British Railway Traffic & Electric Co Ltd v CRC Co Ltd* [1922] 2 KB 260 (KB), 272; *Coventry* (n 14) [101]; *Ranger v Pycraft* [2021] EWHC 502 (QB) [60].

against her (that is, a remedy in response to a '*rights invasion*'). The second category of case is where, to borrow a term coined by Stephen Smith in the context of remedial law,[21] a claimant seeks a remedy (such as a quia timet, prohibitory or desisting mandatory injunction, or declaration) in response to a threat that a defendant will commit a wrong against her (that is, a remedy in response to a '*rights threat*'). The case law indicates that all tort actions fit within one of these two distinct cases. Either claimants seek a remedy in response to a rights invasion, or they seek a remedy in response to a rights threat (or both remedies simultaneously).

This point may seem elementary. It is important, however, because it suggests that neither damages nor an injunction can constitute tort law's primary remedy. In a rights-threat case, the award of the injunction prevents the defendant from infringing the claimant's rights in the future. Accordingly, if claimants were restricted to bringing rights-threat actions only, they would not be able to seek relief for the damage or loss they would suffer if a defendant committed a wrong against them. Conversely, in a rights-invasion case, the award of damages (or a restorative mandatory injunction) remedies the claimant for her damage or loss. Accordingly, if claimants were restricted to bringing rights-invasion actions only, they would be unable to prevent or stop a defendant from infringing their rights, provided the defendant had the means to pay a damages award continually. Thus, damages and injunctions work together in these distinct categories of case to give content to the meaning of a 'right' that is generated by tort law. Neither damages or the injunction can therefore be labelled as tort law's primary remedy.

C. The Injunction is Essential to Tort Law

The second implication, which must follow from the first, is that the injunction has a crucial function in tort. The injunction is the sole mechanism by which courts can directly enforce the primary duties that tort law generates. Although there are other specific remedies available in tort (such as, for example, the remedy of specific delivery in response to conversion, the availability of possession orders in response to trespass to land and the writ of habeas corpus in response to false imprisonment), these remedies are clearly not general tort remedies in the same way that the injunction is. So, without the injunction, there would be no means by which the primary duties in tort law could be directly enforced by way of a court order, rather than indirectly enforced by way of an award of damages. The most that could be said about tort law would be that it creates a set of liability rules that require that damages must be awarded as a *first-instance* response. If this were the case, lawyers would not be required to advise their clients to order their affairs and run their businesses in accordance with the established tort law duties.

[21] S Smith, *Rights, Wrongs and Injustices: The Structure of Remedial Law* (Oxford University Press 2019) 9.

This point highlights the problem with Gardner's contention that tort law can be characterised by the primacy of the reparative. If it is truly the case that repairing a claimant's damage or loss by an award of damages is the most important aspect of tort law, it is difficult to see how tort law could be anything more than a system of law that creates liability rules. It is only by appreciating that both damages and injunctions are equally as important to enforcing the duties generated by tort law that it is possible to see the full picture.

Furthermore, when considering the function of the injunction in tort law, it is worth analysing *how* the injunction operates to enforce the rights generated by tort law. Liability for the commission of a tort is generally determined by reference to the damage or loss suffered by the claimant. Importantly, however, if a defendant intends to commit a tort against the claimant in the future, courts do not confine the defendant's potential liability by making it proportionate to the claimant's likely damage or loss. Instead, courts grant an injunction and employ the primary judicial enforcement mechanism at their disposal: they threaten the defendant with a criminal sanction or sequestration. As explained by the authors of *Arlidge, Eady & Smith on Contempt*, '[b]reaches of injunctions are always traditionally addressed as falling within the category of civil contempt',[22] and therefore a defendant who acts in breach of an injunction can be fined, imprisoned for a maximum of two years or his assets sequestrated.[23]

It is in this way that courts add a further layer of protection to the common law rights generated by tort law. The threat of a criminal sanction or sequestration deters a defendant from deciding simply to pay damages to infringe a claimant's rights for so long as he pleases. Indeed, it goes without saying that no matter how much a defendant is willing to pay to prosecute me maliciously, to defame me on LinkedIn or to crash-tackle me on Broad Street, upon the requisite necessary conditions for injunctive relief being proved, the courts will not hesitate to grant an injunction and restrain the defendant from committing these torts against me. Thus, the clear function of the injunction in tort law is to enable courts to directly enforce the primary duties generated by tort law.

D. Torts are Wrongs

The final implication is that torts create ex ante private law duties that, on a Hohfeldian analysis, simultaneously generate private law rights. In other words, the general availability of injunctive relief in tort confirms that torts are wrongs. We have seen that prohibitory, desisting mandatory and quia timet injunctions have been granted in respect of many different torts. When such injunctions are granted, they obviously do not compensate a claimant for her loss. Rather, the

[22] P Londono (ed), *Arlidge, Eady & Smith on Contempt* (5th edn, Sweet & Maxwell 2019) [3-18]. See also *Scott v Scott* [1913] AC 417 (HL), 456.

[23] See Contempt of Court Act 1981, s 14; Civil Procedure Rules 1998, pt 81.

award of the injunction enforces a duty that the defendant owes the claimant either: (i) after that duty has been breached but in circumstances where the defendant proposes to breach the duty again in the future; or (ii) before that duty has been breached at all. This strongly suggests that all torts, regardless of whether they can be said to protect some pre-existing moral or legal right or interest,[24] must impose legal ex ante duties on defendants that can be enforced by an injunction.

Take, for example, the tort of unlawful means conspiracy. Critics of the rights-based theory have pointed out that this tort does not protect an underlying legal right, as a right not to suffer economic loss (or a right to economic welfare) does not exist.[25] Nevertheless, as we saw in chapter 6, quia timet injunctions have been granted in respect of the tort of unlawful means conspiracy. In such cases, it cannot be said that the courts are compensating the claimant for his or her loss: no damages are being awarded. Rather, the award of the injunction indicates that courts are enforcing the pre-existing duty imposed on the defendant by virtue of the tort's existence. To put it another way, when the tort of unlawful means conspiracy was created, courts imposed a duty on all individuals in our society not to cause loss to another by creating an agreement with third persons to act unlawfully with the intention of causing loss to the other person. That duty is what is being enforced when a quia timet injunction is granted. The effect of the injunction is to restrain the defendant from breaching his duty and infringing the claimant's right.

Thus, the doctrinal findings of this book confirm that, as Lord Reed has put it, '[t]he law of tort is concerned with civil wrongs, that is to say with breach of duties imposed by the law'.[26] The point that the general availability of injunctive relief in tort indicates that torts are wrongs may seem uncontentious. However, there are two reasons why it is important.

First, in recent years, rights-based theories of tort law have come under much scrutiny.[27] While not intending to diminish the importance of this type of scholarship,[28] the authors engaged in such critical analysis seem to have lost sight of a crucial point. It is that regardless of whether a scholar can be categorised as a 'rights-theorist' or not, there is general agreement in the scholarship that torts are wrongs. The findings of this book confirm this conclusion. It is therefore important to highlight that the general availability of injunctive relief demonstrates that tort law is fundamentally about the creation and enforcement of private ex ante

[24] See N McBride, 'Rights and the Basis of Tort Law' in D Nolan and A Robertson (eds), *Rights and Private Law* (Hart Publishing 2012) 331, 336–39 (we must be careful not to place 'artificial limits on what sort of rights underlie tort law').

[25] Murphy (n 18) 464.

[26] *One Step (Support) Ltd v Morris-Garner* [2018] UKSC 20, [2019] AC 649 [31].

[27] See, eg, P Cane, 'Rights in Private Law' in Nolan and Robertson (eds) (n 24) 35; J Goudkamp and J Murphy, 'The Failure of Universal Theories of Tort Law' (2015) 21(2) *Legal Theory* 47; J Stapleton, *Three Essays on Torts* (Oxford University Press 2021); Murphy (n 18).

[28] Indeed, the implications in this section build upon an argument made by Murphy in the context of his broader claim that tort law is not homogeneous.

duties that correspond with private rights. It would be a great shame if the critical analysis of rights-based theories led the courts, the legal profession and students to believe that this was not the case.

Second, it must not be forgotten that in the latter half of the twentieth century, it was widely believed that tort law was primarily a body of law that created fault principles pursuant to which judges could determine which party, in a particular fact scenario, should bear the risk of damage or loss and be ordered to pay compensation according to what was 'fair, just and reasonable'. Consider, for example, this statement made by Denning LJ in the context of considering the principles governing the liability of mentally ill defendants in tort law:

> I am aware that these rules of law have been criticized by some jurists who would make … liability in tort depend on blameworthiness, but I venture to think that this criticism is somewhat out of date. Recent legislative and judicial developments show that the criterion of liability in tort is not so much culpability, but on whom should the risk fall.[29]

Thankfully, this conception of tort law has now largely[30] been abandoned by courts and scholars. The findings of this book raise serious doubts about any last remnants of the idea that 'Tort Law = Compensation for Loss'[31].

E. Potential Objections

It should go without saying that there are several objections that could be made to the foregoing analysis. But each of them misses the mark.

First, it could be said that as there is empirical research evidencing that an award of damages is the remedy that is most frequently awarded in tort cases,[32] the practical reality is that damages are tort law's most important remedy. This argument should be rejected as a *non sequitur*. It does not follow from the fact that a remedy is granted more frequently than other remedies in an area of law that the former remedy is the most important to understanding that body of law.

Second, it could be said that the claim that injunctions are available for all 'torts' fails to take into account the finding in chapter 4 that injunctions are not available in respect of 'torts' that generate primary liabilities, such as the liability that arises for damage caused by defective products under the Consumer Protection Act 1987, and under the rule in *Rylands v Fletcher*. What this demonstrates, the argument would run, is that there are some 'torts' in respect of which an injunction cannot be granted to enforce an ex ante duty.

29 *White v White* [1950] P 39 (CA), 58–59.
30 For an exception related to the tort of negligence, see D Priel, 'Tort Law for Cynics' (2014) 77 *MLR* 703.
31 McBride (n 24) 341.
32 Cane and Goudkamp (n 10) 184–85.

At first sight, this argument is a good one, because the above-mentioned causes of action are classified as 'torts' by the courts. However, there are two reasons why the argument is unpersuasive. First, modern courts have classified these causes of action as 'torts' because it has been reasoned that they create primary duties. It follows that if these causes of action truly form part of tort law, that is because they generate primary duties that can be enforced by an injunction. This means that the causes of action, like all other torts, *can* be restrained by an injunction and the counter argument falls away. Alternatively, with respect, the time has now come to accept that these actions are not torts but fall within the developing category of obligations known as 'primary liabilities'. For the reasons explained in chapter 4, the above-mentioned causes of action are obviously not wrongs. They do not impose a duty on the defendant or proscribe the doing of any act, they simply stipulate that the defendant is liable if a pre-defined event occurs. Accordingly, even though courts have suggested otherwise, these causes of action have been incorrectly classified as torts.[33]

A third retort could be made on the basis that an injunction is classified as an equitable remedy because, ordinarily, the courts' power to grant injunctions derives from the Court of Chancery's inherent power to do so.[34] When the Judicature Act reforms of 1873–75 were passed, these reforms did not change the substance of the law but were purely procedural in effect.[35] Therefore, it could be argued that when an injunction is granted in respect of a tort law right, this indicates nothing about tort law and can only illustrate how equity operates as a distinct body of law.

The difficulty with this argument is that it overlooks a fundamental principle of injunction law that existed both before and after the passing of the Judicature Act reforms: a claimant must establish a legal or equitable right before she can obtain an injunction.[36] The effect of this principle is that when an injunction is granted to restrain or remedy a tort, equity can operate to award an injunction only because of the right generated by tort law in the first place. As Zipursky has observed, when a court grants an injunction in respect of tortious conduct, 'it is doing so because of the parties' rights under tort law'.[37] The grant of an injunction in aid of a tort law right therefore does not create equitable rights (like, for example, the doctrine of proprietary estoppel). Rather, when such an injunction

[33] This point is not a new one. See, generally, J Smith, 'Tort and Absolute Liability – Suggested Changes in Classification' (1916-17) 30 *Harvard Law Review* 241; N McBride and R Bagshaw, *Tort Law* (6th edn, Pearson Education 2018) 12–13.

[34] *Fourie v Le Roux* [2007] 1 WLR 320 (HL) [25]; *Convoy Collateral Ltd v Broad Idea International Ltd* [2021] UKPC 24, [2023] AC 389 [40].

[35] *Salt v Cooper* (1880) 16 Ch D 544, 549; *Ind Coope & Co v Emmerson* (1887) 12 App Cas 300, 309. See, generally, S Degeling and J Edelman (eds), *Equity in Commercial Law* (Lawbook Co 2005).

[36] *Day v Brownrigg* (1878) 10 Ch D 294; *Waterside Workers' Federation of Australia v JW Alexander Ltd* (1918) 25 CLR 434. Although exceptions have been made for some particular types of injunctions: see *Convoy v Broad* (n 34); A Tettenborn, 'Injunctions Without Damages' (1987) 38 *Northern Ireland Legal Quarterly* 118.

[37] BC Zipursky, 'Civil Recourse, Not Corrective Justice' (2003) 91 *Georgetown Law Journal* 695, 713.

is granted, it enforces a *legal* duty that is generated by tort law. In this sense, equity and tort operate together as one body of law: the common law of England and Wales. The award of injunctive relief therefore reveals as much about tort law as it does about equity.

Finally, it could be argued in response that as an injunction is a general remedy that is available in respect of not only torts but also many other causes of action (such as, for example, breach of contract and breach of trust), the remedy is best understood as enabling equity to fulfil a general function of achieving preventive justice. The generality of equity's response when awarding injunctions therefore tends to diminish the weight that can be placed upon injunctive relief to understand tort law.

This argument is premised on the idea that equity's desire to achieve 'preventive justice' operates independently of tort law. While it is arguable that this was the position before the passing of the Judicature Acts of 1873–75, it is doubtful whether it remains the case today. This is evidenced by the fact that the principles governing when courts will countenance the award of an injunction differ depending on the type of cause of action sought to be restrained and its classification within the law of obligations. For example, it was explained in chapter 4 that ordinarily, prohibitory and desisting mandatory injunctions are granted to restrain a future tort where it is shown that the defendant's tort is continuing. Whether damages would adequately remedy the claimant is only a discretionary factor to be taken into account. By contrast, in contract law, it is well established that it must be proved that a monetary sum would be an inadequate remedy before specific performance can be awarded.[38] Further, it is long-established orthodoxy that courts are more willing to grant injunctions in aid of equitable rights in a greater number of circumstances as compared to legal rights.[39] These subtle distinctions suggest that equity does not have some sort of free-standing function to achieve preventive justice that is applied mechanically when an injunction is granted in tort, contract or equity. To the contrary, it would seem that the body of law that generates the right which is being enforced by the injunction shapes the general principles governing the circumstances in which that right can be specifically enforced.

This point confirms that when injunctive relief is granted in aid of a tort law right, tort and equity operate together as the common law of England and Wales. The observation that injunctions can be granted in aid of non-tort law rights in different circumstances should therefore not be used to diminish the weight that can be given to the availability of injunctive relief in understanding the modern law of tort.

[38] *Co-operative Insurance Society Ltd v Argyll Stores (Holdings) Ltd* [1998] AC 1 (HL), 11.

[39] JD Heydon, MJ Leeming and PG Turner, *Meagher, Gummow & Lehane's Equity: Doctrines & Remedies* (5th edn, LexisNexis 2015) [21-020].

III. Injunctions and the Tort/Property Divide

A leading account, if not *the* leading account, of the relationship between property law and tort law has been put forward by Calabresi and Melamed in their classic journal article.[40] In that article, the authors articulate a framework for understanding property law and tort law 'from a unified perspective'.[41] They explain that when the state gives individuals 'entitlements' (that is, rights),[42] it must decide how those rights should be protected. Calabresi and Melamed contend that there are three ways in which our rights can be protected: by property, liability and inalienability rules. The authors do not specifically state that this framework is an explanatory one, nor do they explain to which jurisdiction their framework is intended to apply. However, their core argument is that their framework is a helpful one because it explains the relationship between property law and tort law, and in areas of uncertainty the framework can assist in determining what the law should be. Indeed, as we shall see, many scholars have since relied implicitly on Calabresi and Melamed's framework to make arguments about what the positive law is in England and Wales.

The findings of this book challenge Calabresi and Melamed's view. Section III.A examines their framework and its implications. Section III.B tests the authors' framework, and further conclusions that have been drawn by other scholars who implicitly rely on the framework, against the doctrinal findings of this book.

A. Understanding the Framework

Calabresi and Melamed's analytical framework centres on the distinction between 'property rules' and 'liability rules'.[43] The authors explain that:

> an entitlement is protected by a property rule to the extent that someone who wishes to remove the entitlement from its holder must buy it from him in a voluntary transaction in which the value of the entitlement is agreed upon by the seller.[44]

Another person is therefore not entitled to infringe, purchase or 'take' a right protected by a property rule without the claimant's consent. Accordingly, as Howarth has explained, a property rule 'is where the court will protect the

[40] Calabresi and Melamed (n 3).

[41] ibid 1089.

[42] Calabresi and Melamed do not explain what they mean by the concept of an 'entitlement'. However, they often equate an entitlement with a right in their analysis. Accordingly, that is what the author will consider the concept of an entitlement to mean.

[43] The findings of this book do not have any implications for what is said to be an 'inalienability rule'. Accordingly, this rule is not addressed in this section.

[44] Calabresi and Melamed (n 3) 1092.

claimant's right by injunction if it is violated or threatened with violation'.[45] By contrast, Calabresi and Melamed explain that '[w]henever someone may destroy the initial entitlement if he is willing to pay an objectively determined value for it, an entitlement is protected by a liability rule'.[46] A defendant facing rights protected by a liability rule but not protected by a property rule can therefore purchase the rights of the claimant, 'since the claimant cannot demand any more than the damages the court imposes as the price of violating her right'.[47]

The clear implication of Calabresi and Melamed's framework is that, as a general rule of thumb, property rights are protected by property rules and all other rights generated by tort law are protected only by liability rules. They do, however, issue certain caveats. First, the authors explain that 'most entitlements to [real and personal property] are mixed'.[48] They suggest by way of example that 'Taney's house may be protected by a property rule in situations where Marshall wishes to purchase it [and] by a liability rule where the government decides to take it by eminent domain'.[49] The authors accept, therefore, that while the default position is that property rights are protected by property rules, there are some circumstances in which they are protected by liability rules. Additionally, Calabresi and Melamed indicate that while the other rights in tort law are protected only by liability rules, the criminal law enables rights to bodily integrity to be protected by a property rule.[50] It seems, therefore, that on the authors' view, it is the function of the criminal law to provide ex ante protection to rights that are not property rights.

In summary, on Calabresi and Melamed's view, property law generates rights that require the consent of the right-holder to be transferred or infringed, and which can therefore be enforced by an injunction to prevent an infringement or the taking of the property right. Tort law, on the other hand, generates rights that can be transferred or infringed without the right-holder's consent, provided a monetary sum is paid after the fact.[51]

B. Implications

The findings of this book present three major problems for Calabresi and Melamed's framework.

First, in chapters 4, 5 and 6 it was shown that ordinary prohibitory injunctions, desisting and restorative mandatory injunctions, and quia timet injunctions can be granted in respect of *any* tort. In chapter 4, for example, it was found that

[45] D Howarth, 'Many Duties of Care – or a Duty of Care? Notes from the Underground' (2006) 26 *OJLS* 449, 467. See also Calabresi and Melamed (n 3) 1127.
[46] Calabresi and Melamed (n 3) 1092.
[47] Howarth (n 45) 467.
[48] Calabresi and Melamed (n 3) 1093.
[49] ibid 1093.
[50] ibid 1124–27.
[51] See, in particular, ibid 1108–09.

prohibitory injunctions have been granted to restrain not just trespass to land and private nuisance, but also assault, battery, harassment, libel, slander, malicious falsehood, misuse of private information, inducing a breach of contract, deceit, causing loss by unlawful means, intimidation, public nuisance, passing off and breach of statutory duty. What these findings make plain is that property rights are not the only kinds of rights that courts will protect by granting an injunction. Rather, an injunction can be granted in respect of *all* rights generated by tort law (apart from those 'torts' that generate primary liabilities). Accordingly, on these findings, there is good reason to doubt Calabresi and Melamed's thesis that property law can be distinguished from tort law on the basis that it is only property law that generates rights that can be enforced by an injunction. The general availability of injunctive relief in tort indicates that a defendant is not permitted continuously to infringe any right generated by tort law.

Second, and even more problematically, the findings in chapter 4 indicate that property rights are much less likely to be enforced by an injunction compared to other tort rights. It is well known that where a defendant is continuing to invade a claimant's property right, in certain circumstances a court will refuse to grant an injunction against the defendant and instead award damages in lieu. Calabresi and Melamed recognise this point in their article by explaining that in some circumstances property rights are protected by liability rules. However, what the authors do not appreciate is that property rights are the *only* types of rights the courts permit to be continuously infringed for a monetary sum determined by the court. In chapter 4, it was found that the only cases in which courts have accepted that damages would adequately remedy the claimant's future damage or loss caused by a defendant's continuing tort concern the infringement of property rights. Indeed, the author was unable to locate a single case in which it was held that damages would be an adequate remedy for the future infringement of any other kind of right generated by tort law.

What this means is that it is inaccurate for Calabresi and Melamed to use the label 'property rule' to describe a rule that, in essence, means that *any* right cannot be infringed (or, using their phrase, 'taken') without the claimant's consent and can be enforced by an injunction. There is nothing 'proprietary' about this rule. In fact, the doctrinal findings of this book point to the opposite conclusion. The cases indicate that, as a general rule, damages will not be an adequate remedy for the continuous infringement of a tort law right. The only exception to this rule is that, in some cases, damages may be an adequate remedy for the continued infringement of a *property right*. Accordingly, contrary to Calabresi and Melamed's framework, a property right seems to be the only type of right that courts will permit a defendant to infringe without the claimant's consent in circumstances where the court determines the objective value of the right, irrespective of the price for which the claimant would have sold the right.

The third implication is that Calabresi and Melamed's definition of a 'liability rule' also misses the mark. According to the authors, where a right is protected by a liability rule, a defendant can violate the right provided he pays damages for doing so. What is assumed in this definition is that a liability rule can only operate to protect rights by requiring defendants to pay money for a rights violation. However, in chapter 5 it was found that a restorative mandatory injunction can also be granted as a remedy in response to a rights violation. Although such injunctions have been granted in very few cases, their award demonstrates that it is not correct to assume that when courts hold a defendant liable for invading a claimant's right, in all cases the defendant will be required to pay a monetary sum. Rather, sometimes a defendant will also (or alternatively) be compelled to take positive action to rectify the consequences of his tort. Further, in the cases considered in chapter 5, restorative mandatory injunctions were granted in respect of trespass to land *and* inducing a breach of contract. It appears that a liability rule can therefore operate to require a defendant to take positive action irrespective of whether the underlying right that was infringed can be classified as a property right.

It necessarily follows that it is inaccurate for Calabresi and Melamed to suggest that a liability rule is limited to providing rights protection by solely requiring a defendant to pay compensation for a rights violation. The better view is that liability rules provide rights protection by operating in *two* ways: first, by requiring the defendant to pay damages for his rights violation; and/or, second, by requiring the defendant to take positive action to rectify the consequences of his rights violation. It is important that this is appreciated when scholars think about the different ways in which rights can be protected.

In the light of the foregoing, the doctrinal findings in chapters 4, 5, and 6 indicate that there is reason to doubt the explanatory force of Calabresi and Melamed's framework. However, given the influence of the authors' article on private law thinking, it would be premature to conclude here. It is arguable that Calabresi and Melamed's framework has led to the making of two errors in private law scholarship.

i. Are Injunctions Indicative of Property Rights?

In *Dimensions of Private Law*, Waddams makes the claims that:

> [a] right that can never be enforced by injunction might plausibly be classified as something less than a proprietary right in the full sense. Conversely, the willingness of the court to grant specific remedies … may itself supply the principal reason for calling the plaintiff's interest 'proprietary'.[52]

Waddams' second claim suggests that when a right can be enforced by an injunction (or another specific remedy), this indicates that it is appropriately termed a proprietary right. Although Waddams does not explicitly cite Calabresi and Melamed, his claim appears to be predicated on their analysis as it accords with

[52] S Waddams, *Dimensions of Private Law: Categories and Concepts in Anglo-American Legal Reasoning* (Cambridge University Press 2003) 177–178.

their definition of a property rule. With the doctrinal findings of this book in mind, it can be determined that Waddams' claim could not be further from the truth. Injunctions can be awarded to restrain or remedy *any* right generated by tort law. The availability of an injunction in respect of a particular right therefore does not mean that the right being protected is a proprietary one. For example, the award of an injunction to restrain ongoing harassment certainly does not indicate that the claimant's right not to be harassed is a property right. If Waddams' claim were correct, every right in tort law would be a proprietary one. With respect, and as Murphy has also argued,[53] such a conclusion is incorrect.

ii. Are Property Rights Better Protected in Tort Law than Other Rights?

In *The Anatomy of Tort Law*, Cane posits that there is a hierarchy of 'protected interests' in tort law. He contends that as 'the protection given to some interests … [is] stronger than that given to others', it can be reasoned that 'tort law values some interests more highly than others'.[54] To make out his claim, one particular point made by Cane is that property rights, after 'interests in one's person', occupy second place in tort law's hierarchy, as they are better protected than 'contractual interests', 'non-contractual expectancies', 'trade values' and 'purely financial interests'.[55] To support this claim, Cane asserts that prohibitory injunctions are granted more readily in respect of property rights because:

> [w]hereas a victim of an interference with property is entitled to an injunction unless, exceptionally, a monetary remedy would be adequate, a victim of an interference with any other type of interest will be awarded an injunction only if a monetary remedy would not be adequate …[56]

According to Cane, this 'reflects the high value which tort puts on interests classified as "property" interests'.[57] Although Cane does not explicitly cite Calabresi and Melamad, their framework is certainly echoed in his argument.

The doctrinal findings in chapters 4, 5 and 6 pose three problems for Cane's argument. First, it was explained in chapter 4 that a claimant is not required to prove that damages would be an inadequate remedy to obtain a prohibitory injunction to restrain a future tort. Cane's contention that such a requirement is necessary for a claimant to seek injunctive relief in respect of a non-proprietary tort is therefore incorrect. Second, as was explained in chapters 4, 5, and 6, the necessary conditions for the grant of an injunction in tort law are general. They do not

[53] J Murphy, 'Tort's Hierarchy of Protected Interests' (2022) 81 *CLJ* 356, 374–75.
[54] P Cane, *The Anatomy of Tort Law* (Hart Publishing 1997) 90.
[55] ibid ch 6. Cane does not explicitly state that these interests have a descending order of importance, but this argument is implicit throughout the chapter.
[56] ibid 100.
[57] ibid 100, 141.

change depending on the tort sought to be restrained or remedied. Accordingly, it cannot be said that the requirements for injunctive relief favour the protection of property rights. Third, in chapter 4 it was found that the only cases in which courts have accepted that damages would adequately remedy the claimant's future damage or loss caused by a defendant's continuing tort concern the infringement of *property* rights. It would seem, therefore, that courts believe that property rights are in fact less worthy of protection by injunction than other rights. For these reasons, Cane's contention that the law favours the grant of injunctions in respect of property rights such that property rights are better protected in tort law may be doubted. To the contrary, the positive law indicates that property rights are *less* likely to be protected by the grant of an injunction.

IV. Injunctions and Negligence

There is significant debate in the tort literature over whether the tort of negligence can be restrained by injunction. Moreover, McBride relies on cases (decided in other jurisdictions) in which injunctions have been granted in respect of negligence to support his view that the duty to take care in negligence is a primary duty, a breach of which is a wrong in itself.[58] The implications of the findings of this book for these debates are considered in turn.

A. Can Negligence be Restrained by Injunction?

It must be accepted that not every case involving negligence is suited to being restrained by an injunction. This is for three reasons. First, it is unlikely that a defendant would propose to repeatedly commit the tort of negligence.[59] The number of cases in which ordinary prohibitory or desisting mandatory injunctions could be granted is therefore limited. Second, in most negligence cases, before a claimant has suffered damage or loss she is unaware that the defendant is acting in a way in which a reasonable person would not act. The number of cases in which a claimant would have the opportunity to seek quia timet relief is therefore also limited. Third, as Smith has observed, even if a quia timet injunction could be brought in circumstances where a claimant is aware that the defendant is engaging in negligent behaviour, it is difficult to prove that 'the claimant in particular is likely to be injured by [such] behaviour'.[60]

Even though there are very few factual situations in which negligence could be restrained by injunction, in chapters 4, 5, and 6 it was found that the necessary

[58] N McBride, 'Duties of Care: Do They Really Exist?' (2004) 24 *OJLS* 417, 427–30.
[59] K Oliphant (ed), *The Law of Tort* (3rd edn, LexisNexis 2015) [8.6]; Smith (n 21) 151.
[60] Smith (n 21) 151.

conditions for the award of a prohibitory, desisting mandatory, restorative mandatory or quia timet injunction do not change depending on the tort sought to be restrained. It necessarily follows from these findings that, even though there is no authority on the point, any type of injunction can be granted in respect of the tort of negligence. This conclusion is supported by the fact that there are now several cases in other common law jurisdictions in which quia timet injunctions have been granted to prevent the commission of negligence. McBride has observed that the tort of negligence has been restrained quia timet in the United States.[61] One example he gives is the decision in *Shimp v New Jersey Bell Telephone Co*, where the Supreme Court of New Jersey granted a mandatory quia timet injunction ordering the plaintiff's employer (a telephone company) to place a ban on smoking in the workplace.[62] More recently, in Australia there is now a body of case law in which quia timet injunctions have been awarded to prevent Ministers of the federal Government from committing the tort of negligence against asylum seekers and refugees in the Government's care.[63] The leading case in which a final quia timet injunction was granted is *Plaintiff S99/2016 v Minister for Immigration and Border Protection*.[64] There, Bromberg J granted a quia timet injunction restraining the defendant Minister from arranging for the applicant, who was a refugee in the Minister's care, to undergo an abortion in Papua New Guinea (or any other place where abortion is a crime), on the basis that the Minister would commit the tort of negligence against the applicant if he required her to undergo abortion treatment in a jurisdiction where abortion is illegal. Bromberg J found that if the applicant underwent such treatment, she would be exposed to a not insignificant risk of 'very serious physical and/or psychological harm', including a risk of death.[65] A quia timet injunction was therefore granted to prevent such a risk from materialising (and thereby preventing the Minister from committing the tort of negligence against the applicant).

The doctrinal findings, as well as the relevant cases in other jurisdictions, strongly suggest that an injunction can be granted to restrain negligence in England and Wales. However, it is often stated by tort scholars that an injunction can *never* be granted in respect of the tort of negligence.[66] This view also seems to be adopted in the tort literature more generally, as even though discussion of the tort of negligence is what dominates the tort books, there is rarely any discussion

[61] McBride (n 58) 428.
[62] *Shimp v New Jersey Bell Telephone Co* 368A 2d 408 (1976). See also *Smith v Western Electric Co* 643 SW 2d 10 (1982).
[63] See T Baxter, 'The Slow Death of Past Damage as an Essential Element of Negligence' (2019) 26 *Tort Law Review* 123, 125–27. See also: *The Owners, Strata Plan 11011 v Integrated Project Services Pty Ltd & Anor (No 2)* [2015] NSWSC 554; *Prisoners A to XX v New South Wales* (1994) 75 A Crime R 205 (strike out application).
[64] *Plaintiff S99/2016 v Minister for Immigration and Border Protection* (2016) 243 FCR 17.
[65] ibid [382], [385], [386].
[66] Oliphant (ed) (n 59) [1.35], [8.6] (assertion); Priel (n 30) 715 (assertion). See also Smith (n 21) 149–52, where Smith concludes that 'the absence of injunctions against negligence is unsurprising'.

of the fact that an injunction can be granted as a remedy for negligence.[67] Most of the authors observe that Lord Denning MR stated in *Miller v Jackson* that:

> [t]he books are full of cases where an injunction has been granted to restrain the continuance of a nuisance. But there is no case, so far as I know, where it has been granted so as to stop a man being negligent.[68]

But this statement is not a helpful one for two reasons. First, it was made in the context of a private nuisance case. Furthermore, Lord Denning MR did not state that negligence can never be restrained by an injunction. He simply observed that there is no case in England and Wales in which such an injunction has been awarded.

Beyond reliance on the dicta in *Miller v Jackson*, the most detailed, and seemingly convincing, argument as to why negligence cannot be restrained by injunction has been put forward by Stephen Smith.[69] As we shall see, however, the doctrinal findings indicate that his argument is flawed.

i. Smith's Argument

Smith begins his argument by stating that courts cannot order defendants by an injunction to simply 'take reasonable care', as such an order would fall foul of the constant-supervision consideration. This point should be accepted. Yet Smith also considers that courts cannot order defendants not to engage in specific actions that would be unreasonable on the facts of a case because such orders 'are likely to be unduly intrusive', and therefore presumably fall foul of the undue hardship consideration. He gives an example of a person's careless habit of leaving a ladder unattended on the side of his house, which is likely to result in the ladder's toppling over and causing property damage to the house next door. Smith states that an order directing the defendant 'not to leave unattended ladders propped against the north side of his house' would be unduly intrusive, because 'An unattended ladder is not a risk if it is secured to a house. Nor is an unattended ladder dangerous if it is fixed to the ground, boxed in, or surrounded by a high barrier.'[70] The same problem, Smith states, arises in respect of mandatory injunctions which compel a defendant to take action that is reasonable on the facts. He explains:

> A failure to take care invariably consists in a failure to perform one of a number of possible precautionary actions (eg slowing down, giving a warning, providing a barrier, and so forth). It is rarely the case that there is only one set of actions that must be followed to ensure that an activity is engaged in safely.[71]

[67] The exceptions are: J Murphy, 'Rethinking Injunctions in Tort Law' (2007) 27 *OJLS* 509; McBride and Bagshaw (n 33) 806-07 (responding to Murphy).
[68] *Miller v Jackson* [1977] QB 966 (CA), 980.
[69] Smith (n 21) 149–52.
[70] ibid 152.
[71] ibid.

The point that Smith is making is that in negligence law there are often several different precautions that the reasonable person could take to meet the standard of care. Accordingly, if a court were to order a defendant not to engage in an activity that could be done reasonably (such as using a ladder) in order to prevent commission of the tort of negligence, this would unduly interfere with the defendant's freedoms. Additionally, if a court were to order a defendant to take a particular precaution when engaging in that activity, this would also be unduly restrictive, because the defendant would be deprived of his freedom to choose which precaution to adopt.

With respect, Smith's argument is akin to Mais J's first-instance judgment in *Kennaway v Thompson*,[72] in that it underestimates the sophistication of injunction law. This is for three reasons.

First, from the outset of the analysis, it is important to recognise that the limits on when injunctive relief is available in tort law (that is, the necessary conditions) have been developed to take into account the need to protect the liberties of defendants. As was explained in chapter 6, it is for this reason that to obtain a prohibitory, desisting mandatory or quia timet injunction, courts require a claimant to prove that there is a real risk (that is, a strong probability) that all the elements of the alleged tort will be committed in the future. And where a claimant has satisfied the demanding burden of proving that there is a sufficiently strong probability that the tort of negligence will be committed, a degree of interference with the defendant's liberties is justified.

Second, in cases where a defendant proposes to do a negligent act in the future that would *never* be done by a reasonable person in the position of the defendant, and which would cause the claimant damage or loss, it is not problematic for a court to grant an injunction restraining the defendant from doing the relevant act. That is because the doing of the act is in itself so unreasonable that restraining the defendant from doing it would not unduly interfere with his freedoms. As Goudkamp and Nolan have observed, 'taking reasonable care may involve discontinuing the activity in question, rather than merely taking additional precautions in the course of the activity concerned'.[73] A good example is found in the Australian case of *Plaintiff S99/2016*,[74] the facts of which have already been outlined. There, the Minister was restrained from arranging for the applicant (who had serious underlying health conditions) to have an abortion in a country where abortion is a crime. Such an act (even with additional precautions) would never be done by a reasonable Minister because it so obviously exposed the already vulnerable applicant to a risk of very serious personal injury (including death). Accordingly, it cannot be said that the injunction unduly restricted the Minister's freedom of action.

By contrast, in cases where the defendant proposes to undertake an activity in the future that would only amount to negligence if the defendant failed to

[72] *Kennaway v Thompson* [1981] QB 88 (CA).
[73] J Goudkamp and D Nolan, *Winfield & Jolowicz on Tort* (20th edn, Sweet & Maxwell 2020) [6-018].
[74] *Plaintiff S99/2016* (n 64).

implement certain precautionary measures to ensure that his activity was undertaken with reasonable care, Smith is correct to state that courts should not grant a prohibitory quia timet injunction restraining that activity altogether. That would unduly burden the defendant's freedoms.

However, the third difficulty with Smith's argument is his suggestion that courts should not grant a mandatory quia timet injunction. The fact that there are many different acts that a court could order a defendant to do to prevent a wrong from occurring is not novel to negligence law. As was explained in chapter 5, where there is a range of different acts a defendant could be ordered to do to prevent, stop or remedy his wrong, courts will favour an order that requires the defendant to take the course of action that is most proportionate to the benefits of the injunction to the claimant. There is no reason why this principle would not be applied in a case where the standard of care can be achieved by taking one of several different precautions.

Consider a hypothetical example based on a leading case in negligence law: *Jolley v Sutton LBC*.[75] In that case, the claimant, then a schoolboy aged 14, started to repair an abandoned and rotted boat that was situated in the grounds of a block of flats owned by the defendant council. The council was held liable in (statutory) negligence after the boat collapsed onto the claimant and caused him paraplegia. But assume a slight change in the facts. Suppose that before the accident occurred, the claimant's mother became aware that her son was working on the boat, and because she was unable to prevent him from doing so, she sought a quia timet injunction against the council ordering it to remove and dispose of the boat. It could be argued that leaving an old boat on one's land is not unreasonable in itself, as numerous precautions could be taken to prevent any risks of damage materialising. For example, the council could erect an enclosed fence around the boat, build a shed in which the boat could be stored under lock and key, or simply remove and dispose of the boat. On Smith's argument, a court should not grant an injunction at all in this case, because the council's freedom would be unduly infringed if a court were to order what particular precaution must be taken. But this analysis is overly simplistic. The better view is that a court would order the council to implement the precaution that is most proportionate to the benefits of preventing the future negligence. On the facts, given that the injunction would reduce a risk of serious injury, it is likely that a court would favour the precaution that would be most effective at reducing the risk of damage, provided that the cost of implementing the precaution would not be exorbitant.[76] This balancing exercise, which is attuned to the competing interests of both parties, is preferable to simply imposing a blanket ban on all injunctions to restrain future negligence. The fact that there are different precautions a defendant could take to meet the relevant standard of

[75] *Jolley v Sutton LBC* [2000] 1 WLR 1082 (HL).

[76] However, as the risk that is being mitigated is a risk of serious injury or death, it is likely a court would expect the council to be required to expend significant costs.

care therefore does not prevent a court from awarding a mandatory quia timet injunction to prevent future negligence.

There is, however, a retort that could be made here. Numerous tort law scholars state that tort duties are negative in form.[77] That is, torts impose a duty on individuals *not* to do something. Weinrib states that all tort duties are negative because they comply with Kant's thesis that 'one person's need does not serve as the basis for obligating another to satisfy that need'.[78] It could therefore be argued that mandatory quia timet injunctions cannot operate in negligence law because their effect would be to require individuals to engage in positive action for the benefit of another person, something that is contrary to the way tort duties are expressed. There are three difficulties with this retort, however.

First, the argument is a *non sequitur*. What it means to say that tort law is 'negative' in form is that, as a law of wrongs, it tells individuals what they cannot do. But this observation has no bearing on what individuals must do to avoid committing the wrongs that tort law proscribes, including whether that might require some positive act on a defendant's part (such as, for example, taking another path when you come across private property or fencing a dangerous piece of machinery). It does not follow from the point that tort law is negative in form that individuals should never be required to take positive action in order to comply with a negative duty.

Second, even if it is right to say that as a general rule individuals should not be required to take positive action in order to comply with tortious duties, there is a principled basis to make an exception to permit a mandatory quia timet injunction to be awarded to prevent the tort of negligence. Where a court is satisfied that there is a real risk that a defendant will commit the tort of negligence against the claimant by engaging in an activity without sufficient precaution, the defendant has by his own activity created a danger (the ordinary meaning of which is 'a possibility of harm or death'[79]) that may cause damage or loss to the claimant. Accordingly, pursuant to the well-known principle in omissions liability that creating a risk of causing damage or loss gives rise to 'a duty to take reasonable steps to avert or lessen the risk',[80] it is straightforwardly the case that courts can impose a positive duty on the defendant to act. A mandatory quia timet injunction compelling the defendant to take a precaution is therefore consistent with the law governing omissions liability in tort law.

Finally, even if one could argue that the omissions liability principle in respect of creating dangers should not apply in injunction cases, objecting to the awarding of injunctions because they are not consistent with a Kantian account of tort

[77] See, eg, R Stevens, *Torts and Rights* (Oxford University Press 2007) 9, 339; A Beever, *Rediscovering the Law of Negligence* (Hart Publishing 2007) 222; Nolan and Robertson (eds) (n 24) 8.

[78] E Weinrib, *The Idea of Private Law* (Oxford University Press 1995) 97.

[79] *Cambridge Dictionary* at https://dictionary.cambridge.org/dictionary/english/danger.

[80] *Mitchell v Glasgow City Council* [2009] UKHL 11, (2009) 1 AC 874 [40]. See also ibid [57]; S Steel, 'Rationalising Omissions Liability in Negligence' (2019) 135 *LQR* 484, 502–03.

law is putting the cart before the horse. Although scholars have theorised that tort law creates negative rather than positive duties, this has never been stated by the courts. Accordingly, objecting to the award of quia timet mandatory injunctions because they do not 'fit' Kant's thesis is misconceived. The better view would be that Kant's analysis is lacking in explanatory force because, as chapters 5 and 6 have shown, mandatory injunctions (in both quia timet and ordinary form) are readily available in tort law.

ii. Overview

The types of case in which an injunction can be granted in respect of the tort of negligence are undoubtedly limited. However, for the foregoing reasons, it is wrong to suggest that a defendant can never be restrained by an injunction from committing the tort of negligence. Where a claimant can satisfy the demanding burden of proving that there is a sufficiently strong probability that the tort of negligence will be committed against her, there is good reason to think that such an injunction can be granted, unless the defendant can make out a countervailing discretionary consideration that persuades the court not to grant an injunction.

B. Is the Duty of Care a Primary Duty?

There has long been debate among tort scholars over whether the duty of care in the tort of negligence is a primary duty. Some scholars contend that the 'wrong' in the law of negligence is the breach of a duty of care, causing damage or loss that is not too remote.[81] Priel goes further and contends that negligence is not a wrong at all but a primary liability, which only requires a defendant to pay damages after committing negligence against the claimant.[82] Conversely, other scholars take the position that the 'wrong' in the law of negligence is the breach of the duty to take care *itself*.[83] McBride has put forward several reasons in favour of this latter view, one of which is that the American cases referred to above demonstrate that courts can award injunctions in respect of negligence to enforce a duty to prevent future carelessness in the absence of damage or loss.[84]

[81] To give just a few examples, see: WW Buckland, *Some Reflections on Jurisprudence* (Cambridge University Press 1945) 114; FH Lawson, 'The Duty of Care in Negligence: A Comparative Study' (1947) 22 *Tulane Law Review* 111, 112; D Nolan, 'Deconstructing the Duty of Care' (2013) 129 *LQR* 559, 561–63.

[82] Priel (n 30) 709–17.

[83] See, eg, B Zipursky, 'Legal Malpractice and the Structure of Negligence Law' (1998) 67 *Fordham Law Review* 649; J Goldberg, 'Duty and the Structure of Negligence' (2000) 10 *Kansas Journal of Law and Public Policy* 149; McBride (n 58).

[84] McBride (n 58) 427–30.

Interestingly, the findings of this book support the view that, as John Gardner has put it, the tort of negligence creates an 'obligation not to injure P by not taking reasonable care not to injure P'.[85]

On the one hand, courts would not disregard the requirement to prove damage or loss (that is not too remote) in negligence if they were asked to award a quia timet injunction in respect of the tort. As was explained in chapter 6, a court will award quia timet relief where there is: (i) a real and imminent risk that a tort will be committed; or (ii) a real risk that a tort will be committed that causes the claimant irreparable harm, in circumstances where the putative tortfeasor refuses to take action to minimise the risk and the claimant is unable to take any further action to avoid the risk. To make out either of these tests, a claimant must establish that *every* element of the tort will be made out in the future.[86] Accordingly, to be awarded quia timet relief in respect of a tort that is actionable only upon proof of damage or loss, a claimant must prove that there is a real risk that she will suffer damage or loss as a result of the defendant's act or omission. For example, in *News Group Newspapers Ltd v Society of Graphical and Allied Trades (No 2)*, Stuart-Smith J granted a quia timet injunction in respect of the tort of intimidation only after finding that there was 'a real risk that [the claimants] will succumb to [the defendants' threats]' and suffer loss as a result.[87]

Hence, to obtain quia timet relief to restrain future negligence, it would not be sufficient for a claimant to prove that the defendant owes her a duty of care and that there is a real risk that it will be breached in the future. The claimant would *also* be required to prove that there is a real risk that the defendant's breach of his duty will cause her damage or loss that is not too remote. Indeed, in the Australian case of *Plaintiff S99/2016*, Bromberg J granted the quia timet injunction to restrain the Minister's negligence only after finding that there was a 'material to very significant' risk that the Minister's breach of his duty of care would cause the applicant personal injury.[88] It follows that, even though a quia timet injunction is granted before damage or loss has been inflicted, the positive law does not align with McBride's contention that a quia timet injunction in respect of negligence enforces some sort of free-standing 'duty to take care' that can be divorced from any consideration of the damage element (or 'actionability requirement') in negligence.

On the other hand, the availability of quia timet relief to restrain the tort of negligence demonstrates that the overarching duty that the tort generates can be enforced ex ante. Where there is a sufficient risk that negligence will be committed

[85] J Gardner, 'Obligations and Outcomes in the Law of Torts' in P Cane and J Gardner (eds), *Relating to Responsibility: Essays in Honour of Tony Honoré on his 80th Birthday* (Bloomsbury Publishing 2001) 111, 122.

[86] See *White v Mellin* [1895] AC 154 (HL) 163–64.

[87] *News Group Newspapers Ltd v Society of Graphical and Allied Trades (No 2)* [1987] ICR 181 (QB) 205.

[88] *Plaintiff S99/2016* (n 64) [494].

in the future,[89] courts can enforce the overarching duty by ordering the defendant to do something that accords with the standard of care applicable on the facts, or to refrain from doing a positive act that is inconsistent with that standard of care. Indeed, the Australian cases in which quia timet injunctions have been granted to restrain a government minister from committing the tort of negligence exemplify that courts are prepared to enforce a defendant's duty not to breach a duty of care causing damage or loss that is not too remote *before* the claimant has suffered damage or loss. Accordingly, Priel's assertion that the tort of negligence is merely a liability rule, and that defendants can act as negligently as they wish provided they are willing to pay damages after the fact, is misconceived.

Furthermore, it is important to recognise that the award of a quia timet injunction to restrain future negligence does not mean that the claimant's rights have been infringed at the time the claimant is exposed to an unreasonable risk of damage or loss. The award of a quia timet injunction responds to a *threat* that a defendant will breach his overarching duty created by the tort of negligence. It therefore cannot be said that the availability of quia timet relief in negligence means that a 'motorist who careers down Piccadilly at 60 miles per hour has violated the rights of all those he *could have* hit'.[90] It is equally important to recognise, however, that where a claimant can prove that the defendant owes her a duty of care, and that the duty has been 'breached' but damage or loss has not yet been caused, this fact provides strong evidence that there is a real and imminent risk that the overarching duty – the duty not to cause damage or loss that is not too remote by breaching a duty of care that is owed to the claimant – will be breached in the future. So, even though the 'duty of care' is not what is being enforced by the injunction, a breach of it is still linked to whether a quia timet injunction will be granted to enforce the primary duty created by the tort of negligence.

Ultimately, therefore, the doctrinal findings of this book support the view that the primary duty generated by the tort of negligence is a duty not to cause damage or loss that is not too remote by breaching a duty of care owed to the claimant, *and* that this duty can be enforced ex ante by an injunction.

V. Conclusion

The aim of this chapter has been to examine what the availability of injunctive relief in tort reveals about tort law itself. The doctrinal findings of this book give rise to three overarching implications for tort law.

The first is that it cannot be said that damages are tort law's 'primary' remedy. Both damages and the injunction work together in distinct categories of case to give content to the meaning of a 'right' that is generated by tort law. The injunction

[89] That is, the necessary conditions for quia timet relief as stipulated in ch 6 can be made out.
[90] Nolan (n 80) 562.

therefore has an essential function in tort law: it enables courts to directly enforce the ex ante duties created by tort law.

The second implication is that tort law and property law cannot be distinguished on the basis that property rights are generally protected by the grant of an injunction, while other tort rights are generally only protected by liability rules. Nor can it be said that the grant of an injunction is indicative that a court is protecting a property right, or that the availability of injunctions in respect of property torts indicates that property rights are better protected than other tort rights.

The third implication is that the tort of negligence can be restrained by an injunction in England and Wales. Nevertheless, one should not conclude from this finding that the duty of care in negligence is a primary duty. The better view is that the primary duty that is created by the tort of negligence is a duty not to cause damage or loss that is not too remote by breaching a duty of care that is owed to the claimant.

8

Conclusion

I. Final Remarks

The primary aim of this book has been to advance our understanding of injunctive relief in tort law by analysing a large body of contemporary and historical cases and literature. Chapter 2 surveyed the historical development of the injunction in aid of legal rights in the Chancery, from the injunction's inception in the seventeenth century up until the passing of the Judicature Act reforms of 1873–75. Chapter 3 identified the distinctions between prohibitory, mandatory and quia timet injunctions. Chapters 4, 5 and 6 analysed the positive law in respect of when injunctions can be granted to restrain or remedy torts. And chapter 7 considered the implications of the findings in the earlier chapters for the law of tort more generally.

The main claims that have been advanced were summarised at the end of each chapter. That was intentional. By producing a summary of each sub-set of the law governing injunctions in tort law at the end of chapters 2 to 6, a number of implications about the nature of tort law were able to be identified in chapter 7. The inevitable effect of presenting the findings in this way, however, is that it would be superfluous to restate the conclusions of each chapter here. What is much more profitable is to consider briefly, and at a higher level of abstraction, what the claims mean for how scholars, practitioners and courts think about and use injunctions and the law of tort.

It is hoped that, when taken together, the claims in this book demonstrate two key points about tort law and injunctions. The first is that when courts consider whether to grant an injunction to restrain or remedy a tort, they follow distinct and principled analytical processes. In the existing literature on injunctions, the way in which the analysis is presented suggests that when courts determine whether to award an injunction, they throw several different considerations into a big discretionary mixing pot and equity reveals to the court what the 'just' result would be. Not only is that not the process that is undertaken by the courts today, but such a process has never been adopted by the courts in any period when awarding injunctions in aid of legal rights. The analytical processes that are used are more principled and have a clear structure depending on the type of injunction sought. The summaries of the way in which a court determines whether an injunction should be granted in tort law that are set out in this book provide a clear account of these analytical processes.

The second key point is that the many cases in which injunctions have been awarded to restrain or remedy torts confirm that tort law does not simply compensate for loss. Through the award of an injunction, tort law functions to change individual behaviour by requiring all individuals in our society to comply with a set of ex ante duties. In the same way that administrative law requires a public officer to uphold his or her public duties, tort law requires a private citizen to uphold his or her private duties. The fact that the injunction was devised as a remedy in the Court of Chancery is neither here nor there. While important to understanding the discretionary considerations that influence whether a court is persuaded to award an injunction in aid of a tort law right, it otherwise distracts attention from understanding how the availability of injunctive relief influences the way in which the modern law of tort operates.

This point has broad implications for both scholars and practitioners. For scholars, it suggests that we must not over-emphasise the award of damages in tort law and neglect to highlight the importance of the injunction. There is now good reason to think that a tort textbook is incomplete if it does not include a full discussion of injunctive relief. The universal theories of tort law also need refinement, given that none of the theories addresses the availability of the injunction over more than a few pages.[1] To make good the claim that they account for the whole of the law of tort, the proponents of such theories must consider the availability of injunctive relief in more detail. Finally, and just as importantly, students need to be taught that injunctions are important to enforcing the rights that are generated by tort law. The common practice of relegating any discussion of injunctions to the latter half of a lecture on nuisance is insufficient.

For practitioners, the point that tort law creates ex ante duties that can be enforced by an injunction requires practitioners to be, adopting a term used by Nicholas McBride, 'idealists'.[2] When a client employs a lawyer to seek advice on whether they can engage in conduct that would infringe another's tort law rights, that lawyer must advise them that they owe a duty not to engage in that conduct *and* that the relevant duty can be enforced by an injunction. That lawyer would provide incorrect advice if he or she were to instruct a client that ordinarily they are free to infringe another's tort law rights provided that the client pays compensation after the fact.

[1] See, eg, Richard Posner and William Landes, *The Economic Structure of Tort Law* (Harvard University Press 1987) 43–48 (discussion limited to property torts); E Weinrib, *The Idea of Private Law* (Oxford University Press 1995) 195; R Stevens, *Torts and Rights* (Oxford University Press 2007) 57–58; A Ripstein, *Private Wrongs* (Harvard University Press 2016) 12 (one-sentence introductory mention), 139–40 (two-sentence mention in respect of nuisance), 240 (one-sentence mention in respect of remedies), 276 (one-sentence mention); J Goldberg and B Zipursky, *Recognizing Wrongs* (Harvard University Press 2020) 164.

[2] N McBride, 'Duties of Care: Do They Really Exist?' (2004) 24 *OJLS* 417, 419.

This is not all to say that the award of damages and the achievement of reparation is unimportant to understanding tort law. This book's core contention is simply that by focusing exclusively on damages and reparation, we have been unable to see the full picture of what the modern law of tort really is. It is time that we stop neglecting to consider the availability and role of the injunction in tort.

BIBLIOGRAPHY

Allen, C, *Legal Duties and Other Essays in Jurisprudence* (Clarendon Press 1931)

Ashburne, W, *Principles of Equity* (2nd edn, Butterworth & Co 1933)

Baker, J, *An Introduction to English Legal History* (5th edn, Oxford University Press 2019)

Barker, K, 'Punishment in Private law – No Such Thing (Any More)' in E Bant et al (eds), *Punishment and Private Law* (Bloomsbury Publishing 2021) 35

Baxter, T, 'The Slow Death of Past Damage as an Essential Element of Negligence' (2019) 26 *Tort Law Review* 123

Bean, D, Parry, I and Burns, A, *Injunctions* (14th edn, Sweet & Maxwell 2022)

Beever, A, *Rediscovering the Law of Negligence* (Hart Publishing 2007)

Bell, J, *The Anatomy of Administrative Law* (Hart Publishing 2020)

—— 'Remedies in Judicial Review: Confronting an Intellectual Blindspot' [2022] *Public Law* 200

Bingham, T, *The Rule of Law* (Penguin 2010)

Birks, P, 'The Concept of a Civil Wrong' in D Owen (ed), *Philosophical Foundations of Tort Law* (Oxford University Press 1997) 31

Buckland, W, *Some Reflections on Jurisprudence* (Cambridge University Press 1945)

Buckley, RA, *The Law of Nuisance* (Butterworths 1981)

—— 'Injunctions and the Public Interest' (1981) 44 *MLR* 212

Burrows, A, *Remedies for Torts, Breach of Contract, and Equitable Wrongs* (4th edn, Oxford University Press 2019)

Brimblecombe, F and Fenwick, H, 'Keeping Control of Personal Information in the Digital Age: Efficacy and Equivalence of Tortious and GDPR/DPA Relief?' (2022) 138 *LQR* 456

Bryan, M, 'Injunctions and Damages: Taking Shelfer off the Shelf' (2016) 28 *Singapore Academy of Law Journal* 921

Calabresi, G and Melamed, AD, 'Property Rules, Liability Rules, and Inalienability: One View of the Cathedral' (1972) 85 *Harvard Law Review* 1089

Cane P, *The Anatomy of Tort Law* (Hart Publishing 1997)

—— 'Rights in Private Law' in D Nolan and A Robertson (eds), *Rights and Private Law* (Hart Publishing 2012) 35

Capper D, 'Undue Influence and Unconscionability: A Rationalisation' (1998) 114 *LQR* 479

—— *Injunctions in Private Law* (Edward Elgar Publishing 2024)

Coke, E, *The Second Part of the Institutes of the Lawes of* England (M Flesher 1644)

—— *The Fourth Part of the Institutes of the Lawes of England* (M Flesher 1644)

Daniell, E, *A Treatise on the Practice of the High Court of Chancery* (J & WT Clarke 1838)

Davies, P, 'Injunctions in Tort and Contract' in G Virgo and S Worthington (eds), *Commercial Remedies: Resolving Controversies* (Cambridge University Press 2017) 127

—— 'Injunctions' in J McGhee and S Elliott (eds), *Snell's Equity* (34th edn, Sweet & Maxwell 2021) ch 18

Dean, A, 'What Did the Judicature Act Really Do?' (1935) 1 *Res Judicata* 13

Dixon, M, 'The Sound of Silence' [2014] *Conveyancer & Property Lawyer* 79

Dixon, O, 'Concerning Judicial Method' (1956) 29 *Australian Law Journal* 468

Drewry, C, *A Treatise on the Law and Practice of Injunctions* (S Sweet 1841)

Dworkin, R, 'The Model of Rules' (1967) 35 *University of Chicago Law Review* 14

—— 'Hard Cases' (1975) 88 *Harvard Law Review* 1057

—— *Law's Empire* (Fontana 1980)

Edelman, J, 'Equitable Torts' (2002) 10 *Torts Law Journal* 64

Eden, R, *A Treatise on the Law of Injunctions* (Butterworth 1821)

Finlason, W, *An Exposition of Our Judicial System and Civil Procedure as Reconstructed Under the Judicature Acts* (Longmans, Green and Co 1877)
Fowler, D, *The Practice of the Court of Exchequer: Upon Proceedings in Equity* (2nd edn, Butterworth 1817
Francis, R, *Maxims of Equity* (3rd edn, Savoy 1746)
Gardner, J, 'Obligations and Outcomes in the Law of Torts' in P Cane and J Gardner (eds), *Relating to Responsibility: Essays in Honour of Tony Honoré on his 80th Birthday* (Bloomsbury Publishing 2001) 111
—— 'Torts and Other Wrongs' (2011) 39 *Florida State University Law Review* 43
Gee, S, *Commercial Injunctions* (7th edn, Sweet & Maxwell 2020)
Gleeson, M, 'Judicial Legitimacy' (2000) 20 *Australian Bar Review* 4
Glister, J and Lee, J, *Hanbury on Modern Equity* (22nd edn, Sweet & Maxwell 2021)
Goldberg, J, 'Duty and the Structure of Negligence' (2000) 10 *Kansas Journal of Law and Public Policy* 149
Goldberg, J and Smith, H, 'Wrongful Fusion: Equity and Tort' in JCP Goldberg, HE Smith and PG Turner (eds), *Equity and Law: Fusion and Fission* (Cambridge University Press 2019) 309
Goldberg, J and Zipursky, B, *Recognizing Wrongs* (Harvard University Press 2020)
Goudkamp, J, *Tort Law Defences* (Bloomsbury Publishing 2013)
—— 'Rethinking Fault Liability and Strict Liability in the Law of Torts' (2023) 139 *LQR* 269
Goudkamp, J and Murphy, J, 'The Failure of Universal Theories of Tort Law' (2015) 21(2) *Legal Theory* 47
Goudkamp, J and Nolan, D, *Winfield & Jolowicz on Tort* (20th edn, Sweet & Maxwell 2020)
Gummow, W, 'The Injunction in Aid of Legal Rights – An Australian Perspective' (1993) 56 *Law & Contemporary Problems* 83
Hazeltine, HD, 'The Early History of English Equity' in P Vinogradoff (ed), *Essays in Legal History* (Oxford University Press 1913)
Helmholz, R, 'The Law of Waste and the Law of Dilapidations: A Comparative History' (2021) 9 *Comparative Legal History* 154
Heydon, JD, Leeming, MJ and Turner, PG, *Meagher, Gummow & Lehane's Equity: Doctrines & Remedies* (5th edn, LexisNexis 2015)
Holdsworth, W, *A History of English Law* (Sweet & Maxwell 1909)
Holmes, OW, 'The Theory of Torts' (1873) 7 *American Law Review* 652
Howarth, D, 'Many Duties of Care – or a Duty of Care? Notes from the Underground' (2006) 26 *OJLS* 449
Hynard, E and Lerch, A, 'The Tort of Collateral Abuse of Process' (2021) 44 *UNSW Law Journal* 714
Jaffey, P, 'Duties and Liabilities in Private Law' (2006) 12 *Legal Theory* 137
Jolowicz, J, 'Damages in Equity – A Study of Lord Cairns' Act' (1975) 34 *CLJ* 224
Joyce, W, *The Doctrines and Principles of the Law of Injunctions* (Stevens & Haynes 1877)
Law, J (ed), *A Dictionary of Law* (9th edn, Oxford University Press 2018)
Lawson, F, 'The Duty of Care in Negligence: A Comparative Study' (1947) 22 *Tulane Law Review* 111
Laycock D, 'Injunctions and the Irreparable Injury Rule' (1979) 57 *Texas Law Review* 1065
—— *The Death of the Irreparable Injury Rule* (Oxford University Press 1991)
Lee, M, 'Tort Law and Regulation: Planning and Nuisance' [2011] *Journal of Planning and Environment Law* 986
Lobban, M, 'Preparing for Fusion: Reforming the Nineteenth-Century Court of Chancery, Part II' (2004) 22 *Law and History Review* 565
Londono, P, *Arlidge, Eady & Smith on Contempt* (5th edn, Sweet & Maxwell 2019)
Loughlan, P, 'No Right to the Remedy? An Analysis of Judicial Discretion in the Imposition of Equitable Remedies' (1989) 17 *Melbourne University Law Review* 132
Lubé, DB, *An Analysis of the Principles of Equity Pleading* (Sweet 1823)
Kerr, W, *A Treatise on the Law and Practice of Injunctions in Equity* (3rd edn, Maxwell & Sons 1888)
Maitland, F, *Equity: A Course of Lectures* (Cambridge University Press 1909)
Malek, H (ed), Phipson on Evidence (20th edn, Sweet & Maxwell 2020)
McBride, N, 'Duties of Care: Do They Really Exist?' (2004) 24 *OJLS* 417

—— 'Rights and the Basis of Tort Law' in D Nolan and A Robertson (eds), *Rights and Private Law* (Hart Publishing 2012) 331
—— 'The Future of Clean Hands' in P Davies, S Douglas and J Goudkamp (eds), *Defences in Equity* (Hart Publishing 2018) 267
—— *The Humanity of Private Law: Part I* (Hart Publishing 2018)
McBride, N and Bagshaw, R, *Tort Law* (6th edn, Pearson Education 2018)
McLaren, JPS, 'Nuisance Law and the Industrial Revolution: Some Lessons from Social History' (1983) 3 *OJLS* 155
Mitford, J and Smith, JW, *A Treatise on the Pleadings in Suits in the Court of Chancery* (5th edn, V&R Stevens and GS Norton 1847)
Munday, R, *Evidence* (10th edn, Oxford University Press 2019)
Murphy, J, 'Rethinking Injunctions in Tort Law' (2007) 27 *OJLS* 509
—— 'The Heterogeneity of Tort Law' (2019) 39 *OJLS* 455
—— 'Tort's Hierarchy of Protected Interests' (2022) 81 *CLJ* 356
Nolan D, 'Deconstructing the Duty of Care' (2013) 129 LQR 559
—— 'Preventive Damages' (2016) 132 *LQR* 68
—— 'Rights, Damage and Loss' (2017) 37 *OJLS* 255
—— 'Injunctions' in W Day and S Worthington (eds) *Challenging Private Law: Lord Sumption on the Supreme Court* (Hart Publishing 2020) 155
Nolan, D and Robertson, A, 'Rights and Private Law' in D Nolan and A Robertson (eds), *Rights and Private Law* (Hart Publishing 2012) 1
Oliphant, K (ed), *The Law of Tort* (3rd edn, LexisNexis 2015)
Parkes, R et al, *Gatley on Libel and Slander* (13th edn, Sweet & Maxwell 2022)
Peñalver, E, 'Land Virtues' (2009) 94 *Cornell Law Review* 821
Pollock, F, *The Law of Torts: A Treatise on the Principles of Obligations Arising from Civil Wrongs in the Common Law* (Stevens & Sons 1887)
Pomeroy, J, *A Treatise on Equity Jurisprudence* (AL Bancroft 1881–83)
Pontin, B, *Nuisance Law and Environmental Protection: A Study of Nuisance Injunctions in Practice* (Lawtext Publishing 2013)
—— 'Private Nuisance in the Balance: Coventry v Lawrence (No 1) and (No 2)' (2015) 27 *Journal of Environmental Law* 119
Posner, R and Landes, W, *The Economic Structure of Tort Law* (Harvard University Press 1987)
Priel, D, 'Tort Law for Cynics' (2014) 77 *MLR* 703
Purlevent, J, *Two Law Tracts: The One Being Reflections Upon Estates for Life, the Doctrine of Waste, and the Principles of Injunctions* (His Majesty's Law Printers 1786)
Raack, D, 'A History of Injunctions in England Before 1700' (1986) 61(4) *Indiana Law Journal* 539
Read, HE, 'Equity and Public Wrongs' (1933) 11 *Canadian Bar Review* 73
Ripstein, A, *Private Wrongs* (Harvard University Press 2016)
Rock, E, 'Resolving Conflicts at the Interface of Public and Private Law' (2020) 94 *Australian Law Journal* 381
Rodger, A, 'Judges and Academics in the United Kingdom' (2010) 29 *University of Queensland Law Journal* 29
Rotherham, C, 'Remedies for Breaches of Rights to Light: Averting a Tragedy of the Anticommons' in B McFarlane and S Agnew (eds), *Modern Studies in Property Law* (Hart Publishing 2019) 145
Sawtell, D, 'Injunctions, Land and the Cynical Breach' (2022) 42 *Legal Studies* 649
Seton, H, et al, *Forms of Judgments and Orders in the High Court of Justice and Court of Appeal* (7th edn, Stevens and Sons 1912)
Sharpe, R, *Injunctions and Specific Performance* (4th edn, Thomson Reuters 2012)
Smith, H, 'Equitable Defences as Meta-Law' in P Davies, S Douglas and J Goudkamp (eds), *Defences in Equity* (Hart Publishing 2018) 17
—— 'Equity as Meta-Law' (2021) 130 *Yale Law Journal* 1050
Smith, J, 'Tort and Absolute Liability – Suggested Changes in Classification' (1916–17) 30 *Harvard Law Review* 241

Smith, S, 'Taking Law Seriously' (2000) 50 *University of Toronto Law Journal* 241
—— *Contract Theory* (Oxford University Press 2004)
—— 'A Duty to Make Restitution?' (2013) 26 *Canadian Journal of Law and Jurisprudence* 157
—— 'Duties to Try and Duties to Succeed' in M Dyson, J Goudkamp and F Wilmot-Smith (eds), *Defences in Tort* (Hart Publishing 2015) 65
—— *Rights, Wrongs and Injustices: The Structure of Remedial Law* (Oxford University Press 2019)
Snell, E, *Snell's Principles of Equity* (Stevens and Haynes 1868)
Spry, I, *Equitable Remedies* (9th edn, Thomson Reuters 2014)
Stapleton, J, *Three Essays on Torts* (Oxford University Press 2021)
Steel, S, 'Rationalising Omissions Liability in Negligence' (2019) 135 *LQR* 484
Stevens, R, *Torts and Rights* (Oxford University Press 2007)
—— 'The Proper Limits of Judicial Law-Making' (Judicial Power Project, 30 September 2016) at https://judicialpowerproject.org.uk/robert-stevens-the-proper-limits-of-judicial-law-making
—— 'Damages for Wrongdoing in the Absence of Loss' in J Varuhas and N Moreham (eds), *Remedies for Breach of Privacy* (Hart Publishing 2018) 97
—— 'Professor Sir Frederick Pollock (1845–1937): Jurist as Mayfly' in J Goudkamp and D Nolan (eds), *Scholars of Tort Law* (Hart Publishing 2019) 75
Story, J, *Commentaries on Equity Jurisprudence: As Administered in England and America* (Maxwell & Sons 1836)
—— *Commentaries on Equity Jurisprudence: As Administered in England and America* (3rd edn, Maxwell & Sons 1843)
—— *Commentaries on Equity Jurisprudence: As Administered in England and America* (7th edn, Little, Brown 1857)
Story, J and Redfield, I, *Commentaries on Equity Jurisprudence: As Administered in England and America* (9th edn, Little, Brown 1866)
Sykes, E, 'The Injunction in Aid of Public Law' (1953) 2 *University of Queensland Law Journal* 114
Ripstein, A, *Private Wrongs* (Harvard University Press 2016)
Tettenborn, A, 'Injunctions Without Damages' (1987) 38 *Northern Ireland Legal Quarterly* 118
—— 'Injunctions' in M Jones and A Dugdale (eds), *Clerk & Lindsell on Torts* (23rd edn, Sweet & Maxwell 2020) ch 28
Tiverios, N, 'Preventing the Infinite Regress: Discretion, Bars to Relief and the Structure of Equity' [2023] *CLJ* 1
Tromans, S, 'Nuisance – Prevention or Payment?' (1982) 41 *CLJ* 78
Turner, P, *Equity and Administration* (Cambridge University Press 2016) 1
Waddams, S, *Dimensions of Private Law: Categories and Concepts in Anglo-American Legal Reasoning* (Cambridge University Press 2003)
Weir, T, *An Introduction to Tort Law* (2nd edn, Oxford University Press 2006)
Weinrib, E, 'Understanding Tort Law' (1989) 23 *Valparaiso University Law Review* 485
——, *The Idea of Private Law* (Oxford University Press 1995) 195
Wilde, M, 'Nuisance Law and Damages in Lieu of an Injunction: Challenging the Orthodoxy of the Shelfer Criteria' in SGA Pitel, JW Neyers and E Chamberlain (eds), *Tort Law: Challenging Orthodoxy* (Hart Publishing 2013) 356
Williams, E and Guthrie-Smith, F (eds), *Daniell's Chancery Practice* (8th edn, Stevens & Sons 1914)
Winfield, PH, *The Province of the Law of Tort* (Cambridge University Press 1931)
—— 'Law and Other Things' (1938) 6 *CLJ* 461
Wright, C, 'The English Law of Torts – A Criticism' (1961) 11 *University of Toronto Law Journal* 84
Zakrzewski, R, *Remedies Reclassified* (Oxford University Press 2009) ch 8
Zipursky, BC, 'Legal Malpractice and the Structure of Negligence Law' (1998) 67 *Fordham Law Review* 649
—— 'Civil Recourse, Not Corrective Justice' (2003) 91 *Georgetown Law Journal* 695
Zuckerman, A, *Zuckerman on Civil Procedure: Principles and Practice* (4th edn, Sweet & Maxwell 2021)

INDEX

www.ingramcontent.com/pod-product-compliance
Lightning Source LLC
Chambersburg PA
CBHW071250180926
51613CB00002B/192
* 9 7 8 1 5 0 9 9 8 9 7 1 3 *